By Any Other Name

By Any Other Name

*Exposing the Deception,
Mythology, and Tragedy of Secularism*

James G. Abernathy

Foreword by Dr. Jon A. Weatherly

BY ANY OTHER NAME
Exposing the Deception, Mythology, and Tragedy of Secularism

Copyright © 2007 James G. Abernathy. All rights reserved. Except for brief quotations in critical publications or reviews, no part of this book may be reproduced in any manner without prior written permission from the publisher. Write: Permissions, Wipf and Stock, 199 W. 8th Ave., Eugene, OR 97401.

ISBN 13: 978-1-55635-204-1
Manufactured in the U.S.A.

All scripture quotations, unless otherwise indicated, are taken from the HOLY BIBLE, NEW INTERNATIONAL VERSION®. NIV®. Copyright © 1973, 1978, 1984 by International Bible Society. Used by permission of Zondervan. All rights reserved.

For my parents

*Who pushed when I needed pushing,
comforted when I needed comfort,
and who laid a foundation of stone for the rest of my life.*

*Your wisdom and knowledge mislead you
when you say to yourself,
'I am, and there is none besides me.'
Disaster will come upon you,
and you will not know how to conjure it away.
A calamity will fall upon you
that you cannot ward off with a ransom;
a catastrophe you cannot foresee
will suddenly come upon you.*

—Isaiah 47:10b–11

Contents

Foreword / ix
Introduction / xi

Part One
The Battlefield

1 · The Issue at Hand: What is the Real Issue? 3

2 · Connecting the Dots: All History is Natural History 19

3 · A Worldview by Any Other Name
The Christian Left: Infiltrated Christianity 38

Part Two
Secular Gnosticism

4 · Gnosticism: Ancient Humanism 77

5 · Secular Gnosticism: Analyzing Secular Mythology 87

6 · Closing Thoughts:
So What Does Jesus Think about All This? 129

Part Three
Takeover

7 · Worldview: Painting the Big Picture 149

8 · Education: Institutionalized Indoctrination 212

9 · The Judiciary: Circumventing the People 238

10 · Terrorism and War: Secular Foreign Policy 259

11 · Random Ideas: A Few Observations 275

12 · A Bit of Theology: Civil Government
and Narnia's Ancient Magic 301

Bibliography / 311

Foreword

OUR TIME requires books like this one. We live, as the saying goes, in an interesting time. Our time is interesting not primarily because of new technologies or challenging events. It is interesting because of the stark clash of ideas that surrounds us. This is a book about ideas. And it certainly clashes.

Some do not care for the clash. Tired of argument, discouraged by what appears to be the failure of ideas to yield results, they prefer conciliation over conflict. In the body politic and the body of Christ, there certainly is room for seeking unity and understanding. But not at the expense of clear thinking. This book demands clear thinking.

Specifically, this is a book about the ideological conflict in the United States between the Christian worldview and the broad array of ideas that can loosely be called secularism. It is a book of applied theology, discussing how ideas inherent in the worldview of Christianity impact social and political issues. It is indirectly a book of apologetics as well, offering reasoning that affirms the cogency of the Christian worldview over alternatives as they impact the public square. Think of it as two parts Francis Schaeffer, one part C. S. Lewis, and one part William F. Buckley.

Of course, this book is all parts James Abernathy. Abernathy writes with muscle. His prose is muscular, and so is his logic. This book, thick with substantial philosophical argumentation and historical analysis, does plenty of heavy lifting. It is informed both broadly and deeply, at once rigorously objective and deeply personal. Those who know Abernathy will hear his distinctive voice, articulating his keen intellect, in every sentence.

Readers can expect this book not to commit the sins of many in its genre. Abernathy is no Chicken Little. He doesn't flay about with apocalyptic language, screaming about imminent doom. Nor is he a fuzzy-cheeked utopian who describes the Eden that his ideas will inevitably yield. Nor does he wistfully yearn for some past "Golden Age" in which his worldview held beneficent sway. Readers sated with such pabulum will taste piquant, meaty realism on this plate. Abernathy has no time for anything that is not real.

Foreword

I for one am refreshed by what I read here. I am personally weary of people who, discouraged by the lack of short-term results from the so-called conservative revolution, are ready to start judging policies by their intentions instead of their ideological foundations and their real-world outcomes. I am weary of those who are ready to experiment again with socialism and pacifism when both history and sound theology argue strongly that socialism impoverishes people and pacifism kills them. I am weary of those too impatient to engage a significant ideological struggle for more than the eighteen months between congressional campaigns. I am especially weary of people who don't want to argue with a strongly held position. I like what I read here not because I agree with all of it—though I agree with plenty—but because I like its readiness to debate.

Let the clash of ideas continue, and may the best idea win.

Jon Weatherly
Cincinnati Christian University
June 2007

Introduction

In his classic *Romeo & Juliet*, William Shakespeare tells the story of two young lovers who happen to have the wrong last names. The hatred between their respective families eventually leads to the couple's demise. Their families hate each other and work to prevent Romeo and Juliet from seeing one another. Love, however, has different plans. It cares not for labels but only for souls. And Romeo and Juliet are soulmates. At one point in the story, Juliet tells Romeo, "That which we call a rose by any other name would smell as sweet." She was saying that a person is not defined by his name but by his essence—his soul. Even if they each had different last names, they would be the same souls and, thus, still be soulmates.

This is also true for characteristics not as romantic as love. For example, the trait of selfishness would still be the same quality regardless of what it was actually termed. The color blue would be the same color even if we began calling it red. That is, it would correspond to the same wavelength of light regardless of what scientists termed it. There is simply no escaping the *essence* of a thing. The same is true for ideas. The packaging of an idea may change with time, but its essence remains the same. Simply slapping a different label on an idea doesn't change the idea, and it certainly won't alter its real-world consequences. An idea, like an emotion, character trait, or a color, has an unchanging essence at its core that defines its existence.

For example, communism is defined by its foundational ideas—ideas that define humanity as merely physical matter, condemn private property and free enterprise, identify religion as "the opiate of the masses," institute wealth redistribution systems, force common ownership of property and labor, and centralize power into one state party that controls the government and economy. Over the last 100 years, Communist movements have labeled themselves "the People's Revolution," the "uprising of the proletariat," or "the People's Democratic Liberation Army." Similarly, Communist nations often refer to themselves as "The People's Republic of *x*" or "The Democratic Nation of *y*."

Each of these movements, however, is communist to the core. The ideas that define communism also define these deceptively labeled movements. Labels such as "The People's Republic of China," for example, ap-

Introduction

peal to terms suggesting free systems of government (like a "republic" or "democracy"). The truth of the matter, however, is that China and other Communist countries are nowhere close to being republics or democracies. They are tyrannical systems of government that oppress their people. The ideas that define Communism lead to a system that creates poverty, abolishes free speech, suppresses alternate viewpoints, and murders political dissidents. These are the real-world consequences of Communist ideas. As such, changing communism's name tag will do nothing to quell its disastrous real-world consequences.

The "repackaging" of ideas has been occurring as long as humans have been on the earth. As Ecclesiastes 1:9 says, ". . . there is nothing new under the sun." The same lie Satan fed (literally) Adam and Eve in the Garden of Eden has been packaged and repackaged a thousand times since; namely, that man doesn't need God and has the potential to realize his own salvation apart from divine intervention. This lie along with its secular presuppositions concerning humanity, morality, and government has spawned the most oppressive and murderous societies the world has ever seen. Though its name may change, the idea remains the same. Whether this *secularism* is termed materialism, naturalism, communism, socialism, feminism, "The People's Republic of . . . ," Nazism, modern liberalism, progressivism, pluralism, postmodernism, humanism, or even "liberal Christianity," its horrendous real-world consequences will remain oppression, poverty, and murder.

The current endeavor is to diagnose the various forms of secularism and reveal *how* secularists are deceptively forcing their elitist vision on America. Thus, this book is about *strategy*. There are many other books that argue in detail the premises that serve as the starting points of *By Any Other Name*. The current endeavor is not to rehash such arguments. My intention is to accomplish two primary goals. The first is to provide the tools and resources necessary to diagnose *why* secularism and Christianity have drastically different visions for America. In doing so, this book will connect secularism with its foundational worldview while placing it in its proper context. The second goal is to expose the methods and strategies used by secularism to achieve cultural dominance and political power.

During World War II, the allied countries didn't need to be told there was a war being waged. That was obvious. What these countries needed to know was *why* there was a war going on and *how* it was going to be won. To do this, they needed to understand *why* their opponents thought the way they did and expose the *strategies* their opponents were employing to defeat them. This is the reason code breaking was vital to a successful

Introduction

war effort. If the Allies knew when and where their enemies were going to attack, they could plan appropriately to foil the enemy's schemes.

The Allies dedicated a great deal of resources to breaking the German Enigma Code—the code German military commanders used to keep their strategic communications secret. After the code was deciphered, it was possible for the Allies to know when, where, and how the Germans were going to attack next. Fortunately for the Allies, the Germans arrogantly believed their code was unbreakable and were unaware the Allies were able to crack it. With the code broken, the Allies could mobilize to defend against specific German attacks and launch their own counterattacks in response.

The same is true for the cultural war occurring in America today. Secularism has been and is waging a war against the theistic—particularly Christian—foundation of America. For years, the ideas inherent in Judeo-Christianity theism provided the basis for the culture and institutions that fostered freedom and prosperity. An alien worldview with drastically different ideas is now battling to hijack the culture and institutions formerly based on these Christian ideas. If Christians (including those who embrace, consciously or unconsciously, the principles of Judeo-Christian theism) are not vigilant in influencing the culture and institutions that comprise the soul of America, the freedom and prosperity brought by these ideas will also deteriorate.

To do this, Christians must understand not only *who* the opponents are, but also the *strategies* they employ. They must identify *why* such strategies are used, as well as *when* and *where* secularism is attacking America's culture and institutions. Only then will Christians know how to directly counter the advances of secularism and lay the foundation of a counterattack designed to influence the culture and institutions (including the church) that shape America's future.

Part One, entitled "The Battlefield," contains three chapters. Chapter 1 identifies the *nature* of the battle. That is, what are the *real* issues causing the cultural rift between the two sides? Sometimes Christians misdiagnose the problem and waste valuable time and resources addressing secondary rather than core issues. Real victories in this battle are only possible if the *core* issues are identified and accurately targeted. Chapter 2 identifies the origin of the cultural rift between secularism and theism as the foundational ideas that define the battling worldviews. Such ideas account for *why* the two sides have drastically different visions for the future of America. Chapter 2 also analyzes why ideas have real-world consequences and *how* such consequences manifest themselves in society. This discussion explains the reasons supporting the "by any other name" concept. Chapter 3 issues

Introduction

an indictment of liberal (politically and theologically) Christianity by labeling it a form of secularism and explaining why some Christians unintentionally find themselves on the side of secularism. This chapter also discusses why it is vital to thoroughly examine foundations to ensure secular ideas don't infiltrate the Christian worldview in general and the church in particular. Chapter 3 was motivated by the observation that the political beliefs of my secular undergraduate professors were nearly identical to those of my Christian seminary professors. This phenomenon prompted me to ask the question, "How can two people who formally espouse mutually exclusive worldviews agree on so many issues?" I learned they don't subscribe to different worldviews after all.

Part Two, entitled "Secular Gnosticism," contains three chapters. Chapter 4 is a brief overview explaining the ancient faith of Gnosticism. Chapter 5 compares the ancient faiths of Gnosticism and pagan mythology with secularism in order to illuminate the mythological nature of secularism, *why* secularism employs the strategies it does and how secularism views itself in relation to the rest of society. Included in Chapter 5 is a discussion of how the two repackaged strands of secularism (i.e., humanism and postmodernism) compare in their respective visions for the future of America, how they are manipulating America's institutions to realize these visions, and why *both* view Christianity as Public Enemy Number One. Chapter 6 summarizes the main points of chapters 1-5 and discusses why America's "separation of church and state" government is *inherently* incapable of curing *any* social ill, what Christ taught about the relationship between ideas and behavior, and a biblical analogy provided by Christ that helps explain the "idea to real-world" paradigm. (Additionally, Chapters 1 through 6 are each followed by a set of questions designed to facilitate group discussion and/or personal intellectual exploration.)

Part Three, entitled "Takeover," is a collection of essays detailing the specific ways secularism is hijacking America's culture and institutions. They each serve as an example of how worldview analysis can expose the methods and motivations of secularists. The essays are divided into chapters that are separated categorically—education, the judiciary, terrorism and war, etc. Each essay deals with a specific contemporary topic (current legislation, recent court decisions, education curriculum, political rhetoric, cultural and economic trends, and current political and cultural debates on such issues as abortion, the war on terror, the war in Iraq, social security, Supreme Court appointees, etc.). Each essay also analyzes *why* the topic relates to the overall battle and discusses *how* it reflects secularism's attempt to forcefully realize its vision of a secular America.

Introduction

My hope is that this book will provide the resources to "break the codes" of secularism; define ways to recognize when and where secularism is infiltrating our culture and institutions; explain why secularism is a "repackaged" worldview proven false numerous times, *why* secularism employs the strategies it does, and *how* secularism views itself in relation to the rest of society. Just as cracking the German Enigma Code enabled the Allies to mobilize, thereby preventing German advances *and* enabling counterattacks, I hope Christians will use this resource to mobilize, counter the advances of secularism, and assertively engage in the battle to safeguard a free and prosperous America.

Part One
The Battlefield

1

The Issue at Hand
What Is the Real Issue?

If you've ever traveled to a foreign country where the dominant language was not your own, you are well aware of the communication problems that arise due to the language barrier. A "language barrier" is a metaphor that illustrates the futility of communication without a common vocabulary. There is no common medium that allows for effective dialogue. For example, if you go to a restaurant in Italy where the server understands and speaks only Italian, you may have problems ordering the meal you want. You have no idea what the Italian server is saying to you, and, likewise, the words you are using have no meaning to the Italian-speaking server. This barrier is often overcome by pointing to a fellow customer who is eating what you want or to a picture in the menu. This solves the problem, because you and the Italian server are now communicating using a medium or "language" (i.e., pictures) with which you are both familiar.

Language is the *foundation* of communication. The success or failure of communication will determine, in this case, what you will eat for dinner—if anything. Without first establishing a foundation upon which to communicate, you and the server have no hope of arriving at a consensus regarding what you want for dinner. In this example, language is the primary issue that needs to be resolved. Only then will the secondary issue (what you would like to eat for dinner) be resolved. Unless you and the Italian server utilize the same foundational *starting points*, there is no hope for consensus regarding *contingent subsequent points* (what you want for dinner).

This concept applies whenever two or more people engage in dialogue about *anything*. Unless those dialoguing utilize the same "vocabulary," progress will remain elusive. This is especially true in the public forum where controversial issues that directly affect the direction of our country are discussed. In our current political system, debate seems useless and often digresses into pointless bantering where little, if any, progress is made.

For example, when conservative and liberal presidential candidates debate one another, they spend most of their time debating contingent secondary issues rather than foundational issues. Little to no effort is expended trying to define terms. Thus, when a conservative supports "free enterprise and equal opportunity," he means something completely different from his liberal counterpart when he, too, claims to support "free enterprise and equal opportunity." In this case, the words may be the same, but they have drastically different meanings—or *essences*. The debaters are uttering the same words, but—like the Italian server and American tourist—they are speaking two different "languages." They are debating what to have for dinner (a secondary issue) in different languages and have little hope of arriving at a consensus. This is because the foundational ideas informing their basic thought process, or "language," are ignored. Such foundational ideas form the "first principles" upon which all thought is based. Only when first principles (or *presuppositions*) are defined can meaningful debate about secondary issues occur.

In his book, *The Post-Christian Mind*, Harry Blamires discusses the importance of first principles. In fact, a chapter in his book is entitled just that, "First Principles." He states, "So far as moral and behavioral problems are concerned, the post-Christian mind operates on a level of derivation and subsidiarity. It bypasses the basic rational *determinants* of the situations it chooses to discuss."[1] (Emphasis added.) In short, our post-Christian (a synonym for secular) generation puts the cart before the horse. Too much time is spent debating *subsidiary* (or *secondary*) rather than *foundational* issues. The foundational issues at the core of the disagreement are too often neglected during dialogue. Consensus on subsidiary issues then becomes an impossibility, leaving us destined to an eternity of struggle. Only *after* the foundational issues of a subject have been identified can there be progress in dialogue.

A Few Examples

Abortion

Take the issue of abortion, for example. Abortion's legality, availability, and funding from tax revenues are *subsidiary* issues. They are conclusions derived from logically prior claims that cannot be empirically proved or reasoned, i.e., foundational presuppositions (Blamires calls them first prin-

---

1. Blamires, *The Post-Christian Mind*, 118.

ciples and rational "determinants"). Before progress can be made toward a resolution, those in dialogue must first answer two *foundational* questions: 1) When does human life begin? and 2) What is human life worth (*unborn* life in this case)?

The first concerns the *beginning* of life. Answering this question will define exactly *what* abortion is. Does abortion end the life of a human being or doesn't it? The second question concerns the *value* of life. Answering this question will define the *moral status* of abortion. If those in dialogue disagree on the first question, there is little hope of agreement on any secondary issues (abortion's legality, funding, etc.). Furthermore, the second question doesn't apply if human life doesn't begin at conception, because unborn fetuses wouldn't fall under the category of "human life."

If the answer to the first question is agreed upon, the second question *still* must be answered, because agreement on the first question doesn't logically require agreement on the second. For example, a pro-life advocate and a pro-abortion advocate may agree that life begins at conception but differ on the *relative value* of the unborn child. The pro-life advocate may hold the value of the unborn child as equal to that of the mother (and every other human), while the pro-abortion advocate may place more value on the mother. Just as disagreement regarding question #1 precludes agreement on subsidiary issues, so does disagreement on question #2. Furthermore, someone (a consistent secularist, for example) who concludes *no* human life has inherent value, may agree with the Christian that life begins at conception but disagree about question #2 because of his commitment to secularism's presuppositions concerning *what* a human being is (merely physical matter guided by physical laws).

The answer to question #2 cannot be empirically proved or concluded based on reason. The claim "Human beings have inherent value" cannot be proved or disproved. It cannot be reproduced in a laboratory. You either believe it or you don't. This is the very definition of a first principle, or "foundational presupposition" (as it will be referred to in this book). If two (or more) people disagree on this presupposition, they will be speaking different languages when discussing subsidiary issues, and they will have no hope of *ever* arriving at a consensus. Reason/logic (terms that will be used synonymously) properly used guarantees this eternal dissonance.[2]

---

2. For a discussion of the proper role of reason/logic, see the essay "No Ruts, No Glory" in Chapter 7.

Apologetics

Another area where it is vital to address foundational issues is apologetics (defending the Christian faith). In dialogue between Christians and secularists, many Christians neglect foundations and fall prey to subsidiary thinking when they "overshoot the bow" of secularists. For example, Christians often cite evidence that, due to the secularist's foundational beliefs, will not and indeed cannot be accepted. A Christian can present a mountain of evidence supporting the resurrection of Christ and other *particular* miracle claims, but such evidence will do little in persuading the secularist. This is because secularists object not to the *particular* miracle claims of the Bible but to the notion of miracles *in general*. Rejection of every *particular* miracle claim in history would require extensive historical and empirical research. Thus, the rejection of miracles usually stems from an objection *in principle* rather than *in particular*. Miracles are impossible within the secular worldview. Therefore, every *particular* miracle claim is false. The Christian must first persuade the secularist that miracles are *possible*. Only then is there hope for consensus.

Trick Questions

Blamires analyzes a real-world example of subsidiary thinking using a situation that reared its ugly head in a British city in the 1980s. Due to a number of factors, addiction to heroin spread among the men and women of the community. To counter this trend, police imposed a limitation on the sale of hypodermic syringes. Addicts began sharing syringes as a result of the decreased supply. This sharing resulted in the spread of the human immunodeficiency virus (HIV) among addicts. Subsequent sexual promiscuity and needle-sharing led to a breakout of HIV in the community—including those who were not addicted to heroin. Thus arose the question, "Should hypodermic syringes be made freely available to drug addicts in light of the way HIV is being spread?" Making syringes freely available to addicts (or even *providing* them) *seemed* like the best way to prevent the spread of HIV.

It should be realized, however, that such a question is secondary. Answering this question and basing attempts to alleviate this problem on such a question will not solve the problems of heroin addiction and the spread of HIV. The more foundational "should" questions are: 1) Should people engage in sexually promiscuous behavior? and 2) Should people be addicted to heroin?

In the name of compassion, the secularist may claim that society has an "obligation" to make hypodermic syringes freely available to heroin addicts, but the Christian will place society's "obligation" prior to the debate regarding the availability of syringes. Blamires claims the word "should" must be clarified. He writes, "This has to be said because the post-Christian mind has become obsessed with sometimes specious 'obligations' which arise only because fundamental obligations have been ignored."[3] Merely addressing the symptoms of a more fundamental problem will accomplish nothing except the raising of false hopes . . . and taxes.

A Christian confronted with the question regarding the availability of syringes must realize the question assumes the *moral* acceptability of a very destructive behavior. Neither a "yes" nor a "no" answer will solve the problem *at its foundation*. The Christian must go beyond the biased question to the foundational issues involved, i.e., sexual promiscuity and drug use. In short, there is no Christian answer to the subsidiary question, "Should hypodermic syringes be made freely available to drug addicts in light of the way HIV is being spread?" Christians who attempt to answer this *trick question* have already lost the debate. The question itself assumes the legitimacy of two behaviors that the Christian finds immoral. Blamires asserts, "Christians cannot possibly have at their fingertips immediate remedies for problems produced by behavior which they utterly deplore."[4]

This will no doubt result in secularists labeling Christianity "impractical." After all, shouldn't we be concerned with fixing the world's problems as they are? It seems as though Christianity will simply ignore everyone who has ever made a mistake. Nothing could be further from the truth. Christians are called to come to the aid of those in need, and we must continue to do so with compassion. But ignoring the root causes of the world's ills will only ensure their continuation and canonize "compassion" as an exploitable political platform. We shouldn't fool ourselves into thinking that, as an individual, state, nation, continent, or world, a problem is solvable apart from the identification of its foundational cause. Society becomes unable to solve its own ills if it loses the ability to identify their foundational causes (much more on this in Chapter 6).

Every issue has foundational questions at its core that must be answered as a prerequisite to effective dialogue. Whether it be abortion, homosexual marriage, gun control, welfare, war, education, health care, or any other issue, it is vitally important to differentiate between foundational

---

3. Blamires, *The Post-Christian Mind*, 123.
4. Ibid., 119–20.

and subsidiary issues. This is especially important for Christians who are called to engage culture with the life-changing message of the Gospel.

"Clash of Orthodoxies"

If Christians are to influence the public forum, they must know *where* to most effectively engage it. The so-called "culture war" taking place in the United States and beyond is not a battle of subsidiaries. It is a battle between foundations. The battle being waged is between secularism and Judeo-Christian theism.

Robert P. George discusses this battle in his appropriately titled book, *Clash of Orthodoxies*. The term "orthodoxy" literally means "right belief" or "correct belief." It is usually used in referencing the officially sanctioned doctrines of a traditional religion. However, George rightly categorizes secularism as having its own orthodoxy. He claims that "secularism itself is a sectarian doctrine with its own metaphysical and moral presuppositions and foundations, with its own myths, and, one might even argue, its own rituals."[5]

Through a coup within the public forum, secularists are uprooting orthodox Christian ideas and replacing them with their own secular orthodoxy. Their primary strategy is the marginalization of every idea, value, and belief that smacks of theism—especially Judeo-Christian theism. Disingenuous respect for the "private" nature of religion is merely an attempt to de-claw theist philosophy in the public forum and forever relegate it to the increasingly harmless church pulpit and family dinner table. George sums up the secularist's vision well when he writes, "Secularism aims to privatize religion altogether, to render religiously informed moral judgment irrelevant to public affairs and public life, and to establish itself, secularist ideology, as the nation's public philosophy."[6]

Secularism is a full-fledged worldview replete with its own orthodoxy and vision for the future of America (and the world). Such a vision must be countered by an equally informed and assertive Judeo-Christian worldview and vision. Until Christians identify the core battle waging in our culture, we will forever resign ourselves to the irrelevant victories and defeats on the subsidiary fringes of society. Christians must not back down from secularists in the battle for a legitimate seat at the table of public discourse, because the future direction of America will be determined by the ideas that triumph in this arena.

---

5. George, *Clash of Orthodoxies*, 7–8.
6. Ibid., 6.

Creation vs. Evolution, the Constitution, or Revisionist History? What is the REAL Issue?

Nowhere is the battle between secularism and Judeo-Christian theism more apparent than in the creation vs. evolution debate taking place in today's public schools. Judges everywhere overturn state and local school board decisions that open science curriculum to ideas beyond what the secular establishment allows. Having failed to get outright creationism included in science curricula, theists now try to influence public school science classrooms by incorporating programs that include discussions of Darwinism's many scientific weaknesses and/or ideas of intelligent design.

The strategy for removing Judeo-Christian theism not only from public schools but also from the public forum in general was (is) twofold. First, Judeo-Christian theism had to be categorized as *unscientific*. Having become America's cultural epistemology (i.e., standard for determining truth[s]), secularized science now controls the public forum's box office. Admission is denied to any and all ideas deemed "unscientific." Thus, the labeling of all ethics, values, legislation, and scientific conclusions open to or based on theism as "unscientific, religious dogma" is the first step in marginalizing all things "religious."

This arbitrary division between *secular public scientific fact* and *private religious values* is necessary to delegitimize ideas and values grounded in theistic worldviews. Secularists humor theists by claiming it's permissible to be religious *at home* or in our *private lives*. Underlying this condescension, however, is the claim that religious ideas and values deserve no hearing in the public forum where debate rages over the direction of legislation, education policy, etc. Thus, secularists view "open *public* dialogue" as one secularist debating another.

Nancy Pearcey, in her book entitled *Total Truth*, discusses this dichotomy when she writes:

> The reason it's so important for us to learn how to recognize this division is that it is the single most potent weapon for delegitimizing the biblical perspective in the public square today. Here's how it works: Most secularists are too politically savvy to tackle religion directly or to debunk it as false. So what do they do? They consign religion to the *value* sphere—which takes it out of the realm of true and false altogether. Secularists can then assure us that of course they "respect" religion, while at the same time denying that it has any relevance to the public realm.[7]

---

7. Pearcey, *Total Truth*, 21.

The 2004 presidential debates between George W. Bush and John Kerry serve as a prime example of "delegitimizing the biblical perspective in the public square." When confronted with a question about abortion, John Kerry responded by saying that, as a Catholic, he believed life began at conception. Kerry went on, however, to say it would be inappropriate for him to force his personal religious values on the citizenry as a whole.

Kerry, whether conscious of it or not, utilized an arbitrary split in his thinking. He believes that all ethical, moral, and scientific opinions grounded in a theistic worldview have no place in the public forum. In other words, for an idea to be allowed a hearing in the "free" marketplace of ideas, it must be grounded in the *secular* worldview.

This barrier erected between the secular and religious must be exposed as intellectually arbitrary and politically motivated. Identifying the foundations, or first principles, of a worldview will do this. Secularists, however, tend not to embrace this kind of "worldview analysis," because it reveals the true nature of competing philosophies and ideologies. Worldview analysis breaks down the barrier between secular and religious worldviews because it shows they are *functionally equivalent*.

For example, a secular philosophy like Marxism performs the same function as a theistic philosophy like Christianity. They both give answers to the ultimate questions humans strive to answer, such as, What am I? Where did I come from? What is the cause of evil and suffering? How do we fix these problems? What is the meaning of life?[8] Additionally, both the Marxist and Christian base their ethical, political, and economic systems on *how* their chosen worldviews answer such *presuppositional* questions. As Robert P. George acknowledged, every worldview has its own orthodoxy.

In one of my undergraduate philosophy classes, a lesbian activist spoke on the issue of gay marriage. It was her opinion that homosexuals should have the same marriage rights as heterosexuals. She believed the current discriminatory marriage laws were a result of private values being forced on everyone else. She claimed that private "religious" values have no place in our country's laws. She said that the law should be value-neutral. The assumption was that value-neutral laws would allow for homosexual marriage. She believed that her claim (in support of legalizing homosexual marriage) was value-neutral. She believed her position was supported by secular public "fact," which is supposedly completely absent of biased religious values.

She was completely oblivious to the fact that her position stemmed from her own personal values rather than some magically objective secu-

---

8. See Chapter 2: Connecting the Dots. Also see Chapter 7: Worldview.

lar method capable of establishing *true* knowledge over against the faulty, dogmatic, and biased knowledge supposedly established by religion. In essence, she wasn't claiming that the law should be based on value-neutral fact, but on *her* value system rather than mine. *Every* worldview, Christian or secular, is a system of *values* based on how it answers fundamentally *metaphysical* questions about reality ("metaphysical" refers to objective or over-arching non-physical realities, such as meaning, purpose, morality, values, etc.).

Secularism, however, views itself as categorically different from theism in that it is not based on metaphysics, philosophy, or unscientific religious dogma. Secularists think they are above these primitive constructs. They believe their conclusions (including ethical and moral conclusions) are based on empirical evidence, which results in the punch of their admission ticket into the public arena.

Claims are rejected outright if they do not pass this secular litmus test. Rejected claims are not labeled as such based on their own merit, but because they have been categorized as "religious" or as "private values" by the secular establishment. (This is how secularists control the "rules of admission" that dictate who does and who doesn't get a seat in the public forum.) The *Humanist Manifesto 2000* illustrates this intellectual arrogance well by stating, "Scientific naturalism enables human beings to construct a coherent worldview disentangled from metaphysics or theology and based on the sciences."[9] By separating their worldview from the rest, secularists begin the marginalization of all religious worldviews. Whoever controls the rules of debate also controls the outcome. If Judeo-Christian theism is denied a microphone, it can never influence public policy or the direction of culture.

The "Dis-"establishment Clause and How We Got There

After religion has been labeled unscientific and private, the second step in marginalizing religion is both legal and cultural. This is where the Constitution comes into play. The First Amendment reads as follows: "Congress shall make no law respecting an establishment of religion, or prohibiting the free exercise thereof; or abridging the freedom of speech, or of the press; or the right of the people peaceably to assemble, and to petition the government for a redress of grievances." Misinterpreting the establishment clause of the First Amendment has been the catalyst for a legal and cultural burning-at-the-stake of religion. First, let us take a brief

---

9. Kurtz, *Humanist Manifesto 2000*, 24.

look at how secularism views religion from a historical standpoint in light of its notion of "freedom." This will expose how misinterpreting the First Amendment became acceptable.

Categorizing religion as unscientific and private wasn't enough. Merely *describing* the presumed difference between secularism and religion didn't lead to religion's expulsion from the public forum. A compelling reason as to *why* religion should be expelled was needed. This was often accomplished by the secularist's appeal to history. Secularists argue that religion divides people and is responsible for most of the oppression, misery, and suffering we see in the world (both today *and* in history); the most obvious example of this would be modern terrorism (although the Crusades is also a favorite example among secularists). If religion is shown to be the cause of all worldly strife, *ipso facto*, it is untrue, dangerous, and should in no way have influence in the public forum.

The problem with this approach, however, is that once you scratch below the surface of this claim, you realize it is patently absurd. First, the behavior (immoral or otherwise) of those who subscribe to a philosophy isn't the only factor in establishing the validity of their philosophical claims.[10] Second, anyone "keeping score" realizes secular philosophies have wreaked more oppression, misery, and suffering on humanity in the twentieth century alone (for example, the ideologies of Soviet Russia, Nazi Germany, Pol Pot, etc.) than all theistic religions have throughout *all* of human history. Secularists will lose *every* time if they choose to center the debate on this issue.

Another strategy used to marginalize religion stems from the secular claim that religion impedes freedom. The battle cry of the French Revolution still resounds today. Because religion causes oppression, it must be replaced with a secular philosophy that will unchain the bonds religion places on human potential. The first step toward social utopia becomes the eradication of religion along with its ideas and systems.[11] This view has been inaccurately projected back into the minds of the founding fathers of the United States. Revisionist historians of a secular persuasion would have us believe the founding fathers were motivated by such a secular vision when they penned the First Amendment. This deception is the basis for the "separation of church and state" interpretation the Supreme Court utilizes in decisions that expel religion from the public forum. (This represents the first of the two-pronged attack secularists are launching on the courts. The first tactic is to convince judges and citizens

---

10. Much more on this in Chapter 2.
11. Much more on this in Chapter 5.

that the original intent of the founding fathers is identical to that of the modern secular agenda. In light of the difficulty inherent in proving such an inaccurate claim, the second tactic is to appoint judges who believe in a "living, breathing" interpretation of the Constitution, which renders the original intent of the founding fathers irrelevant.)[12]

This historical and constitutional rewriting was exactly the catalyst that secularists needed to explain *why* religion should be excluded from the public forum. Secularists claim religion is more than just biased metaphysical mumbo-jumbo blindly believed. It is *the* major threat to freedom. The modern notion of "freedom" (as unencumbered, anything goes whenever and wherever) handed down to us from secularists such as Jean-Jacques Rousseau and Friedrich Nietzsche calls for the annihilation of every restraint on the individual (including but not limited to the church, religion and its moral codes, the family, marriage, etc.). This notion of freedom along with secularism's historical and constitutional rewriting provided the intellectual, cultural, and legal justification for religion's exclusion from the public forum.

Secularists must re-package their failed worldview by revising history in their favor. They teach that history tells us religion is the author of oppression and secularism is the author of freedom; all the while the opposite is true. Thus, the two-step process leading to the exclusion of religion from public schools (and the public forum in general) consists of 1) miscategorizing religion as unscientific and biased private value, and 2) utilizing the influence of rewritten history and manipulating the philosophical shell-game of cause and effect regarding the cause of oppression.

These approaches are strategic means to an end. Theists must realize these strategies when they approach controversial debates (such as the creation vs. evolution debate) occurring today in the context of public schools. The above debate is the perfect example of getting caught up in a secondary rather than a foundational disagreement. The foundational issue is *not* whether creationism or intelligent design is or isn't real science. The answer to that question is easy. (According to the philosophical presuppositions of secularism, it isn't. According to the philosophical presuppositions of Judeo-Christian theism, it is.) The foundational question is, "Which worldview will be taught in public schools?" Whoever wins this battle will determine all the *particulars* of curricula against the backdrop of the victorious worldview's philosophical determinants. The question, then, isn't "Is intelligent design real science?" The relevant ques-

---

12. See Chapter 9: The Judiciary.

tion is, "Which definition of science will be utilized: secularism's or Judeo-Christian theism's?"

The core battle in our public schools is not between creation and evolution, but between secularism and Judeo-Christian theism. The scientific status of creationism and intelligent design is irrelevant. Even if theists prevailed in arguing that creationism *is* legitimate science, secularists would *still* fight against its inclusion in public school science curricula. The separation demanded by secularists is not between the church and state but between *theistic religion* and state.

The Humanist Manifesto 2000 reads, "Humanists everywhere have defended the separation of religion and state. We believe that the state should be *secular*, neither for nor against religion."[13] Like the lesbian activist supporting gay marriage, humanists (who are secularists) arrogantly believe their worldview is value-neutral—a claim that couldn't be further from the truth. Furthermore, it is important to realize that the *state* spoken of here includes *all* its aspects: its laws, programs, policies, *and* elected officials. Of course, sprinkled throughout the *Humanist Manifestos* (there are a total of three) are disingenuous statements that pay lip service to respecting different belief systems in the name of "tolerance." But will the next generation come to tolerate a belief system that is shown everywhere to be disrespected by society, labeled the enemy of freedom, and excluded, by definition, from the public forum? It seems a purging from the ranks is a more likely result than a disingenuous respect in the name of "tolerance."

The First Step

Understanding first principles is vital for Christians who engage the public forum. Analyzing first principles helps in two primary ways. It assists us in realizing the *origin* of an idea as well as its *destination*. In college, we were often assigned to read books in which the authors were presenting a particular argument or thesis. Often, my professors chose not to inform their students of the ultimate thesis being argued by the author. Instead, we had to determine it ourselves without knowing the author's thesis in advance. In such cases, it is difficult to discern the significance of the subsidiary claims the author presents in support of his main thesis.

Because I didn't grasp the author's ultimate thesis from the beginning, I often glossed over very important points and overemphasized relatively minor or insignificant claims. In order to recognize the means, one must first understand the end. Because authors build an overall thesis by prov-

---

13. Kurtz, *Humanist Manifesto 2000*, 30.

ing particular claims *along the way*, it is vital to understand the origin (*why* the author feels the claim is worth mentioning) and significance (*where* it fits into the overall thesis) of each particular claim. This can only be done if the overall thesis is understood from the beginning. For example, in discussing the creation/evolution debate, we identified the overall issue as a battle between whether secularism or Judeo-Christian theism will be the backdrop for determining the content of public school curricula. In doing so, we saw the origin and significance of *particular* arguments, such as the claim that intelligent design isn't "real science" and the claim that theistic religion is unscientific and private.

Additionally, we evaluated some of the strategies (e.g., the cultural and legal "separation of church and state," and secular revisionist history) being used by secularists in their bid to exclude religion from the public forum. By identifying the *goal* of secularists (the complete exclusion of theistic religion from the public forum), it becomes possible to identify the significance of *particular* strategies being employed as their *means*. In doing so, we realize that, as Francis Schaeffer stated,

> Today separation of church and state in America is used to silence the church. When Christians speak out on issues, the hue and cry from the humanist state and media is that Christians, and all religions, are prohibited from speaking since there is a separation of church and state. . . . The consequence of the acceptance of this doctrine leads to the removal of religion as an influence in civil government. . . . It is used today as a false political dictum in order to restrict the influence of Christian ideas.[14]

Regarding Christian apologetics, we saw the core issue as a rejection of miracles *in general* rather than a rejection of Christ's resurrection (or any other biblical miracle story) *in particular*. In the respective cases of abortion and the availability of syringes, we were able to differentiate between foundational and subsidiary questions. We saw revisionist history and the "separation of church and state" as subsidiary means to an end. These realizations allow the Christian to *efficiently* engage the secularist's claim at its core rather than at its subsidiary levels. The examples above are few, but this kind of analysis must be applied to every idea, argument, philosophy, ideology, and policy bombarding American minds.

Identifying the cultural battle in America today as a struggle between secularism and Judeo-Christian theism is the first step in stemming the tide of aggressive secularism. Why Christians have been slow to realize this

---

14. Schaeffer, *A Christian Manifesto*, 36.

in the past is best left for a historical or sociological treatment of the issue. One thing is clear, however: secularists recognized the nature of this battle long before Christians did.

Early in the shift of Western thought from Judeo-Christian theism to secularism, secularists realized their worldview was diametrically opposed to theistic worldviews with no possible rapprochement. They realized the fundamental differences in the respective worldviews would necessarily lead to different conclusions regarding government, law and policy, and society in general. Understanding this, secularists went to work delegitimizing theism in every venue possible: philosophy, science, ethics, politics, economics, etc. To counter the secular ideological tidal wave, Christians must come to realize what secularists realized centuries ago, that the battle for the Western world will not be won fighting on the subsidiary fringes of culture, but by shattering the very foundations of the alternative worldview that is wholly irreconcilable to its antithesis. In other words, one will not be victorious unless it shatters the foundation of the other.

In *A Christian Manifesto*, Francis Schaeffer concludes his chapter entitled "The Destruction of Faith and Freedom" by claiming Christians need to realize that

> . . . if we are going to do better we must stop being experts in only seeing these things in bits and pieces. We have to understand that it is one total entity opposed to the other total entity. It concerns truth in regard to final and total reality—not just religious reality, but total reality. And our view of final reality—whether it is material-energy, shaped by impersonal chance, or the living God and Creator—will determine our position on every crucial issue we face today. It will determine our views on the value and dignity of people, the base for the kind of life the individual and society lives, the direction law will take, and whether there will be freedom or some form of authoritarian dominance.[15]

Another Christian author, Alister McGrath, wrote an optimistic autopsy of secularism in *The Twilight of Atheism*. He closes his book with the following words:

> Western atheism now finds itself in something of a twilight zone. Once a worldview with a positive [not in the sense of "good"] view of reality, it seems to have become a permanent pressure group, its defensive agenda dominated by concerns about limiting the growing political influence of religion. But is this the twi-

---

15. Ibid., 51.

light of a sun that has sunk beneath the horizon, to be followed by the darkness and cold of the night? Or is it the twilight of a rising sun, which will bring a new day . . . and new influence? We shall have to wait and see.[16]

McGrath's questions remain as yet unanswered. There is no *necessary* outcome in this battle (regarding the pre-Second Coming world). The victor will be determined by the ideas and actions that dominate America's culture and institutions. "Atheism" *per se* may be defeated just as Hitler's Nazism and Soviet Communism were. But the numerous resurrections of the *essences* of these deadly ideas should serve as warning that wolves in sheep's clothing still roam the earth, searching out whom they can devour. Humanism, postmodernism, relativism, multiculturalism, tolerance, liberation ideologies, modern liberalism, and liberal Christianity parade themselves as nouveau enlightenment, promising tranquility and freedom. In reality, however, they are nothing more than the recycled lie that nothing exists but the physical and that human salvation is attainable only from within (or through the state). Unfortunately, linguistic re-packaging of these lies cannot exorcize their tragic, real-world consequences.

Let us examine why.

Chapter 1
Discussion Questions

1. Blamires uses the terms "first principles" and "rational determinants." This book uses the synonymous term "foundational presupposition." What idea do these terms convey?
2. What is the difference between *foundational* and *subsidiary* thinking?
3. What were some of the examples of foundational issues discussed in Chapter 1? What makes them foundational? Can you think of any examples not discussed in this chapter?
4. What were some of the examples of subsidiary issues discussed in Chapter 1? What makes them subsidiary? Can you think of any examples not discussed in this chapter?
5. What does it mean to say that every worldview is "functionally equivalent"?
6. Do you agree or disagree with the claim that there is no such thing as a "neutral" value? Why or why not?

16. McGrath, *The Twilight of Atheism*, 279.

7. What does it mean to say that subsidiary issues are a "means to an end"?

8. According to Francis Schaeffer, how do secularists use the doctrine of "separation of church and state"?

9. Why do you think Christians, as compared to secularists, have been slow to realize that the nature of the battle is foundational rather than subsidiary?

10. What does it mean to "re-package" an ideology, and when does it become necessary to do so?

2

Connecting the Dots
All History Is Natural History

"For as a man thinketh in his heart, so is he."
—Proverbs 23:7 (KJV)

"If you want to be somebody else, change your mind."
—Sister Hazel, "Change Your Mind"

ANALYZING FOUNDATIONAL issues enables the discovery of an idea's significance and origin. Understanding the origin of an idea, however, is only half the game. Ultimately, the reason why first principles analysis is important is because it allows us to weed out bad ideas and employ good ideas in an attempt to make the world a better place. Nothing great in this world ever occurred without a good idea as its origin. Similarly, no tragedy in this world ever occurred without a bad idea as its origin. Author Richard Weaver recognized this and appropriately entitled one of his books, *Ideas Have Consequences*.

The flow of history is never coincidental. History is a study of the ideas that moved the world. In this sense, *all* history is the history of ideas. Looking back on the American Revolution, John Adams wrote in a letter to his wife in 1818,

> But what do we mean by the American Revolution? Do we mean the American war? The Revolution was effected before the war commenced. The Revolution was in the minds and hearts of the people; a change in their religious sentiments, of their duties and obligations . . . . This radical change in the principles, opinions, sentiments, and affections of the people was the real American Revolution.[1]

---

1. Novak, *On Two Wings*, 72.

The American colonists embraced a set of ideas that led to the American Revolution. Had the colonists embraced a different set of ideas, the American Revolution might never have occurred.

"Future history" will be no different. The tragedies and triumphs of tomorrow will be determined by the ideas embraced today. This is why it is vital to understand exactly where our ideas are leading us. "Good" ideas bring prosperity while "bad" ideas lead to tragedy. This is just as true for individuals as it is for nations. Francis Schaeffer discusses this in his masterpiece on Western thought, *How Should We Then Live?*

> People have presuppositions, and they will live more consistently on the basis of these presuppositions than even they themselves may realize. By *presuppositions* we mean the basic way an individual looks at life, his basic world view, the grid through which he sees the world. Presuppositions rest upon that which a person considers to be the truth of what exists. People's presuppositions lay a grid for all they *bring forth into the external world.* Their presuppositions also provide the basis for their values and are therefore the basis for their decisions. (Second emphasis added.)[2]

Every real-world decision you'll ever make—from what you eat for breakfast, to who gets your vote in an election, to whom you marry—will be determined by the ideas you hold to be true (or, as Schaeffer says, your presuppositional "grid"). The same is true for societies and nations in general. Every real-world event (whether personal, national, or global) is a direct consequence of an idea or set of ideas.

The key is to diagnose which real-world events are consequences of which foundational ideas (also called "presuppositions" due to their nature as *a priori* claims). We must "connect the dots" from seemingly arbitrary real-world events to the causal ideas which lead to them. In doing so, we will see that real-world events (for example, the holocaust or the civil rights movement) are never random or arbitrary. Consider a trip you make to the doctor's office. You've been experiencing symptoms (e.g., an earache, migraine headaches, muscle pain, or rash), but you're not quite sure what's causing them. You anticipate the doctor will pinpoint the *cause* of the symptoms (e.g., an infection, poor diet, injury, stress, etc.). Only when the cause is treated will the symptoms permanently subside. If the wrong cause is identified as the reason for the symptoms, any medication that the doctor has prescribed won't solve the real problem. Attempting to alleviate

---

2. Schaeffer, *How Should We Then Live?* 19.

only a symptom will do nothing to alleviate the core problem. In fact, a misdiagnosis will most likely cause additional undesired symptoms.

Isaiah's Observation

This discussion brings us to the quotation at the beginning of this book. The Old Testament prophet, Isaiah, wrote, "Your wisdom and knowledge mislead you when you say to yourself, 'I am, and there is none besides me.' Disaster will come upon you, and you will not know how to conjure it away. A calamity will fall upon you that you cannot ward off with a ransom; a catastrophe you cannot foresee will suddenly come upon you" (Isaiah 47:10b–11). What exactly is Isaiah saying in this passage?

Isaiah begins by discussing the most foundational presupposition of all, i.e., whether or not there is a God. Isaiah believes God exists and claims it is a fundamental mistake for humanity to claim otherwise. In short, Isaiah rejects secularism. Isaiah then discusses the real-world consequences of believing there is no God. If people live according to secular presuppositions, disaster will follow because such presuppositions lead to real-world "calamity" and "catastrophe."

The problem is that when calamity and catastrophe occur, secularists employ secular ideas to ward them off. This is ironic, because secularists do not realize that the very ideas they are utilizing to fix real-world problems are the same ideas that caused the problems in the first place. For example, (consistent) secularism claims humans are merely physical matter at the mercy of physical law and have no objective inherent value. Additionally, the denial of all metaphysical and supernatural realities results in moral relativism. These perspectives lead to decreased respect for human life and all that comes with it, i.e., increased crime, human rights violations, poverty, etc.[3] These are examples of catastrophes secularism could not "foresee" (v. 11). (Because they believe their own worldview will lead to prosperity, not catastrophe.) They are also calamities that secularism cannot fix or "ward off" (v. 11).

Secular proposals to solve such catastrophes are based, consciously or unconsciously, on the basic secular presupposition that humans are automatons at the mercy of physical law—biology and environment. This is the very idea that leads to increased crime, human rights violations, and poverty in the first place! Isaiah is saying that false ideas (such as secularism) will cause disastrous consequences, and that such consequences are not "fixable" by attempting treatments based on those same false ideas.

3. This claim is discussed at length in Chapter 7.

This is why secularists are *incapable* of solving problems caused by their own secular worldview. It's like trying to cure alcoholism with alcohol.

One example is entitlement programs. Secularists are trying to solve the problem of poverty by treating the poor as though they are automatons at the mercy of biology and socio-economic surroundings (which is exactly what secularism claims them to be). They believe that *systemic* engineering through programs that provide money, education, health care, etc. (notice the lack of acknowledgment that poverty could be a *moral* problem) will automatically turn a poor person into a rich person, a criminal into a saint, a war-hungry dictator to a gentle teddy bear. (But it won't change homosexuals. Remember, they're born that way.) This is one of the very ideas that *cause* poverty in the first place. Only when a society enacts policy based on the idea that people are morally free-will beings who have inherent value (conclusions based on Judeo-Christian presuppositions) can social ills, such as poverty, be alleviated.[4]

Negative real-world "symptoms" (e.g., poverty, oppression, war) are caused by "infectious" ideas. To treat negative real-world symptoms, their cause must be diagnosed, i.e., the ideas that caused them must be identified. Once this identification is complete, work can begin to embrace a different set of ideas that bring about different real-world "symptoms."

Secularists and Christians battle over whose ideas will be labeled the "infectious" ideas that cause the negative real-world symptoms (oppression, war, poverty, etc.) here in the United States and abroad. Secularists diagnose theistic religion (as opposed to secular religion), i.e., Judeo-Christian theism, as the cause of negative real-world symptoms, while Christians identify secularism as the cause. Both cannot be right. So which is the culprit (or are both wrong)? One thing is certain: History tells us tragedy will ensue if America embraces the wrong ideas.

All History Is *Natural* History

Obvious examples of historical tragedies caused by "bad" ideas include the Holocaust perpetrated by the Nazis, the murder of millions in the Soviet Union, and the Cambodian killing fields orchestrated by Pol Pot. Such tragedies, however, didn't happen by chance. They happened because they were a *natural consequence* of a set of ideas.

When the villains and dictators of history are examined, it's learned they weren't the uneducated madmen they are made out to be by some. Evil men such as Hitler, Stalin, and Pol Pot were well-read in the philoso-

---

4. Much more on this in Chapters 3 and 6.

phies of secularists such as Jean-Jacques Rousseau and Frederick Nietzsche. Their evil regimes were based upon the ideas peddled by the atheist philosophers of yesteryear.

Viktor Frankl, a survivor of multiple Nazi concentration camps, diagnosed a "bad" idea as the cause of the tragic real-world consequence known as the Holocaust. Ravi Zacharias cites Frankl from Frankl's book, *The Doctor and the Soul*:

> If we present man with a concept of man which is not true, we may well corrupt him. When we present him as an automaton of reflexes, as a mind machine, as a bundle of instincts, as a pawn of drive and reactions, as a mere product of heredity and environment, we feed the nihilism to which modern man is . . . prone. I became acquainted with the last stage of corruption in my second concentration camp, Auschwitz. The gas chambers of Auschwitz were the ultimate consequence of the theory that man is nothing but the product of heredity and environment—or, as the Nazis like to say, "of blood and soil." I am absolutely convinced that the gas chambers of Auschwitz, Treblinka, and Maidanek were ultimately prepared not in some ministry or other in Berlin, but rather at the desks and in lecture halls of nihilistic scientists and philosophers.[5]

But how do we know for sure that the Nazi's concept of man led to the holocaust (other than taking the word of the Nazis themselves)? The key is understanding what exactly an idea is.

Put simply, ideas are attempts to explain reality. For example, the geocentric theory (a *theory* being a set of ideas intended to describe a phenomenon) of the universe is an attempt to explain a *physical* aspect of reality—that the earth is the center of the universe. Similarly, the idea that "murder is wrong" is an attempt to describe a *metaphysical* aspect of reality.

Every truth claim is an attempt to describe some aspect of reality. Even the statement "there is no objective truth" is an objective statement attempting to describe reality! This is where the notion of "good" ideas and "bad" ideas becomes relevant. A "good" idea, or a *true* idea, is one that describes reality accurately. It is a claim that conforms to the reality of that which it describes. (Postmodernism attempts to reject this type of *correspondence theory* of truth. In rejecting the correspondence theory of truth, however, postmodernism must presuppose its truth.) A "bad" idea is one that does not accurately describe reality. For example, because the geocentric theory of the universe is an inaccurate view of reality, it is not true. Hence, it is a "bad" idea, and the consequences of operating

5. Zacharias, *Can Man Live Without God?* 25.

under such a "bad" idea would be tragic. Had we based our space exploration technology on such a premise, the results would have been, at best, inefficient and, at worst, disastrous. On the other hand, the heliocentric view (a set of ideas that claims the earth revolves around a sun which is at the center of the solar system) of the solar system is a "good" idea (a *true* idea), because it conforms to the particular reality it attempts to describe. A space exploration program based on the heliocentric theory would be much more efficient.

While bad ideas regarding *physical* reality have disastrous consequences, they usually pale in comparison to bad *metaphysical* ideas. The tragedies listed thus far (perpetrated by Hitler, Stalin, Pol Pot, etc.) were the result of metaphysical ideas rather than physical. The Nazi concept of man is a metaphysical claim that had tragic real-world consequences. When an individual, group, or nation embraces an idea, *they necessarily embrace the future real-world consequences of that idea.* In Frankl's analysis, the bad idea was secularism's concept of man. Secularism views man as an intricate combination of physical "stuff" that is best explained by appealing to the physical laws of the universe within a closed cause-and-effect system. Humans are not qualitatively different from tree bark. We are merely a more complex combination of atoms (which is a *quantitative* rather than *qualitative* difference).

What does this mean? It means that the same physical laws that cause an apple to drop to the ground after it disconnects from a tree also cause human personality, thoughts, decisions, and actions. As Frankl noted, such worldviews see man "as an automaton of reflexes, as a mind machine, as a bundle of instincts, as a pawn of drive and reactions, as a mere product of heredity and environment . . . or, as the Nazis like to say, 'of blood and soil.'"

Humanist Manifesto II embraces this description of humanity unapologetically. It reads, ". . . science confirms that the human species is an emergence from natural evolutionary forces. As far as we know, the total personality is a function of the biological organism transacting in a social and cultural context."[6] In other words, humanists, like the Nazis, believe man is a product of "blood and soil." If a real-world consequence of an idea embraced by the Nazis was something as horrible as the Holocaust (or the millions "purged" in Soviet Russia), should we not heed the warning provided by logic and history when we see the same idea embraced and re-packaged years later by an ideology deceptively labeled "humanism?" If something as beautiful as a rose smells just as sweet by any other name, it

6. *Humanist Manifestos I and II*, 17.

follows that something as odious as feces smells just as foul by any other name as well.

The Foundation of Foundations

The most important question a worldview answers is this: What is a human being? *Every* belief regarding political systems, economic systems, war, abortion, education policy, gun control, welfare, the role of cultural institutions, etc. will be determined by the idea adhered to in answering this question. If this question is answered with an untrue idea—one that is not an accurate description of what man *actually* is—disastrous consequences will follow.[7]

This is because just as there are disastrous consequences for ignoring or rejecting the *physical* laws of the universe, there are disastrous consequences for ignoring or rejecting the *metaphysical* realities of the universe *that are equally real*. *Metaphysical*, here, refers to moral laws that cannot be reduced to physical "stuff" (e.g., moral claims such as "murder is wrong," "adultery is wrong," "it is wrong to exploit the poor," "helping the poor is good," "genocide is evil," etc. or the opposite claims saying those things are permissible or even good) and the presuppositions upon which such moral claims are based (e.g., a human is a free-will being created in the image of God, every person has inherent value, etc. or the opposite presupposition claiming humans are merely physical stuff with no inherent value).

Recalling a quote from *Humanist Manifesto 2000*, cited in Chapter 1, we see that secularism rejects all transcendent (objective) metaphysical realities. It reads, "Scientific naturalism enables human beings to construct a coherent worldview disentangled from metaphysics or theology and *based on the sciences*."[8] (Emphasis added.) In other words, if something can't be observed by one of our five senses, it doesn't exist. Unfortunately, just as it is obviously absurd and disastrous to ignore the physical laws of the universe, it is equally as absurd and disastrous to ignore the metaphysical laws of the universe.

If an aerospace engineer decides to reject the accurate physical laws of the universe and design a jet engine based upon his own inaccurate version of physical law, there is going to be a lot of crashing planes and dead passengers. Similarly, a society that rejects the accurate metaphysical realities of the universe in favor of its own inaccurate views of such realities will also suffer *natural* consequences; *natural* because ideas and their real-world

---

7. See the essay entitled "Reality: The Undisputed Champion of the World" in Chapter 7.
8. Kurtz, *Humanist Manifesto 2000*, 30.

consequences exist in a cause-and-effect relationship, just as physical laws and their outcomes exist in a cause-and-effect relationship.

For example, the spread of HIV and Autoimmune Deficiency Syndrome (AIDS) are natural consequences of sexual promiscuity (which is, in turn, based on embracing certain ideas about reality), just as plummeting to the ground is a natural consequence of walking off a building's rooftop and experiencing the physical law of gravity. "Gravity" is simply a term scientists use to describe the relationship between two (or more) objects with mass. All objects with mass are "attracted" to one another (let's ignore quantum mechanics for a moment). Thus, scientists conclude a "force" exists that explains this repeated and consistent observation, i.e., "gravity." (Recently, "gravity" is thought to describe how mass bends space-time rather than how an actual "attraction" exists between objects with mass. This analogy, however, still holds.)

Why isn't the same type of "force" (or objectively existent phenomenon) posited in the realm of human ideas, actions, and consequences? Ideas lead to actions and actions most assuredly have consequences. For example, single parenthood, abortion, emotional trauma, broken relationships, sexually transmitted diseases (STDs) such as HIV and AIDS, and poverty are always consequences in a culture that accepts and/or embraces sexual promiscuity. Why don't secular social scientists do what their physical science counterparts do? Namely, why don't they posit the existence of a causal force behind a relationship that is repeatedly and consistently observed in reality?

Christianity labels this causal "force" as *morality*—an objective system of metaphysical realities woven into the fabric of the universe at creation, which manifest *actual*, consistent, and observable consequences dependent upon the free-will reactions of human beings to them. (The belief in such an invisible yet observable force is no more an act of "faith" than believing in the equally invisible and observable force of gravity.) This "force" is what has been robbing the United States of its prosperity for years—and will continue to do so as secularism becomes more and more dominant.

So, why isn't such a metaphysical force posited? The answer is because secularism, by virtue of its rejection of the supernatural and metaphysical, necessarily rejects the existence of any objective morality. After all, something that doesn't exist cannot influence the real world. Therefore, secularists must find the cause of the aforementioned ills (along with many others) in something *other* than morality. The remaining options? The *physical* realities of genetics and environment. That's right, blood and soil.

This is the context in which secularism answers the all-important question, "What is a human being?"

Physical Chains and Metaphysical Freedom

Our physical selves are required to adhere to the physical laws of the universe but, due to our God-given free will, our moral selves are *not* required to adhere to the *metaphysical laws* of the universe. Unfortunately, this freedom regarding the latter often leads to the conclusion that such metaphysical laws do not exist—that we are free to engage in any type of behavior we want without consequence, or, even more arrogantly, that each person is free to *create his own* metaphysical reality.

The latter is the conclusion of secular moralists (including secular humanists)—those who, in light of their rejection of transcendent moral claims, still attempt to posit *some* kind of metaphysical reality concerning personal or social purpose and meaning. *Humanist Manifesto II* reads, "But we can discover no divine purpose or providence for the human species. While there is much that we do not know, humans are responsible for what we are or will become. No deity will save us; we must save ourselves."[9] Unlike Judeo-Christian theism, which claims that metaphysical realities have their origin in the character of God, secularism claims that such metaphysical realities do not externally exist and, therefore, have their origin within humanity—with no need of the transcendent or divine.

Returning to Frankl's assessment, the leadership of Germany in the 1930s and 1940s embraced a set of ideas that eventually led to the Holocaust and World War II. Similarly, the leaders of Soviet Russia embraced ideas that led to millions being murdered and countless more being oppressed behind the Iron Curtain. Obviously, this is not to say every secularist lives like Hitler, Stalin, Mao, or Pol Pot. Nor is it to say that every religious person lives a perfectly moral life. The relevant point is that Judeo-Christian theism provides the objective presuppositional claims that serve as a foundation for the refutation of values espoused by men such as Hitler and Stalin. In virtue of its rejection of transcendent metaphysical realities, secularism provides no such foundation and must refrain from *all* moral condemnation.

In his book, *Can Man Live Without God?* (an excellent assessment of how and why secularism is the enemy of freedom and the author of tragedy), Ravi Zacharias writes ("antitheism" is what Zacharias calls atheism),

---

9. *Humanist Manifestos I and II*, 16.

It is *true* that not all antitheists are immoral, but the larger point has been completely missed. Antitheism provides every reason to be immoral and is *bereft of any objective point of reference* with which to condemn any choice. Any antitheist who lives a moral life merely lives *better* than his or her philosophy warrants. All denunciation implies a moral doctrine of some kind, and the antitheist is forever engaged in undermining his own mines.[10]

Zacharias elaborates,

A Stalinistic-type choice is one that the philanthropic atheist is hard-pressed to rail against once he or she has, by virtue of atheism, automatically forfeited the right to a moral law. And that is the inescapable quandary. The ground of autonomous, individual morality can give rise to any choking weed that saps the life from all else. Is this, indeed, the utopian humanistic dream?[11]

Intellectual finger-pointing has become a favorite tactic for secularists. Secularism and its believers would like to claim religion is the source of all the world's ills and that its removal is necessary for secular salvation. (Ironically, secularists have no problem positing some kind of "force" which underlies *this* supposed causal relationship between metaphysical ideas and the real-world.) The *real* culprit, however, will be seen when secularism looks in the mirror. While Judeo-Christian theism has often been abused in history to bring about oppression, two conclusions can be drawn: 1) Secular worldviews have wrought much more oppression and suffering than Judeo-Christian theism; and 2) Regardless of historical circumstances, Judeo-Christian theism provides an intellectual foundation to reject oppressive truth claims (such as those of secularists like Hitler and Stalin, or of Christians who abuse their own worldview), while secularism does not. In other words, it is a contradiction of the Judeo-Christian worldview to murder and oppress others, while there is no such contradiction within secularism.

Like parents of a spoiled child who believe their son or daughter can do no wrong, secularists refuse to take responsibility for the real-world consequences of their own worldview. They mistakenly attribute to Judeo-Christian theism the oppression and suffering wrought by their own ideas, and they attribute to their secular worldview the prosperity and freedom brought about by the Judeo-Christian worldview. To once again quote Zacharias, "One of the great blind spots of a philosophy that attempts to

---

10. Zacharias, *Can Man Live Without God?* 31–32.
11. Ibid., 27.

disavow God is its unwillingness to look into the face of the monster it has begotten and own up to being its creator."[12]

Secularism has never, and will never, deliver on its promise of a godless utopia based on reason. It is inherently unable to do so due to its inaccurate presuppositions that attempt to describe reality. "In *God* we trust" is the foundation of free laws, governments, and societies and the basis for the *true* potential and high value of humanity. "In *man* we trust" leads us down the road of purposelessness, oppression, and despair.

From an Idea to the Real World

So what's at stake? In short, *everything*. The ideas you adopt influence everything, including the clothes you wear, who you vote for, who you marry, what you consider to be right or wrong, your career, and whether or not you'll keep reading this book. The relationship between your ideas and actions is a microcosm of how the world works. Ideas influence what kind of governments exist; what kind of policies are embraced; the role of cultural institutions, such as the family, marriage, and the church; the education curriculum taught to our children; foreign policy; war; how the press behaves; entertainment; etc.

Schaeffer opens *How Should We Then Live?* with the words,

> There is a flow to history and culture. This flow is rooted and has its wellspring in the thoughts of people. People are unique in the inner life of the mind—what they are in their thought world determines how they act. This is true of their value systems and it is true of their creativity. It is true of their corporate actions, such as political decisions, and it is true of their personal lives. The results of their thought world flow through their fingers or from their tongues into the external world. It is true of Michelangelo's chisel, and it is true of a dictator's sword.[13]

But *how* exactly do ideas move the world? That is, how do the real-world consequences of an idea (or set of ideas) come to fruition? How does someone's worldview, or "thought world" as Schaeffer calls it, bring about real-world consequences? There must be some sort of medium that serves as a catalyst in the transition of an idea to its real-world consequence. For individuals, it is their actions. When discussing society, the medium that does so most prevalently is culture and its institutions.

---

12. Ibid., 22.
13. Schaeffer, *How Should We Then Live?*, 19.

In his book, *Restoring the Good Society*, civil society advocate Don Eberly claims culture "consists of the basic beliefs, ideas, and values of a people that shape and define individual lives."[14] The ideas that dominate a society's culture will be the determining factor in what real-world consequences manifest. But what happens in a pluralistic society where many *different* ideas are embraced? This is the situation America finds itself in today. There is a different set of ideas at every street corner pushing and shoving for cultural dominance.

I contended earlier that the two main sets of ideas competing in America are secularism and Judeo-Christian theism. Every conflict concerning subsidiary issues boils down to a clash between secular and Judeo-Christian presuppositions (this was illustrated in Chapter 1). But who or what will determine which worldview will bring about its real-world consequences? Is it simply a matter of numbers—whichever worldview claims more adherents wins? Or will it be some sort of combination of worldviews that triumphs?

If Eberly is right in claiming culture "consists of the basic beliefs, ideas, and values of a people that shape and define individual lives," then it is culture that *governs where there is no government.* The staple of democracy is limited government. Limited government is only possible when private citizens embrace a culture that contains the virtues which lead to the self-regulation that keeps government limited. A virtuous citizenry that meets its own needs has no need of an encroaching government that appropriates such responsibilities for itself. Government will remain limited in its proper realm only if a nation's culture breeds virtues such as a quality work ethic, honesty, justice, compassion, love of neighbor, family values, respect for life and truth, personal responsibility, and other traits that motivate communities and families to meet their own needs.

The United States had a similar culture at its founding (though it was far from perfect). The Constitution was written to limit the powers of government, ensuring the rights and responsibilities of private citizens. The founding fathers knew that democracy and freedom were contingent on a citizenry who lived in a way that kept government limited. To once again quote John Adams, "The only foundation of a free Constitution, is pure Virtue, and if this cannot be inspired into our People, in a great Measure . . . They may change their Rulers, and the forms of Government, but they will not obtain a lasting Liberty."[15]

---

14. Eberly, *Restoring the Good Society*, 34.
15. Novak, *On Two Wings*, 72.

As we all know, however, culture can change over time. This fact was not lost on the founding fathers. They knew that governments and laws were based upon the culture of the people. As long as the evolving culture (which includes evolving technology and its moral implications) doesn't violate the basic values spelled out in the Constitution (which is the *republic* aspect of our democratic republic), the country's laws may change as the culture changes. This is why they wrote into the Constitution a *specific method* that allows for change in America's laws. (Ideally, of course, people undergo such cultural changes without appealing to coercive laws to force the change, because, as our founding fathers knew all too well, the government can be manipulated to rob people of their rights, assume the responsibilities of the citizenry, and repress the people.)

Changing the law is a difficult process because of how the Constitution was written. Before an idea can be codified into law, it must pass two tests: 1) It must not violate any tenet of the Constitution (unless the proposed change is a constitutional amendment, in which case a "super-majority" is necessary), and 2) It must be passed by the people either through a direct vote or through the legislature (be it local, state, or federal).

Why was the legislature chosen as the conduit of change in the country's codified values, i.e., its laws? Because it most accurately reflects the will of the people; it is the most difficult branch of government to convince or "sway," because it is the largest; and it is the *least* likely to be manipulated by a powerful minority. Therefore, *if and when* an idea is codified into law, it is the role of the legislature (be it local, state, or federal) to do so.

First and foremost, however, culture should be maintained and regulated by the citizenry, not the government. The founding fathers knew that there are and will be times when a minority culture will attempt to circumvent the will of the majority. To do this, the minority must force its will either at the point of a bayonet or through coercive government laws (two things which, ultimately, are the same thing). With the lawmaking responsibility of government residing with the legislature, however, it is exceedingly difficult to do this for the above stated reasons. Therefore, for a minority set of ideas (and those who hold them) to gain controlling influence in society, one of two things (or both) must be accomplished: 1) The culture of the people must be changed from the ground up (making it no longer the minority), subsequently resulting in control of the legislature, and/or 2) The non-legislative branch(es) of government must be manipulated to circumvent the will of the majority. Thus, either the people in general must be convinced to subscribe to such ideas, and/or there must be an ideological coup in the non-legislative branches of government.

Institutional Manipulation

Institutions play a major role in determining society's direction. Institutions are formed and maintained based on the culture of a society. Their function is shaped by a purpose given them by culture. Institutions such as the family, marriage, the church, schools, the legislature (discussed above), and the judiciary perform specific functions in a society. They preserve and reflect the values that provide them with their respective purposes. Thus, an *institution* is any formalized medium that transmits and/or reflects a society's culture. Whichever ideas control society's culture also control its institutions . . . at least in theory.

How an institution is "used" by a society is determined by the dominant culture at the time. Just as in any society, America utilizes institutions for certain purposes. For years, the family was "used" by society as a place where one man and one woman could experience the joys of marriage and children and pass on the dominant Christian theistic cultural values to the next generation. Schools were "used" by society to pass along knowledge and values as they were contained within the same dominant theistic culture. The legislature was "used" to create the laws of the nation. The judiciary was "used" to *interpret* laws passed by the legislature. The Christian church existed to take the gospel of Christ to the world. As culture changes—as the *ideas embraced by the people* change—how institutions are "used" also changes.

Because of this, institutions influence culture just as they reflect it. For example, the family both reflects the current values of the culture *and* influences what values will comprise tomorrow's culture. The same is true of our education system, legislature, and judiciary. So goes society's institutions, so goes the society (ironically, the reverse is true as well). The direction of America is steered by its institutions and the cultural values that inform them.

As stated above, there are two ways a minority culture, i.e., *a group of people who subscribe to a minority set of ideas—or worldview—yet wish to see their ideas determine the direction of society*, may gain controlling influence in society. First, the minority culture could change the ideas of the people from the ground up (making it no longer the minority); or it could manipulate the nonlegislative branch(es) of government to circumvent the will of the majority. Secularism is utilizing *both* methods.

Secularism is accomplishing this by manipulating two of America's most undemocratic and influential institutions: the education system and the judiciary. The education system is being used to accomplish tactic #1: the changing of the culture from the ground up.[16] The judiciary is being used to accomplish tactic #2: the circumvention of the will of the people through a nonlegislative branch of government.[17] In fact, tactic #2 is often utilized to achieve tactic #1.

These are the two main fronts of the culture war in America today. Thus, it is no coincidence that secularists are extremely passionate about victory in these two venues. Regardless of its minority status, if secularism successfully infiltrates these two institutions and establishes itself as the controlling worldview within them (a process which began decades ago), it is only a matter of time before America becomes a shell of what it was yesterday, is today . . . and could be tomorrow.

What Is at Stake?

"So what?" you may ask. "Why does any of this matter?" Just over 60 years ago, the world was on the brink of destruction. The armies of Hitler and Tojo were marching on the world. We've all heard the phrase, "All it takes for the triumph of evil is for good men to do nothing." This timeless dictum was a possibility in the mid-20th century. Fortunately, during this time, the West had the good men to fight against evil, because the worldview that informed America's culture and institutions was *basically* Christian in its makeup (perhaps more *leftover* than anything, but still enough to influence culture). In the 1940s, when Western culture was put to the test, it did not collapse because its Judeo-Christian base was sufficiently strong. (Claiming America is a "Christian" nation doesn't mean every early American citizen or founding father was a devout Christian—although many were. It means that the presuppositions of the Judeo-Christian worldview were utilized in forming government, society, and institutions—presuppositions often embraced by non-Christians as well.)[18]

(While it is true that Communist Russia—a country not founded on Judeo-Christian principles—fought against evil during World War II, it did so for drastically different reasons than the United States. This difference in values is perfectly illustrated by Soviet Russia's post-war expansionism. The United States and Great Britain installed democratic

16. See Chapter 8.
17. See Chapter 9.
18. See Chapter 3.

governments in the countries they liberated and then withdrew, leaving intact the sovereignty of these nations. The Soviets maintained oppressive control over the nations they "liberated"—what came to be known as the Eastern Bloc. History, once again, provides a clear picture of the real-world difference between the secular and Judeo-Christian worldviews.)

Today America is being bombarded from two directions. Defeat in the first realm results in totalitarianism due to internal decline, while defeat in the second realm results in totalitarianism from decline due to external forces. As America is removed from the Judeo-Christian presuppositional moorings upon which it was founded and upon which it has prospered, the more vulnerable she becomes to repression and totalitarianism from within. As this occurs, the more vulnerable our country will become to external pressure such as terrorism. Without a foundational core that breeds the intestinal fortitude and resolve to identify and defend our way of life (an impossible task when one way of life is viewed as just as legitimate as any other way of life), there's little hope of standing against the external forces of tyranny.

Just as adversity reveals the inner character of a person, it also reveals the strength of a culture. Like a weak bridge crumbling under the weight above it, a culture founded on presuppositions that don't accurately reflect reality will falter when those adversarial and unforgiving forces of reality encounter it.[19] Today the United States is faced with the same obstacles to freedom that have been rearing their ugly heads for millennia: internal tendencies (moral decadence, apathy, and overarching government power) and external pressure (attacks from foreign tyrants and oppressive ideologies). Only time will tell if the United States musters the moral and ideological fortitude necessary to once again preserve that which has been so fleeting for so many in history: freedom. Schaeffer writes,

> A culture or an individual with a weak base can stand only when the pressure on it is not too great.... It is this way with the lives and value systems of individuals and cultures when they have nothing stronger to build on than their own limitedness, their own finiteness. They can stand when pressures are not too great, but when pressures mount, if *then* they do not have a sufficient base, they crash .... Culture and the freedoms of people are fragile. Without a sufficient base, when such pressures come only time is needed—and often not a great deal of time—before there is a collapse.[20]

---

19. See Chapter 6 in addition to the essay entitled "Reality: The Undisputed Champion of the Universe" in Chapter 7.

20. Schaeffer, *How Should We Then Live?* 23.

Humanity is free to choose the direction of history. The ideas we embrace today will determine the future in which we live. We are free to "make our own bed," so to speak. But once we make it, we are forced to lie in it because such freedom doesn't give us the ability to simply neutralize the undesirable real-world consequences that arise from embracing bad ideas. To alter undesirable outcomes, we must first embrace different ideas. *Real-world consequences can always be changed, but change must first occur at the foundational rather than subsidiary level.*

The Myth of Moral Neutrality

There is no such thing as a neutral idea. *Every* idea has a real-world consequential counterpart. This is just as true for the ideas that influence nations and governments as it is for those that influence individual behavior. Unlike the claims of secularism, humanity and society are not mere products of environment, of "blood and soil." Humanity and society are the products of the ideas people freely embrace. As John W. Whitehead writes, "We are more than mere products of our environment. Men and women project their inward thoughts out into the external world where, in fact, their thoughts affect their environment. Ideas thus have consequences, which can be productive or destructive depending upon their basis or foundation." [21]

Proper diagnosis of real-world events is vital. Without such diagnoses, secularism will continue to falsely claim freedom and prosperity as its offspring. Secularists are deceived into believing this falsehood for two reasons: 1) Their worldview incorrectly predicts this, and 2) A cultural lag effect can suggest secularists are correct. The first reason was discussed briefly in Chapter 1 and will be handled in-depth in Chapter 5. The second acknowledges that real-world events sometimes lag behind the institutionalization of a set of ideas. In this case, even though secularism has come to dominate modern American culture and many of its institutions, the real-world consequences of several hundred years of Judeo-Christian influence (freedom and prosperity) are still being experienced. Many mistakenly attribute current freedom and prosperity to the *current* dominant worldview (secularism). In reality, however, the tragic consequences of secularism are slowly becoming a reality (some more quickly than others).

A half a millennia of Judeo-Christian influence can't be exorcized in a day. One need only observe modern Europe for a prognosis of America's near future if it continues to embrace secularism: high unemployment, runaway poverty, weak defense capabilities (if any), nihilistic economic

---

21. Whitehead, *The Second American Revolution*, 25.

and social deals with totalitarian regimes, social unrest resulting in alienation and riots, etc. Fortunately for Europe, the United States is there to ensure the freedom threatened from without. But who will preserve freedom if the United States relinquishes its ability to do so? Judging from entities such as the United Nations (which has no power outside the influence of the United States), the answer to that question doesn't provide much promise.

Secularism claims humans and societies are the product of "blood and soil." Humans have no control over the future. Judeo-Christian theism, on the other hand, claims humans and societies are the products of the ideas they freely embrace. The quality of life for individuals and societies is determined by how well the embraced ideas "line up" with the metaphysical realities woven into the fabric of the universe by the Creator. While the ultimate outcomes of history are the overthrow of evil, the redemption of God's people through Christ, and the subjection of the new heavens and new earth under the authority of Christ—within the realm of the freedom we have been granted, *we* will determine the *particular* outcomes of our *ongoing* history.

Will there be freedom or tyranny? Will human life be respected or neglected? Will the innocent prosper or suffer? Will justice be brought to the guilty? Will there be peace or oppression? *We* are the ones who have answered these questions in the past, and *we*—*not* blood or soil—will answer them in the future. Embracing the Judeo-Christian worldview (which doesn't necessitate the entire world's conversion to Christianity), consciously or unconsciously, is the world's only hope in preserving freedom and prosperity. As such, it is vital that this worldview not be corrupted by poisonous secular ideas. As the only barrier between secularism and its tragic consequences, Judeo-Christian theism *must* remain pure. Otherwise, its effectiveness in holding back secularism's real-world consequences is compromised.

Sadly, however, Christianity has been infiltrated—not by those who openly decry it as false and dangerous, but by those who wholeheartedly identify themselves as Christians—a much more dangerous phenomenon. There is no hope of confronting secularism if the Judeo-Christian worldview itself becomes just another version of the disastrous ideology first proffered by Satan at the beginning of time. If this happens, "Christianity" will be thrown in with all the other politically expedient and re-packaged terms that secularism appropriates to disguise its lies. The once beautiful rose of Christianity will turn a secular shade of black, and the consequences will leave its thorns covered in blood.

Connecting the Dots

Let us identify what infiltrated Christianity looks like, why it is so dangerous, how it came into existence, and what can be done to restore Christianity's purity, thus restoring secularism's only possible opponent.

Chapter 2
Discussion Questions

1. What does it mean to say "ideas have consequences"?
2. Why is it important to diagnose which real-world events are consequences of which ideas?
3. Summarize Isaiah 47:10b–11. How does this illustrate the relationship between ideas and their real-world consequences?
4. What is an example of a foundational cause? What is an example of a *symptom* of a foundational cause? How are they related?
5. What does it mean to say that all history is *natural* history?
6. What is the correspondence theory of truth? Why must postmodernists presuppose its accuracy in their attempt to reject it?
7. Why do secular social scientists reject the notion of a "force" (similar to gravity) operating behind the causal relationship between ideas, actions, and consequences?
8. Do you agree with the claim that secularism must abstain from all moral condemnation? Why or why not?
9. What is *culture*?
10. What is an *institution*? How does it *both* influence and reflect the culture of a society?
11. Why is the legislature the most difficult branch of government to manipulate?
12. What must a minority ideology accomplish in order to gain/maintain controlling influence in a society? How is secularism accomplishing this?
13. What is a *cultural lag effect*?
14. Do you believe the claim, *Humans will determine our ongoing history*, compromises the sovereignty of God? Why or why not?

3

A Worldview by Any Other Name
The Christian Left: Infiltrated Christianity

"Preach the Word; be prepared in season and out of season; correct, rebuke and encourage—with great patience and careful instruction. For the time will come when men will not put up with sound doctrine. Instead, to suit their own desires, they will gather around them a great number of teachers to say what their itching ears want to hear. They will turn their ears away from the truth and turn aside to myths."
—2 Timothy 4:2–4

"Sincere incompetence is still incompetence."
—Anonymous

An observable pattern should emerge regarding the relationship between foundational ideas and their respective real-world events if there exists a cause-and-effect relationship between the two (i.e., patterns which reflect an unseen "force" as discussed in Chapter 2). Indeed, this is exactly what the study of history tells us. For example, socialist/Marxist societies arise when secular ideas dominate a culture. In turn, socialist principles produce socialist economic and social policies. This inevitably leads to a stagnant economy, high unemployment, a lower standard of living, increased poverty, the suppression of free speech and the right to dissent, totalitarianism, and genocide. This is a real-world example of author Richard Weaver's claim that ideas have consequences.

Notice Weaver did not entitle his book *intentions* have consequences. Nor did he entitle it *formal ideological affiliations* have consequences. He entitled it *ideas* have consequences. Thus, when subsidiary beliefs and real-world events are evaluated, they must be judged according to the logically prior ideas upon which they are dependent rather than the intention, identity, or formal ideological affiliation of the "idea-bearer." If intent and formal ideological affiliation have no bearing on real-world events, they should be excluded from worldview analysis. After all, don't most people have the same intentions? Even the most zealous ideological opponents want the same outcomes: peace, prosperity, equal opportunity, etc. The differences reside in *how* such outcomes are achieved. The answers to the vitally important "how" questions result from the foundational *ideas* that are embraced, not the *intentions* that are embraced. The two are often miles apart. Thus, regardless of intent, identity, or formal ideological affiliation, those who embrace similar foundational ideas work together (consciously or subconsciously) to bring about the real-world consequences of such ideas. An observation I've made in my own experiences illustrates this well.

Changing Opponents

The identity of our opponents changes as our contexts change. I've learned this throughout my educational experiences over the last decade or so. As a Christian conservative undergraduate at Miami University (in Oxford, Ohio) studying Comparative Religion and Philosophy, I was in the minority. Only one or two of the dozen or so professors who comprised the Comparative Religion Department could be considered even nominal believers; the rest were nonbelievers. Similarly, of the dozen or so professors who comprised the Philosophy Department, none could be considered even remotely conservative (none that made it known at least). Thus, I was a minority on two counts in 90% of the classes I took as an undergraduate.

In such a "diverse" academic environment, I clung to any idea, student, book, ideology, or scholar who even remotely resembled being politically conservative, because it was impossible to bring Christian scholarship into the classroom. For example, I was planning an independent study with fellow students and a philosophy professor during my junior year. I suggested we study the works of C. S. Lewis (how naive I was!). The philosophy professor (a feminist) responded via e-mail saying such an option was off the table because the Philosophy Department "doesn't consider C. S. Lewis a philosopher nor his work philosophy."

My loyalties had to be realigned, because Christianity as an intellectual alternative was excluded from the academic setting. Inside the classroom, I couldn't be a political conservative *and* a Christian—*only* a political conservative. The only legitimate battle I was allowed to fight in the academic setting was *political* rather than "religious," because the secular establishment felt it had so thoroughly discredited Christianity (years ago) that it no longer deserved a hearing in the public forum. That which labeled secularism false (Judeo-Christian theism) was excluded outright. Thus, it was *impossible* for secularism, the established religion on campus, to have or be an opponent. Secularism was *unquestionable*. The secular establishment must approve "opponents." This is why the only battle I was allowed to fight was a political one. While secular priests and priestesses on campus ruled out Christianity as a viable alternative, they *reluctantly* allowed my political conservatism a hearing . . . as long as it remained a *secular* form of political conservatism. Thus, academically I joined arms with even the most anti-Christian conservatives out of necessity. Case in point: I suggested the independent study cover some of the works of Ayn Rand, an ardent political conservative/libertarian but also a zealous anti-religionist.

Martians in Montana

I made a name for myself in a course entitled *Philosophy of Education* by being quite talkative (six of the eight students in the class along with the professor were liberals, so we had a lot to talk about). Some of the liberal students were shocked that I, a conservative, could hold my own in an intellectual discussion. Spurred on by my "Bush/Cheney 2000" sticker I proudly displayed around campus, a fellow classmate commented, "James, I respect you as an intellectual peer, but how is it that you can support George W. Bush?" Having been dipped in the baptismal waters of secular education since the age of five and having adopted the dominant worldview therein, her thought process was so warped that the terms "intellectual" and "conservative" were, *by definition*, at opposite ends of the spectrum. In her mind, it was simply impossible to be conservative *and* intelligent at the same time. She had been so conditioned by her worldview that she wasn't aware of the debate raging between liberalism and conservatism in today's culture (a debate nonetheless being smothered on secular campuses everywhere). For her, and for so many other secularists, the secular view is so obviously reasonable and correct that any idiot should be able to figure it out.

C. S. Lewis speaks of this in his book, *Abolition of Man*. Lewis discusses an English textbook used in the schools of his day (although he doesn't mention its title). The textbook tells the student that when Samuel Taylor Coleridge (1772–1834, an English poet and philosopher) described a waterfall as "sublime," he wasn't saying anything about the actual waterfall, but only something about his personal emotional response to the waterfall. The textbook says that when humans make such statements (statements describing an objective truth), we "*appear* to be saying something very important" (emphasis added) when in reality we are "*only saying something about our own feelings.*" (Emphasis added.)

The student who reads this will be inclined to draw a similar conclusion regarding *all* statements describing objective truth—be they physical or metaphysical (morality, values, meaning, etc.). According to the textbook, the observer constructs reality subjectively. The student is unaware he is being taught a lesson in philosophy rather than English. Lewis writes, "It is not a theory they put into his mind, but an assumption, which 10 years hence, its origin forgotten and its presence unconscious, will condition him to take one side in a controversy which he has never recognized as a controversy at all."[1] My self-described "intellectual peer" believed conservatism was obviously absurd, because she was *subconsciously* utilizing a biased presupposition based on an education that never presented a viable alternative to secularism. This is an example of the immense influential power of education and why those scrambling for cultural dominance desperately want control of this institution.

In class I aligned myself with all types of conservatives in attacking political liberalism. It came to the point where I didn't care if I aligned myself with atheists, Jews, Muslims, Buddhists, civil libertarians, or any other subset of theism or conservatism, as long as they were *politically* conservative. Schism over the seemingly "smaller" issues was a luxury I simply couldn't afford.

I had subconsciously accepted the secular–religious barrier institutionally advanced by the secular academic establishment. I began to accept the naturalism peddled by secularists as the only truly objective epistemology (i.e., the method used to determine what is considered knowledge), because my Christian worldview was rejected outright once I stepped into the classroom. My Christianity was unknowingly defused and rendered impotent on the altar of the all-knowing secular college epistemology. This was one of the reasons my ideological loyalties opened up to a broader, more *political* demographic. Inside the classroom, a Christian is homeless, constantly struggling to find a legitimate identity. I identified myself as a political conservative rather than as a Christian, because that was my only path of membership into the academic community.

In his book, *The Outrageous Idea of Christian Scholarship*, George Marsden claims there should be a place in contemporary academia and scholarship for the Christian perspective. For several reasons, however, theistic perspectives (especially Christian) are disqualified from contention by definition. To be admitted into the academic community, one

1. Lewis, *Abolition of Man*, 5.

must set his theistic beliefs aside. Marsden writes, "The fact is that, no matter what the subject, our dominant academic culture trains scholars to keep quiet about their faith as the full price of acceptance in that community."[2] As an undergraduate, I fell in line with the demands of the secular establishment so I could be included in the intellectual community, i.e., so I could "play along."

Marsden identifies this marginalization of theism as a tactic used in pushing the agenda of secular religion. Contrary to the "tolerance," "diversity," and "multiculturalism" on which academia supposedly prides itself, such a marginalization creates a uniformity of thought worthy of the most effective methods of totalitarian propaganda. Marsden claims,

> Peoples of diverse cultures are welcomed into respectable academic culture, but only on the condition that they leave the religious dimensions of their cultures at the door. The result is not diversity, but rather a dreary uniformity. Everyone is expected to accept the standard doctrine that religion has no intellectual relevance.... Such "neutrality," of course, is not neutrality at all, but rather conformity to the standards of a modern mainstream academic culture. In this area, at least, the claims to diversity and multiculturalism have masked the opposite.[3]

I subconsciously fell into this secular trap. I conformed my intellectual pursuits and epistemology to what the secular establishment required. This resulted in a change in the identity of my opponents. Who my opponents were was dictated by the rules of the game. *Because theism is excluded from the debate, secularism cannot be seen as an opponent* (because that which identifies secularism as an opponent, i.e., theism, is excluded). In this environment, secularism becomes so hegemonic that *diverse thought need not be repressed, because it is not possible*. An ideology, army, or nation becomes the *de facto* victor if all opposition is removed. "Diversity" becomes the presence of different *kinds* of secularism rather than the presence of legitimate philosophical alternatives such as Judeo-Christian theism.

As C. S. Lewis discussed in *Abolition of Man*, students and scholars are conditioned such that they subconsciously take one side in a debate without recognizing the existence of a controversy in the first place, i.e., without realizing the existence of the other "side" in a debate. It would be like politicians in Congress discussing the political interests of Martians living in Montana. We need not provide a place in the public forum for

---

2. Marsden, *The Outrageous Idea of Christian Scholarship*, 35.
3. Ibid., 35.

Martians in Montana, because such a demographic along with its opinions and ideas does not exist. A generation from now, the words "Christian," "conservative," and "capitalism"—along with the ideas they describe—may be as absurd as the political demands of Martians in Montana. They certainly were for my "intellectual peer" in my *Philosophy of Education* course.

In light of the overall battle between secularism and Christian theism, debate over the salvific role of baptism, the present-day gifts of the Holy Spirit, and arguments about the end times suddenly seem pointless. I find it absurd that while we are living in a secular culture that rejects the basic notion of God, Christians are busying themselves passionately debating whether it will be the rapture or Christ that comes first at the apocalypse. Inter-family squabbles regarding subsidiary theological questions are less than helpful, considering the first step to effective witnessing is simply getting the secularist open to some vague notion of the supernatural in general. America's culture and institutions have been hijacked by secular totalitarians and are everyday converting an entire generation to their "traditions of men" and "deceptive philosophies" (Colossians 2:8). It's time for Christians to look at the "big picture."[4]

On to Grad School

It blew my mind when Talbot School of Theology rejected my application for graduate school. I was applying for their Master's in Philosophy of Religion and Ethics program but was rejected by the admissions committee because of a minor doctrinal issue (minor from my perspective, at least). To this day, I still have no idea what this doctrinal issue had to do with a M.A. in Philosophy of Religion and Ethics. I made the rather innocuous claim in my application that I believed it was God's will for someone to believe, confess, repent, and be baptized during the conversion process.

So there I was, a 22-year-old student looking forward to studying with cutting-edge scholars such as William Lane Craig and J. P. Moreland in the area of philosophy of religion and ethics, and I was rejected because I believed baptism was part of God's will during the conversion process. I believed my calling in this world was (and still is) to influence culture with the gospel of Jesus Christ, and the perfect place to educate myself with fellow Christian conservatives was Talbot School of Theology. I would join the great cultural battle between secularism and Judeo-Christian theism, and I would utilize Talbot as a major step in acquiring the intellectual resources to do so. Unfortunately, however, while our culture is spiraling downward in a hand-basket, Talbot's admissions committee is dividing our forces based on subsidiary theological issues that have no relevance to the overall issue at hand.

As a result, I applied across town at Fuller Theological Seminary (Talbot is in La Mirada, California, while Fuller is in Pasadena, California), although my decision to attend Fuller had more to do with the fact I had been telling people for over two years I was going to attend graduate school in California—and I didn't want to disappoint. In any event, I ended up at Fuller—a far cry from the political perspectives of Talbot's faculty.

As a graduate student at Fuller Theological Seminary, my context changed from that of a secular university (Miami). Because the student body and faculty consisted of professing Christians, I wondered, *With whom will I banter?* I had been forced to join hands with *any* political conservative on Miami's campus. At Fuller, however, there were nothing but Christians inside *and* outside the classroom. Christianity was not rejected as a viable philosophical alternative. In fact, it was *the* philosophical alternative. For a moment (albeit a very *short* moment), everyone seemed to be on "my side." What was someone "born to banter" to do? Who would be my *new* allies and my *new* opponents? It didn't take long to find out.

While the religious atmosphere on Fuller's campus was drastically different from Miami's, there was very little change in the *political* atmosphere—an interesting intellectual phenomenon. (After all, how can people who *supposedly* embrace two drastically different worldviews agree on so many subsidiary issues? This is discussed later.) Sure, the students and faculty at Fuller were born-again Christians, but the majority was politically liberal, and nothing chaps me more than a pacifist, "pro-choice" Christian. My new opponents: politically liberal Christians. My new allies: politically conservative Christians.

My first year at Fuller was 2002–2003, which you may remember included the spring the United States invaded Iraq. The liberals in southern California (including those on Fuller's campus) were out in full force, doing what they do best: protesting and holding candlelight vigils. To this day, I vividly remember a bumper sticker on the office door of a prominent Fuller professor that read, "When Jesus told us to 'love our neighbors,' I'm pretty sure he meant not to kill them" (a notion based on a serious hermeneutical flaw which is discussed later). You couldn't travel a single block without seeing a "War is not the answer" poster.

Something had to be done. In the name of diversity (a concept secularists obsess with when it comes to race, gender, and sexual orientation—but have no need for in the realm of ideology), my roommates and I decided to start a student group. We named it *Students Promoting the*

Acceptance of Reality, or SPAR. We didn't really recruit other members as much as simply post pamphlets and signs all over campus. Our first project was placing signs that read: INVADE IRAQ. Underneath those words we added a quote attributed to John Stuart Mill (taken from an unofficial web site, of course), which read:

> War is an ugly thing, but not the ugliest of things. The decayed and degraded state of moral and patriotic feeling which thinks that nothing is worth war is much worse. The person who has nothing for which he is willing to fight, nothing which is more important than his own personal safety, is a miserable creature, and has no chance of being free unless made or kept so by the exertions of better men than himself.

A few days later, we posted pamphlets around campus introducing exactly what SPAR was, what we stood for, and a few comments debunking liberal myths regarding affirmative action, gun control, school vouchers, etc. We even received an e-mail from the liberal (and largely pacifist) group, *Students for Peace and Justice*, informing us that we couldn't put our publications on their campus bulletin board, because it was reserved solely for them. Just what the pacifists constituting *Students for Peace and Justice* would have done to stop us had we continued to post, however, is beyond me.

If any of my liberal professors at Fuller are reading this, I can rest assured knowing they are most likely either grinning about the cute little conservative that survived southern California or cringing because they don't want Fuller's name associated with a die-hard conservative who believes it is God's will to fight tooth and nail against pacifism, welfare, public education, the United Nations, and unions. In fact, I recently embraced a lifelong mission to make Talbot forever regret rejecting me and to make Fuller forever regret accepting me.

Due to a few circumstances life threw at me, I finished my last credits of grad school closer to home at Cincinnati Christian University. Politically conservative Christians were teaching me for the first time in my educational career. While plenty of issues were open for debate with the professors and students, I found I had to get my political debating "fix" elsewhere.

So What?

So what if our opponents and allies change as our contexts change? The truth of the matter is that this shift occurs within the cultural battle between secularism and Judeo-Christian theism. It is in this context that I consider non-Christian conservatism an ally and liberal Christianity an opponent, even though many who subscribe to the former may be atheists, while those who adhere to the latter are theists. Whom I consider "allies" and "opponents" may seem ironic, because I believe ideas are not "respecters of persons" or "respecters of men." It doesn't matter which individual, community, or nation adopts them. Their real-world consequences will be the same (see Chapter 2). The "idea to real world" relationship operates independently of subjective factors such as motivation, identity, intent, and formal religious or ideological affiliation.[4]

This is simply to say that, for example, John may abstain from pre-marital sex to glorify God and follow his will. Kevin, on the other hand, may abstain from pre-marital sex for selfish reasons. John and Kevin are two entirely different individuals with diametrically opposed motivations and different (even mutually exclusive) formal ideological affiliations. Yet both will reap the rewards of abstinence before marriage, i.e., not having to worry about contracting a disease, getting a girl pregnant, emotional and spiritual trauma, broken relationships, paying child support, etc. This is what it means to say that ideas are not "respecters of men" (which, of course, includes women). Their real-world consequences will manifest themselves regardless of the identity or motivation of whom it is adhering to the ideas. The idea of sexual abstinence, if acted on, manifests the same real-world consequences regardless of *why* someone acts on it. The relationship between ideas and real-world consequences operates independently of subjective factors such as motivation, identity, intent, and formal religious or ideological affiliation.[5]

Viewing fellow Christians as "opponents" may carry with it the connotations of schism and division. This, however, is not my intention. By explaining the phenomenon, I hope to purge the beachhead that secularism has established within Christendom. In so doing, Christians will be more effective than ever in bringing Truth to the world. With this in mind, it becomes necessary to establish the *connection* between non-Christian conservatism and the Judeo-Christian worldview on the one hand, and the *disconnect* between modern political liberalism and the Judeo-Christian worldview on the other.

---

4. See essay entitled, "He Who Laughs Last," in Chapter 7.

5. As I explain in the essay, "He Who Laughs Last" (in Chapter 7), this-worldly consequences pay no attention to intent, motivation, or identity. Eternal and spiritual consequences, however, *do* take these factors into account. This also brings new meaning to the notion of God's "blessings" and "curses."

Redemption in Individuals or Systems?

Whether non-Christian conservatives (who include many civil libertarians) realize it or not, their political philosophy has the Judeo-Christian worldview as its base. Using Nancy Pearcey's worldview framework, we can see that conservative political philosophy (for example, that of our founding fathers) is the real-world political consequence of the Judeo-Christian worldview. In her book, *Total Truth*, Pearcey claims every worldview, religious *and* secular, answers the same three questions regarding the nature of existence. (This is why it makes sense to claim that every worldview, secular or religious, is *functionally equivalent*.)

Pearcey's first question concerns the issue of *creation*. Because every worldview acknowledges existence itself, every worldview provides an explanation for it. Such an explanation answers the questions, "How did the universe get here?", "How did we get here?", and "What are we?" The second question concerns the issue of the *fall*. Because every worldview acknowledges the evil and suffering so easily observable in our world, every worldview has an explanation for it. In short, the question answered is, "What went wrong?" Third, every worldview has a prescription for how to fix what went wrong, i.e., its own method of *redemption*. Thus, a worldview's prescription for *redemption* answers the question, "How do we fix what went wrong?"

The Christian worldview claims that God created the universe *ex nihilo* (from nothing). It also claims humans are created by God in his image. This is the foundation for believing in the inherent value of each human, man's free will, creative ability, moral capacity, ability to think and reason, etc. Regarding the fall, Christianity claims sin is the problem, i.e., man's rejection of God's will in favor of a fragmented autonomy controlled by sin. Evil and suffering are the real-world consequences of man abusing his free will. Such an abuse makes him sinful and separates him from God. At its core, sin is a *moral* problem. Thus, humanity's problems are *moral*. Redemption in Christianity consists of Jesus Christ taking on the penalty for humanity's sin, removing the reason for humanity's separation from God, and providing the avenue of reconciliation between sinful man and holy God. Additionally, holy living in submission to God's moral laws (regardless of motivation) reduces this-worldly evil and suffering.

These Christian presuppositions provide the groundwork for a society to value individual human life, each person's free will, and an overarching purpose and meaning in the universe. Such is the foundation for freedom and democracy. Utilizing these presuppositions (whether formally acknowledged as "Christian" or not) is the only way to bring about and preserve free societies that respect the inherent value and dignity of human life.

The secular worldview, on the other hand, claims the universe is not the result of divine action but of physical necessity.[6] The universe was not created by anyone or anything. *All* that exists is physical "stuff." As Carl Sagan said in his utterly non-scientific and dogmatic (not to mention *mythological*) statement, "The cosmos is all there ever was, is, or ever will be." *Everything* that exists can be reduced to physical stuff, or materials (hence the term "materialism"). This includes humans. Secularism claims humans are nothing but a complex combination of physical "stuff" comprised of molecules, chemicals, and firing synapses—and, as such, are subject to the same physical laws of nature that rule everything else in the universe. There is no qualitative difference between a hydrogen atom, a rock, a tree, and a human other than their respective levels of complexity. Just as an apple is pulled to the ground by gravity after disconnecting from a branch, human thoughts and behaviors are also dictates of physical laws. In other words, like the Nazis and secular humanists believe, humans are a result of "blood and soil." (Any secularist who denies these claims is being inconsistent with his own worldview.)

To a secularist, human thoughts, personality, decisions, and lifestyles are results of purely physical factors (heredity and environment). In short, free will is an illusion. For free will to exist, there must be something essentially *non-physical* (non-material) about a person (which, according to secularism, doesn't exist) which is not governed by physical law. Thus, all history (the ideas and actions of humans) is attributable to genes and environment. Because a human is the sum total of its responses to physical stimuli (biological and social), everything a person thinks and does is determined by such physical stimuli, i.e., a person's genes or the environment (or *system*) in which a person exists. This is just as true for individual behavior and general social trends as it is for less complex materials. For example, water doesn't "choose" to turn to ice when it reaches its freezing point. It does so at the mercy of physical law. There is nothing non-physical about water that provides a "place" for free will. Human actions are determined the same way.

For example, an individual who robs a bank may have done so because he grew up in a poverty-stricken neighborhood, didn't have two parents who raised him, etc. A person is poor because he was born into an oppressive economic system and is incapable of "moving up." Someone is homosexual for genetic reasons, i.e., someone is "born gay." In the general

---

6. See the essay entitled, "Chance, Choice, or Chosen" in Chapter 7.

sense, crime is caused by poverty, poverty is caused by lack of education (as is racism, hatred, etc.), and so on and so forth. Thus, all human behavior—including that which causes evil and suffering—is determined by physical "input."

Secular reasoning goes something like this: Bad (oppressive) systems (and/or bad genes) beget bad humans. Bad humans beget bad thoughts and actions. Bad thoughts and actions beget evil and suffering. Therefore, systems and/or genes are the foundational cause of evil and suffering. Inversely, secular reasoning also claims the following: Good physical input (systems and genes) beget good humans. Good humans beget good thoughts and actions. Good thoughts and actions beget good real-world consequences (no suffering or evil). Redemption (*fixing* society), therefore, lies in instituting and maintaining the physical input (systems and genes) that produces good human thoughts and actions. This logical relationship is why Marxism, an ideology obsessed with systems, is the *necessary* political and economic ideology of secularism. This analysis also explains why secularists focus on *systems* when attempting to improve society. (The disastrous consequences of genetic engineering aren't discussed here. However, there were numerous horrible examples of this in Nazi Germany.) Similarly, this analysis explains why Christians (with their beliefs about the inherent value of the individual and his free will) focus on *individuals* when attempting to improve society.

Returning to the big picture for a moment, secularism provides no foundation for the belief that individual life is *inherently* valuable. Nor does it provide a basis for a value demanding respect for the human conscience, i.e., the freedom to dissent (free will) or a value that infuses meaning and purpose into existence. Such objective, metaphysical claims are not physical things and are not derivable from physical "stuff." Therefore, according to secularism, they do not exist. This results in a moral vacuum that, as history tells us, will be filled by *something*. Which, or whose, ideas fill this vacuum is determined by whoever achieves power.

Where the Rubber Meets the Road

The crux of the issue is the real-world consequences of a worldview. The motivation of anyone who gets involved in cultural dialogue and debate is to make a difference in the world; to "right the wrongs" of society and to fix the evil and suffering in this world. Thus, our journey into first principles is an attempt to *expose the presuppositions* that ultimately lead to real-world consequences—good *and* bad.

Thus, while Pearcey's first-principle issues of *creation* and the *fall* are logically prior to the question of *redemption* (and therefore *must* be answered first), it is a worldview's explanation of *redemption* that directly manifests the *observable* real-world consequences that form the subsidiary issues most often debated in the public forum. A worldview's theory of redemption also informs the purpose given to the institutions that influence the direction of a society. *How* a person proposes to fix what he sees as a problem will be determined by how he views *redemption*. In other words, it matters not which basic worldview a person (or society) *formally* espouses. Real-world events are the result of whichever worldview's presuppositions are utilized in attempting to *actually solve* real-world problems. Once again, we see that ideas are not "respecters of men."

As briefly stated above, a secularist who wishes to influence society will do so based on his presupposition that salvation lies in instituting the right *systems* (and, often, the right genes). Conversely, a Christian theist wishing to influence society will do so based on his presupposition that salvation lies in changing the heart of the *individual*. This explains why secularists (a group that includes modern liberals—even Christian liberals, as explained later) try to change society through *systems* (such as welfare, socialized medicine, massive public education, and wealth redistribution) *and* why they hold external factors such as racism, poverty, lack of education, and economic oppression (all things that comprise the environment of an individual) responsible for the ills of society.

Secularists who blame evil and suffering on the aforementioned external factors and try to change society through massive systemic changes such as those stated above *are merely being logically consistent with the presuppositions they use to organize their opinions and lives.* Thus *it should come as no surprise* that secularists genuinely support systemic programs such as welfare, affirmative action, socialized medicine, and public education, as well as those politicians who support such programs. If human thoughts and actions are products of systems, it logically follows that government programs that forcefully attempt to change the system will be successful in manipulating human behavior for the better. Salvation is just on the other side of a little social engineering.

Similarly, it should come as no surprise that non-secularists/conservatives (especially Christians) reject such explanations for social ills along with their prescriptions for social redemption. It's not a coincidence that they reject programs such as welfare and socialized medicine and vote for politicians who embrace legislation that emphasizes the behavior of individuals. They believe secular/liberal programs will not help "fix" society.

Attempting to forcefully change systems through government programs will not manipulate human behavior for the better, because humans are *not* merely the product of physical input (i.e. systems and genes). *Such non-secularists/conservatives are merely being logically consistent with the presuppositions they use to organize their opinions and lives.*

This is also true for the type of curricula chosen to educate children (*how* to educate children, i.e., which ideas will be taught), *how* to fight the war on terrorism, *how* to achieve economic prosperity, etc. For example, *everyone* claims that we must win the war on terror. *Everyone* claims we should educate our children. *Everyone* claims we want economic prosperity. *Everyone* claims they want equality throughout society. In this sense, the language used to describe goals is the same for the secularist and Christian, Marxist and capitalist, Democrat and Republican, etc. The difference resides in *how* each group wants to achieve the goal.

How a person or group believes these things will be accomplished is entirely contingent upon the basic ideas they hold to be true. Therein lies the difference between a pacifist who believes all conflicts can be resolved diplomatically and a military hawk who believes some conflicts can only be resolved through force; a Democrat who supports welfare and wealth redistribution and a Republican who despises welfare and socialist wealth redistribution programs; someone who believes more education will solve society's problems and someone who believes society's problems are moral in nature rather than merely knowledge-based;[7] a pro-abortion advocate who staunchly believes accessible abortion is vital for a healthy society and a pro-life activist who believes abortion is murder, and so on and so forth.

Someone once told me that before we can solve the problem of global terrorism, we must first solve the problem of global poverty. This is a perfect example of employing secular presuppositions to diagnose the cause of a type of undesirable human behavior (terrorism). Because she believed (consciously or not) human beings are created by the systems that surround them, she *must also* believe the problem has to be solved by appealing to such systems.

Thus, while we both claimed we must defeat terrorism, we had very different views on *how*. Therein lies the reason why I want to forcefully restrain terrorists to get rid of them (because each terrorist freely chooses his behavior), while she wants to institute a global wealth redistribution system to get rid of them (because poverty causes the terrorist "lifestyle," not terrorists themselves). These two methods look very different when it comes to foreign policy and legislation. We are at opposite ends of the

7. Discussed in Chapter 5.

spectrum regarding this subsidiary political issue (in this case, foreign policy). (This also explains why many secularists blame America for terrorism. If America has created an oppressive environment in a foreign country through economic exploitation or violence motivated by oil prices, America is then responsible for fostering an environment that breeds hateful people and their actions based on such hate.)

To know *why* we arrived at diametrically opposed solutions for the same problem, however, one must examine our respective beliefs regarding the foundational question concerning what a human being is—a question answered differently by our respective worldviews. The fact that her subsidiary belief concerning foreign policy came to be "liberal" was because secularism served as her foundation. My subsidiary belief concerning foreign policy ended up on the "conservative" side because Christianity served as my foundation. In the end, ideological (or "political") conservatism is the logical result of the Judeo-Christian worldview. Ideological liberalism is the logical result of the secular worldview. Thus, an ideologically conservative secularist is a logical contradiction. Similarly, a Christian who is ideologically liberal is also a contradiction. (A politically liberal Christian is usually guilty of either "worldview borrowing" or embracing a common hermeneutical flaw. Both will soon be discussed.)

A Worldview by Any Other Name . . .

Identifying someone as a "conservative" or "liberal" can be difficult. One method is to simply list several different issues such as abortion, welfare, war, capital punishment, taxes, economics, church and state issues, etc. A general trend usually emerges by asking what a person believes regarding each of these issues. If someone agrees with the "conservative side" of these issues more than the "liberal side," it can usually be said that such a person is a conservative (and vice-versa for a liberal).

Understanding first principles, however, enables us to see the subsidiary nature of the issues on this list. It's not that a person is liberal or conservative because they believe certain things about subsidiary issues. *A person believes certain things about subsidiary issues because he is a conservative or a liberal*, i.e., a Judeo-Christian theist or a secularist (or a person who is at least acting on a particular worldview's presuppositions—consciously or subconsciously). Beliefs regarding subsidiary issues are determined by prior foundational presuppositions. It is at the level of presuppositions that a person should be identified as a conservative or liberal—*not* at the level of subsidiary issues. A person who ends up being conservative on subsidiary issues began with

Judeo-Christian presuppositions (consciously or not). Inversely, someone who ends up being liberal on subsidiary issues began with secular presuppositions (consciously or not).

If someone told me his opinions regarding creation, fall, and redemption, I could most likely predict his opinion on subsidiary issues *if* he remained logically consistent with his presuppositions. This is often a difficult task, however, because people don't always remain consistent within their own worldview. A perfect example of this is a secularist who believes in nonphysical objective values such as "helping the poor is good," "rape is wrong," "murder is wrong," and/or "exploiting Third World countries for economic gain is wrong." A secularist may, indeed, hold such metaphysical claims as true, but his worldview, in virtue of its rejection of the metaphysical, doesn't provide the intellectual foundation to do so. Because this secularist doesn't accept the consequences of his own worldview (that there is no such thing as morality), he "reaches over" (albeit subconsciously) into another worldview and "borrows" presuppositions that *do* allow for belief in morals.

The inconsistency (for the borrowing secularist) lies in the fact that the presuppositions that enable belief in objective morality (provided by Judeo-Christian theism) are contradictory to the secular presuppositions the secularist *formally* espouses. If the presuppositions of one are true, the presuppositions of the other are *necessarily* false. Another problem is that the consistent secularist has no basis for condemning those who believe rape is fun or that exploiting the poor is permissible to make an extra buck. Thus, in order to condemn other value claims, the secularist must "borrow" Judeo-Christian presuppositions that allow him to do so.

It is interesting to note that secularists will borrow Judeo-Christian presuppositions *as a basis* for valuing the poor (or valuing *anyone* for that matter), yet they will employ their own secular presuppositions when *attempting to alleviate* the actual real-world problem of poverty. For example, the basic fact that secularists value the poor and wish to alleviate poverty and oppression is the result of borrowing the Christian presupposition that humans have inherent value. When it comes to actually getting rid of poverty and oppression, however, secularists will revert back to secular presuppositions concerning humanity, i.e., presuppositions that claim humans are merely physical stuff at the mercy of systems (a claim that, as we already have seen, rejects the inherent value of the individual and provides no motivation to alleviate poverty). Thus, secularists try to actualize (manifest in the real world) a Christian presupposition by employing secular methods. Such a contradictory process is doomed to failure. *Christian* methods must be utilized to actualize *Christian* presuppositions.

This is why welfare and entitlement programs (*systems* designed to alter human behavior) won't solve problems such as poverty and crime. They are attempts based on secularism that try to actualize a Christian value. In essence, secularists are prescribing secular medicine in their attempt to bring about values that are, by necessity, uniquely *Christian*.

This is why secularists (which include liberal Christians; see discussion that follows) are often the most staunch supporters of welfare and entitlement programs. They (subconsciously) maintain the Judeo-Christian presupposition that humans have inherent value (a Christian presupposition "written on their hearts," Romans 2:15), but they abide by secular presuppositions when attempting to solve the problem. Christianity's presuppositions provide both the secularist and the liberal Christian with the *motivation* to help the poor. However, the presuppositions appealed to when attempting to *solve* the problem, rather than the presuppositions appealed to for the basis of valuing poor people in the first place, will ultimately determine the real-world consequences, i.e. the success (or lack thereof) of the attempt to alleviate poverty. This is a perfect example of how the relationship between ideas and real-world events operates independently of subjective factors such as motivation, identity, intent, and formal religious or ideological affiliation.

Secularists, however, don't have a monopoly on "worldview borrowing." Christians who hold beliefs or support programs (such as pro-abortion policy, welfare, socialized medicine, pacifist foreign policy, education as a salve for all our ills, etc.) based on the secular explanation of humanity and redemption are guilty of the same. This is the case with liberal Christians. They combine the Christian worldview with the secular presupposition regarding what a human being is (i.e., merely physical stuff whose thoughts and actions are determined by physical stimuli). If asked outright, liberal Christians will reject basic secular presuppositions (because they are obviously unbiblical). Yet when attempting to alleviate a social ill in the real world, liberal Christians unknowingly (and often enthusiastically) embrace the secular presuppositions they *formally* reject.

Despite a sincere Christian faith, liberal Christians contribute to the manifestation of the disastrous real-world consequences inherent in the secular presuppositions they transplant into their Christianity—consciously or subconsciously—when attempting to solve real-world problems. Because ideas are not "respecters of men," it doesn't matter that the inconsistent Christian is genuine. The disastrous consequences of secularism will rear their ugly heads regardless of who's infusing its presuppositions into our culture or why they are doing it.

This is why liberal Christians are on the wrong "side" in the overall cultural battle between secularism and Judeo-Christian theism. The secular presuppositions they utilize to *solve* a problem that is *initially* identified by a Christian value (or basic presupposition) preclude the real-word manifestation of the Christian value and results in the manifestation of the disastrous real-world consequences inherent in secularism. Liberal Christians are double agents and don't know it. Sincerity may save their souls, but it is of no help in making *this* world a better place. Secular explanations of reality have infiltrated their now tainted Judeo-Christian worldview and corrupted their beliefs regarding subsidiary issues such as abortion, homosexual marriage, welfare, socialized medicine, pacifist foreign policy, massive entitlement programs, global wealth redistribution plans, public education, and other policies that treat humans as the mindless automatons secularism claims they are. Liberal Christians maintain Christianity's basic presuppositions (or basic *values*) about humanity and justice, yet they abide by secular presuppositions in their attempts to actualize such values. Liberal Christians must realize that *secular* methods will yield the real-world manifestation (a world where humans have no inherent value or dignity) of *secular* presuppositions (that humans are merely physical "stuff").

Worldview Borrowing

Something is wrong when two people who formally espouse mutually exclusive worldviews agree on so many subsidiary issues. One or both of them is probably "borrowing" a presupposition or two from the other's worldview.[8] This explains why my Christian seminary professors and secular undergraduate professors held nearly identical subsidiary beliefs despite their formal adherence to mutually exclusive worldviews. They were subconsciously borrowing each other's presuppositions. My secular undergraduate professors unknowingly borrow Christian presuppositions to provide an *objective moral foundation* for those pesky values they can't exorcize (which are "written on their hearts") while my Christian seminary professors unknowingly borrow secular presuppositions to derive their *methods to solve* the world's ills.

Why is this a problem? Because both groups base their proposed solutions for the world's ills on secular presuppositions. Thus, they maintain the same subsidiary beliefs. In turn, because ideas are not "respecters of men," secular values will be manifested (resulting in a world where humans do not have inherent value and dignity) *rather than* Christian values

---

8. See the essays entitled, "Democracy and Consensus: Parts 1 & 2" in Chapter 7.

(which would result in a world where humans *do* have inherent value and dignity). Regardless of the initial Christian foundation (held consciously by my seminary professors but subconsciously by my secular professors), secularism's real-world consequences carry the day because its methods are being utilized for *redemption* purposes.

A secularist who claims society should help the poor is borrowing the Christian presupposition that humans have inherent value and should be treated as such. A Christian who thinks poverty or lack of education is the cause of out-of-wedlock children, crime, and/or terrorism is borrowing the secular presupposition that humans are physical automatons determined by their environment. Similarly, atheist conservatives are borrowing the Christian presuppositions that underlie conservative political ideology.

Similar to liberal Christians who infuse secular presuppositions into our culture and unknowingly contribute to the disastrous real-world consequences of secularism, atheist conservatives who infuse Judeo-Christian presuppositions into our culture are unknowingly contributing to the positive real-world consequences of Judeo-Christian theism. Both are being inconsistent within their own worldview. Because real-world consequences do not compensate for inconsistency, however, atheist conservatives are making *this* world a better place while liberal Christians are not.

Because objective values, i.e. moral *laws*, are written into the fabric of the universe just as physical laws are written into the fabric of the universe, there are consequences to breaking (or ignoring) both.[9] The *sincerity* and *identity* of the lawbreaker, however, matters little. An aerospace engineer may have sincerely good or diabolical intentions when designing a jet engine or airplane according to his own flawed set of physical laws, but the real-world consequences will be the same: Crashing planes and dead passengers.

Similarly, a liberal Christian who supports socialist policies (that arise from secular presuppositions) and supports liberal politicians may be doing so sincerely, but such sincerity will not change the resultant real-world consequences: high unemployment and a sputtering (to say the least) economy; less religious freedom; 4,500 unborn children slaughtered each day (in America alone); a secular monopolistic public school system passing on secular ideas to the next generation; pacifist foreign policy resulting in decreased peace and increased upheaval; an overall devaluation of human life; euthanasia; increased crime; decreased political freedoms, etc.

Besides, sincerity will not comfort the Kurd whose family was raped, tortured, and killed by Saddam Hussein and his henchmen. Nor

---

9. See the essays entitled, "Poverty, AIDS, and Objective Morality" and "Reality: The Undisputed Champion of the Universe" in Chapter 7.

will it comfort the unborn children who have their lives abruptly and violently destroyed. Sincerity didn't comfort the six million Jews murdered by Hitler. Nor did it comfort the 100 million murdered in the name of communism in the twentieth century. These tragic, real-world consequences occurred from embracing bad foundational ideas, and they would have occurred regardless of whether those who did the embracing were Christians, secularists, Marxists, capitalists, Buddhists, republicans, democrats, or Martians in Montana. They also occur regardless of how secularism is repackaged (e.g., as tolerance, multiculturalism, liberalism, progressivism, humanism, postmodernism, etc.).

This relationship between presuppositions and real-world consequences is why you might find otherwise diverse individuals and groups allying themselves with one another in certain contexts. People who hold common presuppositions are usually found in like company regardless of the worldview they *formally* espouse. This is why you often see liberal Christians standing alongside atheist Marxists during a rally (or candlelight vigil) protesting a war, a tax cut, a pro-life and pro-free-market Supreme Court Justice, or capital punishment. This is also why you often see Christians standing alongside atheist conservatives during a rally supporting pro-life legislation, a particular war, free-trade agreements, tax cuts, etc.

Ultimately, the *connection* between atheistic conservatism and Christianity is that the former is built on the presuppositions of the latter—consciously or subconsciously, sincerely or insincerely. The *disconnect* between liberal Christianity and biblical Christianity is that the former is *not* based upon the presuppositions of the latter but on the presuppositions of secularism—consciously or subconsciously, sincerely or insincerely. Real-world consequences, however, are a result of presuppositions employed rather than sincerity. This is why I include politically liberal Christians when I reference secularism or secularists. This is also why the bulk of the essays in this book use the term "liberal" or "liberalism" to refer to the opponent of Christianity rather than "secularism." For the above stated reasons, they are essentially the same.

Hermeneutics and God's Politics

No amount of sincerity will prevent the real-world consequences of the ideas humanity embraces. Because "future history" will be determined by the ideas we choose to embrace today—be they "good" or "bad"—we must align our ideas with the metaphysical realities written into the fabric of the universe. This is vital, because aligning our beliefs with ideas that don't accurately reflect the objective metaphysical realities of the universe results in disaster. We must learn exactly what realities are written into the fabric of the universe. Like most things accomplished in this world, there is an easy way and a hard way to do this.

The hard way is blindly leading ourselves through history, employing every idea that comes our way in some sort of trial-and-error method. Eventually we may find what ideas "work," but pragmatism such as this is inefficient, shortsighted, and *requires* a great deal of suffering before progress can be made. Furthermore, considering humanity's impatience, complete progression through this process is highly unlikely. The easy way is to listen to the One who created the fabric of the universe in the first place. If we want to know the details and purpose of a building, we go to its architect. If we want to know the details and purpose of the universe, we go to its Designer. Luckily, we have that option.

God reveals himself to us in two non-contradictory ways: 1) General revelation and 2) Special revelation. General revelation includes (among other things) our ability to think and reason, experience emotions, observe the world around us, create (art and science), and experience human relationships. Special revelation is personified in Jesus Christ and the Scripture God provided for us, i.e., the Bible. Both forms of revelation, uncorrupted by "human tradition" and "deceptive philosophy" (Colossians 2:8), reveal God. A healthy mix of both, combined with a proper hermeneutic, and we are well on our way to discovering the metaphysical ideas written into the fabric of the universe.

Another benefit of analyzing first principles is the ability to accurately apply Scripture to contemporary life. Many Christians (as well as non-Christians) are often quick to point out that the Bible doesn't mention anything specific about subsidiary issues such as political or economic systems, social entitlement programs, military buildup, the separation of church and state, or socialized healthcare—let alone *endorse* any of these notions. The great thing about analyzing first principles, however, is that it isn't necessary for the Bible to do so!

If subsidiary issues are determined by presuppositions, we need not scour the Bible for specific references to subsidiary contemporary issues (especially issues that didn't exist in the first century). Instead, we must identify the presuppositions that *are* provided by the Bible. From there, we can determine the biblical or "Christian" position on subsidiary issues.

If we discover what the Bible says about the *creation*, *fall*, and *redemption* paradigm, we can, in turn, discover the biblical position on subsidiary issues such as abortion, foreign policy, entitlement and wealth redistribution programs, socialized medicine, the environment, and the proper roles of government and education. Any opinion, program, or form of government based on non-biblical presuppositions regarding creation, fall, or redemption should be considered unbiblical and, therefore, an inaccurate reflection of the physical and metaphysical realities written into the fabric of the universe. Thus, they are "bad" ideas that will result in disastrous real-world consequences (which is where *all* inaccurate or "bad" ideas lead). Once we determine a particular worldview's presuppositions, then we must determine which subsidiary opinions, programs, and ideologies are the conclusions of that particular worldview. Once again, we see the importance of being able to discover the *origin* of a subsidiary idea.

For example, Marxism (socialism, communism, etc.) is an unbiblical political ideology, because it is derived from secular presuppositions that are inherently contradictory to those provided by the Bible. (See prior discussion, "Redemption in Individuals or Systems?") Therefore, every belief or program based on Marxist or socialist principles, i.e., secular presuppositions, is unchristian by definition. This is why the pro-abortion position, the criminal justice system seen as a rehabilitative institution rather than an institution meant for punishment, massive wealth redistribution and entitlement programs, pacifist foreign policy, secular environmentalism, the notion that societal ills are caused by ignorance rather than immorality, the "separation of religion and state," euthanasia, totalitarian regimes, using the judiciary as the legislature, shattering the traditional notion of the family, and secular "safe sex" education methods (to name a few) are all unbiblical, i.e., "unchristian." They are attempts to bring about redemption through systemic methods based on secularism's materialistic presuppositions concerning humanity. (Most of these examples are discussed in the essays throughout Part Three.) Only beliefs, programs, and ideologies derived from presuppositions provided by the Bible can properly be considered "Christian." The key to exposing the "Christian-ness" or "unchristian-ness" of a piece of legislation, policy, or politician is to identify the usually unstated presuppositions (regarding creation, fall, and redemption) of the proposal or person.

Liberal Christianity: Theologically Liberal Christianity

How, then, did secular presuppositions infiltrate Christianity? If liberal Christianity is not based on biblical presuppositions, it may be helpful to hypothesize how this happened. Before this question is answered, however, it should be noted that "liberal Christianity" takes two forms: 1) Theologically liberal Christianity and 2) Politically liberal Christianity. While most theologically liberal Christians are politically liberal, not all politically liberal Christians are theologically liberal.

I was first exposed to theologically liberal Christianity as an undergraduate studying Comparative Religion in a secular religion department at Miami University. This exposure took the form of reading books authored by scholars who consider themselves to be "Christian." For example, you may read books by the liberal scholar John Dominic Crossan or see him being interviewed in a documentary on television. During such interviews, he claims to be a Christian, but what he means by "Christian" is drastically different from what most people think when they use or hear the term "Christian."

Like most, Crossan uses the title "Christian" to indicate he is a follower of Jesus. Crossan's Jesus, however, is much different from the biblical Jesus whom orthodox Christians confess. Crossan's Jesus (as well as that of The Jesus Seminar) is a secularized version of the Jesus described in the Bible. Because Crossan begins with secular presuppositions, he is forced into secular conclusions. Thus, Crossan's Jesus is utterly un-supernatural; he performed no miracles, and there was certainly no resurrection. Crossan's Jesus never claimed to be the Messiah, nor did he claim divinity. Crossan's Jesus did not prophesy the coming of a supernatural kingdom of God that would overthrow evil and redeem God's people. Furthermore, Crossan contends the vast majority of what the Gospels say about Jesus is completely fabricated—an invention of the later church.

Crossan's self-prescribed "Christianity" is basically a commitment to the feel-good Jesus of the Sermon on the Mount (which, according to Crossan, is about the only truthful account of Jesus in the Gospels), who tells everyone to be nice to one another. Exactly how this Jesus sets himself apart from all the other "be nice to one another" prophets in history, however, is beyond me. Needless to say, Crossan is not a Christian in any meaningful sense of the term. His attempt to salvage a meaningful Jesus within his secular worldview leaves him with a banal teacher naively dreaming of a utopia perpetually beyond humanity's reach; a glorified hippie-Jesus easily embraced by secularists.

A more honest treatment of Christianity by a secularist can be found in the writings of Dale Allison. He is a secularist who acknowledges that Jesus did, indeed, claim to be the Messiah. Allison believes Jesus prophesied of a coming supernatural kingdom where God would set things right and redeem his people. Being a secularist, however, Allison simply concludes that Jesus was wrong. Thus, like Crossan, Allison concludes there were no miracles and no resurrection. Presenting the conflicting, yet ultimately similar, claims of Crossan and Allison is a secular religion department's idea of "diversity."

Theologically liberal Christianity is the result of secular Enlightenment philosophy infiltrating biblical studies. Instead of approaching the Bible with an open mind regarding its claims, the Bible is investigated using a secular methodology that presupposes the impossibility of the supernatural. Once again, the proverbial "deck" is stacked in favor of secularism.

Some within this Enlightenment movement, like Crossan, attempt to retain a meaningful and relevant Jesus. But, as mentioned earlier, this results in assigning undue honor to a rather trite individual. Others, like Allison, aren't worried about salvaging a meaningful Jesus or a remnant of Christianity. Either way, orthodox Christianity is debunked as naïve superstition.

Liberal Christianity: Politically Liberal Christianity

Politically liberal Christianity, on the other hand, is a much more interesting development. While politically liberal Christianity is also the result of secular Enlightenment philosophy infiltrating biblical studies, it is also the consequence of a common hermeneutical flaw. For some, this flaw is an honest mistake, but for others it is merely a way to justify a preferred set of political beliefs. I see this flaw at work within four main groups: 1) People who have converted to Christianity after being witnessed to by a politically liberal Christian, 2) Political liberals who convert to Christianity and wish to maintain their previous political persuasion, 3) People who buy into modern liberal clichés that *sound* really good but fail to examine them below the surface, (after all, one must really be an insensitive dolt to disagree with statements like "Everyone should have health care" or "We should all help the poor"), and 4) Those who have much to gain from liberal politics.

Before we launch into this hermeneutical flaw, however, it will be helpful to mention the ways politically liberal Christianity is different from its theological counterpart. Unlike theologically liberal Christianity, it is much more theologically conservative. In fact, there may not be much difference in the doctrinal beliefs of a politically liberal Christian and a politically conservative Christian. In general, they both accept the miracle claims of the Bible, including the bodily resurrection of Christ. They both believe the Bible was written by first-generation Christians who did not misrepresent Jesus' teachings and claims concerning his own identity.

Thus, the validity of the Bible and the reliability of its historical claims are generally held in high regard.

I was first exposed to the idea of this hermeneutical flaw while taking Dr. Jack Cottrell's[10] "Doctrine of God" course at Cincinnati Christian University. Dr. Cottrell explained what he termed the *Christological Fallacy*. It is the belief that Jesus Christ in his role as redeemer (i.e., in the incarnation) is the true and only basis for ethical obligation and the primary source for determining our beliefs regarding subsidiary issues (e.g., ethics, politics, economics, etc.). The fallacy also involves attempting to explain the attributes of God by only referring to Jesus Christ's earthly ministry. Viewing Christ's earthly ministry as the sole standard for determining subsidiary beliefs leaves us with a drastically incomplete conception of God and his will.

If someone *does* base his ethical and political beliefs solely on Christ's ministry, however, it should come as no surprise that he ends up supporting massive entitlement programs and welfare, weak (or no) criminal punishments, and pacifist foreign policy (just to name a few). After all, Christ spent an enormous amount of time instructing us to care for the poor, turn the other cheek, and to love our neighbors (although many liberal Christians ignore the equally real "not-so-nice" Jesus also found in the Gospels). If these teachings are applied to government, the logical result is (among other things) socialist economic policy and pacifist foreign and criminal justice policies.

The aforementioned bumper sticker on the office door of a Fuller professor, which read, "When Jesus told us to 'love our neighbors,' I'm pretty sure he meant not to kill them" is a perfect example of the Christological Fallacy. The professor believed that the role and methods of civil government must conform to the standards of Christ's earthly ministry *only*. This is one reason why many genuine born-again Christians embrace socialist and pacifist policies that are actually based on secular presuppositions. *Secularists* embrace them because they believe redemption is through systems. *Politically liberal Christians* embrace them because they mistakenly believe Christ demands them (due to the Christological Fallacy). Regardless, secularism's disastrous real-world consequences manifest.

---

10. Cottrell, *What the Bible Says About God the Creator*, 166–171.

Love and Holiness:
Not Two Sides of the Same Coin

Determining God's attributes by only referencing Christ's earthly ministry has tragic consequences of its own. Instead of a loving *and* holy God who demands punishment for sin and provides humanity with salvation, the God of the Christological Fallacy is a God who sweeps sin under the rug and expects nothing from his believers. It is true that God wants people to come to him through Christ *as they are*, but he is not content to let them stay that way. Liberal Christians often forget the latter truth. God's holiness is seen as merely a weak aspect of God's love (which is seen as his *true* attribute) rather than an attribute in itself.

I'm reminded of a recent television commercial for the United Methodist Church. The setting is a church where the congregation is sitting in pews while listening to a sermon. As we soon learn, the pews have ejection seats in them. As the camera pans the congregation, certain people are ejected. The ejectees include racial minorities, someone with a disability, an elderly woman, and a homosexual couple. (Such is the United Methodist Church's perception of theologically conservative churches and denominations.) At the end of the commercial, the screen displays the message: "God doesn't reject people. Neither do we." The Bible is clear that it is not sinful to be a racial minority, have a disability, or be elderly. The Bible is *also* clear, however, that homosexuality is sinful and, like every other sin, God expects his people to live repentant lifestyles as free from sin as possible. Conversion is only the first step. A lifetime of honoring God is a process that continues until Christ returns and fully redeems his people. No matter what sins the believer struggles with—be it lying, lust, rage, violence, swearing, gossip, greed, or homosexuality—he must acknowledge the sin in his life and submit to the Lord's headship. In short, there's no such thing as an unrepentant Christian, because such a Christian has not submitted to Christ's lordship—the very essence of "Christianity."

Liberal Christians are usually very good at presenting the "Come as you are" message, but they fail miserably at delivering the "Submit to the Lord's headship" message. This results in a God who accepts everyone *and* the sin in their lives. God certainly does the former, but for him to do the latter would go against his very nature. God is holy and must be separate from sin at all times. It is his holiness, not his love, that demands punishment for sin. As sinners, we cannot be in the presence of God and must suffer physical and spiritual death as the penalty for our sins (see Romans 6:23). However, by removing our sin and suffering the punishment for sin on the cross, Christ, through his sacrifice, made it possible for us to be in God's holy presence. Thus, those who do not accept Christ's sacrifice and thereby have their sin and punishment diverted to Christ, cannot be in God's holy presence.

While God rejects *no one* who chooses to accept Christ, he *certainly will* reject unrepentant sinners at the final judgment. Thus, the phrase "God doesn't reject people . . ." is patently unbiblical. Unfortunately, the Christological Fallacy results in a God who accepts every sinful behavior and lifestyle. This results in a church comprised of unrepentant sinners and explains why liberal Christianity ordains homosexual pastors as well as acknowledges less and less behavior as sinful (such as cohabitation, premarital sex, abortion, etc.).

A God without holiness and wrath is a God without love or, at best, a God who cannot show his love. John 3:16 reads, "For God so loved the world that he gave his one and only Son, that whoever believes in him shall not perish but have eternal life." God's love is perfectly manifested in what he *did* for us. Unless we understand exactly what God *did* for us, we will never fully understand his love. In other words, *why* was it such a big deal for God to sacrifice his only Son? In short, because the punishment must fit the crime.

Not only does sin separate us from God, it also brings us under his wrath. As if eternal separation from God isn't bad enough, being the eternal object of God's wrath is infinitely worse. I think it is accurate to say that God's wrath is the worst thing *ever*—worse than Satan himself and evil itself. In fact, God's wrath *is* hell. With this in mind, Christians must acknowledge that hell exists because of God; not in the sense that God willed sin into the world, but in the sense that God's attribute of holiness *demands* hell's potential in a world without sin and hell's real existence in a world with sin. Thus, the penalty for sin is separation from God and being the object of God's wrath. Herein lies the ability to comprehend the immense depth of God's love. Whatever may have happened on the cross, we can know that Jesus Christ experienced *at least* two things: 1) Separation from God the Father, and 2) suffering as the object of God's wrath. Unfortunately, because everyone sins and *already* deserves such punishments, God himself was the only potential candidate for the job. The amount of love it took for *God himself* to sacrifice and experience these two things is mind-boggling.

What many liberal Christians don't realize is that *without* a holy and wrathful God, Christ's death accomplished nothing—nor was it necessary. A God who only loves need not punish sin. After all, if being the

A Worldview by Any Other Name

object of God's wrath and experiencing separation from God are necessary consequences of sin required by God's holiness, the absence of said holiness necessitates the absence of said consequences. Thus, there is no "gap" between God and man necessitating the need for redemption, i.e., there is no reason for Christ to suffer and die on the cross. The cross becomes, at best, unjust and, at worst, absurd. Instead of the crucifixion being the perfect manifestation of God's holiness and love that *actually* accomplished mankind's redemption, it becomes a senseless event that accomplished absolutely nothing. Jesus' ministry and death are reduced to quaint examples of how everyone should be able to get along with one another (i.e. an educational experience); Jesus becomes the trite hippie-Jesus of John Dominic Crossan and a Gnostic liberator rather than a divine redeemer.[11]

There are many places in the Old and New Testaments that reveal God's wrath, but Jesus gives us a good taste of it when he is praying in the Garden of Gethsemane. Why he was going to die wasn't a mystery to Jesus. He knew exactly the reason. On the eve of his death, he was intensely praying to God. Matthew 26:39 reads, "Going a little farther, he fell with his face to the ground and prayed, 'My Father, if it is possible, may this cup be taken from me. Yet not as I will, but as you will.'" This may not seem significant at first glance—merely a prayer indicating Christ's submission to the will of God. For a first-century Jew, however, referring to the term "cup" meant a great deal more than it does to us today.

The term "cup" is often used in the Old Testament as a reference to God's wrath. Isaiah 51:17 reads, "Awake, awake! Rise up, O Jerusalem, you who have drunk from the hand of the LORD the cup of his wrath, you who have drained to its dregs the goblet that makes men stagger." A few verses later in 51:22, Isaiah writes, "This is what your Sovereign LORD says, your God, who defends his people: 'See, I have taken out of your hand the cup that made you stagger; from that cup, the goblet of my wrath, you will never drink again.'" Similarly, Jeremiah 25:15 reads, "This is what the LORD, the God of Israel, said to me: 'Take from my hand this cup filled with the wine of my wrath and make all the nations to whom I send you drink it.'"

Jesus knew well the full price of redemption. He knew very well what awaited him on the cross and that his vicarious atonement on Calvary was God's loving reaction to his own holiness. As painful as crucifixion is, experiencing God's wrath is infinitely more painful. *This*—not the physical pain of crucifixion—is what Christ was praying intensely about in the

---

11. Discussed in Chapters 4 and 5.

Garden of Gethsemane. *This* is what caused him to sweat blood. Indeed, God himself dreaded being the object of his own devastating wrath.

Redemption, Not Revelation

Often, the Christological Fallacy stems from a misunderstanding of the main purpose for the incarnation; that is, thinking the incarnation was for the purpose of *revelation* (knowledge), including the revelation of ethical norms. However, the main purpose of the incarnation was *redemption* rather than revelation. Humanity's problem is *not* a lack of knowledge. Humanity's problem is sin, a *moral* problem. Besides, God had a plethora of ways he could have delivered more revelation to his people. He certainly didn't need to send his Son to die to give us such revelation. In short, while Jesus did give us revelation, the main purpose of the incarnation was *redemption* (his vicarious, atoning death on the cross) *not* the delivery of knowledge. This is the perfect illustration of how humanity's problem is immorality rather than ignorance.[12] *Christ did not come to educate. He came to redeem.*

We should not think of the Gospels, i.e., the life of Jesus, as a complete and exclusive textbook on ethics, politics, economics, or any other subsidiary issue. The teachings of God are not limited to the red-letter portions of the Gospels. Paul writes in 2 Timothy 3:16, "All Scripture is God-breathed and is useful for teaching, rebuking, correcting and training in righteousness." The *whole* Bible is our guide for determining our worldview and positions on subsidiary issues. Only when we realize this can we completely submit to Christ's lordship.

What Paul says about government in Romans 13 is just as inspired as the teachings delivered by Jesus recorded the Gospels. Furthermore, the Christological Fallacy fails to deal with apparent contradictions between Christ's commands, such as "turn the other cheek," and the commands in the epistles that government is to punish wrongdoers. If Christ's words were meant to apply to government, they blatantly contradict the words of Paul and Peter later in the New Testament. For example, 1 Peter 2:13–14 reads, "Submit yourselves for the Lord's sake to every authority instituted among men: whether to the king, as the supreme authority, or to governors, *who are sent by him to punish those who do wrong* and to commend those who do right." (Emphasis added.) Similarly, Paul writes in Romans 13:4, "For he [government] is God's servant to do you good. But if you do wrong, be afraid, *for he does not bear the sword for nothing. He is God's servant, an*

---

12. This concept is discussed at length in Chapters 4 and 5.

agent of wrath to bring punishment on the wrongdoer." (Emphasis added.) The liberal Christian has quite a struggle ahead of him if he attempts to reconcile Jesus' "turn the other cheek" teaching with Peter's claim that government exists to punish wrongdoers, and with Paul's designation of government as God's "agent of wrath" meant to bring punishment to the wrongdoer.

The answer to this apparent "dilemma," of course, is that Christ's words do not apply to civil government. This conclusion, however, is impossible without viewing the entirety of Scripture, Old Testament and New, as "God-breathed" and "useful for teaching, rebuking, correcting and training in righteousness."

A Word About Opponents

As Christians, we must honor the God-given, inherent value of every individual. We must also keep in mind the "big picture." To do this, two verses come to mind: 1 Peter 3:15 and Ephesians 6:12. The first verse reads, "But in your hearts set apart Christ as Lord. Always be prepared to give an answer to everyone who asks you to give the reason for the hope that you have. But do this with gentleness and respect." The Great Commission calls us to go throughout the world, making disciples along the way; but we must always do so in accordance with the divinely infused value of *every* human being—including everyone's free will to reject Christ. (The biblical form of government is *not* a theocracy. Nor does it require any spiritual coercion.) After all, this belief in the inherent value of humans (believers *and* nonbelievers) is the defining issue separating Christianity from secularism—as well as a few other religions.

The second verse, Ephesians 6:12, reads, "For our struggle is not against flesh and blood, but against the rulers, against the authorities, against the powers of this dark world and against the spiritual forces of evil in the heavenly realms." Throughout this book, I try to refer to *ideas* as the opponents rather than *people*, i.e., "secularism" rather than "secularists." Unfortunately, this is often easier said than done.

As humans, we tend to demonize or deify people rather than ideas. We must keep in mind that, as Paul said, our struggle is not against flesh and blood but against the cosmic powers of evil and its methods. Since the Garden of Eden, "bad" ideas are the Enemy's main way of leading humanity astray, and, as such, *they* must be our targets—*not* the humans who hold them.

Likewise, we must not deify ourselves as saviors of the world as secularism does its adherents. As with the apostles in the book of Acts, it is the power of Christ that enables us to do great things. We must not mistake the source of our amazing potential as being internally grounded. We must always remember that it is submission to God and *his* will and *his* ideas that allows us to fulfill our purpose.

A human being is capable of great good and great evil. Whichever he accomplishes will be determined by the ideas he embraces. As Proverbs 23:7 reads, "For as a man thinketh in his heart, so is he." (KJV) Engaging the public forum in America is vital, because it can also be said, "For as a *nation* thinketh, so is it."

☙ ☙ ☙

Addendum to Chapter 3: What I'm *Not* Saying

To avoid confusion, it may be helpful to discuss what I'm *not* saying in this chapter.

Civil government is a legitimate institution set up in this world by God (although God does not necessarily establish every *particular* government or government leader). Whether or not civil government will exist after the second coming (when God establishes the new heaven and new earth), I don't know. I also don't know if it was part of the plan before the fall. What I do know is that, as the world is today, civil government has a specific purpose regarding what it should do, should not do, and *how* it should fulfill its function.

What this does *not* mean is that every Christian has a responsibility to be politically active. I think the same is true regarding every institution ordained by God, i.e. the church, the family, marriage, etc. Not everyone is required, or "called," to be active in every institution. For example, being a Christian does not require that I work in the formal ministry (i.e., church leadership . . . of course, I'm called to be part of the church, but not necessarily a leader). Similarly, I'm not required to get married simply to participate in the God-ordained institution of marriage. Nor am I required to have children in order to participate in the God-ordained institution of parenthood/family.

But *if I do participate in one of these institutions, I'm called to do so a biblical manner.* Thus, I'm free to choose for myself whether or not to engage in any of these institutions but I am not free to shirk the biblical worldview once I am in the midst of one of these institutions. Therefore, if a conservative Mennonite (most likely someone who abstains from all political involvement) wishes to walk his Christian faith through compassion and mercy, so be it. This is a legitimate thing to do *in the realm within which he is acting*. But this is enormously different from claiming the civil government should abide by standards that are to be displayed in a *different* realm, i.e. the church, personal relationships with others, etc.

The critique in Chapter 3 is not aimed towards those Christians who wish to use a peace/compassion/mercy standard in realms *outside* the civil government. In fact, I believe this is the standard that *should* be used within the realms/institutions of the church, personal relationships, etc. My contention is that such standards are not proper methods in the realm of civil government.

For example, it would be wrong for *me* or the *church*, within the purposes they've been given, to kill someone because he killed my sister. But it would *not* be wrong for the civil government to do so in its capacity as civil government (as long as it did so justly). Similarly, the church is charged with bringing the gospel to the world through love, compassion, and mercy. Civil government has been given no such role and it would be improper if it combined its role of justice-deliverer with the spreading of the gospel—which, in history, has usually taken the form of forced conversion. The church should not use the methods of civil government (i.e. punishment, justice-delivery, wrath, force, etc.) just as civil government should not use the methods of the church (love, compassion, mercy, etc.).

Perhaps it is incumbent upon me to explain my theory for the purpose of civil government. Here is the short version. Like every other institution established by God, civil government has a specific purpose. That purpose is to maintain peace through punishment, i.e. to be an "avenger of God's wrath" (Romans 13, 1 Peter 2:13-14, 2 Peter 2:9-10), not in an eternal sense, but in a this-worldly sense. Civil government exists to *protect* the inherent value and rights of every human (*not provide them*).

Compassion, mercy, and other similar traits, in my opinion, are not methods to be utilized by civil government. However, such traits *are* proper in realms such as the church and personal relationships, for example, and *should* be utilized in those contexts, i.e. Christians are obligated to act according to those traits within those contexts.

From a subjective perspective, the conservative Mennonite displaying peace, compassion, and mercy is a far cry from a committed secularist. And, as long as the conservative Mennonite utilizes those traits within realms such as the church and personal relationships, his ideas will produce positive real-world consequences (because those traits properly line up with the function of those realms/institutions). Once the conservative

Mennonite proscribes those same traits to civil government, however, the "ideas are not respecters of men" paradigm holds and the consequences will be no different than if a committed secularist had employed the ideas.

Therefore, while the origin of the now politically active conservative Mennonite's activism may be based on a hermeneutically incorrect view of Scripture (i.e., the Christological fallacy) and thus, not a direct result of an encroaching secular epistemology, the real-world consequences of his activism (should they be employed) will be identical to that of the formal secularist because both of their presuppositions lead to the same political conclusions regarding the purpose and methods of civil government. Thus, as mentioned earlier, the sincerity of the conservative Mennonite may save him, but such sincerity does little in making *this* world a better place—at least when it comes to the real-world consequences caused by the actions of a wrong-headed civil government.

I would only have a problem with the conservative Mennonite's positions if he claimed civil government is not an institution ordained by God; or if he claimed all Christians are called *not* to participate in civil government. Therefore, I'm *not* saying that it is sinful for a Christian to abstain from involvement in politics. What I *am* claiming is that *if* a Christian gets involved in politics, he is called to do so from a biblical worldview.

I'm also *not* saying that a Christian must support every act of government. For example, a Christian is called *not* to support immoral legislation, unjust punishment for criminals, or unjust wars. (There are even *rare* occasions when Christians are called to defy the civil government.) But this is a far cry from the categorical claim that government has no right whatsoever to punish criminals or engage in war. These rights are actualized *when the circumstances call for it*. They are *not* actualized when the circumstances do *not* call for it. A Christian is called to disagree with his government when it steps outside the bounds of its specific function or when it attempts to fulfill its purpose based non-Judeo-Christian presuppositions (but this does *not* necessarily mean a revolution or overthrow is in order).

Is America Special?

Thus, I'm *not* saying the United States is infallible (far from it). A Christian is first and foremost a citizen of *God's* kingdom. The United States of America has *not* been granted special status by God, nor is it God's kingdom here on earth. In fact, the very existence of this book is a testament to the fact that the United States itself is just as capable of decadence as any of the totalitarian nations I condemn throughout these pages. One need only look at the 4,500 unborn children who are murdered in the United States *each day* to understand this (and this is just the tip of the iceberg).

Therefore, do not mistake my patriotism for a belief that God has granted special ancient Israel-like status to the United States. He simply has not done so.[13] The United States should not receive a free pass regarding its morally reprehensible faults. Nor is every endeavor undertaken by the United States automatically blessed by God. The United States has, does, and will continue to engage in immoral endeavors, and Christians are called to condemn their own country's wrongheaded acts accordingly.[14] In fact, much of Chapter 6 is dedicated to why the United States is becoming a nation that is *incapable* of proper moral judgment. I spend a good deal of time critiquing the decadence, totalitarianism, and oppression of many nations in South America, Europe, and the Middle East, but you can rest assured knowing that the United States isn't far behind if she continues to reject the metaphysical realities of Judeo-Christian theism.

My intent is not to hold up America as a perfect Judeo-Christian nation or as a model of all that is right and good. It most assuredly is not. This is perhaps most noticeable in our culture's general rejection of objective moral truth and the outright denigration of Christianity and its adherents. Much of the Judeo-Christian ethic I *seem* to equate (although I do not) with the United States is a latent Christianity underlying many of our institutions (the separation of powers, how our government works, etc.) as a result of its *former* cultural dominance.[15] Thus, much of America's current prosperity is a result of a latent Judeo-Christian ethic rather than the more recent rejection and denigration of Judeo-Christian theism—which has *already* begun resulting in disaster (for example, the aforementioned 4,500 abortions performed each day in the United States). If our culture continues to reject Judeo-Christian theism, even this latent Christianity will be discarded. (See discussion of the cultural lag effect in Chapter 2.) Then *nothing* will stand between the United States and the tragic real-world consequences of secularism.

Additionally, you will likely notice that many of the essays in Part Three take an "us vs. them" tone. However, when the "us" is the United States, Republican Party, or some other historically contingent entity, I am not suggesting these groups have a divinely granted status over and above

---

13. The essay "He Who Laughs Last" in Chapter 7 thoroughly discusses this issue.

14. This analysis also applies to political parties, interest groups, etc.

15. Even then, however, this was largely an imperfect cultural dominance. There has never been a Christian "Golden Age" in America or anywhere else—nor will there ever be in this world.

simply being more closely aligned with presuppositional truth than their opponents. Such entities are fallible and easily corrupted by untrue ideas, and Christians are called to critique/condemn them accordingly.

The United States cannot bring salvation to the world. Only the gospel can accomplish that. As Christians, we are called to spread the gospel of Jesus Christ, not the gospel of the United States of America. The United States has been a catalyst in bringing this-worldly freedom to much of the world (and hopefully this can continue). But Christians must distinguish this-worldly political freedom from eternal freedom offered only through Jesus Christ. Governments (including those who comprise them) are called by God to protect the former. Christians are called by God to spread the latter.

These two callings, however, are by no means mutually exclusive. If a Christian participates in the realm of government, he is called to protect this-worldly freedom using the methods proper to the institution of government (which does not include spreading personal salvation via the gospel of Jesus Christ per se). In his non-governmental capacity, he is called to bring the gospel of Jesus Christ to the world making disciples along the way (using the methods proper to the realms of the church and personal relationships).

Furthermore, as discussed in Chapter 3, a government based on Judeo-Christian presuppositions (a so-called "Christian government" or "Christian nation") is *not* a theocracy. Civil government is not the administrator of salvation, nor does it care what religion or ideology a person subscribes to as long as the person respects the value and rights of other citizens.

This is what it means to be "American." It has nothing to do with skin color, class, or even religion. It is a set of beliefs about yourself, others, and the world. America is the most diverse country in the world, yet it is the most peaceful. Typically, diversity and peace are not found together. In America, however, they coexist. This is because America isn't quite as diverse as one may think.

There is a common belief system underlying this diversity; one that, at its core, respects the *inherent* value and rights of every human being. If someone subscribes to this "lowest common metaphysical denominator," he (or she) is good to go. Unfortunately, this underlying set of objective values is being undermined by worldviews that reject objective truth. As this trend continues, America will be increasingly plagued by the tribalism, oppression, and fragmentation that have come to define many nations in the Middle East, Europe, and South America—a process that has already begun.

Regarding whether or not the conservative Mennonite, at the end of his life, has served the kingdom of God, I believe that he will have done so in the context where his methods were appropriate, i.e. the church and personal relationships. But if he incorrectly employs those methods within the role of civil government, I believe he is not acting within God's will because he is forsaking the biblical worldview regarding the methods and purpose of civil government.

Perhaps civil government is something that will only exist pre-Second Coming. I don't know–nor have I thought about the theological consequences of this claim down the logical road. But I can say with assurance that 1) Civil government is a legitimate God-ordained institution (when it acts within its bounds), 2) a civil government based on Judeo-Christian theism will lead to positive real-world consequences, and 3) it is God's will that civil governments be structured according to Judeo-Christian presuppositions.

Chapter 3
Discussion Questions

1. Do you agree with the claim that the idea-to-real-world relationship acts independently of subjective factors such as intent, identity, or the formal ideological affiliation of the idea-bearer? Why or why not?

2. Why is it impossible to view secularism as an opponent on today's secular campuses?

3. How have the secular ideas of diversity and multiculturalism led to a "dreary uniformity" (to use George Marsden's words)?

4. If our opponents change according to the context in which we find ourselves, when (if ever) do you think it is proper for Christians to debate doctrinal issues that often become "inter-family squabbles," such as baptism, end-times issues, etc. When is it not proper to do so?

5. In your own experiences (or even in your own opinions), have you observed how people who formally espouse mutually exclusive worldviews often agree on subsidiary issues? If so, discuss some examples.

6. In light of the examples of John and Kevin abstaining from pre-marital sex, what implications are there for our understanding of God's so-called "blessings" and "curses?"

7. What does it mean to say that all worldviews are *functionally equivalent*? Why is this important to realize?

8. In attempting to alleviate the world's ills, why do secularists focus on systems while Christians focus on individuals?

9. Do you agree that Marxism is a logical necessity flowing from secular presuppositions? Why or why not?

10. What does it mean to say ideas are not "respecters of men"? What are the implications of this idea for liberal Christians?

11. Why are liberal Christianity and atheistic conservatism logical contradictions?

12. Why is it possible to predict someone's opinions on subsidiary issues simply by knowing how he answers questions relating to creation, fall, and redemption? When is this not possible?

13. Regarding Christians who borrow secular presuppositions and secularists who borrow Christian presuppositions, why do secular consequences "carry the day" for both of them?

14. If sincerity plays no role in the manifestation of this-worldly real-world consequences, what role (if any) does it play elsewhere?

15. Why is it not necessary to locate specific passages of Scripture that deal with subsidiary issues in order to find the biblical/Christian view of such subsidiary issues?

16. What is theologically liberal Christianity?

17. How are the claims of John Dominic Crossan and Dale Allison different? How are they ultimately similar?

18. What is politically liberal Christianity?

19. What is the Christological Fallacy and what are its ramifications?

20. In what sense is it true that "hell exists because of God's holiness"?

21. What was the main purpose of the incarnation? What was *not* the main purpose of the incarnation?

22. How does the purpose of the incarnation reflect humanity's problem?

Part Two
Secular Gnosticism

4

Gnosticism
Ancient Humanism

GNOSTICISM WAS a tradition influential during the second, third, and early fourth centuries A.D. There were several "Christian" sects of this tradition, but none of these versions could be considered orthodox. Gnosticism has its own tradition with its own story to tell. Like every worldview, it provides answers to the three questions Pearcey claims every worldview answers, i.e., creation, fall, and redemption. It is within these answers that the similarities between Gnosticism and secularism reside. But first, a brief overview of Gnosticism is necessary.

Gnosis

Strictly speaking, *Gnosticism* (and *gnostic*) is derived from the Greek word *gnosis*, which is usually translated "knowledge." The goal of Gnosticism is to achieve a *particular kind* of knowledge that brings salvation. Such salvific knowledge, however, is not the rational knowledge we think of today when we hear the term "knowledge." We tend to think of knowledge as a collection of information and facts, i.e., propositional knowledge. This is *not* the kind of knowledge aspired to by the gnostic.

Some scholars of Gnosticism believe the term "insight" comes closer to the actual meaning employed by gnostics. Such insight is gained not through scientific observation and experiment or by employing reason as a framework that guides rational thought, but through direct experience resulting in a heightened state of consciousness. Stephan Hoeller writes that "there occurs a significant altering of consciousness that transports the knower beyond the limitations of personal consciousness and, indeed, beyond the limitations of the very world we live in."[1]

Gnosis gained through unique mystical experience is considered *esoteric*. Something that is esoteric is intended for or understood only by a

---

1. Hoeller, *Gnosticism: New Light on the Ancient Tradition of Inner Knowing*, 6.

particular group or a restricted number of people. *Esoteric* knowledge is not disclosed to the general public. It is impossible for those who do not experience this altered state of consciousness during a mystical transportation to acquire *gnosis*. Kurt Rudolph writes, "It is a knowledge given by revelation, which has been made available only to the elect who are capable of receiving it, and therefore has an esoteric character."[2]

Central to Gnosticism is the claim that within every individual is a divine spark that is, in essence, God. Every individual's ultimate origin was in God. While Orthodox Christianity claims God created humans in his *image*, this is *not* the claim of Gnosticism. Gnosticism claims every person in existence was and is God himself—or itself.

Unfortunately, this spark is imprisoned in the physical creation, which includes our bodies. Like many pagan religions, Gnosticism is dualistic. *Dualism* is the belief that the physical world is inherently evil, while the spiritual world is inherently good. According to Gnosticism, salvation is the release of the divine spark from the cumbersome physical creation. After this release, the spark (a person's true self, his soul) engages on a heavenly flight through multiple realms of the heavens until it is eventually reunited with God—or the *pleroma*. Hoeller writes, "It is as though the body and the mind were bars of a cage in which the soul (or spirit) is trapped. When a captive entity exits the cage and flies aloft, it rises to spiritual realms where ultimate meaning and happiness abide. Soaring through these regions, it finally reaches its primordial home, the Divine."[3]

Hoeller cites Harold Bloom who characterizes salvific gnosis in two ways. First, it is an "acquaintance with God who is unknown to and remote from the world, a god in exile from a false creation" and, second, it is "recognition that one's deeper nature was no part of creation but was and still is part of the fullness that is God."[4] *Gnosis* releases the individual soul from the physical creation that limits it, thus allowing the soul to realize its full potential as the divine entity it is.

This extensive quote from Hoeller is helpful in understanding gnostic salvation. He writes:

> From this ultimate essentiality [God, or the *pleroma*] the sparks or spirits that are the essence of human souls come forth, and to it they seek to return. Each spirit entity is a pure spark or atom of divine consciousness and is of the same essence as God. Yet

---

2. Rudolph, *Gnosis: The Nature & History of Gnosticism*, 55.
3. Hoeller, *Gnosticism: New Light on the Ancient Tradition of Inner Knowing*, 15.
4. Ibid., 6.

though these sparks are ontologically united with the Divine, they are existentially separated from it [due to the physical creation]. This separation needs to be undone.... A certain painful, often indistinct, longing for something greater, more meaningful, and more enduring than can be experienced in earthly embodiment is the beginning of the undoing of this great separation. Liberating gnosis, resulting in transcendent consciousness, is the effective end of the separation.... The lid that seals in our universe is lifted and we behold the vast ocean of boundless light, of which we are temporarily exiled sparks. Such was and continues to be the vision of the Gnostics.[5]

Reality, Humanity, and Redemption

According to Gnosticism, the ultimate divinity from which each of us originated and to which each of us longs to be reunited is not the Creator God of Judeo-Christian tradition. The ultimate divinity, or "God" (heretofore referred to as the *pleroma* to avoid any association with the monotheistic God) did *not* create the cosmos. This claim follows from Gnosticism's dualistic foundation. If physical creation is inherently evil, it could not have originated from ultimate good, i.e., the *pleroma*. Thus, something else must have been responsible for the physical creation.

This "something else" is a being called the *demiurge*. "Demiurge" literally means "half-maker," which reflects the gnostic belief that the demiurge didn't create the *pleroma* or its sparks that eventually became imprisoned in physical bodies. It only created the cumbersome *physical* world that distracts us from our true destiny, i.e., unity in the pleroma. Together with the *archons* ("petty rulers" in Greek; beings similar to yet less powerful than the demiurge), the demiurge rules the physical creation and works to keep our divine souls entrapped.

Hoeller cites Plato's analogy of the cave to help explain the gnostic view of reality. Trapped deep inside the cave are people who are chained to the cave floor. They are forced to face the back wall of the cave. Behind them is a fire that casts their shadows on the cave wall in front of them (although the cave dwellers can't see the fire itself). Thus, for these trapped individuals, the shadows on the wall in front of them constitute total reality. They are unaware of both the fire behind them and the liberating world outside the cave.

5. Ibid., 11–12.

Plato believed knowledge of particulars (the physical world around us) was not true knowledge of ultimate reality. Like Plato, gnostics believe this physical world is equivalent to the shadows on the cave wall. For the imprisoned soul, the shadows constitute total reality. The released soul who has experienced salvific gnosis, however, has broken free from the chains of physical creation (with its cumbersome laws and regulations) and has flown freely upward to knowledge of ultimate reality; the divine within itself has been united with the pleroma.

Hoeller explains that gnostics believe humans have the ability to turn away from the shadows and "commune with reality directly." He writes:

> This is the basis for an important point: The created world, including a major portion of the human mind, is seen as evil by the Gnostic primarily because it distracts consciousness away from knowledge of the Divine. . . . What the Gnostic struggles against is not so much the cosmos as the alienation of consciousness from the ultimate reality underlying the cosmos, which in monotheistic language is called "God." Since to the soul without gnosis the cosmos [the physical world] appears to be the only reality, it is an obstacle to the Gnostic's true objective, which is the raising of consciousness above all physical and mental substitute realities to the true reality, beyond matter and mind.[6]

Understanding this dualistic view of reality is vital in understanding the gnostic worldview. The cause of evil and suffering is not found within humanity but in the *external* factors of physical creation and its rulers (the demiurge and the archons, who serve to hinder the divine in all of us). Physical creation did not *become* flawed; it was *created* flawed (and thus is inherently evil) by a flawed being, the demiurge. If there is evil and suffering in this reality (and Gnosticism acknowledges such), the creator of this reality is the one responsible for it. The human dilemma is not sin, but ignorance—the exorcism of which comes with gnosis.

The demiurge became identified as the creator God of the Old Testament, Yahweh. Christ, a "messenger of Light" sent to awaken the divine spark within us, is juxtaposed to Yahweh. Christ's "father" in the New Testament is not the arbitrary ruler described by the Old Testament but instead is a completely different entity, the pleroma. In short, the "God" of the New Testament is completely different from the God of the Old Testament.

---

6. Ibid., 15–16.

Due to their origin in the demiurge and *this-worldly* nature, the gnostics viewed the Old Testament laws with disdain. Such laws were given to humanity by the demiurge in order to keep us distracted from ultimate divine reality, because they prevent us from realizing our true identity and potential. The myths and laws proffered by the demiurge are simply a way for the demiurge to maintain its power over entrapped souls. Hoeller explains:

> People are generally ignorant of the divine spark residing within them. This ignorance serves the interests of the archons, who act as cosmic slave masters, keeping the light sparks in bondage. Anything that causes us to remain attached to earthly things, *including the mental concepts we hold*, keeps us in enslavement to the lesser cosmic rulers.[7] (Emphasis added.)

The italicized portion of this quote indicates that the corrupt physical world includes the oppressive *ideas* (i.e., moral codes, laws, etc.) that serve to subjugate humanity.

The demiurge "tricks" humans into believing salvation comes by way of adherence to moral codes; i.e., codes that not only distract souls from ultimate reality but also prevent them from realizing their divine identity and potential for salvation from within. There is no external being or moral code necessary for salvation. Rudolph explains, "The Gnostic thus acts in conformity with his nature and destiny; he is enabled to do so by the freedom from the constraint and tyranny of the cosmos which he has recovered. There is for him no redemption given by nature which he has not achieved for himself."[8]

If ultimate reality (spiritual reality) is categorically separate from physical reality (which includes our physical bodies along with the demiurge's moral laws and deceptive ideas), then there is no such thing as sin in *this* world. This is why many early church fathers labeled Gnosticism as *antinomian*, which is defined as "opposed to or denying the fixed meaning or universal applicability of moral law"[9] or as "one who rejects a socially established morality."[10] Because Gnosticism is primarily concerned with the soul's *spiritual* (rather than *physical*) state of consciousness when it comes to salvation, external action in *this* world is not an indicator of moral standing. In fact, committing sin in this world actually becomes a sign of having acquired gnosis.

7. Ibid., 18.
8. Rudolph, *Gnosis: The Nature & History of Gnosticism*, 118.
9. www.Dictionary.com.
10. www.merriam-webster.com.

Gnostic Elitism

Those who have acquired gnosis are, by definition, incapable of sinning because the gnostic notion of "sin" is *ignorance*, which is necessarily alleviated upon the arrival of gnosis. Hoeller explains, "Gnostics look to salvation not from sin . . . . but from the ignorance of which sin is the consequence. Those who know the Divine through gnosis shed all sin, while those without gnosis cannot help but persist in transgressions. Ignorance—which means ignorance of spiritual realities—is dispelled by gnosis."[11]

Notice the language used by Hoeller (a sympathetic gnostic himself). Referring to those without gnosis, i.e., the ignorant, he claims they "cannot help but persist in transgressions." They are utterly incapable of not only realizing their true potential as divine beings but also of living an authentic existence free of the physical and moral transgressions that so easily entangle. If you haven't noticed already, gnostic elitism is rearing its ugly head.

In trying to avoid the label "elitist," Hoeller draws attention to the gnostic doctrine concerning "messengers of Light." While salvation through gnosis is inherently available within every man and woman, awakening from the ideas and world that entrap our divine souls must often be "spurred on" by beings who have come forth from the pleroma (Jesus is one such being). A true gnostic is one who has been awakened by such a "messenger from God."

Exactly *how* this doctrine relieves Gnosticism of the charge of elitism, however, escapes me. Adding the phrase "chosen by God" (or "chosen by the pleroma" in the gnostic's case) does little to humble the select few who are privy to knowledge of ultimate things. Of course, the Bible often uses this language when referring to God's people, i.e., the Israelites in the Old Testament and all believers in the New Testament, but these passages must be combined with passages such as 1 Timothy 2:3–5, which reads, "This is good, and pleases God our Savior, *who wants all men to be saved and to come to a knowledge of the truth*. For there is one God and one mediator between God and men, the man Christ Jesus." (Emphasis added.) Hoeller attempts to backtrack by writing,

> "Some call this view [the gnostic notion of salvation] elitist, and the contemporary egalitarian mindset tends to rebel against elitism. But there is a difference between an arbitrary, self-interested elitism that sets oneself and one's fellows apart as a chosen group,

---

11. Hoeller, *Gnosticism: New Light on the Ancient Tradition of Inner Knowing*, 19.

on the one hand, and the inevitable existence of elite persons, on the other."[12]

I'm not sure such a statement makes me, an entrapped and unenlightened soul, feel any better about my ignorance and resulting inability to avoid transgression. In fact, Hoeller doesn't claim that I'm not elite because I'm not chosen. He claims I'm not chosen because I'm not elite. How comforting!

Hoeller cites a gnostic text, *The Apocalypse of Peter*, wherein Peter complains that the people witnessing the crucifixion cannot see Jesus' true nature (Jesus was merely a spirit and did not suffer on the cross). While laughing and glad, Jesus replies, "I have told you: Leave the blind alone." Hoeller explains, "That is, the majority is always blind. To try to explain to the blind what they are constitutionally incapable of seeing is a waste of time and effort. The hidden meanings of events, teachings, and indeed of life is known only to a few."[13] This is the very definition of elitism.

Creation, Evil, and the Fall

Because Gnosticism is generally interested in the symbolism and meaning of sacred texts rather than their historical, this-worldly claims, it is often difficult to clearly understand gnostic claims regarding creation (which, I suppose, is the point of gnosis; knowledge that cannot be contained in texts or propositional statements but only in esoteric experiences that enlighten). Nonetheless, it remains possible to uncover Gnosticism's answer to the question of creation by examining its interpretation of the biblical creation story in Genesis.

The traditional interpretation of Genesis goes something like this: God created the world good. God created humans (Adam and Eve) in his image. Satan tempted them to rebel against God, which they did by eating of the tree (the tree of the knowledge of good and evil) from which God forbade them to eat. Thus, sin entered the world, corrupting both human nature and physical creation. Adam and Eve were kicked out of paradise, the Garden of Eden. The evil and suffering present in the world are due to this sin and the sin committed by each and every human who has ever existed.

Without altering the basic events and characters in the Genesis creation story, Gnosticism interprets its content and meaning very differently. It helps if we remember the identity of the Old Testament creator God,

---

12. Ibid., 20.
13. Ibid., 201.

i.e., Yahweh. Gnosticism identifies Yahweh as the demiurge, the evil being who created the world to imprison divine human souls. The demiurge's prohibition against eating from the tree of the knowledge of good and evil was motivated by envy and was meant to prevent humans from acquiring higher knowledge of ultimate realities. In short, the prohibition was to keep people in ignorance, as subjects imprisoned in a world ruled by the demiurge and his archons.

In this scenario, the serpent that tempts Eve isn't the evil tempter and adversary (Satan) of all that is good, but the wisest creature in paradise who wishes to free Adam and Eve from the world that imprisons. The serpent informs Eve of the *real* truth concerning her identity and origin. Adam and Eve subsequently partake of the tree of the knowledge of good and evil, and they acquire gnosis. They realize the full divine potential inherent within themselves by forsaking the lies of the demiurge and embracing the truth that salvation comes from within. Rudolph writes, "The 'tree of knowledge' in paradise according to various gnostic texts imparts to Adam his appropriate God-like status over against the lower creator God [the demiurge], who pronounced his prohibition of the enjoyment of the tree only out of envy."[14] As a result, the demiurge, because of his spite and jealousy, punished Adam and Eve by kicking them out of the Garden of Eden—a far cry from the Judeo-Christian interpretation of Genesis.

Hoeller cites gnostic scripture that claims "their eyes were opened"—which he identifies as a metaphor for gnosis. Hoeller continues, "The first humans could then see for the first time that the deities who had created them were loathsome in appearance, having the faces of animals, and they recoiled in horror at the sight of them. Although cursed by the Demiurge and his archons, the first human pair had acquired the capacity for gnosis."[15]

At this point you may be wondering how the demiurge came into existence. Without getting too technical, it "emanated" from the pleroma. However, such an "emanation" should not be considered a direct act of creation by the pleroma. The pleroma doesn't create anything, and it is wholly separate from anything other than itself. The demiurge, on the other hand, *did* create the visible world and the ideas, rules, and regulations that entrap the divine sparks (which also "emanated" from the pleroma). If you're expending mental energy trying to grasp the difference between direct creation and "emanation," don't bother. Such an understanding is probably esoteric anyway, requiring a heightened state of consciousness and a heavenly flight through the various levels of existence until you are

14. Rudolph, *Gnosis: The Nature & History of Gnosticism*, 94.
15. Hoeller, *Gnosticism: New Light on the Ancient Tradition of Inner Knowing*, 29.

ultimately reunited with the Divine. And, even then, this piece of knowledge is *gnosis*... which means you wouldn't be able to explain it to anyone upon your return.

Picking up the story a few chapters later in Genesis, we come to the stories of Noah's flood and Sodom and Gomorrah. Biblical Christianity teaches that the flood was sent to destroy humanity because of its wicked licentiousness. Sodom and Gomorrah were later destroyed for the same reason. According to Gnosticism, however, Sodom and Gomorrah were not destroyed because of their wickedness. Gnosticism viewed Sodom and Gomorrah's licentiousness as a telltale sign of gnosis—freedom from demiurge-induced ignorance. The Gnostic interpretation claims that Sodom and Gomorrah are not examples of God punishing the sinfulness of humans, but they are instead examples of destruction wrought by the demiurge out of envy and anger because he could not tolerate people acquiring salvific gnosis and enjoying the freedom that follows. The wicked lifestyles and licentious acts of those inhabiting Sodom and Gomorrah were not sins against a holy God; they were fruit of the liberation that comes with gnosis. Liberating gnosis includes liberation from this-worldly moral codes and inhibitions. Thus, immorality such as sexual promiscuity and homosexuality are signs of salvific gnosis rather than sinful rebellion against God.

In Gnosticism, humans are not "guilty" of sinning against God. In fact, absolutely no blame whatsoever should be placed on humans. Evil is inherent in the physical world with its cumbersome ideas and regulations; a world human souls are ontologically separate from and yearning to escape. When a human soul transcends this world through gnosis, it also transcends the evil inherent in it. Once this occurs, engaging in evil of any sort becomes impossible. This is why the inhabitants of Sodom and Gomorrah were liberated Gnostics rather than wicked sinners. Gnostic "original sin" is ignorance brought about by the demiurge, not immorality resulting from humanity's rebellion against God.

Conclusion

You may have already noticed some similarities between Gnosticism and secularism. This is possible because they provide similar answers to the questions of the fall and redemption. They also have similar definitions for freedom, i.e., the deconstruction of objective truth claims that demand obedience to an oppressive external standard rather than a subjective internally-created reality. This includes the observation that disobedience to cumbersome moral codes is indicative of internally-based freedom. The next chapter will illuminate these mythological similarities and analyze how the two most popular re-packaged forms of secularism, humanism and postmodernism, compare in their respective visions for the future of America.

Chapter 4
Discussion Questions

1. What is *gnosis*? How is it different from our modern notion of knowledge?
2. What is *dualism*? Is Christianity a dualistic religion? Why or why not?
3. What is the difference between the origin of humanity according to Christianity and the origin of humanity according to Gnosticism?
4. What is Plato's analogy of the cave? What is it attempting to explain about reality? To what extent do you believe this analogy is accurate?
5. How does the demiurge subjugate humanity? Do you recognize this line of thinking in any modern worldviews?
6. Why are those who have achieved gnosis *incapable* of committing sin?
7. How does Gnosticism interpret the Genesis creation story?
8. How do the gnostic and Christian views of sin differ?
9. Why does Gnosticism consider moral decadence a telltale sign of salvific gnosis?
10. According to Gnosticism, why were Sodom and Gomorrah destroyed? How is this different from the Judeo-Christian interpretation of the same account?

5

Secular Gnosticism
Analyzing Secular Mythology

WORLDVIEW AS a concept is valuable beyond its use in cross-cultural comparison. As a *method*, it exposes the functional equivalence of competing belief systems. No longer can one worldview claim esoteric status as the sole bearer of an unbiased epistemology. Worldview analysis exposes the religious nature of secularism and enables the critical examination of its two ideological offspring, humanism and postmodernism (one farther along the "logical timeline" than the other). The consequences of these "offspring" are disastrous for society—especially within the disciplines of cultural interpretation (anthropology, sociology, etc.) and the institutions of education and the judiciary. Comparison of secularism to the ancient faiths of Gnosticism and paganism enhances this analysis.

Logical Timeline

"Logical timeline" refers to the intellectual (subsidiary beliefs) and real-world (practical policies, institutions, and events) consequences of a set of presuppositions that naturally work themselves out over time. In this case, secular humanism is an *early* consequence of secular presuppositions, while postmodernism is a *later* consequence of secular presuppositions. Viewed from this perspective, secular humanism is logically and experientially prior to postmodernism. It is often said that secular humanists are *optimistic* modernists, while postmodernists are *pessimistic* modernists ("modernist" being another term for secularist). How can two seemingly different ideologies be based on the same secular presuppositions?

The French Revolution and the years immediately following it are a good real-world microcosm of secularism's logical timeline. The secular revolutionaries violently overthrew the ruling monarchy with the intention of creating an egalitarian society based solely on secular tenets. It was thought that humans would fulfill their immense potential once cumbersome religious dogma was removed (a very *mythological* claim pre-dated by both Gnosticism and Promethean paganism).

What happened? Many of the initial revolutionaries were beheaded as a result of the revolution they began. Thousands were murdered in the name of egalitarianism. In the end, a new tyrant, Napoleon, replaced the recently overthrown French monarchy. In light of such subsequent events, many lost faith in the supposedly boundless potential of humanity proffered by Enlightenment secularism. The zealous hope of a humanistic society based purely on secular presuppositions faded into an ideology that scrambles around on the kitchen floor looking for any scrap of meaning it can find. If secularism can't provide salvation and social harmony, nothing can. Obviously the answer certainly wasn't to return to religion. Thus, objective truth claims (provided only by theistic religion), along with the meaning and purpose they provide, are lost forever. The only hope for a meaningful life lies in the subjective construction of such by the individual. The hopeful optimism described earlier is *secular humanism*, while the resultant pessimism can properly be labeled *postmodernism*.

Secular humanism (i.e., the notion that a truly egalitarian society that respects human rights can be built solely on reason and experience, without the aid of religious dogma or metaphysics) is usually the *initial* result once secular presuppositions take hold. Secular humanism is the product of infusing secularism with meaning and morality from an outside worldview, i.e., "worldview borrowing" (because secular presuppositions can't provide meaning and morality themselves).[1] Secularists who posit the existence of morality do so because it is very difficult to exorcise the values "written on their hearts" (Romans 2:15), i.e., God's image (*imago dei*) in each of us that provides the basis for legitimate meaning and morality. Deep down, no secularist wants to live in a world without meaning and morality; no one wants to live in a world without purpose and no moral difference between Adolf Hitler and Mother Theresa. This deep desire is a bound and gagged *imago dei* gasping for air. Postmodernists, however, complete what secular humanists could not finish: a full *imago*-ectomy. Secular humanists want to have their cake and eat it too. They want morality, meaning, and purpose within their secular worldview. *Consistent* secularism, however, requires believing in an amoral and meaningless world.

Postmodernism rears its ugly head when secular presuppositions, upon which secular humanism is also based, *are consistently applied* in the areas of meaning and morality. Postmodernism, not secular humanism, is the outcome of allowing secular presuppositions to successfully exorcise

---

1. Discussed in Chapter 3.

the last remnants of meaning and morality *written on the heart*. James Sire writes in his classic, *The Universe Next Door*, that postmodernism ". . . is the last move of the modern, the result of the modern taking its own commitments [secular presuppositions] seriously and seeing that they failed to stand the test of analysis."[2] Postmodernism is the surgeon who cuts out the unique essence of humanity—the *imago dei*.

A *consistent* secularist is eventually forced to come to terms with the inevitable conclusion that his own presuppositions simply do not allow for the existence of meaning or morality. Postmodernism claims meaning must be created by the individual from within, and, even then, such meaning is not somehow willed into *objective* existence. A surprisingly high number of postmodern secularists acknowledge this necessary consequence, but there are plenty of secular humanists who refuse to acknowledge the nihilism wrought by their own worldview.

Refusing to accept a world without meaning or morality, however, secular humanists "borrow" such notions from other worldviews—such as Judeo-Christian theism—which allow them to make moral claims, inconsistent though such claims are with their own *formally* adopted presuppositions. A secular humanist is someone who has yet to consistently follow his presuppositions through to the end (or has refused to do so). Secular humanism and postmodernism have an "inter-family squabble" within secularism, because the former strives to maintain the inevitably impossible balance between secular presuppositions and the intuitive meaning and morality *written on men's hearts* by God, while the latter dutifully rejects meaning and morality in the name of logical consistency. Kudos to postmodernism for at least being consistent.

Promethean Redemption

It is no coincidence the name of the publishing company that published the *Humanist Manifestos I & II* is "Prometheus Publishing." (Isn't it ironic that secular humanism, a worldview supposedly free of metaphysics, compares itself to an ancient *myth*?) The mythological story secularists claim as their own serves as an apt parallel between secularism, pagan mythology, and Gnosticism. Just as Prometheus was the conduit of deliverance for ancient man, secularism believes itself to be the conduit of deliverance for modern man.

Prometheus helped Zeus and the other gods fight against the Titans. Even after the victorious gods became powerful, however, Prometheus did

---

2. Sire, *The Universe Next Door*, 173.

not have much respect for them (including Zeus). Prometheus cared more for humanity than for the gods. Thus when Zeus refused to take interest in the lives of mortal men, Prometheus felt he had to act on their behalf. Believing the knowledge and divine gifts necessary for civilization would be wasted on humans, Zeus intended for humans to live primitive lives without the advantages of civilization. Zeus warned Prometheus not to interfere with this plan, but taking pity on the cold and suffering mortal humans, Prometheus delivered that which Zeus withheld. Defying Zeus and the gods, Prometheus climbed Mount Olympus and stole fire from the chariot of Helios. He delivered the fire to Earth, and humans used it to warm themselves.

This single act began a domino effect that resulted in the massive advancement of human civilization. No longer were humans kept ignorant by the gods, destined for a pathetic life of frostbite and suffering. Human potential—the divine spark within all of us—was realized by releasing humanity from the inhibiting control of the gods. Unfettered by the yoke of the gods, humans have the ability to save themselves. Prometheus initiated the deliverance humanity had within itself—and he paid dearly for it, because Zeus punished him.

The myth of Prometheus and the Gnostic interpretation of the Genesis creation story both have a great deal to say about humanity and the gods (or God). Both begin with humanity in a state of forced ignorance induced by God or the gods (the demiurge and the archons according to Gnostic doctrine, and Zeus as the culprit according to ancient mythology). The demiurge purposefully keeps humans ignorant so it can maintain its power over them. The demiurge's power would be overthrown if humans realized their true identity and potential. Similarly, Zeus repressed humans because of his lack of faith in humanity's potential.

In both cases, *ignorance* is the problem rather than sin. Thus, *knowledge* is the cure for the human condition; this is understood as esoteric gnosis according to Gnosticism and, according to ancient mythology, knowledge leading to the advancement of human civilization (something very similar to our modern notion of knowledge). Either way, salvation comes from within (even though it may often need to be spurred on by a "messenger of Light" or Promethean hero). Religion (Zeus and the demiurge) only serves to hinder humanity. It is a yoke that must be thrown off. The liberator in these two creation stories is the being who opens the eyes of humanity and awakens them to the ability they had inside all along. This liberator is the serpent according to the Gnostic interpretation of Genesis, and it is Prometheus according to ancient mythology. They revealed knowledge that the gods wanted hidden for a myriad of reasons (usually power). Secularism may couch its claims in a supposed unbiased "scientific" epistemology, but secular science is a repackaged language conveying the same old myth—a new mask on the same face.

The role of liberator in every worldview is indispensable. Whether it is a personified character or a set of ideas, someone or something must play that role. Modern-day secularism is no different. In fact, it is rather mundane. As examined earlier, there was nothing novel about the ideology of the zealous French revolutionaries. The same ideas were alive and well in Gnosticism and ancient mythology thousands of years before the Enlightenment. Man has been searching for meaning and purpose since the dawn of time. As has been the case since time immemorial, meaning is found in two places: internally (meaning is created from within) or externally (meaning is infused into reality by God). This is nothing new. As the author of Ecclesiastes wrote in 1:9–10,

> What has been will be again,
> what has been done will be done again;
> there is nothing new under the sun.
> Is there anything of which one can say,
> "Look! This is something new"?
> It was here already, long ago;
> it was here before our time.

If German philosopher Friedrich Nietzsche is right and God really is dead, then we should expect humans to fill the vacuum with something else. Humans are by nature religious creatures, and if they aren't formally worshipping the monotheistic God, they are worshipping something in his place. It's not simply a matter of being "religious" or "not religious," but a matter of *which* religion one professes: an internal religion or an external religion. Once again, we see the *functional equivalence* of all worldviews.

As Blaise Pascal said centuries ago, inside the heart of every person is a God-shaped hole. First principles analysis reveals the religious nature of the ways humans attempt to fill that hole. Whether the hole is filled by Christ or communism, the guillotine or class warfare, Darwinian evolution or intelligent design, global utopia or anarchy, atheism or Judaism, the characters and ideas that fill the hole are functionally the same. They serve to answer the inherently religious questions every human wants answered: Who and what am I? What is the meaning of life? What went wrong? Why is there evil and suffering? How can the world be made a better place?

Secular Humanist Liberation

Paralleling the Promethean myth and the Gnostic interpretation of Genesis, secular humanism views ignorance as the problem and knowledge as the cure. Human life burdened under the cumbersome yoke of religion is a life of repression. Like the demiurge who perpetuates its repressive power by utilizing false religion to hinder the potential that lies within humanity, secularism views religion as the "opiate of the masses" that serves to subjugate those who ignorantly accept its tenets.

Secularism sees itself as the wise serpent in the Gnostic interpretation of Genesis, as a harbinger of the freedom that comes with breaking the chains of oppressive religion. Secularism also sees itself as Prometheus, a sympathetic martyr who delivered humans from their plight of living under the oppressive foot of the gods. Humanity already has everything it needs to be saved. Reason and experience will save. No supernatural help is necessary.

Consider the following claims made in the *Humanist Manifestos I & II*.[3] Following each will be a brief translation and worldview analysis (or, first principles analysis) of the claim.

Humanist Manifesto I (1933)

- ". . . humanists regard the universe as self-existing and not created."[4]

Translation

The universe did not have a beginning. It has always been here. As Carl Sagan would say on his television series *Cosmos*, "The cosmos is all there was, is, and ever will be."

Worldview Analysis

If secularism is true and only physical stuff exists, the above statement *must* be true. After all, if *nothing* exists outside the cosmos (as Carl Sagan so eloquently claimed), the cosmos can't originate from such nothingness; that would break the scientific law of conservation of energy—out of nothing, comes nothing. This is why secular scientists first rejected the notion of an expanding universe (and why secularists first rejected the idea of a "Big Bang"). An expanding universe must have a beginning, and ev-

---

3. Kurtz, *Humanist Manifestos I and II*, 4–22
4. Ibid., 8.

erything that has a beginning must have a cause. Because something with a beginning cannot cause itself, it must be caused by something other and prior to itself, i.e., something outside the cosmos. This secular claim is a necessary philosophical conclusion rather than a claim based on empirical evidence.

- "Humanism believes that man is a part of nature and that he has emerged as the result of a continuous process."[5]

Translation

Humans deserve no special status above anything else in nature, because we are a product and a part of nature itself, i.e., Darwinian evolution.

Worldview Analysis

Once again, if secularism is accurate, this *must* be the case. There are no other alternatives, and all evidence must be forced into this secular paradigm. Furthermore, there is nothing special about humanity's current form. It is merely a step in the evolutionary process that will soon be obsolete.

- "Humanism recognizes that man's religious culture and civilization . . . are the product of a gradual development due to his interaction with his natural environment and with his social heritage."[6]

Translation

People's surrounding environment determines their beliefs, actions, and lifestyles.

Worldview Analysis

This claim coincides with the secular conclusion that human beings are merely physical "stuff" at the mercy of the physical laws of the universe. The individual is a complex collection of matter, organs, chemicals, and firing synapses that respond to external stimuli. This is also true for societies and cultures in general.

- "Humanism asserts that the nature of the universe depicted by modern science makes unacceptable any supernatural or cosmic guarantees of human values."[7]

5. Ibid.
6. Ibid.
7. Ibid.

Translation

When determining morality and ethics, it is unacceptable to appeal to God or divine revelation for moral direction, because they cannot be accounted for empirically.

Worldview Analysis

Because secularism denies the supernatural, secular humanists must look elsewhere for a foundation upon which to base moral claims. Postmodernists scrap this endeavor entirely, but the humanist (who wishes to maintain some kind of morality even though this contradicts his own presuppositions) must come up with a non-supernatural base for morality—an impossible task.

- "... humanism considers the complete realization of human personality to be the end of man's life and seeks its development and fulfillment in the here and now."[8]

Translation

The purpose of life is to cultivate your own personality and then die.

Worldview Analysis

Because there is no objective meaning to life grounded in the supernatural, all meaning must be created within each person's personality (or by individual societies). Thus, the meaning of life is the selfish realization of the self (or the realization of whatever values a society invents). Additionally, there is no afterlife. When someone dies, his personality simply vanishes from existence.

- "Man will learn to face the crises of life in terms of his knowledge of their naturalness and probability."[9]

Translation

Problems cannot be solved or averted by appealing to knowledge based upon divine revelation. Humans must learn to solve the crises of life and society by utilizing a secular version of the scientific method. Because every event in history (including all human thoughts and actions) is the result of physical laws, such events should eventually be completely predictable.

---

8. Ibid., 9.
9. Ibid.

Worldview Analysis

This claim flows from the notion that true objective knowledge can only be gained through a secularized scientific method. Everything else is marginalized as private values, religious dogma, etc. Because *everything* (individual beliefs, cultural values, historical events, and social institutions and systems) is determined by purely physical causes, it should be possible to reach a level of omniscience by employing a secularized scientific method. If everything that *is* is "natural," then it should be able to be predicted. This statement also has interesting ramifications for environmental morality. If *everything* that happens in the cosmos is "natural," it follows that nothing is unnatural. This would include depleting the o-zone, polluting streams, cutting down the rain forests, etc. If humans are simply another part of nature, nothing they do can be labeled "unnatural"—including destroying the environment.

- "The humanists are firmly convinced that existing acquisitive and profit-motivated society has shown itself to be inadequate and that a radical change in methods, controls, and motives must be instituted. A socialized and cooperative economic order must be established to the end that the equitable distribution of the means of life be possible. The goal of humanism is a free and universal society in which people voluntarily and intelligently cooperate for the common good. Humanists demand a shared life in a shared world."[10]

Translation

Because capitalism (a bad system) is responsible for the world's economic ills, massive socialist wealth redistribution programs must be instituted globally.

Worldview Analysis

As was mentioned earlier in this book, socialism (communism, Marxism, etc.) is a natural real-world consequence of secularism, because it is the political and economic outworking of the presupposition that humans are purely physical stuff and, as such, are solely a product of physical factors such as biology (genetics) and systems. Thus, to alter undesirable human behavior, the genetics (a *very* scary thought that is examined later) or systems that cause such behavior must be altered first. Written in 1933, those who authored *Humanist Manifesto I* did not have the chance to observe

10. Ibid., 10.

the atrocities of Soviet Communism. This *might* have been excusable except for the fact that those who authored *Humanist Manifesto II* (1973) and *Humanist Manifesto 2000* (2000) *still* embraced socialism.

- "Man is at last becoming aware that he alone is responsible for the realization of the world of his dreams, that he has within himself the power for its achievement. He must set intelligence and will to the task."[11]

Translation

Humans must rely on themselves and the value they create to realize the world they wish to live in.

Worldview Analysis

Man alone is responsible for salvation, because there is no such thing as the supernatural. Furthermore, by virtue of their intelligence (reason and knowledge), humans have the potential to achieve such salvation without divine help (which includes "help" in the form of divinely given moral codes).

Humanist Manifesto II (1973)

- "Traditional moral codes and newer irrational cults both fail to meet the pressing needs of today and tomorrow. False 'theologies of hope' and messianic ideologies, substituting new dogmas for old, cannot cope with the existing world realities. They separate rather than unite peoples."[12]

Translation

Traditional morality no longer meets the needs of individuals or societies. Moral codes (i.e., religion) divide people rather than unite them.

Worldview Analysis

"Traditional moral codes" are usually based on a religion's sacred Scripture, which is seen as divine revelation. Since there is no such thing as the supernatural, such codes are based on superstition and not grounded in human reason or experience and, therefore, are incapable of aiding humanity in establishing worldwide social harmony. Furthermore, such "codes" not only prevent the possibility of unity but actually *cause* divi-

---

11. Ibid.
12. Ibid., 14.

sion (an interesting claim, considering secularism has caused more division and suffering in the twentieth century alone than theistic religion has in all of human history). As with the demiurge and Zeus, traditional moral codes inhibit humanity's potential.

Concerning religion:

- "We believe . . . that traditional dogmatic or authoritarian religions that place revelation, God, ritual, or creed above human needs and experience do a disservice to the human species. . . .We find insufficient evidence for belief in the existence of a supernatural; it is either meaningless or irrelevant to the question of the survival and fulfillment of the human race. As non-theists, we begin with humans not God, nature not deity."[13]

Translation

All religions do a disservice to the human species, because the knowledge they provide is based on superstition and folklore. Our secular version of the scientific method proves that there is no evidence for the existence of the supernatural, and, therefore, the questions of God and his will are irrelevant when it comes to human life. Thus, knowledge is grounded in the only remaining possibility, the self.

Worldview Analysis

All knowledge relevant to human life must be empirically based and legitimated by a secularized scientific method. Knowledge not based on secular presuppositions is, at the least, irrelevant and, at the most, a lie; therefore, it is unsuitable when considering policy, legislation, morality, lifestyles, etc. Keep your religion to yourself. This also reflects how secularism views its values as "neutral"—as opposed to religious values, which are biased and superstitious.

- "But we reject those features of traditional religious morality that deny humans a full appreciation of their own potentialities and responsibilities. Traditional religions often offer solace to humans, but, as often, they inhibit humans from helping themselves or experiencing their full potentialities."[14]

---

13. Ibid., 15–16.
14. Ibid., 16.

Translation

Religion diverts man's attention from himself to the supernatural. This causes man to neglect his own potential in bringing about salvation in *this* world. While belief in the supernatural and the afterlife is comforting to some, it inhibits humans from acting in *this* world.

Worldview Analysis

This is a subtler version of the "opiate of the masses" argument put forward by Karl Marx. Unfortunately for secularists, belief in the supernatural and the afterlife is the only legitimate foundation for condemning immoral ideologies and valuing our fellow man in *this* life. (Furthermore, it is interesting to note that this belief claims religion prevents people from helping themselves. This is ironic in light of modern liberalism's—a political ideology based on secularism—insistence on the necessity of government programs that help *precisely because individuals are inherently incapable of helping themselves*.)

- "But we can discover no divine purpose or providence for the human species. While there is much that we do not know, humans are responsible for what we are or will become. No deity will save us; we must save ourselves."[15]

Translation

There is no objective purpose for humanity. While we don't know everything about the universe, there is no need to appeal to the supernatural to explain phenomena we don't yet understand. There is no God. *We* are responsible for social and personal salvation.

Worldview Analysis

If the cosmos is all there is, there's nothing outside of it that infuses any ultimate meaning or purpose to existence. Because of secularism's commitment to materialism, it can't, by definition, appeal to the supernatural to explain that which is unknown to us at this time. We can be fully confident that it's only a matter of time before we will discover a materialistic explanation that will uncover what we currently do not know. (It is important to distinguish my claim that humans will determine many particular outcomes of our ongoing history from the secular claim that "humans are responsible for what we are or will become." The secular claim requires the *invention*

---

15. Ibid., 16.

of metaphysical realities. My claim requires the acknowledgement of the metaphysical reality woven into the fabric of the universe by God.)

- "Modern science discredits such historic concepts as the 'ghost in the machine' and the 'separable soul.' Rather, science affirms that the human species is an emergence from natural evolutionary forces. As far as we know, the total personality is a function of the biological organism transacting in a social and cultural context."[16]

Translation

There is no such thing as the soul. A human being is *merely* physical stuff. That's *all* he is. Human beings are the result of a meaningless and purposeless process. Each of us is a result of "blood and soil." There is no such thing as free will. (See essay entitled "Chance, Choice, or Chosen?" in Chapter 7.)

Worldview Analysis

If human beings are *only* physical matter, they are at the mercy of the physical laws of the universe, as is an apple that falls to the ground. This is because there is no fundamental difference between an apple and a human. The only difference is that a human is a more complex collection of physical stuff than an apple. Thus, every human thought, belief, and action is the direct physical effect of a prior physical cause. For free will to exist, there must be something non-physical about a human. Within the secular worldview, however, this is not a possible conclusion. *Genes and social context determine everything a person is, believes, and does.* Once again, this is Marxism to the core. (Are you beginning to see why Marxism is a *necessary* consequence of secularism?) Humanists believe human beings are a result of "blood and soil." How Nazi-like of them . . .

- "There is no credible evidence that life survives the death of the body. We continue to exist in our progeny and in the way that our lives have influenced others in our culture."[17]

Translation

There is no life after death. When a person dies, he ceases to exist. The only way a person "survives" after death is through his children or his influence on those who are still living.

16. Ibid., 17.
17. Ibid.

Worldview Analysis

Once again, this is a necessary conclusion that follows from secular presuppositions.

Concerning ethics:

- "We affirm that moral values derive their source from human experience. Ethics is autonomous and situational, needing no theological or ideological sanction. Ethics stems from human need and interest. . . . Human life has meaning because we create and develop our futures."[18]

Translation

Morals should be based on human experience *only* rather than divine revelation. Morality and ethics should change depending upon the human needs and interests at the moment. The only meaning that exists is that which we create for ourselves.

Worldview Analysis

This is an attempt to ground morality and ethics in something other than the supernatural. Because such a moral or ethical system cannot be objective, it must be open to change depending on the context. Only something supernatural can infuse *objective* morality and meaning into the universe. Without the supernatural, only personal arbitrary meaning can be constructed—a relativistic metaphysical reality that extends no further than the individual (or collectively social) mind.

Concerning the individual:

- "Although science can account for the causes of behavior, the possibilities of individual freedom of choice exist in human life and should be increased."[19]

Translation

Even though our worldview provides no basis for a belief in free will, we nonetheless believe free will exists, because it makes us feel good.

---

18. Ibid., 17.
19. Ibid., 18.

Worldview Analysis

This is a blatant example of worldview "borrowing." When the secular worldview requires secularists to believe something that makes them uncomfortable (for example, that there is no such thing as free will), they simply borrow a presupposition from a rival worldview that allows them to sleep at night. As previously mentioned, this discomfort stems from having basic notions of truth "written on their hearts" by God. God's image within us is difficult to exorcise; it takes years of indoctrination . . . although 18 years are usually enough (ages 5 through 22 in public schools).

- "The many varieties of sexual exploration should not in themselves be considered 'evil.' Without countenancing mindless permissiveness or unbridled promiscuity, a civilized society should be a tolerant one. . . . Moral education for children and adults is an important way of developing awareness and sexual maturity."[20]

Translation

Because there is no such thing as objective right and wrong, no sexual act can be considered evil . . . except, for some reason, mindless permissiveness and unbridled promiscuity. And, by the way, we are going to utilize the education system to teach this to your children.

Worldview Analysis

This is a blatant example of the inherent contradiction in saying there are no objective morals, yet then making objective moral claims, i.e., society should be tolerant but not countenance mindless permissiveness or unbridled promiscuity, and education should be used to promote sexual awareness, etc.

Concerning democratic society:

- "All persons should have a voice in developing the values and goals that determine their lives."[21]

Translation

Everyone is free to believe what he wants to believe and live how he wants to live.

---

20. Ibid., 18–19.
21. Ibid., 19.

Worldview Analysis

Because there is no objective morality, there is no standard by which to compare competing moral claims. This is another example of the contradiction between claiming there is no universal morality, then claiming "All persons should have a voice" when determining their own lives. Exactly *why* should people have this right?

- "People are more important than decalogues, rules, prescriptions, or regulations."[22]

Translation

People are more important than rules . . . except this rule.

Worldview Analysis

This is another example of contradictory metaphysical claims (i.e., claiming there is no objective morality, followed by making an objective moral claim). From whence does this secular attempt to instill *inherent* value in the individual come? After all, if ethics are based strictly on experience and should change as contexts change, shouldn't we—in the spirit of situational ethics and tolerance—hold open the possibility that sometimes rules might be more important than humans? (The closest secularism comes to instilling value in humans is an attempt based on the utility or the "usefulness" of a person or group—as subjectively determined by those who have power over said person or group. See the essay entitled "Abortion: Ethical Rapprochement and Legal Contradictions" in Chapter 7.)

- "The separation of church and state and the separation of ideology and state are imperatives. . . . It [the state] should not favor any particular religious bodies through the use of public monies, nor espouse a single ideology and function thereby as an instrument of propaganda or oppression, particularly against dissenters."[23]

Translation

The state shall not favor any one belief system over another nor spend tax dollars instilling any belief system into its people . . . except *our* belief system, including our desire to use education to instill our sexual values (as mentioned earlier).

---

22. Ibid.
23. Ibid., 19–20.

Worldview Analysis

This is a result of secularism thinking it is categorically different from other worldviews. Because secular knowledge is based on the only truly objective epistemology (a secularized scientific method), it should be utilized in the public square. Religious knowledge, on the other hand, should be marginalized to the private sphere and kept out of the public arena. Like the lesbian activist who visited my undergraduate philosophy class, many secularists don't realize "neutral" values do not exist. It is impossible for a society *not* to embrace a set of values.

- "We believe in the right to universal education. Everyone has a right to the cultural opportunity to fulfill his or her unique capacities and talents. . . . Innovative and experimental forms of education are to be welcomed."[24]

Translation

Even though we claim there is no such thing as universal morality or values, we believe education to be an objective value, and a universal moral obligation exists for society to provide it.

Worldview Analysis

This is an example of the underlying claim that ignorance is the cause of the world's ills. If ignorance is the problem, education will solve all our ills. This is opposed to the Judeo-Christian claim that worldly ills are caused by sin, i.e., immorality.

Concerning the world community:

- "We deplore the division of humankind on nationalistic grounds. We have reached a turning point in human history where the best option is to transcend the limits of national sovereignty and to move toward the building of a world community in which all sectors of the human family can participate. Thus we look to the development of a system of world law and a world order based upon transnational federal government."[25]

Translation

Because reason and experience (empirical observation) are available to every human, there is no reason why every human and nation shouldn't

---

24. Ibid., 20.
25. Ibid., 21.

be able to come together and live in peace. Nationalistic sovereignty, patriotism, and loyalties are misguided and divisive.

Worldview Analysis

Humanist faith in humanity is extremely high, because salvation is from within. Secular humanism mistakenly views reason as a tool that necessarily leads everyone to the same conclusions regarding morality and what is best for society.[26] They also want one enormous federal government to govern the entire world.

- "This world community must renounce the resort to violence and force as a method of solving international disputes. We believe in a peaceful adjudication of differences by international courts and by the development of the arts of negotiation and compromise. War is obsolete."[27]

Translation

Because the human faculty of reason is capable of bringing everyone to the same conclusions, all disputes can be resolved by appealing to reason rather than force.

Worldview Analysis

Pacifism is a natural real-world consequence of secular humanism because of its faith in human reason. Reason alone is enough to settle all disputes. For example, as long as we can get all disputing parties to sit down at a table and use reason, their disputes can be solved rationally without force or violence.[28]

- "We would resist any moves to censor basic scientific research on moral, political, or social grounds."[29]

Translation

Because knowledge is the cure for the world's ills, it should be pursued at all costs.

---

26. See the essay entitled "No Ruts, No Glory" in Chapter 7.
27. *Humanist Manifestos I and II*, 21.
28. To see why this is *not* true, see "No Ruts, No Glory" in Chapter 7.
29. *Humanist Manifestos I and II*, 22.

Worldview Analysis

Only knowledge gained through a secularized scientific method is considered legitimate. Therefore, research based on such a method will lead to knowledge that will help us relieve the crises and tensions in the world. Of course, the "moral, political, or social grounds" mentioned are of the religious variety only. After all, secularism is supposedly neutral and not tainted by biased metaphysics.

- "We must expand communication and transportation across frontiers. Travel restrictions must cease."[30]

Translation

All immigration policies must cease. National borders must be completely open.

Worldview Analysis

This is a natural real-world consequence of believing humanity is capable of living together in peace via the faculty of reason. The existence of different nations supposedly results from the dominance of biased religious and political dogmatism rather than "neutral" secular epistemology based on reason and experience. After all, everyone should be able to get along if they utilize reason.

Far from accepting the nihilistic conclusions inherent in secular presuppositions, secular humanism is full of moral claims about how humanity should behave. Needless to say, secular humanism has trouble justifying such moral claims. This is why humanist intellectuals dedicate a great deal of time and effort to finding a foundation for the moral claims they espouse. Acknowledging their moral claims are borrowed from mutually exclusive worldviews, such as Judeo-Christian theism, is not an option. They must find a way to ground their moral claims within the limits of their own secular presuppositions. Unfortunately for secular humanists, this has never been done—nor is it possible.

Friedrich Nietzsche, an ardent secularist, prophesied that a temporary moral vacuum would result when society realized God did not exist. He said that in the short term, this would result in anarchy, because there would be no basis for *any* form of morality. Eventually, however, someone (a figure or ideology he termed the "uberman" or "superman") would come along and provide a morality built on secular presuppositions.

---

30. Ibid., 22.

Nietzsche's prophecy was right in that moral anarchy is the result of believing "God is dead," but he was deathly wrong when he predicted this moral vacuum would be filled by a person or ideology that would bring peaceful moral stability. History tells us the deconstruction of objective metaphysical moral claims results in the rise of "supermen" such as Hitler, Stalin, and Pol Pot—a far cry from the transnational world utopia promised by secular humanists.

Postmodern Liberation

Postmodernism is the consistent application of secular presuppositions to *every* area of life. The first step is applying secular presuppositions to the realms of meaning and morality. This inevitably leads to the conclusions that there is no objective meaning to life or the universe, and there is no objective morality around which everyone can base their lives. The second step is applying secular presuppositions to the realms of science and reason. The postmodern skepticism that leads to the deconstruction of metaphysics (i.e., meaning and morality) is directed toward deconstructing modern science and Western thought (i.e., logic). Objective claims about reality, science, and logic are deconstructed as narrow traditions told as part of a narrative—a demiurgical narrative designed to oppress.

If you place a pencil in a glass filled with water and view it from the side, it appears as though the pencil bends or breaks at the surface of the water. The senses we use for observation tell us the pencil is bent or broken, but, in reality, it is not. Thus, our senses (in this case, vision) are not accurately observing that which is external to us (the pencil). This phenomenon is a microcosm of postmodernism. Postmodernism claims that objective, external reality (physical *and* metaphysical) is, at best, inaccessible and, at worst, nonexistent. The only hope for humanity is for each individual to construct *his own* reality. For the postmodernist, reality is *internal only* rather than external. Thus, in postmodernism (just as in Gnosticism), ultimate reality is found within.

Before subjective realities can be *constructed*, however, old realities must be *deconstructed*. Deconstruction is the reduction of a physical or metaphysical claim to its most basic constituent components. Some call this process the "nothing buttery" of postmodernism, because deconstruction says that x is "nothing but" y. For example, traditional religion with all of its historical claims, moral codes, and supposed personal fulfillment is "nothing but" a psychological concoction, a crutch that humans have created to help us deal with the loneliness and meaninglessness of life. Karl

Marx takes this analysis a step further and reduces traditional religion to a disease caused by the repressive lifestyle lived by the proletariat; a disease exploited by the bourgeoisie to maintain its power. Additionally, capitalism is "nothing but" a system that perpetuates the oppression of the lower class by the upper class—a kind of capitalist demiurge—who controls the means of production. Religion is "nothing but" a modern demiurge preventing freedom and inhibiting humanity.

In short, postmodernism claims that deconstruction allows us to see a phenomena for what it "really" is. Once again, *true* knowledge saves the day. It is like a window that allows us to see through the cumbersome wall separating us from a beautiful garden on the other side. In fact, *this book* could be accused of deconstructing the strategies of secularism's bid to dominate culture. This is true to a point. The difference, however, is that I am not deconstructing simply for the purpose of deconstructing. Postmodern deconstruction serves to reduce everything en route to realizing the nonexistence of any and all objective truth claims. The current endeavor in this book is to *uncover* objective truth rather than destroy it.

A Critique of Postmodernism

Postmodern deconstruction as a method is *self-referentially incoherent*. A claim is self-referentially incoherent if a consequence of it being true is the falsification of the claim. For example, the claim that there are no absolutes is self-referentially incoherent, because if there are no absolutes, then the absolute statement of "there are no absolutes" is false. Deconstruction is used to "see through" opinions, ideologies, and systems. It exposes them as the subjective myths they are—most likely created by modern demiurges and meant to oppress. In order for deconstruction to do this, however, it must itself be something *universally true* and capable of being applied in every situation—something considered an impossibility in postmodernism.

Why not deconstruct deconstruction? To do so would be for postmodernism to undermine its own premises. Ultimately, postmodernism would have to be seen as just another subjective myth—as equally valid as the Judeo-Christian theism that rejects it. Postmodernism then becomes simply another interest group jockeying for legal and cultural dominance through crafty manipulation and/or brute force.

It is absurd to deconstruct first principles, such as logic, because deconstruction itself is based upon some first principle, i.e., logic itself. In the concluding words of *Abolition of Man*, C. S. Lewis summarizes the postmodern dilemma:

> But you cannot go on "explaining away" forever: you will find that you have explained explanation itself away. You cannot go on "seeing through" things forever. The whole point of seeing through something is to see something through it. It is good that the window should be transparent, because the street or garden beyond it is opaque. How if you saw through the garden too? It is no use trying to "see through" first principles. If you see through everything, then everything is transparent. But a wholly transparent world is an invisible world. To "see-through" all things is the same as not to see.[31]

Postmodernism claims that all truth claims *not* constructed by the individual from within must be exposed and disposed. This is especially true for objective truth claims, i.e., worldviews and subsidiary beliefs that claim truth is externally objective and *cannot* be constructed from within. Traditional religions fall under this category, as do science, logic, capitalism, free-market economics, and most other ideas associated with America. By deconstructing objective truth claims and their supernatural foundation, every individual becomes free to construct his own reality—including his own morality. (Such "personal reality construction" has become the postmodern definition of "freedom"—a notion very similar to gnostic antinomianism. In both worldviews, the rejection of objective moral codes is indicative of liberation.)

This consequence is also true for society in general and its ability to construct reality from scratch. When Nietzsche claimed "God is dead," he wasn't saying that God suddenly stopped existing (Nietzsche was an atheist). He was saying society had done away with God as an active player in forming laws, governments, culture, and morality. God was no longer relevant, nor were the implications of belief in God. Nietzsche knew that God's death removed any hope of society-wide agreement on absolute truth. Society, truth, and power become a "free for all" with no anchor or standard for resolving disputes.

Years ago it was possible to debate who was right and who was wrong. When two or more people came together to debate a particular issue, there was an underlying assumption that *someone* was, indeed, right, and *someone* was wrong. The existence of objective truth was an unspoken understanding. Arriving at the objectively right answer was a possibility.

Debate in the context of objective truth can be fruitful, because the disputing parties are using the same epistemological standard. Consensus is *possible* in such a context. *Only then* does the utilization of reason for peaceful resolution become a possibility. Today, however, objective truth

---

31. Lewis, *Abolition of Man*, 81.

is *not* an unspoken understanding. How often have you seen two people debate an issue only to conclude that "what is right for you isn't necessarily right for me"? Dialogue stops at that point, because there is no reason to debate the issue further. The disputing parties are irreconcilable, because there's no objective standard by which to compare the validity of their mutually exclusive claims. They are both equally valid. Debate becomes meaningless without the backdrop of objective truth.

Logic itself assumes objective truth (which is why it is rejected by postmodernists). It is based on the law of non-contradiction. The law of non-contradiction states that something cannot be both x and not x at the same time in the same way. For example, my eyes cannot be blue and not blue at the same time in the same way (physical). My dog cannot be a golden retriever and not a golden retriever at the same time in the same way (physical). Murder cannot be both wrong and not wrong at the same time in the same way (metaphysical). Rape cannot be wrong and not wrong at the same time in the same way (metaphysical).

Postmodernism, however, attempts to reject logic, because it views logic as only one epistemological standard among many; it is no more valid than the next. Because objective reality (especially metaphysical reality) is either nonexistent or inaccessible, the claim that logic is universal is rejected outright. Thus, logic is removed as a standard for resolving disputes.

In such a cultural and intellectual milieu, dialogue and debate are replaced by crafty manipulation, at best, or force and violence, at worst. After all, what's the point of dialogue if it gets us nowhere in resolving disputes? Instead of political parties and interest groups vying for cultural influence through dialogue and democratic processes, disputing groups resort to brute force to establish cultural, political, and institutional dominance. Moral relativism is utterly incapable of establishing or maintaining peaceful democratic societies, because it provides no foundation for dialogue and peaceful resolution nor a mutual respect among disputing individuals and parties.

Metaphysical reality must be constructed from within by each individual, because objective reality (physical *and* metaphysical) is inaccessible (or nonexistent). Because there is no standard by which to compare the validity of each constructed reality, every constructed reality is equally valid. Thus, Marxism is as equally valid as capitalism. Atheism is as equally valid as Christianity. Being pro-abortion is as equally valid as being pro-life. Supporting capital punishment is as equally valid as being against capital punishment. Viewing black Americans as property is as equally valid as fighting for civil rights. Hitler's "Final Solution" is as equally valid as the

Western democracies that fought against Nazi Germany and Imperialist Japan. So on and so forth. When people with different ideologies clash within a culture of postmodern relativism (as our culture is becoming/has become), there is no hope for reconciliation, diplomacy, or tolerance—only endless dissonance resolved through force.

Postmodern Storytelling

Postmodernism claims every person or group has their own story, or *narrative*. A person's narrative is the reality each individual constructs to organize his lifestyle and beliefs. For example, Christians have chosen Judeo-Christian theism as their narrative. Marxists have chosen materialism as their narrative. Environmentalists have chosen environmentalism as their narrative. Buddhists have chosen Buddhism as their narrative. In short, a person's narrative is his worldview, and, according to (consistent) postmodernism, every narrative is equally valid. This has become the new definition for "tolerance." Rather than a notion of acceptance based upon the objective truth claim that every individual has inherent value, tolerance now means every truth claim is as equally valid as another—even truth claims that reject the inherent value of the individual.

With no absolute truth *and* no way to access truth (even if such absolute truth existed), there is no ultimate purpose or goal for society, the person, or existence in general; social existence is nothing more than individual opinions vying for power. James Sire writes:

> The horizon defining the limits of our world has been wiped away. The center holding us in place has vanished. Our age, which more and more is coming to be called postmodern, finds itself afloat in a pluralism of perspectives, a plethora of philosophical possibilities, but with no dominant notion of where to go or how to get there. A near future of cultural anarchy seems inevitable.[32]

Postmodernism uses the notion of *language* when describing the nature of narratives. In this context, however, the term "language" doesn't refer to spoken languages such as Spanish, English, or German. It refers to the particular way a person or group constructs reality. For example, a Christian utilizes the *language* of Judeo-Christian theism to organize his lifestyle and beliefs. An atheist uses the *language* provided by secularism. Ultimately, the language used for construction will determine a person's subsidiary beliefs. This is what is meant when today's young individuals try

---

32. Sire, *The Universe Next Door*, 174.

to "find themselves." They're not searching for some sort of external standard (for example, God's standard) around which to organize their lives. They're trying to *create from within* a reality in which they're comfortable.

Postmodernism doesn't have a problem with narratives as long as each individual freely chooses his own. (In case you're wondering, belief in an ability to freely choose one's own narrative contradicts the unpopular yet consistent secular conclusion that free will doesn't exist.) Postmodernism rails against *metanarratives*. A *metanarrative* is a narrative that claims to be objectively true for everyone. Postmodernism claims a metanarrative is merely a narrative trying to exert control over other individuals. For example, when I claim that Christianity is objectively true, I'm trying to manipulate someone else into adopting my own personal narrative as his own. If I am successful, I have power over that person, because I control how he organizes his lifestyle and beliefs (because he has accepted *my* language). Thus, all metanarratives (i.e., worldviews and subsidiary beliefs claiming objective truth) are, by definition, oppressive, because they prevent an individual from constructing *his own* reality. We see in the gnostic parallel how the demiurge maintained his power over humanity by convincing Adam and Eve to accept *his* metanarrative (which contains supernatural moral codes and rules) rather than letting them realize their own narrative.

Power is gained by convincing as many people as possible to live by *your* constructed reality rather than their own. All metanarratives are seen as "power grabs." This is why postmodernism views theistic religions, with their objective moral claims founded on supernatural revelation, as oppressive. They are all metanarratives. Such religions stifle the human potential to create a personal reality. Once again, traditional religion with its strict moral codes plays the role of the demiurge and Zeus, while postmodern deconstruction (and the re-construction which follows) are gnostic and Promethean liberators.

Postmodernism often labels influential leaders and thinkers as "strong poets." They are persons who have convinced a large group of people to accept their own narrative. For example, Jesus Christ is a strong poet because so many people throughout history and in the world today use *his* language when constructing their reality. Sigmund Freud is a strong poet because he has so heavily influenced the modern field of psychology and psychoanalysis. Charles Darwin is a strong poet because his language of natural selection and speciation rules modern secular science. Other strong poets include Adam Smith (capitalism), Karl Marx (communism), Adolf Hitler (Nazism), etc.

Strong poets, however, need not be personified in individuals. They can also take the form of particular movements in society, e.g., the feminist movement, the civil rights movement, the prohibitionist movement, etc. The important point to remember is that postmodernism views past, present, and future history as a collection of power struggles—narratives fighting one another for political and cultural dominance. And because dialogue is meaningless due to the absence of an objective backdrop, such struggles most often take the form of coercive manipulation or brute force.

In *theory*, the moral relativism inherent in postmodernism promotes complete individual autonomy. In *fact*, however, with no possibility of rapprochement between disputing narratives, coercion through manipulation and/or violence is the only medium for "resolution" between such disputing narratives. The "winner" of the struggle becomes the dominant narrative by either forcefully converting everyone or, when that fails, simply exterminating them. Thus, to the victor go the spoils.

More Equal than Others

Secular *theory* claims that secular moral relativism results in autonomy and freedom, while theistic religion leads to oppression. This theory leads to the secularist's disdain for objective truth claims. Opinions are respected as long as they are narratives, not metanarratives. This is why modern secularists *claim* to respect different views, but, in reality, they only respect relativistic views free from oppressive metanarratives, i.e., traditional religion (which, in America, is usually Christianity). All opinions and beliefs stemming from such demiurgical "religious" worldviews must be suppressed, because they hinder freedom (the freedom to construct one's own reality) and lead to oppression.

This situation reminds me of George Orwell's *Animal Farm*. The farm animals overthrow the farmer in an attempt to form their own utopia. After the revolution is successful, the animals set up a system of rules to govern their new and improved farm. The rule by which they will live is, "All animals are equal." After awhile, however, someone (an animal interested in gaining power) sneaks into the barn and paints a new rule on the wall. The new rule is, "All animals are equal . . . but some animals are *more equal* than others." (Emphasis added.) Because secularists believe objective truth claims (i.e., theistic religion) cause division and oppression, they feel they must silence such claims. Thus, claims grounded in secularism are "more equal" than those grounded in religion. Thus, destroying religion in the public forum is a primary way secularists "fight for freedom."

History tells us that when there is an absence of order in society, order will be *imposed*. Without the backdrop of objective truth, the type of order that will be imposed is determined by whoever gains power—most likely through violence. Once this happens, the ruling narrative represses all other narratives. This is how secular "diversity" becomes totalitarianism. Judeo-Christian diversity is based on the objective truth claim that every individual is created in the image of God and thus possesses inherent value. Secular diversity, on the other hand, is not based on any objective truth claim and, when push comes to shove, provides no reason to respect the inherent value of the individual. Thus, "dialogue" becomes a matter of ideological selection—those in power choosing which worldviews to accept and which to repress. (Who's the demiurge now?)

Secularists claim to respect and tolerate all views, but due to their mythological (gnostic and Promethean) interpretation of liberation and "freedom," they are prevented from applying such "respect" and "tolerance" to demiurgical worldviews, such as Judeo-Christian theism, and the subsidiary claims (capitalism, the pro-life position, abstinence, etc.) founded on them. In fact, not only must theistic worldviews not be respected, but they also must be prevented from influencing the direction of society (because they inhibit "freedom"). We are now back to the issue discussed in Chapter 1: The banishment of theistic worldviews (Judeo-Christian theism specifically) from the public forum. Isn't such banishment simply the logical conclusion of a worldview that sees religion as a prison for divine human potential, the "spark" of potential capable of creating the perfect world? We saw this myth in Gnosticism and paganism 2000 years ago, and we're seeing it again today in the deceptive, re-packaged language of secularism.

Freedom and Social Contract Theory

Underlying the claim that deconstruction and construction bring liberation is a particular notion of *freedom*; one that is based on the interpretation that humans are at their core completely autonomous beings, wholly independent of one another. Enlightenment social contract theorists label the completely independent and autonomous individual as existing in the "state of nature." It was believed that humans lived in this primitive state before they came together to create society. Such a primitive state of nature was characterized by selfish fulfillment, violence, manipulation, and absolutely no concern for others. (Ironically, this sounds exactly like the postmodern world described previously.)

Only when living in this primitive state of nature became untenable did individuals come together to form rules and institutions (society) that made life a bit more pleasant. The ultimate goal of individual existence (fulfilling one's selfish desires) was difficult to do in the "state of nature," because everyone went around killing everyone else. Culture (with its values, mores, taboos, and institutions) was merely a means to an end—a way to fulfill selfish desires more efficiently. However, the ultimate goal of humanity—selfish individual fulfillment—did not change.

Thus, social contract theorists believe values such as the Ten Commandments and institutions such as the family, marriage, and the church are merely social constructs that allow individuals to more efficiently fulfill selfish desires. When such social constructs inhibit personal fulfillment, however, they can be disposed of, because in the end, they exist to serve the individual. They are not objective physical and metaphysical realities that are written into the fabric of the universe, as Judeo-Christian theism claims. Thus, when marriage ceases to please a husband or wife, he or she can simply dispose of the cumbersome commitment. When a particular set of values hinders someone's selfish sexual or financial desires, they can be disposed of in favor of a more conducive set of values. As you can see, Social Contract Theory's emphasis on the self fits nicely with postmodernism. Like postmodernism, Social Contract Theory requires the deconstruction of demiurgical metanarratives that oppress.

Eventually, the constructed morality systems (e.g., the Ten Commandments) and institutions (e.g., marriage, the family, etc.) originally meant to increase selfish fulfillment begin to oppress humans. This is what Jean-Jacques Rousseau meant when he said, "Man is born free, yet everywhere he is in chains." He didn't mean that humans were literally bound by chains. He meant that the primitive human is born unrestrained by any set of values or institutions (because, objectively, there aren't any). As the human grows, however, he is placed under the yoke of moral codes and social expectations. Rousseau, like many secularists, longed for the return of humanity to the "state of nature" and, ironically, appealed to totalitarian governments to forcefully peel away society's values and institutions (yet another example of how secularism leads to totalitarianism).

Unlike Social Contract Theory, Judeo-Christian theism claims that humans are *not* essentially individual and autonomous creatures whose purpose is selfish fulfillment (which includes the freedom to construct, or not construct, metaphysical reality), but they are creatures created to be in relationship with God and other humans. The Ten Commandments (objective morality) and institutions such as marriage, family, and the church are divinely ordained and basic realities of creation—not subjectively constructed entities to be manipulated for individual gain. The Ten Commandments are reflective of the objective morality written into the fabric of the universe. Similarly, marriage, family, and other institutions are reflective of the personal and social needs that arise due to the characteristics inherent in being created in God's image.

Considering Social Contract Theory's explanation for what a human is, it should come as no surprise that *freedom* comes to be defined in the negative sense as an unencumbered state wherein the individual may do whatever he wants whenever he wants. Thus, freedom becomes a matter of tearing down socially constructed values and institutions in the name of individual fulfillment—very similar to the postmodern ideas of deconstruction and narrative-building. Only when an individual is able to create his own reality absent from the coercion of objective truth claims ("metanarratives" according to postmodernism), can it be considered *free*. The rules and regulations of the demiurge must be rejected in favor of a reality constructed from within each of us. Constructing reality is no longer a job for God. It is now the right of every individual.

This definition of freedom accounts for the secular humanist rejection of theistic religion and the postmodern obsession with the deconstruction of objective truth claims. The rejection of theistic religion and the deconstruction of objective truth claims are seen as strategic steps leading to freedom. The demiurge and his coercive rules and regulations must be overthrown. Humans must be given the chance to fulfill their own divine potential through the Promethean revelation provided by secularism. Also, as seen with Rousseau's appeals, this accounts for why secularism leads to totalitarianism—only a totalitarian government would be able to forcefully rid a society of its objective value claims and institutions (including a totalitarian educational system and judiciary).

Within every worldview, freedom is defined against a *teleological* backdrop. *Telos* is the end of a goal-oriented process.[33] The *telos* of something is its ultimate *purpose* for being. For example, the *telos* of an acorn is to become an oak tree. The *telos* of an insect larva is to grow into an adult insect. The *telos* of a table is to have things sitting upon it. A worldview's definition of freedom will depend on its claim regarding the *telos* of humanity, i.e., humanity's purpose for being.

Secularism and Judeo-Christian theism have very different definitions of freedom, because they prescribe different purposes for humanity. Postmodernism (and its Social Contract Theory adherents) sees the purpose

33. www.dictionary.com.

of humanity as complete, selfish individual fulfillment via the deconstruction of objective values and institutions, followed by the construction of a personal reality. Secular humanism views the purpose of humanity as the destruction of traditional religious dogma in an attempt to create a utopia based on reason alone. (Notice *both* require the deconstruction of objective truth claims, i.e. religion.) Either way, rejecting objective morality becomes a telltale sign of being "open-minded" or a so-called "free thinker." Like Sodom and Gomorrah to their gnostic predecessors, secularists view increased moral decadence as a side-effect of true freedom.

Judeo-Christian theism, on the other hand, claims humanity's *telos* (purpose) is to glorify God and experience his goodness. Fortunately for humanity, God has revealed exactly *how* to do this through general revelation (reason) and special revelation (Christ, Scripture, the Holy Spirit). To be free is to *submit* to God's will for our lives as spelled out in his revelation to us. This is why *freedom* and *submission* go hand-in-hand, although in secularism they are seen as two concepts utterly opposed to one another. In short, *Christian freedom* is acknowledging and submitting to an *external* standard. *Secular freedom* is constructing a personal standard *from within*—a hopelessly purposeless task.

Secular Gnosis

Prometheus and gnosis are not redeemers. They are *liberators*. *Redemption* is for those who cannot save themselves, while *liberation* is for those who have their salvation within themselves. Redemption is moral, while liberation is enlightenment. Christianity claims it brings redemption, while secularism claims it brings liberation. These fundamental differences are why secularism is elitist and Christianity is not.

Christianity claims *everyone* is a sinner in need of redemption. Eternal salvation does not reside in a person's level of knowledge, good deeds, race, gender, class, or ethnic group. Salvation is only through the blood of Jesus Christ, and this gift is offered to everyone equally. The apostle Paul writes in Galatians 3:28–29, "There is neither Jew nor Greek, slave nor free, male nor female, for you are all one in Christ Jesus. If you belong to Christ, then you are Abraham's seed, and heirs according to the promise." It doesn't matter who you are. If you accept Christ as Lord and Savior, you are adopted into God's "family" and are able to receive the inheritance of eternal life.

The salvation Christianity offers arrives externally as a gift from God. It is not something humans think or do *within themselves*. The gnostic, pagan, secular humanist, and postmodern claim that salvation is an autonomous act from within is completely and utterly false; it is a lie Satan has literally been feeding humanity since the Garden of Eden. While humans may choose whether or not to accept Christ, salvation is *God's* act. Paul writes in Romans 3:22–24, "This righteousness from God comes through faith in Jesus Christ to all who believe. There is no difference, for all have sinned and fall short of the glory of God, and are justified freely by his grace through the redemption that came by Christ Jesus." All humanity is in need of redemption because all have fallen; and only through Christ can the effects of our fall be reversed (Acts 4:11–12).

These two passages alone provide the justification that all men are equal. The phrase "All men are created equal . . . " is a direct consequence of the biblical claim that *all* humans are created in God's image. Similarly, the equality of men is also based on the fact that *all* have *fallen* equally. Even for those who are saved, there is no justification to mistreat those who have not accepted Christ. For it is the sustaining blood of Christ that redeems the saved rather than anything a believer has accomplished internally (or externally, for that matter). The difference between the saved and the unsaved is not their relative value, but the fact that the former are forgiven. The inherent value of the individual (based on being created in God's image) remains intact regardless of a person's particular beliefs. This is why God wishes *everyone* to be saved (1 Timothy 2:3–5). He loves everyone equally, and the actions of Christians must reflect such love. In short, if the Bible is read fairly, it is impossible to claim that biblical Christianity is elitist.

Secularism, on the other hand, is a worldview offering liberation rather than redemption; liberation based on reason and knowledge. Secularism claims humanity can achieve the utopia we desire if we shed the chains of religion and embrace reason as a guide. *Every* person is capable of reasoned thinking (well, almost everyone—as will be discussed below). Because of this, the humanist faith in humanity is extremely high. Secular humanism views reason as a tool that will lead everyone to the same conclusions regarding morality and what's best for society. (Such an interpretation of reason is grossly inaccurate. Reason is dependent upon presuppositions. The method of reason itself doesn't determine truth. It only forces you to remain consistent with the presuppositions provided by your worldview.)[34] For example, according to secular humanism, if everyone were reasonable (the terms *reason* and *logic* are used synonymously), we would come to the same conclusions in debates about creation and evolution, abortion, the separation of church and state, the role of government, taxes, education

---

34. See the essay entitled "No Ruts, No Glory" in Chapter 7.

curriculum, etc. In other words, there would be no disputes, no war, no exploitation, and no oppression.

Humanists believe if people disagree, it is because one or all are being unreasonable. After all, if everyone is utilizing reason, they should arrive at the same conclusion. Knowledge through reason is the key to realizing social utopia. The more knowledge the world has, the more peaceful its societies (or the transnational society) will be. Because there is no such thing as sin (and therefore, no sinful human nature), humans will automatically act morally if they are given sufficient knowledge (and secular education is the *system* that distributes this knowledge—which, in turn, alters human behavior). Just as in Gnosticism, humanism claims ignorance is dispelled by the arrival of knowledge. This is why knowledge is seen as the cure for the world's ills. Humanism (like Gnosticism and pagan mythology) embraces the myth that ignorance, not immorality, stands between humanity and utopia. Immoral behavior ("undesirable behavior" would be more accurate) is considered simply a collection of decisions made without all the facts at hand (or without the right systems in place).

As the medium that instills knowledge, education is seen as the catalyst that brings knowledge to its students, thus producing desirable behavior. According to secular humanism, there is no problem or dispute in this world that can't be solved by increased knowledge delivered through education. This is why liberals in America and abroad see education as a fundamental right that should be provided by society. It's interesting to observe that modern liberals prescribe education as the cure for nearly everything. How do we decrease STDs and teenage pregnancy? By providing education about safe sex. How do we decrease poverty? By providing free education (including free college education). How do we alleviate hatred and racism? Through culturally diverse education curricula. Education has become the quintessential system utilized by secularism to alter human behavior.

Secularism believes educating someone will automatically make him moral. This stems from the belief that humans do not have a sinful nature. Like Gnosticism, secularism believes humans shoulder no blame whatsoever for the ills of the world (bad biology and/or systems cause them). Humans may be chained to a cave floor and forced to gaze upon a wall of shadows, but it isn't their fault. A demiurgical metanarrative (oppressive worldviews and systems) keeps them in their chains. If people simply have all the right information (knowledge) and are grown in the right petri dish (environment/system), they will shed such chains and make the right decisions. (Of course, the question arises, "'Right' according to whom?" The answer? Those in power.)

I wish it were this easy. Moral behavior is not a necessary consequence of increased knowledge. Case-in-point (one of *many*): Germany in the 1930s and 1940s was the most educated nation in the world, yet one of the most immoral, murderous, and oppressive ideologies in history arose and flourished among Germany's highly educated population. Additionally, most of the twentieth century's worst dictators were highly educated. What secularism doesn't understand is that, as British author G. K. Chesterton once quipped, putting devils inside a classroom will not make them angels. It will only make them educated devils. Education is of no help unless it is teaching the right ideas—especially regarding morality.

Elitism as Esoteric Disdain

Secularism views progress as the widespread availability of education leading to increased knowledge. Everyone has the capacity to be reasonable. If someone has a wrong opinion, he only need be "educated" to be brought in line. If someone is a Christian, he needs to be educated with the secular knowledge that will free him from cumbersome Christian dogma. A political conservative needs to be "enlightened" with secular knowledge regarding how the world *really* works. Christians and conservatives must be shown that the ideas they embrace are demiurgical shadows on the cave wall.

Those who have been enlightened with such knowledge see it as their duty to enlighten others. If someone doesn't agree with the enlightened, it is because he is being unreasonable or because he doesn't have enough knowledge (in other words, he is "uneducated"). Those who consistently disagree with the enlightened are flawed in their thinking and must be corrected. The relationship between the enlightened and unenlightened is analogous to the relationship between parent and child. A parent must teach the child the ways of the world. Similarly, the enlightened must teach the unenlightened how the world *really* works. In this context, it is easy to see how the enlightened often view the unenlightened with condescension (a tell-tale sign of elitism). The enlightened come to view their knowledge and resultant position as *esoteric*—just as the gnostics did.

The claim that a secularized version of science provides humanity with true knowledge is a basic tenet of secular humanism. Secularists decry attempts to interpret science through a supernatural or religious lens. Such attempts, secularists say, are unjustified and only arise out of a need to oppress others or to overcome the fear of metaphysical purposelessness. Therefore, it's not just knowledge that must be instilled in humanity, but a *particular kind* of knowledge deemed acceptable by the secular establishment. Religious and any other supernatural ideas are primitive constructs that hinder freedom and must be rejected if society is to embrace *true* knowledge capable of improving society. (*This* is the real reason secularists fight the inclusion of intelligent design in educational curriculum; their claim that creationism isn't "real" science is not the true reason.) Those who hold to such religious and supernatural ideas are viewed as foolish children in need of enlightenment. Such an elitist and condescending attitude is perfectly displayed in *Humanist Manifesto 2000*, where it says, "We think it time for humanity to embrace its own *adulthood*—to leave behind the magical thinking and mythmaking that are substitutes for tested knowledge of nature."[35] (Emphasis added.)

Because secularists believe utilizing reason and knowledge *necessarily* leads to consensus, they believe those who consistently disagree with the enlightened (i.e. Christians and conservatives) are either intentionally refusing to use reason (they are too stubborn) or they are incapable of using it (they are too stupid or too blinded by religion). Either way, the enlightened can do only so much to convince the unenlightened of the divine spark within. Viewing the stubborn or the stupid with disdain soon comes to characterize how the enlightened view the unenlightened. This disdain grows exponentially if the supposed "enlightened" are in the minority. They view the masses as unenlightened children who need to be directed—against their will if need be.[36] A child may *think* he knows better, but the parent would be unwise to let such a naive person run the household.

In secularism, the role of the enlightened educated is twofold: 1) To educate the uneducated or, if the uneducated refuse to be enlightened, 2) to disregard them (and their opinions) and run the "household" in an educated manner without them. It is no coincidence that the education establishment in America is perhaps the most elitist institution in the country. After all, it has been granted the role of savior, i.e., the role of enlightening the masses with the gnosis that will usher in the transnational, peaceful utopia prophesied about by secular prophets. Because there is no God, it is the elites that provide the right of freedom to the masses—a very important task, one only achieved through the actions of a very special class of people, i.e. gnostic "messengers of light" sent to liberate divine human potential. Anyone or anything standing in their way hinders such freedom (such as parents, private education, and homeschooling).

Hoeller's comments cited in Chapter 4 describing Gnosticism begin to make sense in the context of secular elitism. "Some call this view

35. *Humanist Manifesto 2000*, 26.
36. See essay entitled "Kibble for Fat Cats" in Chapter 7.

Secular Gnosticism

[the gnostic notion of salvation] elitist, and the contemporary egalitarian mindset tends to rebel against elitism. But there is a difference between an arbitrary, self-interested elitism that sets oneself and one's fellows apart as a chosen group, on the one hand, and the *inevitable existence of elite persons*, on the other."[37] (Emphasis added.) Secularists, especially when in the minority, begin to view their enlightenment as ordained from "above"—a result of the social Darwinian gods having smiled upon them.

For secular humanism and postmodernism, the goal of education is to deconstruct objective truth claims grounded in religion, thus freeing the formerly unenlightened student to create his own reality complete with its own set of values. No longer is the purpose of education to teach about external reality—a physical and metaphysical metanarrative (as grounded in the Judeo-Christian tradition). This is because objective truth claims regarding external physical and metaphysical reality are hindrances to personal "freedom."

Furthermore, according to the Judeo-Christian worldview, knowledge (facts, propositional knowledge of physical reality, etc.—that which leads to the applied sciences and technology) is taught as a means of fulfilling the cultural mandate (the command to "subdue the earth" in Genesis 1:28). Objective *metaphysical* reality (morality and meaning) is taught as a standard the adherence of which to ensures freedom and prevents this-worldly suffering (i.e. as the means of achieving the best world possible in the here and now). Secularism, on the other hand, teaches that objective metaphysical claims *hinder* freedom (and thus, must be deconstructed and marginalized) and that salvation in the here and now is achieved by utilizing propositional knowledge of *physical* reality in combination with the creation of a subjectively-created society-wide metaphysic.

If educating the unenlightened fails, it isn't the fault of the educators. It is the fault of the unenlightened oafs who are too stubborn, too dumb, or too blinded to receive enlightenment. When this happens, it is the job of the enlightened minority to circumvent the will of the unenlightened masses in the name of progress. In America, this is primarily done by stripping away control of the education system from parents (and private citizens in general) and manipulating the judiciary to bypass the will of unenlightened private citizens. *This* is why public education and the judiciary are two of the most elitist institutions in America. It is through them that the enlightened minority condescendingly saves society from the ignorant masses who refuse to accept, or are unable to accept, secular gnosis.

---

37. Hoeller, *Gnosticism: New Light on the Ancient Tradition of Inner Knowing*, 20.

Secularism United: Secular Humanism and Postmodernism Combined

Secular humanism and postmodernism ("Secularism United") may be squabbling within their own household, but their enemy is the same: Judeo-Christian theism. They have been and are setting themselves up against Judeo-Christian theism in a battle for America's culture and institutions. *Both* engage in the deconstruction of Christianity and the construction of a secular utopia through the manipulation of culture, institutions, and government (*especially* government). With the aid of "Messengers of Light" such as public education and the judiciary, human beings are divine agents that usher in salvation. Judeo-Christian theism, on the other hand, claims that salvation comes to us externally through Jesus Christ. Only through the internal acceptance of God's external and objective "breakthrough" into history, can humanity experience salvation. Thus, Judeo-Christian theism sees neither government nor cultural institutions as divine conduits of ultimate (or *this*-worldly, for that matter) liberation.

Furthermore, Judeo-Christian theism claims the way to make *this* world a better place is by diagnosing *immorality* as the cause of society's problems. Only moral solutions can alleviate moral problems. In virtue of its rejection of all objective morality, secularism (humanism and postmodernism) is *incapable* of identifying immorality as the cause of the world's ills. It is forced to locate the cause of the world's problems elsewhere. Secularism does so by attributing the world's ills to *physical* causes, i.e., genetics and systems (which include demiurgical metanarratives). (Systems have come to be seen as the primary culprits because the in-depth study of genetics has only been a recent emergence. On the other hand, the study of systems has had much more time to develop. Let this be fair warning: As genetic science progresses, expect it to be used as yet another tool to mold the kind of humans secularism desires to produce. The genetic experiments used by Hitler and the Nazis in their bid to produce the perfect race illustrate this phenomenon.) Thus, all attempts by secularism to solve such ills will address genetics or systems. This is modern liberalism in a nutshell—the same presuppositions that led to the atrocities of Nazi Germany and Soviet Russia (among other tragedies).

These two diametrically opposed visions for the United States are the source of today's cultural battle—with secularists (Secularism United) and Christian liberals on one side and theists, Christians, and atheist conservatives on the other. In his book, *The Second American Revolution*, John W. Whitehead writes, "When a state claims divine honors, there will always be warfare between Christ and Caesar, for two rival gods claim the same jurisdiction over man. It is a conflict between two kingdoms, between two Kings, each of whom claims ultimate and divine powers."[38]

Christians reject secularism because the self and the state become false gods promising an impossible salvation. Secularism United rejects Christianity because it is the only barrier between secularism and the "freedom" it desires to force on society. When the standards for truth and justice are external and unchangeable, individuals and states are hard-pressed to manipulate the institutions and culture based on such standards. By rejecting objective metaphysical truth claims, however, truth and justice can be whatever those in power (e.g., public education elites, judges, dictators, tribal generals, etc.) say they are. As Francis Schaeffer wrote, "No totalitarian authority nor authoritarian state can tolerate those who have an absolute by which to judge that state and its actions."[39] Objective truth claims are the biggest barriers to Secularism United. Thus, Judeo-Christian theism—America's most dominant worldview that claims objective metaphysical reality—becomes Public Enemy Number One.

Conclusion

The particular characters may change but the mythological framework remains the same. Gnosticism, Promethian paganism, and secularism share a mythology that claims humans do not need redemption from an external supernatural source. In fact, belief in such hinders the divine spark in all of us. Humanity is capable of its own liberation from within. The deconstruction of religion along with its moral codes and institutions (the family, church, etc.) is vital in allowing the self to create its own reality–the postmodern definition of "freedom." Culture is seen through the eyes of Social Contract Theory and education is used as a tool for deconstruction.

By briefly outlining Gnosticism and Promethean mythology, the presuppositional nature of secularism can be compared to two ancient faiths and their similar prescriptions for the liberation of humanity. The mythological framework ascribed to secularism by this analysis exposes the motivation behind the humanistic and postmodern agendas ("Secularism United") that call for the deconstruction of cultural institutions as well as the manipulation of our judiciary and educational systems as tools for such deconstruction.

---

38. Whitehead, *The Second American Revolution*, 18.
39. Schaeffer, *How Should We Then Live?* 26.

Addendum to Chapter 5
What I'm *Not* Saying

Throwing the Baby out with the Bath Water?

I agree that there are elements of postmodernism and humanism which lead to legitimate perspectives of the gospel and legitimate critiques of the contemporary church. But this is not to say that postmodernism and humanism, in themselves, offer any methods or perspectives that can't already be found in the Judeo-Christian worldview. I don't deny that certain elements of postmodernism and humanism can lead to legitimate ways of addressing issues important to Christianity and culture. What I claim is that these worldviews, in themselves, are unbiblical because they are based on secular presuppositions.

Any legitimate element within those worldviews are either a result of "worldview borrowing" or ideological coincidence—a similar subsidiary belief based on a different presupposition. Regarding the former, such elements can already be found in the Judeo-Christian worldview—*if* we grasp a well-rounded and complete Judeo-Christian theism. Regarding the latter, it doesn't matter how similar two subsidiary beliefs may *seem*, they will have different real-world outcomes if they are based on mutually exclusive presuppositions.[40]

Regarding the belief that there are elements of humanist and postmodern thought that parallel much of what the Christian gospel requires: Isn't it true that if the Christian gospel requires something, it should already be included in the Judeo-Christian worldview? We, as Christians, need not borrow elements from an obviously unbiblical worldview if what we wish to borrow is already contained within our own Judeo-Christian worldview. If certain subsidiary elements of humanism and postmodernism are truly required by the Christian gospel, then, by definition, they are already part of the Christian worldview and, thus, not uniquely humanist or postmodern. Thus, neither humanism nor postmodernism has anything to offer Christianity that Christianity doesn't already contain within itself.

---

40. See Chapter 2.

Additionally, I do *not* equate modernism with Judeo-Christian theism. In my rejection of postmodernism, many within Christendom who are sympathetic to postmodernism (for example, postmodern Christians, "Emerging Church" adherents, etc.) believe that I equate the Judeo-Christian worldview with modernism. Enlightenment modernism is as foreign to the Christian worldview as is its reactionary counterpart, postmodernism. In the end, however, *both* are forms of secularism because their foundational presuppositions are secular. They have an inter-family squabble because one (modernism/humanism) can't seem to exorcise the *imago dei* in each of us that is written on our hearts (which includes morality, values, etc.) while the other (postmodernism), in the name of consistency, successfully exorcizes that which humanism can't come to let go of–the *imago dei* in each of us.

A Christian need not embrace a foreign worldview to recognize a legitimate perspective or critique levied against Christianity. For example, it isn't necessary to endorse postmodernism in general in order to acknowledge a critique (proposed by a postmodernist) of how a particular Christian denomination approaches the issues of biblical inerrancy and infallibility. The Judeo-Christian worldview itself is perfectly capable of exposing the invalid beliefs of its own adherents.

Those who adhere to postmodern Christianity should realize that "postmodern Christianity" is, by definition, a contradiction in terms. The very concept violates the law of noncontradiction. It is akin to claiming a square circle is a possibility. The presence of one negates the presence of the other. It makes absolutely no sense to utilize a foreign worldview to critique your own worldview (or vice versa). *Of course* there are going to be critiques. In fact, logic demands it. Something is wrong if there are *not* critiques. (If a worldview is unable to critique another worldview, the two probably aren't different worldviews.)

For example, an article entitled "A Postmodern Critique of Christianity" is absurd. Similarly, an article entitled "A Christian Critique of Postmodernism" is equally absurd. Much more intriguing and worthwhile articles might be entitled "A Judeo-Christian Critique of the American Church," "A Postmodern Critique of Moral Relativism," or "A Biblical Critique of Charismatic Views of Scriptural Inerrancy." The worldview, ideology, or subsidiary belief under examination must be critiqued by the same standard to which it holds itself. Otherwise, you're just pointing out the obvious: Different worldviews are different.

Different worldviews are different because they provide different answers to the most basic foundational questions. Those within a worldview must evaluate their own beliefs in light of the presuppositions provided by the worldview to which they ascribe. If someone feels that his worldview's subsidiary beliefs are inadequate or wrong, he must examine the presuppositions of his own worldview (and his own logic in applying them). If someone feels that his worldview's presuppositions are inadequate or wrong, this requires him to change worldviews—not evaluate an alternative worldview's presuppositional and subsidiary beliefs using a worldview's presuppositions. Evaluating one worldview using a different worldview's presuppositions is a categorically futile endeavor. It would be like measuring the color blue with a ruler, or measuring inches with a metric tool. (Cross-worldview dialogue is possible but it must be done "from scratch," so to speak, building on one presupposition at a time. Once there is disagreement on a presupposition, it must be measured against whatever epistemological standard is being utilized—which itself is a presupposition open to disagreement. The more presuppositional disagreements there are, the more subsidiary disagreements there will be.)

Judeo-Christian theism itself should be the standard against which our own Christian beliefs are judged. Alternative worldviews are often helpful in shaking Christians out of episodes of intellectual laziness, but this is a far cry from accepting subsidiary beliefs that are based on obviously non-biblical presuppositions. (As we saw in Chapter 3, this will produce tragic real-world consequences regardless of intent.) This is a major way Christianity becomes infiltrated by foreign worldviews. Christians become intellectually lazy and susceptible to enticing worldviews that seem, on the surface, to have legitimate critiques against Judeo-Christian theism. Christians must remain intellectually vigilant, continually learning and challenging their own view of Judeo-Christian theism. The finite nature of our minds demands this. This process of self-evaluation will yield plenty of critiques on its own.

Education

I'm also *not* saying education is useless. In fact, education is extremely valuable—*if* it teaches the right ideas. What I disagree with is the foundational claim that ignorance is the source of society's problems. I am against any educational system based on this presupposition. I'm also against any educational system based on the secular view that a human is at the mercy of purely physical stimuli. An educational system based on this presupposition sees itself as merely another *system* that is being utilized to manipulate human behavior. Education based on either of these ideas will fail society because such ideas, being the inaccurate presuppositions they are, have tragic real-world consequences.

I also do not believe education is the responsibility of the government—especially a "separation of church and state" government. Such a government is limited to viewing education in one of the two ways mentioned in the previous paragraph.[41] Thus, I'm *not* saying education is useless or evil. Like most things in this world, it has its legitimate place it its proper context. Also like most things, however, it will become disastrous when not viewed or utilized in its proper context.

Knowledge as Gnosis, Knowledge as Values

Obviously, someone must *know* correct values to practice them. Thus, in a way, someone must have *knowledge* of moral values. However, this type of moral knowledge can more accurately be described as *awareness*. Using the phrase "moral awareness" may help in distinguishing the Judeo-Christian call to acknowledge (and live by) an objective metaphysical reality from the secular view of knowledge as gnosis. The difference resides in the presuppositional baggage underlying each view.

Therefore, I'm *not* against knowledge properly defined. (In fact, humans *should* strive to gain knowledge through scientific and rational endeavors. This is an essential aspect of Judeo-Christian theism.[42]) What I'm against is "knowledge" as gnosis and the salvific role assigned to it by secularism.

---

41. See Chapter 6.

42. For a discussion on why science is a logical consequence of Judeo-Christian theism (and not a consequence of other worldviews), I highly recommend *The Victory of Reason* by Rodney Stark.

Chapter 5
Discussion Questions

1. What is a *logical timeline*?
2. How did the French Revolution differ from the American Revolution?
3. Of the humanist claims cited, which surprises you the most? Why?
4. What is postmodernism? What is *deconstruction* and why is it necessary?
5. Why is debate meaningless in a relativistic context?
6. What is the difference between a narrative and a metanarrative, and why does postmodernism view the latter as oppressive?
7. Do you agree with the claim that moral relativism is incapable of sustaining freedom and democracy? Why or why not?
8. Why do secularists believe that to promote freedom, they must suppress traditional religion?
9. What is Social Contract Theory?
10. How does Social Contract Theory view objective value claims and cultural institutions?
11. How does Social Contract Theory define *freedom*?
12. How do humanism, postmodernism, and Christianity differ when it comes to the purpose each ascribes to humanity? How does a worldview's notion of purpose influence its definition of "freedom"?
13. What is the difference between *redemption* and *liberation*?
14. According to secularism, what is the role of education? Do you agree or disagree?
15. Why has the education establishment become elitist?
16. Why do both humanism and postmodernism (Secularism United) see Christianity as being Public Enemy Number One?

6

Closing Thoughts
So What Does Jesus Think about All This?

"Listen to me, everyone, and understand this. Nothing outside a man can make him 'unclean' by going into him. Rather, it is what comes out of a man that makes him 'unclean.'. . . Don't you see that nothing that enters a man from the outside can make him 'unclean'? For it doesn't go into his heart but into his stomach, and then out of his body. What comes out of a man is what makes him 'unclean.' For from within, out of men's hearts, come evil thoughts, sexual immorality, theft, murder, adultery, greed, malice, deceit, lewdness, envy, slander, arrogance and folly. All these evils come from inside and make a man 'unclean.'"
—Jesus of Nazareth (Mark 7:14b–23)

BEFORE WE launch into the "practical strategies" section that begins with the next chapter, it will be helpful to close this section of the book with a few thoughts. Summarizing the content of the first five chapters will prepare you for the essays in Part Three that use worldview analysis (or "first principles analysis") to expose secularism's methods of cultural infiltration and coercion.

First, as you might have noticed, I have used several different terms to refer to secularism. This is reflective of the overall thesis of this book, i.e., that secularism has been re-packaged using deceptive and politically expedient language that allows for its stealthy infiltration into America's culture and institutions. Whether the term is humanism, postmodernism, post-structuralism, materialism, naturalism, progressivism, socialism, Marxism, communism, modern liberalism, theologically liberal Christianity, politically liberal Christianity, or "The People's Republic of *x*," the essence is secularism, and, as such, disastrous real-world consequences are the result. Remember, secularism *by any other name* smells just as foul.

Second, ideas have consequences. This point cannot be emphasized enough. Ideas determine the direction of societies, the actions of individuals, and the purpose of existence. There is no such thing as a "random" event or action. Genocide, war, oppression, and poverty don't randomly pop into existence. Similarly, freedom, charity, and justice are not coincidences that arise for no reason. They are the real-world consequences of foundational ideas. This is not to say that people don't have free will. They most assuredly do. What this means is that the ideas people freely embrace are the paradigm within which a person experiences the world and acts within it. The same goes for societies and nations as well. It is impossible for the real-world consequences of ideas *not* to manifest.

Secularism will never lead to the real-world consequences inherent in Judeo-Christian presuppositions. Similarly, pure Christianity not infiltrated by secular presuppositions will never lead to the real-world consequences inherent in secular presuppositions. For example, if I leave Cincinnati (my hometown) and head north on Interstate 75, I will end up in Detroit, Michigan. If I leave Cincinnati and head northeast on Interstate 71, I'll end up in Columbus, Ohio. Interstate 75 doesn't lead to Columbus, and I-71 doesn't lead to Detroit—no matter how badly I may want them to. Which interstate I choose predetermines my eventual destination. This is how logic works. Once I pick a "wave to surf," I'm forced to ride it through to its conclusion.[1]

The Heart of It All

I'm reminded of the slogan printed on Ohio's license plates: "The heart of it all." Ohio's slightly east-of-center location within the United States spawns comparison of it to the heart of the country—insinuating Ohio plays a fundamental role in the direction of the United States. Jesus Christ consistently recognized a similar analogy in his own ministry. (This section will be especially helpful for those guilty of buying into the Christological fallacy. This will show that the Christological fallacy shouldn't lead to modern liberalism after all.) When the Pharisees asked Jesus which commandment in the Law was the greatest, Jesus replied:

> 'Love the Lord your God with all your heart and with all your soul and with all your mind.' This is the first and greatest commandment. And the second is like it: 'Love your neighbor as yourself.' All the Law and the Prophets hang on these two commandments. (Matthew 22:37–40)

---

1. See the essay entitled "No Ruts, No Glory" in Chapter 7.

These two commandments were the foundation of the Law. If people follow these two commandments, all the others will naturally fall into place. Because the outward actions of a person are caused by what is in the heart, the real-world consequence of embracing these two foundational commandments would be living out the remaining commandments. As Proverbs 23:7 reads, "For as a man thinketh in his heart, so is he." (KJV)

Earlier in Jesus' ministry when he healed a demon-possessed man, the Pharisees accused him of doing so by the power of Beelzebub. Jesus responded, "Every kingdom divided against itself will be ruined, and every city or household divided against itself will not stand. If Satan drives out Satan, he is divided against himself. How then can his kingdom stand?" (Matthew 12:25–26) The healing of the demon-possessed man was a consequence of the good in Jesus. Good comes from good. Evil comes from evil. It is impossible for good to stand if it is mixed with evil (this is why infiltrated Christianity is so dangerous). Had Jesus been evil, he could not have healed the demon-possessed man; the healing was a real-world consequence of the goodness in Jesus' heart.

A few verses later, Jesus says,

> Make a tree good and its fruit will be good, or make a tree bad and its fruit will be bad, for a tree is recognized by its fruit. You brood of vipers, how can you who are evil say anything good? For out of the overflow of the heart the mouth speaks. The good man brings good things out of the good stored up in him, and the evil man brings evil things out of the evil stored up in him. But I tell you that men will have to give account on the day of judgment for every careless word they have spoken. For by your words you will be acquitted, and by your words you will be condemned. (Matthew 12:33–37)

What is obviously true for trees is also true for people (and worldviews). It is impossible for a good tree to bear bad fruit and for a bad tree to bear good fruit. (Thus, as Jesus noted, it was impossible for the Pharisees to say anything good.) Furthermore, you can recognize what kind of tree it is (good or bad) by the fruit it bears. The necessary relationship between the core of the tree (whether it's good or bad) and its fruit reflects the idea-to-real-world relationship. Good fruit (i.e., good real-world consequences) indicates a good core (i.e., worldview). Bad fruit (i.e., bad real-world consequences) indicates a bad core (i.e., worldview). (Notice that Jesus *didn't* say, "Make the fruit good and the tree will become good. Make the fruit bad and the tree will become bad.")

Inside Out

This is why it is vital to determine which fruits (i.e., which real-world events) are the result of which tree (i.e., which worldview). It would be devastating to attribute a set of real-world events to the wrong worldview. For example, secularists claim oppression and totalitarianism necessarily result when theistic religion (especially Judeo-Christian theism) dominates a culture. If this were true, the best way to avoid oppression and totalitarianism would be to institute secular ideas as the dominant cultural foundation. The problem is that secularists have incorrectly attributed a negative set of real-world consequences/events (i.e., oppression and totalitarianism) to a worldview that, in reality, *prevents* oppression and totalitarianism—a misdiagnosis with tragic consequences. On the flipside, the worldview that secularists claim *prevents* oppression and totalitarianism in reality *causes* oppression and totalitarianism. Thus, secularists are trying to close an open wound by ripping it further apart. They are trying to cure alcoholism by prescribing alcohol. This is the danger of "idea misdiagnosis." (We must also learn to discern when a worldview's adherent is acting inconsistently. For example, when a Christian engages in hateful behavior or forced conversions or when a secularist claims society has a moral obligation to help the poor. These "fruits" do not result from the adherent's formally adopted worldview. They result from borrowed or inconsistently applied presuppositions.)

On a personal level, the fruit (or behavior/actions) of a person results from what is "stored up in him." A person's words are the overflow of the heart. Jesus tells the Pharisees that it is *impossible* for evil men to say anything good. On the other hand, Jesus claims that the good man acts good as a result of the good in his heart. ("The good man brings good things out of the good stored up in him, and the evil man brings evil things out of the evil stored up in him." —Matthew 12:35) Jesus can then say a man will be judged by his words (i.e., actions), because they are a direct indicator of what is in his heart. Thus, judging someone based on his words (actions) is the same as judging what is in his heart. There is a *direct relationship* between what's in a man's heart (i.e., his worldview) and his external behavior (i.e., real-world events).

At this point, someone may point to a secularist who performs good actions and claim such actions are the real-world fruit of the secular worldview he embraces in his heart. As discussed earlier, however, the secularist must borrow presuppositions from a theistic worldview in order to intellectually justify the "oughtness" of his actions. Secularism alone does not provide this justification. Anyone who believes an action is morally obligatory does not truly embrace consistent secularism in his heart. Such a person has yet to completely exorcize the *imago dei* within.

In another confrontation with the Pharisees, Jesus addresses the issue of unclean foods. The Pharisees noticed Jesus' disciples eating food with unwashed hands. According to the Law, this made the food they were eating unclean. After the plotting Pharisees brought this to Jesus' attention, Jesus responded, "Listen to me, everyone, and understand this. Nothing outside a man can make him 'unclean' by going into him. Rather, it is what comes out of a man that makes him 'unclean.'" (Mark 7:14–15) Later, Jesus explains to his disciples:

> "Don't you see that nothing that enters a man from the outside can make him 'unclean'? For it doesn't go into his heart but into his stomach, and then out of his body. What comes out of a man is what makes him 'unclean.' For from within, out of men's hearts, come evil thoughts, sexual immorality, theft, murder, adultery, greed, malice, deceit, lewdness, envy, slander, arrogance and folly. All these evils come from inside and make a man 'unclean'" (Mark 7:18–23).

It is in the heart where the ideas of a person take hold. The heart is the seed out of which a person's words, thoughts, and deeds originate. *Good and evil actions are ultimately the results of the ideas embraced in the heart of a person, not the systems which "enter a man from the outside."* Jesus lists 13 real-world consequences in this passage and identifies their origin as the heart. According to Luke's account, Jesus says, "People do not pick figs from thornbushes, or grapes from briers." (Luke 6:44b) It is simply impossible to manifest contingent real-world consequences that are not *already inherent* in their prior presuppositional ideas.

Another interesting conclusion that can be drawn from Jesus' words is the fact that real-world consequences, i.e., good and bad human behaviors, have their origin in the heart of the individual rather than in the person's political, social, or economic environments—all things that "enter a man from the outside." For Jesus to locate the cause of the world's ills any place other than the sinful human heart would be for him to deny God's truth regarding the identity of humanity, i.e., that we are free-willed creatures created in God's image, yet corrupted by sin. It is also interesting to observe what Jesus says about the destination of what goes into the body; namely, it is turned to excrement and ejected from the body during a bowel movement—an apt analogy describing the effectiveness of secular attempts to manipulate human behavior via systemic changes such as entitlement programs, pacifist foreign policy, public education, and the like.

The moral status of an action, therefore, is judged according to its origin. That is, the moral status of a real-world consequence is judged according to the godliness or ungodliness of the idea from which it spawned. For example, a massive entitlement program based on the secular notion of humanity disrespects God, because it is based on a "human tradition" (Colossians 2:8) that runs counter to God's truth (this is why the Christian left's methods are "unchristian"). While such programs are thought by many to reflect the moral conscience of a nation (i.e., the more a country spends on entitlement programs and welfare to "help the poor," the more "moral" that country is), what they truly reflect is the rejection of Judeo-Christian principles in favor of a secular worldview that brings disaster.

(Likewise, a nation that commits a great deal of resources to military and defense isn't necessarily doing so because it is imperialistic and loves war, violence, and revenge. A strong military results from embracing two *biblical* presuppositions. First, it is a logical consequence of acknowledging the sinful aspect of human nature and humanity's potential for evil. Second, it results from a proper view of the purpose of civil government—to *protect* our rights, not provide them. This second presupposition is most often *the* distinguishing belief separating conservatives from liberals. For example, the relevant question isn't, "Should we care for the poor?" The relevant question is, "In light of the different purposes assigned to the different institutions, whose responsibility is it to care for the poor?")

Many don't realize that secularism's tendency to view humans as a product of biology and environment (of "blood and soil") is the catalyst leading to elitism and the justification of a big government that subsumes the responsibilities of other institutions. If desirable human behavior (which is what leads to the perfect society) is only a systemic overhaul away, there must be an entity that *forces* this systemic change *from the outside*. After all, individual humans can't precipitate change *from within* a bad system, because their bad behavior is a direct *result* of the bad system. According to secularism, bad systems cause bad human behavior. Only a good system produces good human behavior. There is no good behavior without a good system. Therefore, positive social change brought about by good behavior requires a prerequisite good system to be imposed on humans *from the outside* (or from *above*), because, according to secularism, a personal change of heart *on the inside* of a person—separate from external determining factors—is impossible. (Furthermore, as discussed earlier, according to secularism, the biblical notion of an "inside" or a "heart"

Closing Thoughts

of a person—something non-physical such as a soul—doesn't exist. This is because *everything* that exists is *only* physical *material* at the mercy of physical law.) What entity is used to force a good system on people? That's right, government—the *only* entity with the coercive power to do so.

Once this view of government is understood, it's easy to understand why the modern gnostics who comprise our government and institutions (especially the judiciary and public education) are elitist "messengers of light." They are charged with bringing salvation to the helpless masses stuck in a vicious cycle of ignorance and oppression caused by the systems in which they find themselves. It is ironic that the secular (mostly humanist) faith in humanity's ability to achieve utopia by utilizing reason falls by the wayside when it comes to real-world political systems. The human goes from being a god-like user of reason, capable of his own salvation, to a mindless cockroach whose behavior is strictly a set of responses to external stimuli. Unfortunately, this usually results in the person being treated as such, too—yet another reason secularism leads to totalitarianism. Those in power who are charged with bringing salvation become god-like in status, while the masses of citizens are seen as automatons who must be manipulated, or "educated," into behaving in a desirable manner.[2]

A Helpful Analogy

Returning to Jesus' comparison of humans to trees for a moment, we can also apply this relationship to a worldview and its real-world consequences. Picture a tree. For our purposes, this tree represents the human enterprise—from its core (in the heart of a person) to its real-world consequences. Its roots are the worldview. Without a worldview, there is no tree. The worldview feeds the tree and allows it to live. The roots are usually unseen, which is also true of a person's worldview; it often operates unbeknownst to the person utilizing it. This doesn't mean, however, that the worldview is unimportant. Just as roots fulfill their role whether seen or unseen, so does a worldview. The presuppositions (how the worldview answers the questions of creation, fall, and redemption) provided by the worldview comprise the trunk of the tree. Just as a trunk is the foundation of a tree and provides for its stability, presuppositions are the foundation of thought and the departure points for logic.

The branches of the tree are subsidiary beliefs. Just as the trunk supports branches, subsidiary beliefs are determined by presuppositions. The fruits of the tree are real-world consequences. This is where the proverbial

2. See the essay entitled "Kibble for Fat Cats" in Chapter 7.

"rubber meets the road." Just as Jesus said a tree would be recognized and judged by its fruit, the same is true for a worldview (*if* its adherents are being logically consistent). The key is discerning which fruit is caused by which subsidiary beliefs (the branches), which subsidiary beliefs are caused by which presuppositions (the trunk), and which presuppositions are caused by which worldview (the roots). This process of discernment is exactly what worldview analysis is all about. If this analysis is successful, it becomes possible to expose the methods and strategies of each worldview in its attempt to manifest its vision for society. The remaining chapters of this book will expose the methods and strategies of secularism and why its elitist vision—even according to secularism itself—must be *forced* on the American people.

A Contradiction in Our Midst?

By now you may have noticed an apparent contradiction between two claims put forth in this book. The first claim concerns what I have described as a necessary feature of secularism, i.e., that human free will is forfeited due to the secular presupposition that physical matter is all that exists (argued in Chapter 2). The second claim concerns the assertion that human behavior is determined by ideas. I have stated that there is a causal relationship between the ideas people embrace and their resultant behavior. Both claims posit a causal relationship between behavior and some logically prior factor (*physical matter* and *physical law* according to secularism and *ideas* according Christianity), yet I have asserted that Judeo-Christian theism preserves free will. These two claims may seem contradictory. The second claim, however, does not necessitate the conclusion that humans have no free will. Two reasons for this apply.

First, people are free to choose which ideas to embrace. Second, people are not forced to remain consistent with the ideas they embrace. This is what it means to be *illogical*—to do or believe something inconsistent with a logically prior claim. Understanding worldview analysis, the proper role of reason/logic, and the direct relationship between ideas and real-world consequences enables one to diagnose the logical inconsistencies in his own thought as well as the thought of others. For example, those who formally espouse a secular worldview have an especially difficult time avoiding contradiction, because they must constantly fight against that which is the essence of every person: God's image (which includes values "written on the heart"). For example, most secularists believe individuals have inherent value (a belief that contradicts secularism's presuppositions).

Closing Thoughts

As previously discussed, humanism is a form of secularism that hasn't yet exorcised the hobgoblin that haunts every form of secularism: God's image in each of us. Furthermore, people are free to believe and act according to *no* particular idea or set of ideas, i.e., people are free to act according to emotion, impulse, etc.

The point is that any worldview espousing the existence of a non-physical aspect of humanity (as does Judeo-Christian theism) is not bound by physical limitations regarding the human will. By definition, free will *must* either be a non-physical entity or be "located" in something non-physical (i.e., a soul). Otherwise, it is subject to physical law and ceases to be "free" in any meaningful sense.

A Foundation Built on Rock

If you close this book only remembering one thing, let it be that the direct relationship between ideas and real-world consequences cannot be underestimated. The United States of America has been prosperous because the ideas instituted as the foundation of its culture, society, and laws *naturally* lead to the real-world consequences of prosperity and freedom.[3] These foundational ideas also motivated the United States to help maintain the freedom of the entire Western world, as well as the freedom of many nations across the globe. However, as these foundational ideas change, so will the real-world consequences.

Today the United States is still relatively prosperous and free (especially when compared to the rest of the world), but we would be foolish to believe this will automatically remain the case forever. Since the beginning of humanity, there has never been a time when someone (or a group of someones) wasn't actively plotting to overthrow the freedom of others. Throughout human history, freedom has been the exception, not the rule.[4] Vigilance is required to establish and preserve freedom, and it starts in the world of ideas. Courageous men and women with courageous ideas are the origin of free nations. The United States is no different. Indeed, the world is no different. The world will eventually "get what it deserves." It will reap the real-world consequences of the ideas it embraces.

The words of Jesus in Luke 6:46–49 seem particularly relevant here. Jesus says,

---

3. See the essay entitled "He Who Laughs Last" in Chapter 7.
4. See the essay entitled "Freedom and Death: Strange Bedfellows" in Chapter 7.

> Why do you call me, 'Lord, Lord,' and do not do what I say? I will show you what he is like who comes to me and hears my words and puts them into practice. He is like a man building a house, who dug down deep and laid the foundation on rock. When a flood came, the torrent struck that house but could not shake it, because it was well built. But the one who hears my words and does not put them into practice is like a man who built a house on the ground without a foundation. The moment the torrent struck that house, it collapsed and its destruction was complete.

The foundation of the United States has been, until recently, true ideas about reality (regarding creation, fall, and redemption) as given to us through both general and special revelation (though it has been employed imperfectly and has been deteriorating for years). Herein lies the difference between free and prosperous nations and those that experience totalitarianism and oppression; namely, free nations have embraced true ideas while oppressive nations have embraced untrue ideas (or have had untrue ideas *forced* on them—as is often the case under totalitarian regimes). Nations built on a foundation of rock (God's truth)—consciously or unconsciously, formally or informally—will thrive.[5] Nations built on a foundation of sand will collapse against the "torrents" and be destroyed.

I am in no way suggesting the United States instituted true presuppositions perfectly. Nor am I suggesting that this country has a perfect track record of consistently applying these presuppositions. (In fact, the Christian worldview *expects this not to be the case* due to its explanation of humanity and sin.) What I *am* suggesting is that America's foundation is *generally* based on the core ideas inherent in the Judeo-Christian *worldview*—ideas that form a foundation of rock. This foundation is why, even at a relatively young age of 231, the United States is the oldest democratic republic on earth. While other governments and nations based on a foundation of sand have collapsed due to realities their worldviews refuse to acknowledge, America has withstood these same realities—physical *and* metaphysical realities woven into the fabric of the universe at its creation by God.

These physical and metaphysical realities can be the greatest gift or the greatest curse given to humanity. Which they will be depends on how we react to them. If we embrace these realities (i.e., God's moral law) wholeheartedly, live by them the best we can, and base our culture, laws, and institutions on them, they will bring prosperity and freedom. If we reject or ignore them and attempt to create our own realities, they will

---

5. See the essay entitled "He Who Laughs Last" in Chapter 7.

bring disaster similar to what the world has been witnessing since our ancient ancestors were kicked out of the Garden of Eden.

Physical laws can be our best friend or worst enemy. If objective physical laws are acknowledged and respected, we will witness great technological advancements. This is the essence of science—to *discover* (not create) the physical laws of the universe and use them to prosper. If they are acknowledged and used to guide our endeavors, they are a blessing. However, if physical laws are ignored (or rejected), disaster will ensue. Instead of being the source of technological prosperity, they become the source of disaster. Consider the fate of someone jumping off a 10-story building in an attempt to fly, or the folly in designing a jet engine according to an engineer's personally created system of physical laws. Would *you* get on that plane? I sure wouldn't. *Metaphysical laws are no different.*

Impartial Message: Impartial Results

In Luke 10, we read of Jesus choosing seventy-two people to send out ahead of him. They are to preach to the towns that Jesus himself will eventually visit. Jesus sends them with a particular message. He tells them:

> When you enter a town and are welcomed, eat what is set before you. Heal the sick who are there and tell them, 'The kingdom of God is near you.' But when you enter a town and are not welcomed, go into its streets and say, 'Even the dust of your town that sticks to our feet we wipe off against you. Yet be sure of this: The kingdom of God is near.' I tell you, it will be more bearable on that day for Sodom than for that town. (Luke 10:8–12)

Notice that the seventy-two are to deliver the *same message* to both those who will come to accept them *and* those who will come to reject them. Yet this message had very different ramifications depending on how people reacted to it. For the people who accepted its truth, it was a blessing. For those who rejected it, however, the truth was a curse that would bring horrible consequences. It is a joyous, fulfilling, hopeful, and loving message for those who believe. For those who reject it, however, it is the source of unspeakable torment and disaster—in *this* world and the next. God's moral laws written into the fabric of the universe, if followed, lead to amazing blessings such as peace, prosperity, and freedom. If rejected, however, these laws will bring about "curses" such as oppression, war, and disease.[6] It matters not who breaks or ignores these moral laws or why. The *this*-worldly consequences will be the same.[7]

Some reject these moral laws by pretending they don't exist. Others reject them by creating their own morality from within. Both are futile endeavors. Temporal prosperity will elude societies that engage in such moral reconstruction. Likewise, eternal prosperity will elude individuals who do the same regarding belief in Christ. There is only one standard that brings prosperity—God's standard. The disaster that ensues after walking off a 10-story building is of the same consequential type as the disaster that ensues after a society embraces, for example, sexual promiscuity. Both disasters are necessary consequences of cause-and-effect relationships that God built into the universe—one *physical* and one *metaphysical*. Furthermore, these cause-and-effect relationships operate independently of an individual's or society's intent, identity, or formal ideological affiliation.

Such impartiality (in the sense of *universal applicability*) should be sufficient to keep the believer humble. It is *God* who gives us (and everyone else in the world) our value, not anything *we* have accomplished independent of him. One of John the Baptist's first messages was directed to prideful Israelites who believed God showed partiality toward them. John preached that their status before God would be determined by their acceptance or rejection of God's truth and their behavior resulting from that decision rather than their race, position, or formal religious affiliation. John said in Luke 3:8–9, "Therefore bear fruits in keeping with repentance, and do not begin to say to yourselves, 'We have Abraham for our father,' for I say to you that from these stones God is able to raise up children to Abraham. Indeed the axe is already laid at the root of the trees; so every tree that does not bear good fruit is cut down and thrown into the fire." (NASB) If he desired, God could make Christians of the stones around us—definitely a humbling realization.

After Peter witnessed the outpouring of the Holy Spirit on Cornelius (a gentile), he realized the impartiality of God's truth. It can be a man's best friend or his worst enemy. Acts 10:34–35 reads, "Opening his mouth, Peter said: 'I most certainly understand now that God is not one to show partiality, but in every nation the man who fears Him and does what is right is welcome to Him.'" (NASB) God's truth, i.e., the physical and metaphysical laws he wove into the fabric of the universe, shows no partiality. Furthermore, God wishes for *all* to come to repentance (2 Peter 3:9). Since this is the case, the existence of nonbelievers should be enough

---

6. See the essay entitled "Poverty, AIDS, and Objective Morality" in Chapter 7.

7. See the essay entitled "He Who Laughs Last" in Chapter 7.

Closing Thoughts

to show that salvation is contingent on the individual's reaction to God's free gift of grace. The rejection of God's salvation has tragic eternal consequences. Likewise, even in this world, rejecting God-ordained metaphysical realities concerning humanity, free will, objective morality, sin, and evil will bring about the unforeseeable calamities Isaiah warned us about thousands of years ago—calamities we will not be able to "conjure away" (Isaiah 47:11). To reject any aspect of reality is to invite destruction at the hands of reality's "torrents."

For example, foreign policy based on a pacifism grounded in the secular (especially humanist) worldview is utterly incapable of dealing with a particular aspect of reality, i.e., evil hearts and minds not interested in reason, peace, or prosperity (one example of a "torrent"). Case-in-point: Had the Western world embraced pacifism during the 1930s and 1940s, freedom in the West would be a thing of the past. Thankfully, the allies embraced ideas that posited the existence of such a reality (sin) and its real-world consequence (evil humans such as Hitler who kill, oppress, and destroy), and they acted on that belief by seeing the need to *forcefully* stop Hitler and the Nazis—violently if necessary. (Whether this realization came from consciously embracing Christianity in particular or merely Christianity's basic presuppositions is irrelevant. Remember, ideas are not "respecters of men." See Chapter 3.)

When this reality (or "torrent" as Jesus called it) struck in the 1930s and 1940s, the allied nations, whose house was built upon a rock, withstood the attack. A secular humanist society that embraced pacifism would have been wiped from the face of the earth, because its house would have been built on the sand of secularism. It would have tried to solve the problem of evil men by appealing to methods based on secular humanist presuppositions that deny the existence of the very phenomenon posing the threat—i.e., sin and evil. If ignorance had been Hitler's problem, we could have taught his evil out of him. If bad systems were his problem, we could have rehabilitated him in a cushy jail cell accompanied by a 12-step program. Neither of these was Hitler's problem. Attempts to stop him based on such diagnoses would (and did) fail miserably. These faulty methods were unable to "conjure" him away. Methods based on false presuppositions cannot stand against "torrents" of reality such as Hitler.

Nongravityism

Let's return to the example of someone plummeting off a 10-story building. A worldview that denies the physical reality of gravity (let us call this worldview "nongravityism" and its adherents "nongravityists") would predict that a person could continue walking in mid-air even after a person walked off the ledge of a building's roof (similar to what Wile E. Coyote did before he would look down). The problem is that this worldview's denial of gravity has no effect on the actual external existence of gravity. Thus, a nongravityist would be utterly shocked when he walked off a building's roof and plummeted to the ground.

Nongravityists now have a dilemma. They have to explain why someone plummets to the ground when he walks off the top of a building. Nongravityists have two options. They can either change their worldview (either by slightly altering it or by scrapping it entirely) or they can appeal to their own worldview for an explanation. If they choose the latter, they are limited to explanations that are consistent with nongravityism's presuppositions, i.e. they must explain the cause of a real-world consequence of gravity without appealing to gravity. That is, they must explain why people plummet to the ground when they walk of a building's ledge *without* appealing to gravity. Perhaps they'll blame lack of education. If the person only knew enough about walking off buildings, he would be fine. Or maybe an oppressive architect who imposed his own view of buildings on the plummeter is to blame.

Attempts by nongravityists to alleviate the social ill of plummeting to one's death would then take the form of providing free education to people so they could be educated as to how one walks off a building safely. Or perhaps such an attempt would require censoring the bigoted architect who imposed his oppressive gravity metanarrative on society. The problem is that no matter how sincerely or passionately these attempts are employed, they will do nothing to prevent the phenomenon they are meant to alleviate, i.e. falling off buildings. The only way to prevent such catastrophes is to acknowledge the reality of gravity and live in a way that allows gravity to be a blessing rather than a curse. For those who accept gravity's truth, gravity can be used in positive and meaningful ways. Gravity is a dangerous "torrent" of reality, however, for those who deny its truth. *A worldview that denies the existence of that which causes an undesirable real-world event can do nothing to prevent or alleviate that real-world event.* Therefore, any and all nongravityist attempts to alleviate the social ill of plummeting to one's death (which is caused by gravity) will be completely futile. The same is true for consequences caused by breaking or ignoring *metaphysical* realities.

This futility is perfectly illustrated by secularism's denial of objective morality. Secular attempts to alleviate ills such as poverty and crime are examples of how secular methods are rendered impotent (and disastrous) by the "torrents" of reality. Because poverty, crime and war, for example, are the real-world consequences of ignoring, denying, or breaking a basic reality that secularism claims doesn't exist (objective morality), secularism is impotent when trying to alleviate them. It prescribes the wrong medicine. Secularism prescribes medicine (e.g., welfare, entitlement programs, weak criminal sentences, criminal rehabilitation rather than punishment, education, pacifist diplomacy, etc.) based on its fallacious claim that humans are the product of their environment. In the final analysis, secularism has no idea what causes poverty, crime, and war! Thus, it has no way to provide a cure! For secularism, similar to those in Luke 10, the message (in this case, objective morality) is a torrent rather than a blessing.

Only medicine designed to treat *immorality* can effectively treat poverty, crime, and war. (I'm *not* saying it is immoral to be poor. I'm saying poverty is one consequence of immorality, although not *necessarily* any immorality of the poor person. People can be poor due to the immoral acts of those who oppress them. This is especially apparent in nations led by dictators.) Similarly, only a medicine designed to treat the evil of sin can effectively treat oppression and genocide. Thus, the factor indicating a worldview's ability to "cure" a worldly ill is whether or not it acknowledges the basic reality of the ill's cause (or causes). Secularism falsely views the causes of crime, poverty, oppression, and Hitler as bad systems and/or ignorance. Thus, secularism is incapable of curing such problems. Judeo-Christian theism, unlike secularism, acknowledges the existence of an objective morality and, thus, is able to identify the cause of crime, poverty, oppression, and Hitler for what it *really* is: immorality (i.e., evil, the abuse of man's free will in rejecting God's will). Therefore, institutions, cultures, and nations based on Judeo-Christian theism (consciously or unconsciously) are able to effectively treat the consequences of immorality, or "torrents" as Jesus calls them—the causes of which are misdiagnosed by secularism. (Of course, this-worldly torrents pale in comparison to the eternal reality of God's holiness and judgment at the Second Coming—a blessing for those who accept Christ, but a torrent for those who do not.)

A Massive Yet Impotent State

This is why the "separation of church and state" (in actuality it is the separation of *theistic religion* and state) has disastrous real-world consequences. If the ability to cure the ills of society is contingent upon the identification of their cause, only worldviews that acknowledge the existence of such causes will be able to provide that ability. Since it is *only* a religious worldview (the Judeo-Christian worldview in particular) that acknowledges the existence of such a cause (breaking or ignoring *objective morality*), its removal from the public forum (and replacement with a secular worldview incapable of such acknowledgement) precludes the ability to cure any and all ills. In short, the more society exorcizes theistic religion from the public forum, the more ineffective society will be in alleviating social ills and preserving prosperity and freedom.

The cause of the world's ills is immorality. Only worldviews that posit the existence of objective morality can make this proper diagnosis. Secularism denies the existence of objective morality, thus rendering itself unable to identify the cause of society's ills. Thus, it can never solve them. It views ignorance and environment as the causes of the society's ills. Therefore, every attempt by a secular government to solve a problem will reflect these two incorrect presuppositions.

This is already obvious in the case of government-run programs that attempt to ameliorate ills such as poverty, crime, teen pregnancy, the spread of STDs, domestic abuse, etc. By institutionalizing "the separation of church and state," secularists have forever rendered impotent the ability of government to solve *any* social ill. The government's ability to interpret the cause of the ills it is attempting to alleviate is limited to secular explanations. Thus, the methods utilized to fix such ills are limited to secular methods. Social ills are consequences of embracing and institutionalizing secular ideas in the first place. It is ludicrous to believe that social ills can be alleviated by employing methods based on the very ideas that caused them.

For example, if some government program (or person working in a government program) claims teen pregnancy or the spread of STDs is caused by immorality and should be treated as such, it would be labeled as "intolerant" and accused of forcing one person's or one group's set of morals (or "religion") on others. When morality is mentioned, the inevitable question of "Whose morality?" is invoked—insinuating the postmodern claim that objective truth claims (or "metanarratives") are oppressive. Morality and religion become attached at the hip, and secularism has no problem throwing the baby out with the bath water.

In a secular government, only secular causes (based on secularism's view of the human) can be offered as explanations, such as bad systems or bad genes. In turn, only secular solutions (medicine) can be attempted, i.e., massive entitlement programs, nationalized health care, more public (secular) education, etc. This illustrates the vicious cycle of government power. A secular government is put in charge of diagnosing the causes of social ills and, due to "the separation of church and state," *must* conclude the causes are secular in nature. Then the government inevitably concludes that secular methods (programs that attempt to force systemic change) must be used to alleviate said ills. And because the government is the only entity that has the power and capability (discussed in Chapter 5) to institute such methods, it concludes the government must do the saving. Thus, the government must expand to take on these new responsibilities.

A government that is allowed to claim social ills are caused by immorality (rather than systems or ignorance) is able to conclude that something *other* than a systemic government program may be their cure. In fact, such a government will most likely conclude a systemic government program would *not* work, because it would be considered as medicine prescribed based on a faulty diagnosis. In short, a secular government—one based on the principle of "separation of church and state"—is inherently incapable of solving *any* social ill because it cannot identify its cause. Without religion (Judeo-Christian theism in particular), a proper diagnosis of social ills is impossible. Secular society is defenseless when the "torrents" of poverty, crime, oppression, war, teenage pregnancy, and AIDS strike. It has no idea what causes them and has no chance to fight them off, or "conjure" them away—as Isaiah so eloquently predicted. This is why using secular methods to solve the world's problems will inevitably fail.

A Note on "Practical Strategies"

Lastly, by labeling the following part of this book the "practical strategies" section, I don't want to imply the first six chapters are irrelevant intellectual jargon. Hopefully this point is already obvious, considering the number of "real-world" examples cited in the first six chapters. While each essay in Part Three is written to stand alone (which explains some of the conceptual repetitions in them), the content of the first six chapters illuminates their intricacies and unifies them under a common purpose. Reading the essays without first reading Part One and Two is certainly feasible, but the purpose of the essays is to train the mind to use the analysis presented in the previous two parts to "decode" the deceptive and politically expedient language and methods of secularism.

In short, while the first six chapters discussed the *what* and *why* of secularism, the essays to follow discuss the *how* of secularism. We should fully expect the methods of a worldview (i.e., *how* it attempts to manifest its vision of society) to directly reflect its basic presuppositions. For example, if secularism claims people are automatons at the mercy of biology and environment (the sum total of DNA and socio-economic systems), that's exactly how it will treat people in its attempt to bring about its vision. Thus, no one should be surprised when individual human dignity is compromised in the name of social change, systemic overhauls, or biological engineering. It should also come as no surprise that secularism views massive systemic programs such as socialist economic and education policies (as well as those who enforce them) as liberators capable of ushering in the perfect age of acceptance, tolerance, and freedom for all. If the essays are the puzzle pieces, then Parts One and Two are the box cover with the picture on the front, allowing us to envision both the foundation and goal of the overall project. The first two parts show us how *and* why the pieces fit together.

Ultimately, I hope all three parts of this book will enable *you* to analyze the world around you. Now that we've *explained* the conflict, *identified* the "sides," and discovered *why* two drastically different visions exist for the future of America, let us expose *how* one of these visions is being forced on the American people.

Chapter 6 Discussion Questions

1. Why is it vital to determine which real-world events are consequences of which worldview?

2. What does it mean to say that the moral status of an action should be judged according to its origin?

3. Why is it impossible for someone within a bad system to bring about positive social change or act in a desirable manner?

4. Explain the analogy of the tree. Is this a helpful analogy? Why or why not?

5. Why is it *not* a double standard to claim that free will is forfeited in secularism but maintained in Christianity?

6. What are "torrents" of reality, and why are untrue worldviews incapable of standing against them? Can you think of any "torrents" not discussed in this chapter?

7. Why is a secular government *incapable*, by definition, of alleviating a society's ills?

PART THREE
Takeover

7

Worldview
Painting the Big Picture

Poverty, AIDS, and Objective Morality

It seems we can't go a season without another concert or summit dedicated to alleviating the global ills of poverty and AIDS. The futility of such endeavors would be laughable if it weren't so tragic. The fundamental reason these concerts and summits are failing and will always fail is that those who lead and attend them are incapable of identifying the cause of that which they seek to alleviate.

Notice I said *incapable*. I'm not questioning their sincerity. *If* they could rid the world of such problems, I'm sure they would. What I'm questioning is their ability to interpret reality in a way that allows them to achieve their desired goal. A worldview that doesn't posit objective moral truth will be blind to the remedy for ills caused by the rejection of said truth. Many of those who participate in such summits and concerts subscribe to secularism (consciously or subconsciously) and its necessary moral relativism.

AIDS is a moral problem. Plain and simple. It is not a class/economic problem. It is not a racial problem. It is not an ethnic problem. It is not an education problem. And until it is viewed as a moral problem, AIDS will ravage humanity.

No one can argue with the fact that we could stop the worldwide spread of AIDS immediately. The solution is simple: Stop having extramarital sex, thus relegating all sexual acts within the bounds of a marriage between one man and one woman. Although for the sake of argument, this plan would work even if homosexuals were given the right to marry, as long as they live by the same moral code regarding sexual activity within a monogamous marriage. AIDS would be wiped off the face of the earth within one generation. (Of course, those with AIDS would have to make the moral decision *not* to have children.)

The reason this solution is not an option for many who participate in these concerts and summits is that their rejection of absolute moral truth prevents them from condemning any behavior or lifestyle—no matter how destructive it may be. With no absolute moral truth, one lifestyle is just as good as another. Therefore, the behaviors and lifestyles that breed the AIDS epidemic cannot be condemned. Thus, the cause of the current AIDS epidemic remains a mystery to these activists passionately trying to stop it. Because of this, the cause of the AIDS epidemic must be found in something other than immoral behavior (remember, according to secularism, there is no such thing as condemnable immoral behavior).

In keeping with the salvific faith secularists have in knowledge and systems, many claim the problem lies in lack of education and/or access to proper "health care." If the world could be taught the educational value of safe sex and have access to birth control (condoms, abortion, etc.), epidemics such as AIDS and unwanted pregnancy would be alleviated. Others claim such epidemics are caused by economics (i.e. economic *systems*). Because of industrial nations like the United States, Third World countries have been relegated to the poverty dump of the world. Such nations lack the education, resources (read: condoms and abortion), and proper motivation to prevent many societal ills. Once again, "blood and soil" are responsible for the behavior that causes AIDS.

All the education and condoms in the world won't eliminate poverty and AIDS unless that education includes the reinforcement of the absolute morality that prevents such epidemics in the first place. Education won't solve anything unless you're teaching the right things.

Similarly, poverty won't be eliminated (or decreased) until the immoral behavior (perpetrated by *both* the rich and the poor) that created it is ceased. Any plan to eliminate global poverty not based on a theistic foundation for free will and its resultant free-market capitalism is destined to fail. Much of the poverty in Third World countries is created by highly regulated economic systems, totalitarian regimes, socialist/communist ideals, and dictatorships—*not* "expansionist" American policy.

Free-market capitalism, however, is not enough on its own (just as education by itself isn't enough). The right values and principles must be at work within the system. Poverty exists even within relatively free capitalist societies, but, in general, it is caused by behavior and lifestyle. A 70% illegitimacy rate among African-Americans contributes to the high poverty level in that demographic. Children raised with a chip on their shoulder and an anti-authoritarian attitude contribute to poverty. Poor individuals being convinced (usually by wealthy politicians) that economic mobilization among the classes is impossible contributes to poverty. Promiscuous sexual behavior contributes to poverty. High crime rates contribute to poverty. Those in power who exploit the poor contribute to poverty. The list could go on. *These behaviors have nothing to do with race, gender, sexual orientation, or class.* They have everything to do with foundational moral claims and the behaviors that ensue from them.

The United States didn't become the most prosperous nation in history by accident. It happened because the right principles, values, and morals were instituted and passed on from generation to generation. To create similar prosperity across the globe, these same principles, values, and morals need to be adopted in struggling nations. Sending food and monetary assistance is only a Band-Aid on a gaping wound. As Thomas Sowell (senior fellow at The Hoover Institution and conservative columnist) has said, knowledge (this refers to adopting certain values, *not* the kind of knowledge based on the secular myth of gnosis) is one of the few things you can give away and not have less of afterward. Why don't we pass along the values that create the prosperity instead of inefficiently attempting to redistribute it? (And no, this has nothing to do with "Christianizing" the world. One need not accept Christ to experience the *this*-worldly blessings of living the moral life. Remember, ideas are not "respecters of men.")

Until a worldview that posits an objective morality is utilized, the real cause of ills such as poverty and AIDS will go undetected. Unfortunately, not understanding the cause of a problem results in the futility of attempts to solve it. AIDS is a moral problem, and until it is treated as such, it will continue ravaging the globe.

Reality: The Undisputed Champion of the Universe

In the last essay, I wrote about an inability by many to recognize the cause of worldwide poverty and AIDS. This inability stems from a fundamental denial of absolute morality. The denial of absolute morality, however, is only one symptom of a more general problem. This problem goes deeper than particular policy issues, as it cuts to the very core of the human enterprise.

There are physical laws of the universe by which humans are forced to abide. If we choose to ignore them, there are consequences—often disastrous ones (e.g., plane crashes, collapsed buildings, nuclear meltdowns, hitting a finger with a hammer, cancer caused by smoking, etc.). We can't escape or defy the physical laws of the universe. Our relationship with the *moral* world, however, is different. We are not forced to live according to absolute moral laws in the same way we are forced to live according to physical laws. This often leads to the erroneous conclusion that there are no moral laws.

While we as humans are not forced to live according to the moral law, *there are still consequences to breaking such a law*. AIDS is a perfect example. Humans aren't forced to reserve sexual relations for the marriage bed, but consequences arise if we do not. Sexually transmitted diseases, unwanted pregnancies, broken relationships, and broken homes are but a few of the consequences of sexual promiscuity. Reality dictates this to us. These consequences aren't a widespread conspiracy by right-wing fundamentalist Christians who wish to force their morality on everyone else. Real-world consequences are a cause and effect phenomenon. Ills such as AIDS and poverty don't spring up out of nowhere. They are caused by particular actions based upon foundational ideas.

Every political or moral theory has as its foundation a particular understanding of reality, i.e., creation, fall, and redemption. The subsidiary features of a political or moral theory are the consequences of how such foundational questions are answered. A political or moral theory will fail if it wrongly answers these questions. For example, secularism claims that there is no inherent human nature (although many secularists/Marxists/Socialists inconsistently believe human nature is basically good). Human beings are a result of materialist Darwinian evolution and are subject to the same physical laws that govern all other physical matter in the universe. Human thoughts and behaviors are caused by the systems that influence them. This is why systems are so important in Marxist thought. Humans are a product of the systems in which they exist. Crime, poverty, oppression, and every other ill of humanity are not faults of the individual, but rather the results of the oppressive systems surrounding the individual. Thus, for the secularist, salvation lies in instituting the perfect systems (through education, wealth redistribution, health care, etc.) that, in turn, will create perfect humans.

The problem is that secularism's explanation for the cause of human behavior is sorely inadequate. It doesn't line up with reality. Secularism attempts to create its own reality in spite of what reality actually is. The reality is that human beings are not mindless drones at the mercy of the scientific laws that govern cause and effect. The materialist universe presupposed by secularism doesn't exist.

Humans have free will and are able to choose what standard of morality by which to live. Secularism fails (along with its political theory—Marxism) because its proposed solutions to all of the world's ills are based on a set of presuppositions that do not accurately diagnose the cause of the behaviors that lead to such ills.

It is impossible to rewrite reality. Attempts to do so are futile and tragic. Only theories (or worldviews) that are accurate descriptions of reality can achieve their desired goals. It is reality that dictates the consequences of human choices. The dictates of reality should be the standard by which we, as free humans, determine our choices. This is how God created the universe. In addition to guilt before God, sin also has its own "natural" consequences in *this* world. For example, adultery leading to a broken marriage or sexual promiscuity leading to contracting a sexually transmitted disease.

Inaccurate theories of life (or inaccurate *worldviews*) are in constant battle with reality. The problem for these theories is that reality hasn't yet lost a match. It's undefeated. Reality is the undisputed champion in the war over who controls the universe. My advice? If you can't beat it, join it.

He Who Laughs Last . . .

I've often heard people say that America is a nation blessed by God. But what exactly does this mean? Is God constantly intervening within history to make sure that America is prosperous? Or is it more of an indirect blessing? If it's the latter, how exactly does that work?

When we look around the world, it is obvious that Americans have privileges and opportunities that are not available in many other parts of the world. Some would say this is because God has blessed our great country, because it was founded on a Judeo-Christian worldview. God, therefore, is rewarding America because it is a "Christian nation" (or at least it was at some point). My question is this: Is America prosperous today because God has specifically intervened in history due to our Christian heritage, or because America, in virtue of its Judeo-Christian foundation, has instituted the right values and systems that *naturally* lead to prosperity?

Consider the following. John, a born-again Christian, decides to be sexually abstinent before marriage, because he is motivated by his desire to submit to God's will. Because of this, John is blessed with not having to worry about contracting sexually transmitted diseases, getting a girl pregnant, emotional trauma, etc. Many would say that John's resultant physical and emotional health is a "blessing" from God. In other words, God is blessing John's decision to abstain from sex before marriage.

Kevin, on the other hand, is an atheist. For strictly pragmatic and selfish reasons, Kevin decides to abstain from sex before marriage. Kevin has a professional sports career ahead of him, and contracting a sexually transmitted disease (especially a serious one) would hinder such a career. Kevin also has to be worried about rape allegations in an attempt to extort money from him. Additionally, paying child support, in the event he impregnated a woman, would cost him a lot of money. Thus, Kevin—albeit for very different reasons—will experience the same physical and emotional health that John experiences.

While many may say that John is "blessed" by God because of his submission to God's will, I think people may be hesitant to conclude that God is also "blessing" Kevin, considering Kevin's atheism and selfish motives. But isn't it true that John and Kevin are *both* experiencing physical and emotional health? Why would John's health be a blessing from God and Kevin's health not be? As mentioned earlier, it is because ideas are not "respecters of men."

This same scenario can be extended to nations as well. What would happen if a nation instituted biblical principles as a matter of pragmatic efficiency rather than piety? I believe that such a nation would experience the same this-worldly prosperity as the "Christian nation" that instituted biblical principles based on the Judeo-Christian commitment to humbly follow God's will. Why is this the case?

The reason is because right and wrong, good and evil, and correct values (*metaphysical* realities) are written into the fabric of the universe. Just as obeying the physical laws of nature will result in the same real-world consequences regardless of a person's motivation (for example, a jet engine will work properly if it's designed correctly, regardless of its engineer's motivation—both Americans and Nazis built war planes during World War II), obeying the proper values regarding right and wrong and good and evil will result in the same this-worldly prosperity for both Christian and atheist. Just as there are consequences for trying to break or ignore physical and moral law, there are also *benefits* to adhering to both, regardless of motivation.

Thus, God does not need to "bless" America in the sense that he must specifically intervene outside of what naturally occurs when a person or nation aligns its values with those of reality. For example, both John and Kevin will experience the type of prosperity that *naturally* results from abstaining from sex before marriage. This is what it means to claim that America is "blessed" by God even though it has *not* been granted any kind of Ancient Israel-like special status. This also encourages the sober realization that America, because it has not been granted such a status, is not immune from the "natural cursings" inherent in breaking or ignoring objective moral reality. If America continues to reject Judeo-Christian theism, God is not going to step in and save her simply because she's America. He's made no such promise and such an expectation results from an invalid comparison of the United States to ancient Israel or a false belief equating the United States to the kingdom of God.

It is of the utmost importance to realize that this claim is *not* an attempt to remove God from the big picture. This is NOT simply a form of deism. If anything, this claim infuses God into every aspect of life, both moral and physical (but *not* in a pantheistic way). This view is not mutually exclusive with the claim that God can, has, and does intervene in history at specific moments (a claim I believe). What this view claims is that such direct historical intervention is *over and above* what we might call "indirect" or "natural blessings." "Direct blessings" (as we might call them), on the other hand, are performed in virtue of a *specific* purpose or outcome God has in mind.

Jesus says in Matthew 5:45 that God "causes his sun to rise on the evil and the good, and sends rain on the righteous and the unrighteous." In this context, Jesus is exhorting his listeners to love their enemies by referencing God's beneficence to *all* humanity, good *and* evil. In the ancient world, rain was seen as a blessing from God (or the gods), because it caused crops to grow and ensured a bountiful harvest and sustenance for a season. Bountiful harvests from proper management of farmland is a good example of a "natural blessing."

In the Old Testament, we see a similar concept that plays out in the life of Job. Job's friends are telling him that his suffering is a result of the sin in his life. Job disagrees and responds by insisting that his friends observe the world around them. Everywhere the evil prosper while the good suffer. As a general rule, God simply doesn't work in this world the way Job's friends suggest.

In the case of John and Kevin (and, by extension, the Christian and atheist nations), if all prosperity (and misery) is of the "direct blessing" (or "direct cursing") category, it means that God is constantly intervening directly in history to bestow prosperity on the selfish, just as he does the godly. It's as if cause-and-effect doesn't exist. God must constantly intervene to impose order on an otherwise random system. Without this constant intervention, the consequences of sexual promiscuity, for example, would be completely random. It may lead to prosperity for one person or nation and disaster for another person or nation.

On the contrary, I suggest that just as God need not bestow direct worldly *misfortune* and suffering based solely on behaviors, lifestyles, and motivations, he also need not directly bestow worldly *prosperity* based solely on behaviors, lifestyles, and motivations. *Both worldly misfortune and worldly prosperity are first and foremost cause-and-effect consequences determined by how humans react to the natural moral scheme inherent in the fabric of the universe, as it reflects the character of God in his creation.*

We see in the apostle Paul's letter to the Romans that he connects ethics (right and wrong) with nature (the creation). Paul writes in Romans 1:25–27,

> For they exchanged the truth of God for a lie, and worshiped and served the creature rather than the Creator, who is blessed forever. Amen. For this reason God gave them over to degrading passions; for their women exchanged the natural function for that which is unnatural, and in the same way also the men abandoned the natural function of the woman and burned in their desire toward one another, men with men committing indecent acts and receiving in their own persons the due penalty of their error. (NASB)

We see here that Paul is positing a moral dimension to the natural universe.

Some of you may have noticed the modifier with which I've preceded the term "prosperity;" namely, the term *this-worldly*. This is to distinguish the indiscriminate (or "indirect") natural blessings of God (which may include physical health, financial wealth, etc.—blessings that are experienced in *this world*) from the direct blessings he bestows on those who enter into a personal relationship with him (blessings such as salvation and the indwelling Holy Spirit—spiritual blessings experienced in this world *and* the next). Due to his holiness, God is a bit more discriminate regarding those upon whom he bestows the latter type of blessings (which are available to *anyone* who accepts Christ).

God's spiritual blessings, eternal salvation and the Holy Spirit, are available upon the acceptance of Christ and are a direct result of specific divine intervention. While Kevin the atheist may experience the "natural blessing" of an STD-free life, he will never know the spiritual fulfillment John experiences by virtue of his relationship with Christ.

Blaise Pascal—the famous mathematician, physicist, and philosopher—said that each one of us has a God-shaped hole in our heart that can only be filled by God. While we may attempt to fill that hole with passing idols such as money, sex, drugs, etc., we as humans will never experience ultimate fulfillment unless we invite God into our hearts. Blessings of the "natural" type do not lead to ultimate spiritual fulfillment in this life nor to eternal salvation in the next. Only the blood of Christ provides that. While extremely important in their own right, "natural blessings" are utterly incapable of providing *ultimate* and *eternal* fulfillment.

Once again, I want to emphasize that God *can, has, does, and will continue to* intervene within history to establish his specific will in specific situations. My point here is not to promote some form of deism, but to emphasize the importance of acknowledging the moral aspect of objective reality. This is why, as historian and scholar Richard Weaver wrote, ideas have consequences. It is ideas that lead to actions. And it is actions that lead to the real-world consequences of history.

Paul wrote in Galatians 6:7, "Do not be deceived, God is not mocked; for whatever a man sows, this he will also reap."(NASB) Obviously, Paul is not saying that humans don't mock God. We see everywhere that they do. Rather, Paul is telling his audience that God's moral law, which is written into the objective fabric of the universe, cannot be ignored without consequence. God and his creation always have the "last laugh."

Biting the Worldview That Feeds You

In the wake of Pope Benedict's controversial yet historically accurate citation (in 2006) of a fourteenth century Pope (who claimed Islam was spread by the sword), Muslim fascists everywhere gained the moral high ground by burning the pope in effigy and murdering a nun. Touché. If only the Vatican had rejected President Bush's policy of "torture" and war, Muslim fascists would have fallen in line like a bunch of gentle kittens. Wait a minute . . . the Vatican *does* reject such policies. So why don't Muslim fascists adore the Pope? After all, if liberals are correct, rejecting President Bush's policy of "torturing" captured terrorists will suddenly prevent Muslim terrorists from beheading Allied prisoners and hating us to the point of mass murder.

Pope Benedict recently held a meeting with Islamic envoys at his summer palace. At this meeting, the Pope said, "Christians and Muslims must learn to work together . . . in order to guard against all forms of intolerance and to oppose all manifestations of violence." Unfortunately for the Pope, he's been "scooped." The environment of which he speaks already exists . . . and has thrived for years. First, however, let us look where this environment does *not* exist.

Most obviously, this environment does not exist in the Middle East. The Middle East is a hotbed for fascism, dictators, and totalitarianism. The freedom to dissent doesn't exist. Political battles are won through genocide. Freedom of religion is nonexistent. Outside of Israel (and an emerging free

Iraq), democracy is only a dream. It is obvious the Pope's description of a place where Christians and Muslims "work together" and "oppose all manifestations of violence" does not exist in the Middle East.

Nor does this environment exist in Asia and the Pacific Islands. Indonesia is ripe with terrorists and kidnappings. It is a hotbed for plotting terrorists and corrupt officials.

Nor does this environment exist in Europe. For the most part, Muslims haven't been "absorbed" into European society. They live together, work together, worship together, and have no desire to become a part of the broader European milieu. Not that I blame them. There's nothing about Europe in general (or any particular European nation) that inspires collective engagement and patriotism. (The relativistic secularism and postmodernism that dominate European culture are to blame for this.) Europe is dominated by group politics. It's not just Muslims that are constantly fighting for their identity-based agenda. Unions, the young, the unemployed (consistently in double-digit percentages in Europe), students, etc. are constantly fighting for their piece of the pie.

Of course, by "absorb" I don't mean that Muslims would give up any essential doctrines of their faith; that is not required to become "part" of or participate in a society (a *legitimate* society, that is). As predicted, secularism leads to fragmented interest groups vying for control through power grabs, manipulation, and often violence. Without a backdrop of objective truth (as the Judeo-Christian worldview provides), dialogue becomes meaningless. "Dialogue" becomes a manipulative and/or violent free-for-all. To the victor go the spoils.

In an ironic twist, right smack dab in the middle of the country accused by everyone of warmongering and torture, exists the Pope's dream of an environment where Christians and Muslims "work together" and "oppose all manifestations of violence." That's right. The Pope and the Muslim envoys who agreed with his statement all yearn for a world that has been thriving for years in the United States of America—a country the world continually condemns.

Do you know how many Muslims I saw at the grocery store yesterday? Do you know how many Muslims I shopped side by side with at the mall last weekend? Do you know that I voted in a booth next to a Muslim last November (and will probably do so again this November)? Do you know how long the Islamic Center of Cincinnati has peacefully coexisted in an area full of suburban Christians? Since well before *and* after the terrorist attacks on September 11, 2001.

My experience is in no way unique. It is multiplied hundreds of times over across the United States. Every day in the United States, people who subscribe to mutually exclusive religions and ideologies peacefully coexist. But why is this the case? Why has the dreamy papal environment of peace taken root in America, yet seemingly has alluded the rest of the world? In short, because of the worldview upon which America was founded.

The Judeo-Christian worldview provides the foundational presuppositions necessary for the belief that humans, regardless of their religious, racial, or ideological affiliations, have inherent value. From this basic belief results the rights we so often take for granted in America, i.e., the right to free speech, the right to dissent, the freedom of religion, the right to bear arms, the right to assemble, the right to a fair and speedy trial, etc. Modern Europe has embraced secularism and has, therefore, lost touch with basic Judeo-Christian presuppositions. This accounts for the socialism and fragmented ethnic tribalism that plague Europe today. It should come as no surprise that the Middle East, having exorcized Christianity centuries ago (if it had ever been influential in the first place), is dominated by dictatorships and totalitarianism (which is where Europe and South America are headed).

When I say America is based on the "Christian worldview," I am *not* saying that every single American is a Christian. I'm not saying that everyone who wishes to become an American must convert to Christianity. What I *am* saying is that to be "American," one must accept basic ideas that encourage coexistence. For example, one not need be a born-again Christian to believe every human has inherent value. While the origin and intellectual foundation of that belief are most assuredly grounded in Christianity, one need not be a Christian to appropriate the idea into his own set of beliefs (although one needs to be a Christian to do so in a logically consistent manner).

This is what is so great about "America." It matters not who you are, what religion you espouse, or the color of your skin. As long as you accept "ideological Americanism," you're in. Have you ever noticed the opening ceremonies at the Olympics? Most athletes from the various countries all look basically the same. Regarding American athletes, however, this couldn't be further from the truth. This is because their "Americanism" exists in their minds rather than in any particular physical trait.

Isn't it ironic that the most racially, ethnically, and religiously "diverse" country in the world is also the most peaceful (comparatively speaking)? This is because America isn't as "diverse" as one might think. The backdrop of objective truth provided by the Judeo-Christian worldview encourages otherwise diverse people to peacefully coexist because basic moral realities are, consciously or subconsciously, agreed upon. Secularism provides no such backdrop (the issue of whether or not Islam provides such a backdrop will not be discussed here—although judging from non-American Islam in the Middle East, it doesn't seem promising).

The ideas that comprise "America" were written into the Constitution over 200 years ago. In some respects, it has taken the United States a while to realize its own Americanism (i.e. slavery, segregation, etc.). The foundational ideas of the abolition movement were written into the Constitution. The foundational ideas of the civil rights movement were written into the Constitution. (It is also notable that both movements were *Christian* grass roots movements. Just read some of the speeches given by the leading abolitionists of the day or the speeches of Dr. Martin Luther King Jr.)

America is not perfect. It never has been and never will be. But while America is being pulled from its moorings by activist judges and liberal politicians (many of whom include Republicans), it is proper to acknowledge that the founders understood quite well the slow realization of the Christian worldview that was instituted by an imperfect society in 1776. This is why it is possible to say that the abolition movement and the civil rights movement were most assuredly "American" movements. They resulted from acknowledging the Christian worldview that served as the foundation of our Constitution. The legality of slavery and the American Constitution was an uneasy coexistence that many of the founders *intended*. In short, it would have been impossible for the Constitution and legal slavery to coexist for more than a short period in history. Many of the founding fathers intended this to be the case, and American history later bore out their intentions. (Any attempt by liberals to appropriate this argument to justify a "living" Constitution is doomed to failure for two reasons. First, my argument rests upon the premise that the Constitution is a document based on unchanging truths and eternal values. Secondly, secular interpretations of the Constitution [i.e., legalized abortion, the "separation of church and state," socialist economic policy, etc.] are, by definition, secular and thus unconstitutional.)

On the one hand, the world condemns the United States for attempting to "Americanize" the world. Yet on the other hand, the world yearns for what America has to offer. The world vigorously rejects the Christian worldview, yet passionately embraces the fruit of that worldview, i.e., freedom. If the roots of a tree die, so does its fruit. The world hates America, yet yearns for the fruit America produces. "America" has the potential to spread across the globe, because it is a set of ideas—not a gender, skin color, or set of borders.

If people could see past their biased hatred for America, perhaps they would realize that the utopia for which they so passionately long is at its nearest manifestation in the United States of America. Perhaps this epiphany will encourage them to question *why* this is the case.

No Ruts, No Glory

Several years ago, a professor told me about theological ruts. He compared modern theological thinking to the old dirt roads upon which horse-drawn carriages traveled. When it would rain, the roads would turn to mud and wheels would leave ruts in the muddy road. When the mud dried, these long ruts became permanent features in the road.

This required drivers to "choose their ruts carefully," because once their wheels were in a set of ruts, those ruts determined the carriage's direction for a very long time. My professor told this story in the context of discussing hermeneutical presuppositions and their theological consequences, but this is also the perfect analogy for the role of reason and logic in thinking (the terms "reason" and "logic" will be used synonymously).

Reason brings structure to the *process* of thinking. It is *not* the foundation for thinking. Like the uselessness of a car without gas, reason without premises is useless. Premises are the prerequisite for rational thought. Without premises, reason has nothing with which to "work." For example, let's look at a common syllogism:

Cats are green.
Tom is a cat.
Therefore, Tom is green.

Where is the logic in this statement? First I'll tell you where it's *not*. Logic is not in the statement "cats are green," nor is it in the statement, "Tom is a cat." Those are empirical statements determined by an epistemological standard. They are premises—premises not determined by reason itself.

"Tom is green" is a logically necessary truth *given* the two premises. Reason doesn't care one way or the other whether or not Tom is green. All reason cares about is consistency. In other words, *if* you believe "cats are green" (the major premise) and *if* you believe "Tom is a cat" (the minor premise), then you *must* believe "Tom is green."

Reason will lead you to a different conclusion if your premises are different. For example, if your major premise is "cats are blue," your conclusion would be "Tom is blue." The two conclusions ("Tom is green" and

"Tom is blue") are mutually exclusive, but both are equally reasonable/logical conclusions. Individuals subscribing to each conclusion *cannot* be accused of being unreasonable/illogical.

Reason doesn't care about truth. As already stated, it only cares about consistency. Reason/logic is basically the law of non-contradiction and the law of the excluded middle. The law of non-contradiction states that something cannot be itself and its opposite in the same way at the same time. For example, murder cannot be right and wrong at the same time or my eyes cannot be blue and not blue and the same time. Ruts exist because of reason. The direction of the ruts, however, is determined by premises. Once reason is determined as the standard for thought, thinking can begin. Of course, if reason/logic is not utilized as the standard for thought, anything goes. Thought outside of reason is like wandering aimlessly in the desert. You've probably forgotten where you started, you don't know where you're going, and you'll probably die before you get there. If someone admittedly doesn't accept reason/logic as a standard, dialogue ceases to be meaningful. Unless you enjoy wasting your time and energy, I suggest moving on to more worthwhile endeavors.

Once the role of reason/logic is understood, it is easier to understand the vital importance of premises. The question then becomes, "Where do we get our premises?" The answer? A worldview. A worldview gives us the answers to the most fundamental questions of existence. Such answers form our premises. Once you have a worldview, i.e., once you have chosen a set of "ruts," you're stuck with its subsidiary implications down the "logical road."

The premises contained within a worldview predetermine your potential horizon of knowledge and experience. For example, will someone experience compassion toward those who are suffering without the foundational presupposition that those persons have inherent value? Will someone experience motivation to eliminate poverty, homelessness, oppression, discrimination, etc. without a foundational notion of justice? Can someone experience eternal meaning in life's tragedies without a fundamental belief in a personal God? Can someone reach a supernatural conclusion if his worldview rules out the possibility of the supernatural from the beginning?

As an undergraduate at a secular university, I observed that most of the religion professors utilized a secular worldview when studying history and religion. Such a worldview yields materialistic methods that eliminate the possibility of supernatural conclusions concerning religious texts. This bias precludes an investigation of the biblical text on *its own grounds*. Thus, we should not be surprised when secular scholars arrive at secular conclusions. Reason/logic *forces* them to.

Two options can be taken concerning the biblical texts. Either they are God's Word or they aren't. Only someone open to both of these possibilities from the beginning is open-minded enough for a fair treatment of the texts. This rules out the secular scholar. If you want a fair treatment of a text—*any* text—you need not look at the secular religion and history departments across America.

Reason doesn't determine conclusions. *It ensures that the conclusions already inherent in your premises are consistently realized.* This is why the secular humanist faith in reason/logic is misplaced. Secular humanist philosophies have faith that humans have the ability to bring about their own salvation through the faculty of reason. Secularism claims traditional religion hinders the potential of humanity, often to the point of oppression. Secularism claims human nature is basically good (or nonexistent and malleable) and, through the cooperative use of reason, humanity can attain the society for which it longs. Reason is universal, and, as long as every human utilizes it, everyone will arrive at the same conclusions. For the secular humanist, the answer to the question, "Can't we all just get along?" is "Yes, if everybody uses reason."

This misplaced faith is the result of a misunderstanding concerning the function and ability of reason. Reason won't bring about universal conformity. Universal conformity is only possible when everyone begins with the same premises, i.e., the same worldview . . . something not likely to happen any time soon.

Secular humanist philosophies believe that if humans could just be "fixed" through social engineering (read: "education"), everyone would use reason, thus resulting in the eradication of poverty, war, oppression, etc. Civil government is a tool used for such an end. Secular humanist political theories see the fundamental purpose of government and law as something that "shapes" humans rather than a tool that protects humans from one another. Unfortunately, such "shaping" usually takes the form of coercion, oppression, or worse . . . genocide.

Reason is an invaluable tool, but its limitations must be understood. It is at the mercy of the premises brought to the table . . . and it is worldview that determines such premises.

Reason: Man's Best Friend or Worst Enemy?

Several months of studying culminated in December of 2006, when I took the Law School Admission Test (LSAT). Throughout the process of studying, I learned a great deal about how lawyers are trained to think. With this realization came an epiphany. It is this epiphany I would like to share with you.

Why do lawyers get such a bad name? The reasons are numerous, but I'm only going to list a few: 1) Many lawyers don't actually *produce* anything. Like union leaders, they earn a living off of the hard work and/or misery of others. Positions such as these are often justified by rationalizing that the lawyer or union leader is "fighting for the rights of others." Sure, these lawyers sometimes ease the suffering of their clients and hold accountable those responsible, but we should be honest about what is going on here: Like the party or institution responsible for the misery in the first place, the livelihood of these lawyers requires profiting off of the misery of others. Examples include lawyers specializing in divorce, personal injury, and frivolous lawsuits. 2) Many politicians are lawyers. Perhaps the only group more maligned than lawyers is politicians. And because many politicians are also lawyers, that angst is directed toward the field of law in general. 3) High-profile cases that receive national media coverage are often cases in which lawyers get obviously guilty criminals off scot-free. Perversions of justice in cases such as these don't sit well with the majority of law-abiding citizens in this country. 4) Lastly, manipulation is the name of the game. A court of law is full of masters of manipulation. Instead of codified reflections of objective and eternal truths, the laws that govern locally, statewide, and nationally are merely rules seen as either barriers that must be evaded or advantages that must be exploited.

My aforementioned epiphany concerns this last point. This is one reason why lawyers get a bad rap and a major reason why lawyers are so dangerous.

One must understand logic (a term used synonymously with *reason*) to do well on the LSAT. The LSAT does not test legal knowledge or courtroom procedures. It tests the ability to think logically. This includes the ability to understand the sometimes complex relationships between premises, conclusions, arguments, and methods of reasoning. Logic is the main tool of the lawyer.

It is vital to understand that *logic does not care about truth*. Logic does not provide premises. It only requires your conclusions to be consistent with the premises you bring to the table. For the logically consistent individual, everything you will ever believe and do is already inherent in the foundational premises you embrace. *Logic only requires that the conclusions already inherent in your premises be consistently realized.*

This is why logic can be humanity's best friend or worst enemy. If a society embraces premises that lead to freedom and prosperity, logic is our friend. Logic is our enemy, however, if society embraces premises that lead to tragedy such as authoritarianism or genocide. *Both* Mother Teresa and Adolf Hitler were completely logical in their thinking. The differences in their lifestyles didn't lie with the fact that one was logical and one was illogical (or that one was "reasonable" and the other "unreasonable"). The differences reside in the different premises they embraced.

So what? What does all this mean? It means that those who are skilled in the art of logic and thinking have at their fingertips a tool that could either be used for the benefit of humanity or for its destruction. It all depends on the premises that inform the logic. It depends on what one believes about the basic realities of existence.

In a culture dominated by secularism and the necessary moral relativism of its two main offspring—humanism and postmodernism—logic becomes a weapon of mass destruction. When objective truth is denied, logic has no foundation and becomes an arbitrary tool of manipulation utilized according to the whim of an individual or group. Adolf Hitler used logic just as Mother Teresa did. But with no objective truth, it is impossible to condemn one and extol the other. The logical soundness of a person's beliefs is not a standard indicating moral correctness. If it were, *both* Hitler and Mother Teresa would be considered morally upright.

Because secularism has come to dominate our country's education system, the idea of objective truth is not presented to students as a viable alternative. Students are taught, in word and deed, that freedom lies in the construction of their own reality—their own *moral* reality, in particular. Tolerance becomes the virtue of virtues; objective truth is seen as that which oppresses, because it limits the ability to subjectively construct one's own reality—i.e., it hinders the aforementioned modern notion of *freedom*.

Like most educational institutions, secularism dominates the country's law schools as well. This should come as no surprise, considering the secular public education most law school students receive in the preceding 17 to 18 years of their lives. Additionally, the vast majority of the faculty attended schools dominated by secularism.

Thus, those who are expertly trained in the art of logic and thinking do not believe in objective truth (of course, lawyers are not the only people trained like this). The powerful tool of logic is put in the hands of the very people who ought not possess it—people who reject objective truth. Without a belief in objective truth, a nation's laws are not seen to reflect (or not reflect) an external and universal standard that is applicable in all times and all places. Instead, a society's morals, taboos, institutions, and laws are seen through the lens of social contract theory; that is, as arbitrary phenomena invented to facilitate the most effective means of selfish fulfillment. As such, laws have no objective base in reality and can be discarded (or, if necessary, manipulated) at any time and for any reason (this includes the Constitution).

Teaching the art of logic and thinking to those with no belief in objective morality is like giving a gun to a 10-year-old and not training him how to use it. Like logic, a gun can be your best friend or your worst enemy. It depends on the one using it.

Lawyers, as well as many others, are being equipped with the immensely powerful tool of logic but are not given a bedrock standard instructing them how to use it. In fact, this is true for most of the blessings we experience in this life, i.e., sex, money, relationships, knowledge, etc. Denying the objective moral fabric of the universe transforms the very things that make this life worth living, into things that destroy all we care about and love.

Yadda, Yadda, Yadda: Dialogue More Meaningless Than Seinfeld (and Not Nearly as Entertaining)

On the way home from church one Sunday evening, I found myself listening to a radio program hosted by a Muslim who was not of Middle Eastern descent. That is, he sounded like a Caucasian American who converted to Islam (but I could be wrong). His guest was a Roman Catholic scholar who was a supposed expert in the area of Christian/Muslim dialogue. During the 30 minutes I listened, I didn't hear a single thing that would make this world a more peaceful place.

Granted, I only listened for 30 minutes; but one would think that *something* constructive would come out of a conversation (between two men of different faiths) about easing the "tension" (to put it lightly) between different worldviews. I would say this tension exists between Islam and Christianity only, but considering the problem Islamo-fascists have with most of the world (including within its own multi-sect family), this tension is much bigger than a Christian-Muslim spat that can be settled with a few slaps of brick-filled gloves.

The two men droned on and on about the importance of understanding each other's religion. Beyond that, they discussed the inherent difficulty in understanding that which is different from your own belief system. Yadda, yadda, yadda. (No, I didn't yadda yadda the best part.) How about they tell me something I don't know?

Here's the problem for those who believe that lack of dialogue (commonly called "diplomacy") is the major cause of conflict (in this case, terrorism perpetrated by Islamo-Fascists) in the world: *Reason is not able to bring those who begin with different premises to the same conclusions.* (See my prior essay entitled "No Ruts, No Glory" for a detailed discussion of the proper role of reason/logic.) In fact, if reason is properly utilized, it will *never* bring those who hold mutually exclusive premises to the same conclusions.

This is why dialogue between mutually exclusive worldviews is useless. Dialogue between mutually exclusive worldviews can end in only two ways:

Scenario One

Agree to disagree. In this scenario, the two (or more) worldviews in dispute acknowledge they will never come to an agreement, and they agree to leave each other alone. If this happens, one worldview can say and do nothing about *anything* that goes on within the other worldview—good or bad. (For example, worldview A can say and do nothing about a Holocaust occurring in worldview B.)

Scenario Two

Fight it out. In this scenario, the disputing worldviews acknowledge they cannot come to an agreement, and they are not okay with leaving each other alone. For whatever reason(s), the worldviews are not content to simply go their separate ways. Sometimes worldview C is not okay with something going on in worldview D (i.e., genocide, oppression, etc.) and believes it has a responsibility to stop it. Other times, worldview F simply wants to wipe worldview G from the face of the earth (for whatever reason). In this case, worldview G usually feels compelled to defend itself.

There is no Scenario Three. Many today believe mutually exclusive worldviews can coexist peacefully if they simply understand one another—if they simply gather around a table, use reason, and "dialogue" until an agreement is reached. This is not an option. The only way mutually exclusive worldviews can "peacefully coexist" is through Scenario One. Most people, however, do not understand what this entails.

Scenario One means that worldview A must *never* mingle in the affairs of worldview B. This means *never* . . . even if a group of people within worldview B (such as Jews, Christians, homosexuals, Muslims, women, the unborn, people who have green eyes, etc.) are being systematically murdered by the millions, even if women aren't allowed to vote, even if ethnic cleansing rules the day, and—God forbid—even if spotted owls are being killed for fun.

Anyone with an iota of a moral conscience has a hard time swallowing Scenario One—and rightly so. Once again, that pesky *imago dei* in us gets in the way. People often artificially support Scenario One when it is politically expedient, but they subscribe to the possibility of Scenario Two when it comes to an issue on their political agenda.

The key, therefore, is determining whether or not different worldviews are mutually exclusive. If they are, no amount of dialogue will ever fuse them. And, by definition, the premises (or presuppositions) of different worldviews are mutually exclusive. If people agree on a plethora of secondary issues, they most likely adhere to the same worldview (whether they formally acknowledge this or not—as discussed in Chapter Three).

My question for the two men on the radio program is this: What do you do when another person refuses to dialogue? What do you do when the person you are dialoguing with jumps over the table and tries to saw off your head? You have two options: 1) Let him saw off your head, or 2) Kill him before he does so. There is no third option.

The fact that we understand each other's worldview will not help us peacefully coexist. In fact, it is precisely because we *do* understand each other's worldview that a conflict exists. When the real-world manifestation of one worldview necessitates the limitation or eradication of the other, don't expect the threatened worldview to simply lie down and accept such a fate.

Kibble for Fat Cats

Someone told me a story a while ago that illustrated the difference between cats and dogs. A dog sees his owner feeding him, giving him water, walking him, and playing with him, and he concludes, "Wow, my owner must be God." A cat, on the other hand, sees his owner feeding him, giving him water, and playing with him, and he concludes, "Wow, *I* must be God." This humorous comparison serves as an analogy to the attitudes of many politicians today. The attitude of those in power usually falls into one of these two categories. Secularism breeds leaders of the "cat" type.

Secularism claims the ills of society are not caused by the consequences of individual human choices, but by the systems that create such individuals. Rather than influencing the hearts of individuals, the efforts of secularists are focused on perfecting the systems that create individuals. Therefore, salvation for secularists is contingent upon gaining and maintaining the power necessary to institute the proper systems—by force if necessary.

In this view, government control is seen as the most efficient medium (indeed, the *only* medium with this ability) to realizing a society with a perfect system. Because it is the right system that ultimately rids a society of oppression, crime, poverty, and every other ill—and because the government is the only entity that can forcefully institute such a system—*government is seen as that which has the ability to save humanity.*

Thus, our rights as citizens are granted to us by the government, and it is the government that is the source and provider of our rights (because, according to secularism, there is no "higher power" above government that ensures such rights). According to Judeo-Christian theism, *God* grants us our rights. Civil government exists to *protect* those rights. This is a *significant* departure from secularism. This view underlies the language used by President George W. Bush when he discusses freedom. As President Bush repeatedly says in his speeches, when the United States (or any country) frees another nation, the ensuing freedom is not a gift from the United States. It is a gift given by God to every human being. The United States is simply its protector. However, this doesn't make the U.S. government unique. This should be the function of *every* civil government. Civil government is called to protect our rights, not provide them.

Unfortunately, secularism elevates civil government to the level of God. This status and function of government are then transferred to the individuals who comprise the government, i.e., the politicians. Thus, individual politicians see themselves as those who provide our rights and have the power to rescue us from societal ills. No longer are the citizens of a nation seen as capable of saving themselves. This role is reserved for government and the politicians comprising it.

No wonder modern politicians are "cats"! The elitism inherent in secularism has granted Savior status (or "liberator" status, as discussed in Chapter Five) to the elected official (or *appointed* in the case of judges). The role previously assigned to the divine (or to the private citizen) is now assigned to the superheroes filling our government offices. If they can rescue us from certain death, they *must* be special!

Many modern politicians act like God, because that's the role society has granted them. They view the populace with disdain—as sheep who require leading, who are incapable of helping themselves. As citizens, we have no bootstraps and must await an extended hand from a fat cat from Massachusetts to rescue us from the hole in which we've found ourselves. The only thing we depraved, intellect-lacking peons can manage is to inadvertently dig our hole deeper.

Secularism mixed with Judeo-Christian democracy creates a system of bribery and extortion. The politicians convince the citizens that they (the citizens) are incapable of helping themselves. Once this lie is successfully indoctrinated, the politicians hold themselves up as the ones who can and will do the helping.

For example, have you ever wondered why government programs are so important to modern secularists? 1) Such programs are the practical outworking of the government's attempt to save its citizens. 2) They are a way to increase the government's size, power, and influence. The more powerful the government, the easier it is to institute the perfect system. 3) They are the payout for those who voted for the modern secular politicians (who promised to save them). In essence, the symbiotic relationship can be expressed in the following dialogue:

Politician: Vote for me, and I'll give you your programs.
Constituency: Give us our programs, and we'll vote for you.

It is in the best interest of secular politicians to do two things: 1) Convince the citizenry it can't help itself and is in need of the government to make things right. 2) Keep the citizenry from ever actually being "saved." The former is important, because without it the politicians would never *gain* power in the first place. The latter is essential, because without it the politicians could not *maintain* their power. An individual who is convinced a person can help himself won't vote for a secular politician, and a "saved" individual no longer needs salvation from the government. The utopia for which secular politicians supposedly yearn is their worst enemy, for it is a society without victims. And a society without victims is a society without the exploitation that is necessary for secular politicians to grant themselves Savior status. (Keep in mind that whether or not a person or groups of people are *actually* victims is irrelevant. What matters is the perception of victimization.)

Secularism combined with democracy breeds extortion, because the means by which the government provides these programs is pilfered from the coffers of those who have the resources. If secular politicians (as well as activists) can convince 51% of the population (or five Supreme Court Justices) of their ideology, they can possess the power to control the assets of an entire nation's private citizens. Those convinced of secularism's victim ideology appease their consciences by forcing others (and often themselves) to fund the government programs and policies that are vital to the systemic salvation of the citizenry. I'm convinced that if there were a perfect society with no victims, and secular politics were to be introduced, that society would all of a sudden be full of victims.

The cats in our government buildings get fat from the victimization (actual or perceived) of the constituency. Remember that fact the next time you hear a wealthy, white, fat politician claim he is fighting for "your country's tired, poor, and helpless masses."

Chance, Choice, or Chosen?

You'll often hear about how much chance is required for Darwinian evolution to occur. Without a supernatural entity purposefully creating man, nature, and animals, the highly improbable evolutionary steps that brought life about must have occurred by chance. If, however, astronomer/humanist Carl Sagan was right when he dogmatically appropriated secular mythology's claim that the physical cosmos was all that ever was, is, or ever will be (the basic tenet of secularism), not only is chance an illusion, but so is choice (free will).

If all that exists is physical "stuff," then it is also true that the physical laws that guide every physical cause and subsequent effect apply to *all* reality. Every effect is directly caused by a prior effect, which was caused by another prior effect, which was caused by another prior effect, and so on and so forth (every effect serves as a cause for something else). In short, all that is *must* be the way it is. Physical laws determine everything. There is no chance, and there is no choice—only what is "chosen" by impersonal laws of nature.

A tree doesn't "choose" to grow leaves. Nor does it grow leaves by chance. If the conditions are right (conditions necessarily brought into existence according to physical laws), leaves will grow. If conditions are such that leaves won't grow (harsh temperatures, lack of nourishment, etc.), they won't.

Water at the Earth's poles didn't choose to freeze. Nor did it randomly freeze. If the temperature of water drops at or below its freezing point, it *must* freeze. It isn't free *not* to. Nor will water freeze randomly while above its freezing point. Water is at the mercy of physical law. Water does not have free will.

The same is true for humans. If the basic tenet of secularism (i.e., *all* that exists is physical stuff) is true, then every function of the human body is a necessary consequence of a prior physical cause. Our emotions are the effects of how chemicals in our brain function and interact. Our thoughts are directly caused by synapses firing, which in turn were caused by something else physical. Human actions are similarly determined.

Indeed, our entire personalities are simply the result of chemicals and synapses interacting in a manner dictated by physical laws. As cited earlier, *Humanist Manifesto II* claims as much when it says, "As far as we know, the total personality is a function of the biological organism transacting in a social and cultural context." What does this mean? It means that your every emotion, thought, decision, and action are directly caused by internal biology or external social forces.

In short, there is no "you" behind your physical self that is making free-will decisions. "You" are nothing but a complex set of physical things (chemicals, synapses, etc.) necessarily interacting with one another in a manner predetermined by physical laws. Your thoughts and opinions about God, football, abortion, your spouse and/or children, ice cream, and movies are the *necessary* effects of physical phenomena determined by physical laws.

Furthermore, every *action* you perform is similarly explained. "You" don't decide to give money to the poor, buy dinner for your date, or murder a neighbor. Physical phenomena do. Thus, there is no "you" to be held responsible for the actions of "your" physical body (which is all you are). Your body and its behavior are the sum total of dictatorial biological and social (physical) forces. Impersonal physical law "chooses" that the leaf grow, the water freeze, and a man murder his neighbor. In order for chance to exist, there must be real-life possibilities *not* necessarily determined by physical laws. However, since physical stuff is *all* that exists, and all physical stuff is at the mercy of physical laws, *nothing* that exists or occurs is outside the jurisdiction of physical laws.

For choice (human free will) to exist, there must be something essentially non-physical about the human (because only the non-physical falls outside the jurisdiction of physical law). But secularism rules out this possibility *by definition*, i.e., if it were true that something non-physical existed, secularism would be a false worldview. Only a non-physical "soul" of some sort would be capable of making truly free decisions outside the jurisdiction of physical law.

Thus, it is illogical rubbish to claim evolution required "chance." Nothing could be further from the truth. Like the leaf that grows, water that freezes, and human who murders his neighbor, evolution occurred because it *had* to, i.e., it was "forced" to occur by physical law. In fact, *everything* that has occurred and will occur in the universe *had* to occur. Hurricane Katrina *had* to hit. Mount St. Helens *had* to erupt. The movie, "Dude, Where's My Car?," *had* to be made. Caesar *had* to cross the Rubicon. Hitler and the Nazis *had* to murder six million Jews. The United States *had* to drop two atomic bombs on Japan. Terrorists *had* to fly planes into buildings on September 11, 2001. Child molesters *had* to rape the children they did. You *have* to be pro-life or pro-abortion (whichever you are). You *had* to eat what you did for breakfast. I *had* to write this book. You *must* recommend this book to everyone you know. Choice is an illusion. There is no possible string of events in this world other than what actually occurred. Everything that *is* exists necessarily. Additionally, everything that *will be* is already determined.

This belief has tragic consequences for culture, law, and government. Such consequences are already prevalent today because of the influence of modern liberalism and its secular presuppositions—the two most obvious (consequences) of which are a weak criminal justice system and socialist/communist educational, economic, and foreign policy.

Consistent secularists must believe in a world where there is no moral difference between Mother Teresa and Hitler (both were necessities), no such thing as purpose or meaning, and no reason to hold anyone responsible for his behavior—no matter how destructive or revolting. There is no ongoing purpose to history—only necessary outcomes caused by impersonal physical law.

Yet it is secularists who are constantly lecturing us about the moral need to help the poor, protect the environment, provide "free" health care and education, and spend more time trying "diplomacy." Unfortunately for them, their worldview provides no basis for such claims. The secular battle cry, "No objective truth except ours!" is logically absurd. A secularist who claims someone has a moral obligation to do *anything* is a walking contradiction.

But it isn't the secularist's fault. After all, his opinion is the result of interacting chemicals and neurons dictated by physical law. Unfortunately for the secularist, nature has "chosen" him to believe in ridiculous logical impossibilities.

The Ideological Origin of Beautiful Art

In the fall of 2006, television and radio commentator, Bill O'Reilly, dedicated a segment on his show to discussing why Hollywood (the movie and music industries, along with the art world in general) is dominated by liberals. One of his guests was movie critic Richard Roeper (of *Ebert and Roeper*). Roeper claimed such industries are by nature creative. That is, movies, music, and art are creative acts by creative people. Roeper then concluded in an obviously derogatory manner, "Conservatives just aren't creative people."

Is Roeper correct? Are conservatives incapable of creativity? Is there something about conservative ideology that stifles creative thought? To understand this phenomenon, it is important to comprehend the relationship between foundational and subsidiary thinking.[1] Someone doesn't start by saying, "I'm a liberal," and *then* begin to think like a liberal and take liberal positions. Rather, a way of thinking comes first—a way of thinking based on foundational ideas about basic realities. Subsidiary beliefs are (or should be) the necessary logical ramifications of foundational beliefs (a worldview). Thus, a person's beliefs, actions, and decisions are direct results of logically prior foundational ideas concerning the basics of reality. If this is the case, it should be possible to trace the origin of a social phenomenon back to such foundational ideas. The liberal/secular dominance within the movie, music, literature (including poetry), and art industries is no different.

The basic tenet of secularism (and its resultant liberalism) is the claim that only physical matter exists. There is no supernatural. A logical consequence of this claim is the nonexistence of any type of objective morality. Such a reality must be constructed from within by each individual (or, in some cases, by a group or the state). Once again, moral relativism rears its ugly head. These two metaphysical claims will be shown to account for why the aforementioned industries (heretofore referred to simply as *art*) are dominated by liberals.

First, "creativity" must be defined. The denial of objective morality creates a vacuum that humans long to fill. However, only the select and warped few are comfortable with a meaningless universe where there is no moral difference between Adolf Hitler and Mother Teresa. Most must fill this void with something. With the appeal to objective morality ruled out, the only other avenue is subjective construction, i.e., the individual construction of one's own morality. In this scenario, every individual defines

---

1. Discussed at length in Chapter 1.

for himself what is right and wrong, good and bad. Thus, "creation" (or "creativity") is an autonomous *ex nihilo* (out of nothing) act rather than a *reflective* one. After all, there is nothing to reflect if there is no objective reality. (Judeo-Christian morality is *reflective* in that it *describes* an objective moral order grounded in God.)

This is exactly why many artists pride themselves on shocking people out of their comfort zones. Such art is meant to shake people out of a traditional malaise supposedly caused by oppressive objective moral codes (usually religion) that stifle human potential and creativity. Think about it. What value does photographer Robert Mapplethorpe's art have outside of its ability to shock and awe? Do we honestly believe "beauty" is an upside-down crucifix in a jar of urine or a portrait of the Virgin Mary painted with dung? Secularists sure do. *Ex nihilo* originality becomes the standard of "beauty" regardless of how filthy or disgusting it may be.

Secularists/liberals dominate the art industries because such industries provide outlets for their morally relativistic worldviews. There is quite literally no limit to what realities they can create. Art provides an unlimited amount of petri dishes in which to experiment with whatever nouveau philosophy is fashionable at the time. There is no objective standard to rein in the so-called "liberated" mind.

Liberals dominate the art industries as a result of a vicious cycle. As secularism increases its cultural influence, its logical real-world consequences will eventually bear themselves out. For example, the necessary denial of objective morality deteriorates into a world absent of not only morality but also of meaning and purpose. A purely physical world yields no such niceties. Eventually, people realize their subjectively constructed realities extend no further than their own minds. This daunting realization produces the despair, disillusionment, and confusion so reminiscent in the art industries, particularly music and literature.

People often remark that a song or poem really "spoke to them." What does this mean? It means that the song or poem put into words (or music) exactly what the listener is feeling or experiencing. And in a culture that teaches the secular doctrines of Darwinism, relativism, and tolerance, art that reflects such despair and confusion will be well received, especially by the young who are striving to fill the vacuum caused by secularism but are not given the objective tools to do so.

Listen to a Christian radio station for a day. Then listen to a secular radio station the next day. If you can manage to put aside any philosophical or religious biases, you will be left with two very different impressions of the world. Additionally, your demeanor and/or emotional status will be very different. Christian music leaves you with a very definite sense of meaning and purpose (be it true or untrue), while secular music serves to inculcate an element of despair and confusion. This phenomenon is part of the reason secular music doesn't "speak to" many who believe in objective meaning, purpose, and morality. How can a song describing despair and confusion appeal to someone who has a definite sense of meaning and purpose in life? The opposite is also true. Those who "think liberally" are attracted to liberal forms of creativity, and those who "think conservatively" are attracted to conservative forms of creativity (discussed in a moment).

Is the secular definition of creativity as *ex nihilo* originality a fair one? It certainly seems to be, given the secular worldview. A liberal sees a random world absent of meaning, purpose, and beauty. If the world is to have meaning, purpose, or beauty, they must be created *ex nihilo* by subjective minds. This is the exact opposite conclusion drawn by conservatives. Because conservative ideology is based on objective morality (because it's based on the Judeo-Christian worldview), conservatives see a world full of meaning, purpose, and beauty. The universe already has objective meaning, purpose, and morality in it. It's a package deal. They need not be imposed by subjective minds. Thus, "creativity" is *reflective originality* rather than *ex nihilo originality*. Conservative creativity begins with a belief in an objective order to existence.

As discussed in the second paragraph of this essay, the liberal definition of "creativity" (or art in general) is a direct result of secular foundational ideas. Similarly, the conservative definition of "creativity" is a direct result of Judeo-Christian foundational ideas. The way of thinking that has come to be termed "liberal" produces a particular kind of phenomenon; in this case, art industries dominated by the idea that creativity is *ex nihilo* originality—regardless of its content. The way of thinking that has come to be termed "conservative" produces another kind of phenomenon; in this case, art industries dominated by the idea that creativity is *reflective*. But what does art based on the conservative idea of *reflective* creativity look like? A quick answer: Science and mathematics—fields that acknowledge an objective reality that needs to be revealed and mastered for man's benefit, for that is its purpose. (Genesis 1:28-30 is the philosophical foundation for civilization and the Western impetus for the rise of science.) Even as a high school student who didn't particularly enjoy math, I was aware of the intricate and consistent reality mathematics reflected—a reality no less beautiful than any piece of art I was exposed to in the art class down the hall. As a college student taking formal logic (which is basically mathematics with letters), I was amazed by the beauty of the formulas and equations that were reflective of reality—a reality of which we can only see the consequences. I experienced a similar sentiment in my biology, geology, and astronomy classes.[2]

When initially hearing Richard Roeper's comment, "Conservatives just aren't creative people," I responded by saying aloud, "Are you kidding? Conservative creativity sent us to the moon. Conservative creativity is why you drive to work in a car every morning. Conservative creativity is why we have airplanes, modern medicine, and skyscrapers. Don't tell me conservatives aren't creative!" Galileo Galilei, Johannes Kepler, and Nicolaus Copernicus are just as much artists as Michelangelo, Rembrandt, and Jackson Pollock. To be honest, I'm often more impressed with the works of Thomas Edison or Orville and Wilbur Wright than I am with those of Pablo Picasso or Vincent van Gogh (although all are very impressive).

In his book, *How Should We Then Live?* Francis Schaeffer juxtaposes the art of the Renaissance with the art of the Reformation. Philosophically, the Renaissance and Reformation provided different answers to the same question; namely, "What is ultimate?" The Renaissance claimed man was the measure of all things, while the Reformation elevated God as ultimate. The art within each movement reflected how each answered that question. Renaissance art emphasized man as central, while Reformation art emphasized the divine as central.

What one notices when comparing the art of these two movements is that Reformation art is reflective, while Renaissance art attempts to create in man anew that which Reformation art ascribed to the divine. Each movement's art was a consequence of the diametrically opposed ideas that served as their foundations. There is only one being capable of *ex nihilo* originality. Unfortunately for secularists, it's not the human being. This realization, however, in no way lessens the impressiveness of those who engage in reflectively creative acts. True acts of creativity require talent and resolve. Let's not pretend that creative beauty is limited to the traditional areas of art such as movies, music, poetry, literature, painting, sculpture, etc. The inner workings of a jet engine or the impressive foundation of a bridge that brings worlds together is just as beautiful as the Mona Lisa or Sistine Chapel.

Let's also not be so "liberal" with our use of the term *beauty*. As I walk through an art show or exhibit, I am awed by the sublime nature of reflec-

---

2. For an in-depth discussion of how the Judeo-Christian worldview is responsible for the rise of science, I highly recommend *The Victory of Reason*, by Rodney Stark.

tive art rather than the fragmented despair of art which futilely attempts *ex nihilo* originality but only succeeds in reflecting the meaninglessness, hopelessness, and confusion of the ideas on which it is based. That's not beauty. In fact, it's the very definition of ugliness.

The subtle genius of a painting, photograph, sculpture, or invention that captures a perspective of creation heretofore unnoticed by anyone but the artist is a thing of beauty. The unique experiences of an artist that culminate in a perspective-creating experience are the source of great art. (This is why great art/science is often produced by those with weird, unusual, or troubling experiences and eccentric personalities. It is precisely those qualities that lead to the unique perspectives necessary for inspiring art. This is what it means to say that reflective art is *original*. It portrays an aspect of reality that is not perceived by most.) Believe me, there are innumerable facets of existence that have yet to be explored by human perception. Thus, the potential for great art is never-ending. The subtle genius of the incandescent light bulb or the scientific epiphany that brings together years of cloudy observations is a thing of beauty.

The unique ability of humanity to engage in creative art is one of the main characteristics that separates us from other species. Only humans are able to grasp and unveil Truth. God gave humanity the ability, albeit finite, to probe his ways and mind—the source of truth. English poet John Keats said, "Beauty is truth, truth beauty." Not being an expert on Keats' work, I can't comment in detail regarding what *he* meant by the statement. But the phrase perfectly illustrates what I believe true beauty is. Beauty is correspondence to the infinite, omnipotent, unfathomable mind that is the source of all existence and Truth. Once someone catches a glimpse of this beauty, there is no going back. The next time you observe a piece of art (of *any* kind), ask yourself, "What aspect of the infinite does this reflect?" Or just sit back and marvel at the small piece of God's mind manifested before you by a creature fulfilling what it means to be created in the *imago dei*—the image of God.

Positive and Negative Rights

"Rights language" is vital in understanding the proper role of government. Specifically, the difference between a *negative* right and a *positive* right must be properly understood. In one sense, a negative right is "a right *from* . . . ," while a positive right is "a right *to* . . . ." An example of a positive right is a right *to* education or a right *to* health care. An example of a negative right is a right *from* being physically harmed by your neighbor or a right *from* your neighbor stealing your car.

The key to understanding these differences is to define the nature of positive rights. If someone believes the government exists to *provide* rights, then the government is obligated to *provide* whatever is considered a "right." Thus, it becomes necessary for the government to provide "rights" such as education and health care. But there is a flipside to every positive right, i.e., a *burden*. Because the government has no funds of its own but only what it taxes from its people, any positive right requiring monetary sustenance becomes the *moral obligation* of a certain population (those who provide the funds). Thus, every time a positive right is posited, a moral obligation is *necessarily* also posited.

From a functional standpoint, *a positive right is a right that is actualized by enforcing a moral obligation. A negative right is a right that is actualized by preventing infringement upon it.* Thus, a government charged with actualizing positive rights is charged with providing moral redemption for the people by enforcing the people's moral obligations, i.e., enforcing the positive aspect of human nature. A government charged with actualizing negative rights is charged with restraining the negative aspect of human nature. The dominant opinion regarding the fundamental purpose of government is vital, because it leads to the kind of public policy that will be implemented.

A proper understanding of what a human being is leads to the realization that the role of government is *not* to force the best out of humanity, but to restrain the worst of humanity. Thus, positive rights are left to the people, while negative rights are "enforced" by government. Civil government exists to *protect* positive rights *by actualizing* negative rights. Does someone have the right to health care? Absolutely. Is government obligated to provide it? No. The government *protects* your right to health care by preventing others from infringing upon that right. The importance of this distinction should not be underestimated. It is vital for the private citizenry to fulfill its rightful responsibility of ensuring positive rights. If such a responsibility is neglected by the citizenry, then government will gladly fill the void—and will do so with disastrous consequences.

Government increases its powers in two main ways: 1) It assumes the responsibilities of the private citizenry, because the private citizenry has neglected its responsibilities; 2) It assumes such responsibilities through force (either at the point of a bayonet or by deceiving enough people into *believing* the private citizenry has neglected its responsibility).

Governments are constantly utilizing both methods. It is the job of the citizenry to ensure that such attempts are unsuccessful. This is what

Thomas Jefferson meant when he said, "Eternal vigilance is the price of freedom." Freedoms aren't lost by coincidence. They are taken away. And it is up to free citizens to maintain and transmit freedom-preserving values that serve to limit government—which is, much more often than not, the entity responsible for tyranny and oppression (unlike liberal claims that view those in the private sector as threats, e.g., corporations, John Doe and his gun, etc.).

The invention of positive rights is a sure way to increase the power of government. This is one source of the stark difference between liberal and conservative ideologies. Modern liberalism is constantly coming up with positive rights that the government must enforce, while conservatism is more interested in protecting negative rights and allowing the citizenry to fulfill its positive rights on its own, thus limiting the power of government—a necessary feature of democracy.

Every positive right over which the government assumes control, the more powerful it becomes and the less freedom citizens have. Remember this fact the next time someone claims a "right" exists.

Democracy and Consensus, Part 1

In 2001, when pseudo-Republican Jim Jeffords left the Republican Party to become an Independent (giving Democrats temporary control of the Senate—Republicans won the Senate back in 2002), a liberal friend of mine said, "Balance is good for the country." (At the time, Republicans had control of the House.) This friend was a Democrat, so at first I concluded his statement was because he wished his party had been in power. "Balance" is usually a virtue to those in the minority.

But upon deeper reflection, I came to two conclusions: 1) Balance and "consensus," as they are typically termed in modern political rhetoric, are undemocratic notions; 2) Viewing balance and consensus as virtues in themselves is the result of an inconsistent and/or unprincipled worldview. This essay is dedicated to discussing the first conclusion. The next essay will discuss the second.

By claiming "balance is good for the country," my liberal friend wasn't just being a sore loser. He was claiming that the imposition of his own particular view of "good" should be instituted over and above the will of the people. At the time, the Senate was 50-50 with Vice President Dick Cheney being the tie-breaking vote. That's how the American people had voted. The American people had willed a Republican voting majority in the Senate. This didn't matter for my friend, however, as he believed that the government should reflect his own view of what was "good" for the country rather than what the American people willed—a typical liberal vision for government.

When the "gang of 14" (the group of seven Republicans and seven Democrats who compromised on President Bush's filibustered judicial nominees) effectively ended the filibuster on four of 11 judicial nominees, many praised the agreement as a victory for all American people, and it was heralded as a truly democratic moment with balance and consensus winning the day. Unfortunately, this decision was about as far from democratic as one could get.

In a constitutional Republic like the United States, the people's basic rights are protected by a Constitution. This Constitution also serves as the standard by which legislation is passed and law is interpreted and enforced. It also provides the standard used to amend itself. After such issues and rights have been properly protected, however, the people are the ones who decide "what goes" and what doesn't.

In this case, the people decided to have a Republican majority in the Senate (when the Vice-President's tie-breaking vote was included). To put it another way, the people decided to have a Democratic *minority* in the Senate. Thus, when it came to the Senate, Republicans got to say "what goes" and what doesn't. The Constitution is obvious when it calls for a super-majority. For example, a super-majority is necessary to amend the Constitution. A super-majority, however, is not necessary when approving a president's judicial nominees. It is simply ludicrous to conclude that the "advise and consent" clause regarding presidential judicial nominees calls for a super-majority.

What this means is that elections actually mean something. In 2004 Republicans were elected as the majority. Therefore, they were the ones to say "what goes" (according to Constitutional guidelines . . . and approving judicial nominees falls within those guidelines). For some reason, Democrats thought that because they lost that election, they got to determine "what goes." This was why they were utilizing the filibuster to prevent President Bush's judicial nominees from being approved. Essentially, the minority in the Senate had veto power over the will of the people. Truly a "tyranny of the minority." (Although this wouldn't have been possible if Senate Republicans had the backbone to unite against the Democrats.)

It mattered little to liberals that their party was in the minority. They thought their vision for government was right, and they were willing to force it on the American people. Filibustering judicial nominees is the perfect example of "the end justifying the means." In fact, the general attitude liberals have regarding judicial activism is also reflective of such a notion. Like judicial activism, filibustering judicial nominees is the perfect way to bypass the will of the people.

"Balance" and "consensus" are terms used in the political rhetoric of tyrants and totalitarians. In a free society where basic rights are ensured by a Constitution, balance and consensus rarely rear their heads. Insisting on and enforcing consensus in a constitutional Republic renders elections meaningless . . . a desirable goal, I suppose, for an elitist minority.

Democracy and Consensus, Part 2

Viewing balance and consensus as virtues in themselves is the result of an inconsistent and/or unprincipled worldview. This statement may seem a bit harsh and extreme, but it loses some of its bite when it is unpacked.

In July 2005, Pseudo-Republican Arlen Specter said regarding then-Justice Sandra Day O'Connor's potential replacement (before President Bush nominated Judge John Roberts), "When you have these delicate questions, it's helpful to the country to have somebody who is a swing vote, which maintains the balance." Senator John McCain issued a similar statement. Sentiments such as this are echoed a million times over every day. Balance has become a virtue in itself.

First let me define what I mean by "balance." Balance is a "middle ground" between two opposing sides, i.e., opposing worldviews, ideas, theories, etc. By definition, it contains elements of *both* opposing "sides." The problem arises when balance is attempted between two mutually exclusive worldviews (such as secularism and Judeo-Christian theism, liberalism and conservatism). Balance becoming a virtue in itself leads to forcing together the pieces from two different puzzles . . . even when it's obvious the pieces don't fit together.

My essay entitled "Reality: The Undisputed Champion of the Universe" briefly describes what a worldview is and how it works. The example I used was Marxism—the secular worldview underlying political liberalism. Particular morals, political systems, and policies are the outworking of the presuppositions provided by a worldview. If a worldview is an inaccurate description of reality, its consequences (political systems, public policies, etc.) will be disastrous. Thus it's unwise to implement any particular idea or policy stemming from a faulty worldview.

By definition, the "balanced" coexistence of mutually exclusive worldviews demands that at least one of them (or all of them) be wrong (according to the law of non-contradiction). Therefore, if these mutually exclusive worldviews are combined in the name of "balance," the ideas and policies of at least one faulty worldview are guaranteed to be implemented.

I'm not suggesting society should arbitrarily pick a worldview and "go with it" simply in the hope of getting lucky. I'm saying that those who view "balance" as a virtue in itself are sorely mistaken and destined to build a society based on contradiction and at least one set of false ideas that bring disastrous real-world consequences.

If these "balancers" were to understand that they are trying to force together mutually exclusive worldviews, they would (hopefully) cease pushing their contradictory agenda. If there really is a God and humans do make free moral choices, then any policy (political or otherwise) not based on such presuppositions is destined to fail.

When Sandra Day O'Connor was a swing vote on the Supreme Court, I was much more disappointed in her analytical ability than I was her liberal activist counterparts. At least the liberal activist judges were consistent. O'Connor made a decision one day that reflected her allegiance to one worldview, and she made another decision the next day reflecting an allegiance to another mutually exclusive worldview.

Worldview analysis shows us a logical connection in being, for example, pro-life, pro-capital punishment, supportive of defending private property rights, supportive of a free-market economy, an advocate of a strong national defense, and a supporter of tough criminal sentencing. It's no coincidence that those who are pro-life just happen to be pro-capital punishment, that those who defend a free-market economy also support a strong national defense, and that those who are against gay marriage also believe premarital sex is wrong. These are all consequences of adhering to Judeo-Christian presuppositions.

The next time someone praises or calls for balance and consensus, remember these two essays. Most likely someone is either 1) attempting a power grab via coercion and indoctrination in an effort to bypass the will of the people, or 2) working from an incoherent combination of mutually exclusive worldviews. Either way, the inevitable result is the implementation of disastrous ideas and policies.

"Lord of War"
Right on the Mark . . . if There is Such a Thing

In 2005 I saw the movie "Lord of War" starring Nicolas Cage. Having read several reviews and seen the trailer, I knew what the movie was about. The film, based on true events, is a matter-of-fact, documentary-type tale of a private international arms dealer. As expected, the movie takes a few shots at President Bush and portrays the United States as morally equivalent to the private arms dealer who sells guns to anyone (regardless of the buyer's intentions), cheats on his wife, and has a cocaine addiction. What intrigued me, however, is Yuri Orlov's (Nicholas Cage's character) worldview and resultant lifestyle. Orlov perfectly personifies secularism and its real-world consequences.

Yuri (and his younger brother, Vitaly) was born in the Ukraine, but he manages to escape with his parents to the United States at a young age. In order to escape, his family has to pose as Jews in order to blend in with other Jews who are fleeing Soviet oppression (much of the movie takes place before the fall of the Soviet Union). When the Orlovs arrive in the United States, Yuri's father keeps up the charade in order to maintain legitimacy with the feds. He constantly reads the Hebrew Scriptures and attends synagogue faithfully (which annoys his Catholic wife).

A scene near the beginning of the movie shows Yuri sitting with his brother and parents at the diner they own (Yuri is probably in his late 20s to early 30s at the time). Yuri comments on the hat (which is not a Yarmulke) his father is wearing and asks him why he always wears it. His father responds by saying, "It reminds me that there's something higher than ourselves." Yuri's lack of response is telling.

At Yuri's wedding later in the movie, his new bride (whose family had died years prior) wishes her parents were there to witness the occasion. Yuri replies, "They *are* watching." This provides little comfort for his new bride, however, because she knows he doesn't mean what he says. She responds by saying, "I know you don't believe that." Yuri's lack of response is, once again, telling. She knows as well as Yuri does that he doesn't believe in anything "higher than them," let alone in any kind of afterlife.

At one point Yuri even tries to live a non-criminal lifestyle (at the behest of his wife). It lasts about six months. He decides he can't fight who he really is. During the narration (Yuri narrates the entire movie), he discusses this inner battle. He mentions that several months into development, a fetus still has the tail of a reptile. Evolution, he says, makes us who we are. Yuri says, "When you fight biology, you always lose." Yuri couldn't "go straight," because his biology, not his own free will, determined his actions. His morally reprehensible decisions and actions were the result of the same universal physical laws that require an apple to fall from a tree. This is secularism to the core.

From a philosophical standpoint, Yuri can be called several things; among them are secularist, naturalist, Darwinian evolutionist, materialist, and atheist. The point is, however, that Yuri lives and thinks according to a completely secular worldview . . . and he should be commended for doing so consistently. Yuri may be many things (an adulterer, drug addict, murderer, etc.), but a hypocrite he is not.

Without an objective foundation for moral reality, there can be no right and wrong. There's no moral or ethical difference between the evil dictator who violently murders women and children and the inner city social worker who dedicates her life mentoring poverty-stricken children. None. Any secularist who tells you otherwise is spouting incoherent drivel that is inconsistent with his own worldview. This includes secular moralists who defend animal rights or protest the destruction of the rain forests, defend "reproductive choice," complain about America's human rights violations overseas and here at home, rail against the injustices of big business, claim it is our moral responsibility to educate our children or provide a "livable wage" to workers, claim we should help the poor, wish to make condoms and morning-after pills available to teenagers because it is the moral thing to do, etc.

Socrates, the ancient Greek philosopher, said, "The unexamined life is not worth living." But for the secularist, as James Sire notes in his book, *The Universe Next Door*, it is only the *unexamined* life that is worth living.[3] Consistent secularists are hard to find. Have you ever encountered someone who actually believes there is no moral difference between Adolph Hitler and Mother Teresa? In other words, have you ever met a consistent secularist? If you have, you were probably on a college campus somewhere. It is usually there where the morality "written on our hearts" is finally exorcized.

Yuri Orlov is a prime example of a consistent secularist. The climax of the movie takes place in an African country where Yuri and his brother, Vitaly, are about to sell two truckloads of weapons to a general. While Yuri is negotiating the deal, Vitaly wanders around and notices a small village of people living in tents about fifty yards away. A child (probably around ten years of age) wanders too far away from his mother and is then chased by three men with machetes. In an attempt to save her son, the mother chases after him. The three men with machetes proceed to hack the mother and son to death. Vitaly sees this and, struck by a moment of moral clarity, interrupts Yuri's negotiations to privately inform him of the situation.

Vitaly explains to Yuri what just happened and tells him that as soon as they sell the weapons to the general, they will be used to slaughter the villagers below. The hacked-up bodies of the mother and son are plainly seen

---

3. Sire, *The Universe Next Door*, 90.

by Yuri. After a few moments of rationalizing, Yuri seemingly convinces his brother that it's not their problem and returns to negotiating the deal.

Yuri's conclusion was the *only possible logical conclusion for the consistent secularist*. Of course, assuming his biology would let him, Yuri could have refused to sell the guns to the general. *But it wouldn't have been because it was the right thing to do.* In secularist thought, nothing is "out there" to keep Yuri from cheating on his wife, sniffing cocaine, selling weapons to an evil dictator, or hacking up a mother and her child with a machete. Secular epistemology precludes "out-thereness." It may be able to tell us what *is*, but, according to its own presuppositions, it can never tell us what *ought to be*.

The conclusion is this: Anyone who does not believe in a Creator-God cannot believe in the existence of right and wrong. This is why secular worldviews have disastrous consequences. This is why secular politics are so dangerous. The quintessential secular political ideology, Marxism, is itself responsible for over one hundred million murders in the twentieth century alone. Should this surprise us? With nothing "out there," with no foundation for right and wrong, if physical "stuff" is all that exists, why should anyone care about anyone else? After all, "it's not our problem." And why should anyone be held responsible for his actions? After all, "If you fight biology, you always lose."

Ideas have consequences. Secular premises lead to secular conclusions. Yuri Orlov is the perfect example of a consistent secularist. "Lord of War" is right on the mark . . . if there is such a thing.

Superman Returns with the Same Ol' Humanism

Having seen the previews for *Superman Returns*, I knew this movie had potential for an intriguing essay. After seeing the movie, I must say that my original intuition was correct. *Superman Returns* offers plenty of opportunity for philosophical, social, and political commentary.

One preview was so thick with messianic overtones, that a comparison to Christ is unavoidable. Jor-El, Superman's father, makes the comment that he sent his "only son" (Kal-El is Superman's, a.k.a. Clark Kent's, original name) to Earth for the purpose of showing humans the way. Add to this the fact that "El" is a form of the Hebrew term for *God*, and the messianic overtones become even more obvious. The messianic message of *Superman Returns*, however, is very different from the messianic message offered in biblical Christianity. The difference? *Superman Returns* offers humanist *liberation* rather than divine *redemption*.

Because (secular) humanists do not believe in God or the divine, there is no such thing as sin. The Christian concept of sin as disobedience to God and his will is absent in the humanist worldview. Thus, the moral codes offered by Christianity (and other religions) that are based on God's character are mere fabrications constructed by humanity.

Also rejected by humanists is the Christian explanation for the fall of mankind. According to Christianity, evil and suffering were brought about by disobeying God. This disobedience brought sin into both the world and human hearts (which accounts for our "sinful nature") and has had disastrous consequences ever since. Thus, the ills of this world are caused by *immorality*—by our own decision to reject God and his moral code, in favor of a fragmented autonomy; in other words, by our attempt to become gods ourselves. Humans are sinful and, as such, must be separated from the holy God, the Creator of the universe. *That's* our problem. Thus, redemption is needed.

Therefore, salvation resides in having human sin removed (and redirecting sin's punishment from the sinner to Christ), thus allowing reconciliation between a newly pure humanity and a holy God. Humans must be *redeemed*, not *liberated*. It is impossible for any human or group of humans to provide others with salvation, because every human has sinned. Thus, salvation must be offered by the divine, because humans cannot save themselves. Christianity teaches that this was done through Christ's death on the cross (by serving as the punishment for sin and sanctifying those who accept his vicarious atonement).

Humanism, on the other hand, claims the ills of the world are caused by ignorance rather than sin and immorality. Because humans do not have a sinful nature and there is no God to which man needs to be reconciled, redemption isn't necessary. Humans should be capable of overcoming the ills of the world all by themselves. For humans to achieve salvation, they only need to possess knowledge of *how*. Thus, salvation (however one defines it; usually it is considered some version of a social utopia) is within the grasp of humanity. No divine help is necessary.

Humanists believe the human faculty of reason has the ability to unite all humanity under a common goal *and* enable universal agreement on *how* to achieve that goal.[4] The utilization of reason in the pursuit of knowledge will eventually lead to secular salvation, because the accumu-

---

4. To see why this is a gross misinterpretation of the role of reason, see my essay, "No Ruts, No Glory."

lation of knowledge alleviates ignorance, which is the original cause of the world's ills. (Notice how this parallels Gnostic mythology.) In short, humans need only be enlightened (or "educated") to achieve salvation.

According to Jor-El (the alien from Krypton who sent his "only son" to Earth to save humanity), this enlightenment is *exactly* why he sent Kal-El to Earth. Jor-El says, "Even though you've been raised as a human being, you're not one of them. They can be a great people, Kal-El, if they wish to be. They only lack the light to show the way. For this reason above all, their capacity for good, I have sent them you . . . my only son."

The most common metaphor for salvific knowledge is "light" (a favorite term of the gnostics as well). Combined with humanity's good nature, salvific knowledge will necessarily lead to salvation. Humanism's (faulty) assumption is that humans will always use knowledge for good. After all, if we have a good nature, our actions will reflect it. Thus, a major step toward secular salvation is acquiring knowledge that debunks all belief systems (especially Judeo-Christian theism) that claim humans have a sinful nature.

Jor-El said humans "*only* lack the light." (Emphasis added.) All humans need is knowledge gained through either reason or experience. He believes humans have the potential to save themselves without divine aid. This is the essence of secular humanism. Humanist messiahs *show* the way. The Christian Messiah *is* the way. Humanism requires a *liberator*. Christianity requires a *savior*. Christianity claims that humans are *actually* saved by Christ's death and resurrection. Humanist scholars and liberal Christians, on the other hand, believe Christ's life *shows* the way (because secularists don't believe in the divinity of Christ or his resurrection). In secular humanism, the non-divine Jesus and his life offer knowledge usable by humans to fulfill their own salvific potential. In Christianity, Christ's vicarious death and resurrection provide salvation, because they are the bridge between an unholy (i.e., sinful, immoral) people and the holy God.

Superman Returns offers the proverbial "icing on the cake" by including the socialist tendencies that always follow in humanism's footsteps. The antagonist's (Lex Luther's) evil plot is to manipulate alien crystal technology to create new land that only he would own. This new land would begin in the ocean and grow outward, destroying all the current land in existence (and killing billions in the process). Eventually, anyone who wanted or needed land would have to come to Lex Luther to get it. Thus, the evil in *Superman Returns* is private property. Just as in the first Superman movie, Lex Luther's dastardly plot is based on the evils of private property and capitalism. Once again, an oppressive system is to blame. How original.

But does all this make sense when we consider that Lex Luther is a genius? He is as smart as they come. He is precisely the type of person humanism wishes to create—a person who has gained as much knowledge as possible. This knowledge, combined with the person's good nature, will inevitably lead to attempts to create a social utopia. If this is the case, why is Lex Luther evil?

If you'll remember, a major step in achieving humanist salvation is debunking all belief systems that claim humans do not have an inherently good nature (and those that claim humanity needs divine help to be saved). If people subscribe to the idea that humans are not inherently good, they will act accordingly, i.e., not good. Public Enemy Number One, which teaches that humans have a sinful nature, is Christianity. Therefore, a major step toward secular salvation is debunking Christianity *and* all its subsidiary beliefs based upon Christian presuppositions (such as objective moral codes—because they hinder freedom). And guess which economic system is based on Judeo-Christian presuppositions? That's right—capitalism.[5] Lex Luther represents an unenlightened capitalist whose behavior is tainted by a belief system that claims humans do not have an inherently good nature. Put another way, Lex Luther represents the Judeo-Christian worldview.

The ironic part of the story, however, is found in how Superman and Lex Luther view themselves. At one point in the movie, Luther cites the story of Prometheus. Prometheus was a god who stole fire from the gods and gave it to humans. Before being gifted with fire, humans lived miserable lives because they were kept in ignorance of the possibilities of human civilization. The god Zeus intentionally kept humans in this state of ignorance and condemned Prometheus for providing the Earth with fire. Once humans received the gift of fire, however, human civilization skyrocketed. Humans were no longer miserable, because they utilized their newly found knowledge to achieve a kind of salvation. By providing humans with a piece of knowledge, Prometheus had unlocked the vast potential that humans have within to save themselves.

---

5. This is a primary reason why the communist and Islamic worlds equate the threat of Christianity with the threat of capitalism. Christianity is rejected in many parts of the world because capitalism is never long to follow in Christianity's footsteps. For example, many communist countries couldn't care less about the religious aspects of Christianity. But because capitalism follows wherever Christianity goes, the prohibition of Christianity is motivated by political and economic concerns.

Lex Luther claims he is going to come up with a technology that he will share with the world (the aforementioned land-creating crystal technology). Luther's girlfriend then asks him if he wants to be a god. Luther responds by saying something to the effect of, "Gods are capricious. They fly around in red capes and keep their powers to themselves." Luther is condemning Superman by comparing him to Zeus. Luther sees himself as a modern-day Prometheus.

This is ironic, because Superman (and his father) also sees himself as a Promethean liberator. Superman himself does not actually save humanity. As Jor-El instructed his son, humans "only" need to be *shown* the way (the role of a *liberator*), not *given* the way (the role of a *redeemer*). Humans have within themselves the capacity for salvation.

Both Superman and Lex Luther are trying to bring humanist Promethean salvation to humanity. Lex Luther is brainwashed by the ideas of private property and capitalism. Thus, he goes astray. Superman, on the other hand, wants to bring salvific light to humanity and is not corrupted by capitalism, private property, or their Judeo-Christian foundation. Luther brings oppression under the foot of Judeo-Christian beliefs. Superman brings freedom on the wings of humanism.

The term "savior" is used throughout the movie. But this is inaccurate nomenclature. Superman doesn't see himself as a savior. He sees himself as a liberator—setting humans free from the bonds of the ignorance peddled by Judeo-Christian capitalists like Lex Luther.

Freedom from Consequences? Not Likely.

The debate regarding the safety of the RU-486 pill caused me to wonder why liberals are against telling the truth about the pill. The fact is, the pill isn't exactly the safest drug in the world. Many women have died from taking it, and many others have suffered dangerous and painful side effects. There are many doctors who testify to these facts. Yet liberals don't want such information to be disseminated, nor do they think there should even be a discussion about it. (Of course, the existence of side effects doesn't necessarily preclude approved by the FDA. The issue is the fact that liberals want the entire discussion suppressed—or day I say, *censored*.)

Pro-abortionists are so passionate to get their agenda (abortion on-demand) forced on the American people, they don't care what it takes. The RU-486 drug is a major step in meeting their abortion-on-demand objectives. Who cares if a few women suffer and/or die? After all, some collateral damage should be expected in war.

The modern notion of freedom is defined by the ability to do whatever one wants, whenever one wants, and with absolutely no hindrances. Such hindrances may include familial expectations, social taboos, repressive laws, cumbersome religious dogma, or any kind of discrimination. Liberals are doing their best to clear the way for such freedom by deconstructing the family, religion, social taboos, and the church. They are also succeeding through local, state, and federal legislation that is freeing individuals from all responsibility for their actions. And let's not forget they've come up with more forms of "discrimination" than I can recall at the moment.

The barriers to this form of freedom that have been the hardest to remove, however, are *consequences*, i.e., the consequences of a particular action or behavior. Unlike familial, social, and religious expectations that serve to *deter* such behavior through prevention, consequences occur *after* such behavior has occurred (thus they serve as a different type of deterrence). Liberals have been relatively successful in clearing the way for the acceptance of sexual "freedom" (read: premarital sex, sexual promiscuity, etc.) by removing the social taboos, discriminatory laws, familial expectations, and cumbersome religious rules that deter such behavior beforehand. Removing the *consequences* of sexual promiscuity, however, has proven to be a more difficult task.

No matter how hard they try, liberals cannot *completely* remove the real-world consequences of sexual promiscuity—consequences such as sexually transmitted diseases, emotional trauma, broken relationships, feelings of guilt and shame, pregnancy, etc. But this doesn't prevent them from trying.

Feelings of guilt and shame must be removed by changing the values of a culture. Removing God, parental authority, and objective morality are steps toward making the individual the measure of all things. For someone to feel guilt or shame, he must be guilty of violating some external standard such as God's will, parental expectations, etc. If there is no external standard, then there's no reason to feel guilt or shame.

Emotional trauma is removed in a similar way, but because humans are created in the image of God, it is difficult to manipulate the human psyche. Unfortunately, many (especially young girls) are forced to deal with such emotional trauma on their own; the liberal establishment has convinced them that the *only* consequences of premarital sex and sexual promiscuity are *physical*—consequences they are assured will be prevented if they simply engage in "safe sex." The secular world approaches sex from a purely physical and materialistic perspective (which their worldview demands), and this leaves young people in shock when they realize that sex is much more.

Pregnancy spent centuries as the top-ranking consequence that deterred people (mostly women) from sexually promiscuous behavior. The widespread availability of abortion, however, has been the left's attempt to nullify pregnancy as a consequence. Secularists (especially secular humanists) believe humans have the ability to save themselves (create the perfect society) through reason and experience (empirical science). Thus, progress is found in increased knowledge and scientific research.

Technological advancement is a key component toward such a secular salvation. This is why the *Humanist Manifesto II* claims society should resist any attempt to censor scientific research based on moral, political, or social grounds. Scientific "progress" such as abortion allows humans to become "free," because the consequences of certain behavior (the negative consequences that seem to suggest such behavior is inappropriate, impractical, or—dare I say—wrong) are removed.

The problem is that God's character is woven into the fabric of the universe, and his character includes a moral dimension. Just as there are consequences to breaking (trying to break, at least) or ignoring the physical laws of the universe, there are consequences to breaking the *moral* laws of the universe as well. No matter how hard liberalism tries to alleviate the consequences that naturally arise from immoral behavior, it will fail.

For true progress to occur, modern liberalism must change its definition of "freedom." Freedom isn't the unencumbered ability to do whatever one wants whenever one wants. It is the alignment of our will with the *external* standard woven into the fabric of the universe—in short, the alignment of our will with God's will. Only then can we fully achieve the purpose for which we were created—a purpose known and revealed to us by our Creator.

Gay Marriage, Social Contract, and Freedom—Part 1

There has been widespread acceptance of legislation that defines marriage as a sacred institution between one man and one woman. This puts liberals in an awkward position. Once again, their actual position on the issue is so far from the mainstream opinion of the citizenry that honesty isn't an option. As with most of their positions—such as abortion on-demand, high taxes, and pacifist foreign policy—full disclosure of their wish to destroy the traditional family would spell doom at the ballot box.

For this reason, liberals must couch their opposition to the traditional marriage amendment in terms the citizenry won't recognize as radically leftist (and secular). The most popular tactic (especially popular among pseudo-Republicans like Senators Arlen Specter and John McCain) is the phrase, "I believe marriage is a sacred institution between one man and one woman, but I think states should be the ones to decide." Concern for letting "the people" decide the outcome should be alleviated, considering it takes two-thirds of the House and two-thirds of the Senate (two bodies elected directly by "the people") to pass an amendment—in addition to three-fourths of state governors (who are also elected directly by the people).

When liberals use the phrase, they are attempting to label conservatives (who usually oppose federal government and its encroachments) as hypocrites. Liberals claim conservative politicians are merely pandering to their far-right base for political gain. This seemingly explains why a group who usually supports state's rights abandons that value when it comes to this amendment.

In short, liberals claim conservatives are making up this issue out of thin air in an attempt to win votes. Conservatives, on the other hand, claim there is no contradiction between their formally espoused conservatism, which values state's rights, and their current support of the traditional marriage amendment. What liberals don't understand (or refuse to acknowledge) is that conservatives would *love* to put this issue in the hands of the states. In fact, over the last few years alone, 19 states have amended their constitutions with similar amendments.

The problem is that liberal activist judges are taking the issue away from the states by unilaterally overturning such amendments and legislation. The states *are* trying to handle this issue on their own. Unfortunately, no state amendment or piece of legislation is outside the reach of activist judges who use the bench to force the leftist agenda down the people's throat. Short of getting new judges who actually respect the Constitution, the only way to stop them is to pass a constitutional amendment. (Notice the judiciary has absolutely no role in passing a constitutional amendment. This perfectly illustrates how the founding fathers intended the judiciary to be *subservient* to the Constitution—not rewrite it.)

Liberals oppose taking the issue to the people, because that would deal their leftist agenda a death blow. Judging from past attempts, there is no way the citizenry would actually freely adopt the leftist agenda. This is why liberals refuse to let the abortion issue be decided by the people. If the people and the states were to decide, most forms of abortion would become illegal. This is also why liberals spend a great deal of time, energy, and money keeping the abortion issue in the courts. They're the only hope to keeping abortion on-demand legal.

Liberals who believe this issue ought to be "left to the states to decide" are either utilizing a foreign ideology to better package their leftist desire to destroy the family, or they are conveniently forgetting that they never use such a standard when it comes to their socialist economic policies.

Liberals are attempting to neutralize the gay marriage debate through two primary arguments: 1) Claiming there is no threat to traditional marriage from activist judges, and 2) Citing polls that suggest the gay marriage issue isn't anywhere in the top 10 when it comes to issues of interest for Americans. Another form of the second argument comes in the question, "Why should we spend so much time debating this issue when Iraq is a mess, Iran has nukes, and our country is losing jobs to outsourcing?"

The first argument is patently wrong. In fact, a judge has already overturned Nebraska's constitutional amendment protecting marriage. Also, the National Protection of Marriage Act signed into law under President Bill Clinton was conveniently brushed aside in 2006 when the Massachusetts Supreme Court overturned a state law reserving marriage for one man and one woman. That state's high court then commanded its legislature to pass a law legalizing gay marriage—and gave them a deadline by which to do it! What ever happened to the separation of powers?

The second argument is a red herring. What is the Senate supposed to do if not consider the issues and legislation of the day? Also, where was this concern when Senate Democrats were filibustering so many of Bush's judicial nominees?

Don't buy the facade. For all the reasons liberals offer to explain why they oppose the traditional marriage amendment, only one is true. The destruction of the traditional family is a major priority of the leftist agenda.

Gay Marriage, Social Contract and Freedom—Part 2

I concluded the preceding essay by claiming that the destruction of the traditional family is a major priority in the leftist agenda. Why is this the case? What is the origin of the left's passion against the traditional family? As usual, I claim it is a direct consequence of a particular set of ideas; namely, ideas that lead to a particular definition of *freedom*.

Social Contract Theory (SCT) is a theory that has had widespread influence the last three hundred or so years. It has influenced the ideology of leaders, the formation of governments, and countless cultures. At its core,

SCT views a man (all humans) as a completely autonomous individual, disconnected from anyone or anything around him. At some point in the past, before the emergence of civilization and its rules and regulations, humans lived in an uninhibited "state of nature," wherein each autonomous individual was *free* to pursue his own selfish desires.

As one might guess, this didn't make for long and prosperous lives, because everyone went around killing one another in the name of selfish fulfillment. There was no objective moral code to infuse inherent value into anyone other than yourself. Thus, other individuals were merely pawns to manipulate on your way to fulfilling selfish desires. Of course, when manipulation failed, simply killing the other person was usually most expedient.

We existed in this "state of nature" until someone deduced that we could all realize our selfish desires more *efficiently* if we agreed on some ground rules. (As English philosopher Thomas Hobbes stated, life in the "state of nature" was "brutish" and "short.") Thus, human civilization was born. Moral codes as well as cultural mores, taboos, and institutions were constructed as ground rules that provided a more "civilized" environment in which to pursue personal interests. Basically, human civilization merely served to prevent everyone from killing one another. After all, a dead someone isn't someone who can fulfill selfish desires. Thus, humans entered into a social "contract" with one another to abide by the rules of civilization.

One obvious ramification of this theory is the conclusion that the institutions and moral claims of civilization are not objectively true. They are man-made constructions meant to facilitate the realization of individual selfish fulfillment. The Ten Commandments, for example, are not considered timeless truths by which humanity should strive to live. They are situational rules at the mercy of their human creators who may dispose of them if they cease to serve as effective catalysts for selfish individual fulfillment. The family is not an institution established by God and written into the moral fabric of the universe. The family instead is a means to an end—a relationship (or set of relationships) that may be disposed of if it interferes with an individual's selfish fulfillment.

It is vital to notice that while civilization was created, the *goal* or *purpose* for humanity remained the same: selfish individual fulfillment. Therefore, every set of moral codes, social taboos, and cultural institutions must be interpreted through the lens of autonomous individuality. If a moral code, social taboo, or cultural institution begins to inhibit selfish fulfillment rather than promote it, it is no longer serving its purpose and must be thrown out. Instead of being a conduit to "freedom" (which comes to be defined as autonomous selfish fulfillment—a definition directly resulting from the view that humans are essentially autonomous individuals disconnected from everyone and everything), it becomes the tool of oppression, because it hinders individual selfish fulfillment.

Jean-Jacques Rousseau, Genevan philosopher, said "Man is born free, yet everywhere in chains." He wasn't saying humans were literally bound by chains. He was claiming a person is born in a "state of nature" and then, as the child grows into an adult, forced to live according to the rules and institutions of civilization. Instead of promoting freedom, moral codes such as the Ten Commandments and institutions such as marriage, the family, and the church now inhibit a person's freedom.

Therefore, such moral codes and institutions must either be eliminated altogether or, as modern liberalism attempts, gradually be redefined in a process leading to eventual elimination. Unfortunately for modern liberalism, its goal of moral and institutional elimination would utterly fail at the ballot box for two reasons: 1) Humans, in reality, are not essentially autonomous individuals disconnected from others, but rather they are creatures made to be in a relationship with God and with others. Moral codes and institutions such as marriage and the family are objective realities that reflect such a nature. 2) The Christian principles/presuppositions so dominant throughout our nation's history (until recently) haven't been completely exorcized from American culture . . . *yet*.

For these two reasons, modern liberals must utilize the strategy of gradual redefinition. Attacking the institutions of marriage and family directly would be political suicide; therefore, their definitions must be altered. No longer do marriage and family mean what they used to mean. Marriage is no longer between one man and one woman. It is now defined as a relationship between any two consenting adults (although modern liberalism offers no reason why marriage's definition shouldn't be extended to include multiples partners, children, animals, etc.). Family is no longer defined as a father and mother with a child or children. Its definition is now so open it is almost pointless to use the term. For example, the term "single parent family" used to be an oxymoron. Today, the term "family" is applied to any collection of individuals wishing to appropriate the term, regardless of marriage status, parental status, or lifestyle.

A culture with no belief in objective truth has no basis to judge any behavior or lifestyle as better or worse than any other—no matter how revolting the behavior or dire the consequences. Restricting the application of the terms "marriage" and "family" (and the social benefits attached to them) by narrowly defining them according to religious dogma becomes "discrimination" (another term that has been redefined). Moral relativism renders all definition subjective and, by definition, discriminatory.

This nation's culture has changed because we have adopted an explanation of humanity (SCT—a secular worldview) that necessarily leads to a definition of freedom that cannot be realized unless all moral and social restraints are alleviated. This is why a modern liberal and a Christian conservative both use the term "freedom," yet mean two completely different things. Each has a different view of what humanity is, and that explains why each prescribe a different *purpose* (or meaning) for life. Their respective views on the purpose of life, in turn, lead to completely different definitions of freedom. Then, their respective definitions of freedom necessarily lead to different subsidiary values, policy, legislation, behaviors, and lifestyles.

Now we see *why* the destruction of the family is a major priority in the leftist agenda. Its destruction (along with the destruction of all objective moral codes and institutions) releases the chains inhibiting humans from realizing *true freedom*, which, based on SCT's explanation of humanity, is defined as individual selfish fulfillment. If this sounds similar to postmodernism, it's because it is. Social Contract Theory, postmodernism, and modernism are all worldviews based on secular presuppositions regarding the nature of reality and humanity (materialism). Thus, we should expect to see similarities in their subsidiary claims and real-world consequences.

The structure of American government, however, prevents the left from instituting their agenda, because 1) it's blatantly unconstitutional, and 2) the majority of Americans haven't yet embraced the culture of the leftist elites. The left, therefore, must either force their culture on the people through undemocratic methods (exploiting education and the judiciary) or be deceptive about their agenda through gradual redefinition and re-education (accomplished through political rhetoric and public education).

Abortion: Ethical Rapprochement and Legal Contradictions

Laws are interesting phenomena, because they both reflect and influence the values of a citizenry. In light of this observation, contradictory laws are telling because they clue us into an ethical haziness present in the culture. Case in point: The legality of abortion (even up to the point of actual birth) compared to laws that prescribe punishment for those who harm a fetus in the mother's womb, whether such harm is purposeful or inadvertent. What do such contradictory laws tell us about our values?

Abortion used to be illegal because there was widespread acceptance of the presupposition that a human being comes into existence at conception and is thus deserving of legal protection. Human life in itself was valued, because such a value existed externally—i.e., society held to the objective truth that each and every human being is valuable regardless of one's own personal value system. When such a value is universally acknowledged as true for everyone, it is often codified into law.

The codification of a value into law is a process impossible without appeal to the transcendent nature of the value in question. Otherwise, the value never rises to the level of universal application to all times, in all places, and for all people. In the case of abortion, when the culture no longer ascribed to the transcendent and universal nature of individual human value, the law that reflected such a value was taken off the books (although, in the case of abortion, this was accomplished by judicial *fiat* rather than via the people).

Curiously, however, there still exists laws protecting the fetus from certain criminal acts—be they accidental or purposeful. How can the existence of such laws be explained? They can be explained in two ways. 1) They are laws created and promoted by pro-lifers who still hold to the transcendent nature of individual human value; or 2) they are laws reflecting subjective values legitimated by the individuals who construct them rather than an appeal to objective transcendence.

The second explanation is illustrated in the relativistic, postmodern claim that "values are what we make them to be." Every individual is free to define for himself what is right and wrong and how one should live. What is right for one person may not be right for another. Each individual is free to construct an entire value system based upon his own personal standard. Values no longer carry with them the connotation of transcendence, nor are they universally applicable to all people, in all places, at all times.

Thus, a new definition of freedom is born. The new definition of freedom means being completely unencumbered by anything (or anyone) external to the self. Not only does the self prioritize its own values into a kind of hierarchy, but such personally constructed values are also projected onto external reality. The self becomes the measure of all things—internally *and* externally.

The problem with secular ethics is that the denial of the transcendent renders culture (societies, etc.) incapable of condemning subjectively constructed ethical systems that bring about monumental disaster, e.g., Nazism, communism, genocide, etc. No backdrop exists that allows cross-ethical comparison. For example, a secularist cannot claim there is an objective ethical difference between Charles Manson and Charles Spurgeon.

Without appeal to the transcendent, the value a person places on something external to himself cannot be challenged. For example, you may value the family dog and, therefore, project worth into Fido; but that doesn't mean Fido *actually possesses* inherent worth. Because of this, you have no recourse against *my* personal value regarding the family dog—which, by the way, projects *no* worth into Fido.

Therefore, you have no grounds upon which to protest the fact that I choose to physically torture Fido. Only if Fido has inherent and objective worth that is external to our respective selves—a value not contingent upon subjectively created values (such as whether you or I choose to believe for ourselves that Fido has value)—can my act of physical torture be considered morally repugnant . . . which brings us back to our example of contradictory abortion laws.

Ask yourself: What is the *real, actual* difference between a fetus who is aborted in a community clinic and a fetus accidentally terminated when a woman, for example, is assaulted and robbed at gunpoint (or a fetus terminated by an angry and physically abusive boyfriend who wants the mother to have an abortion but refuses)? The answer? From a biological and ontological standpoint, absolutely nothing.

Yet, according to American law, the former has absolutely no rights whatsoever—leaving "it" legally susceptible to horrendous tortures (the details of which I will spare you) while the latter is protected by laws that punish those who would do him harm. In short, the former has no rights, while the latter has a right to life, liberty, and the pursuit of happiness. Why is this?

The difference between the rights of the respective fetuses lies in the value projected on each from an external values-builder, i.e., the mother. The only difference between the two is the fact that the mother getting the abortion projects no value onto "her" (as if it's possible to own another human being) fetus, while the mother whose fetus is harmed during a crime *does* project value onto "her" fetus. The value of the unborn human being is completely contingent upon the arbitrary value system imposed on "it" by the person with power—i.e., the mother. Without a belief in the transcendent and supernatural-based claim that humans have inherent value, the ruled will always be defined by the value assigned them by the ruler.

Secular and postmodern ethics results in those having power forcing their values onto those not in power (in this case, the mother over the unborn—but it is easy to extrapolate this relationship to other groups as well). "Might makes right" when there exists no possible rapprochement between conflicting value systems. When this occurs, the values represented by those in power constitute the ethical hegemony forced on the citizenry as a whole.

As Friedrich Nietzsche said, when God is killed, there will exist an ethical vacuum that must be filled. Whatever (or whoever) fills this vacuum wields unchecked power. We've seen the disastrous consequences when people like Hitler, Stalin, Pol Pot (no doubt well familiar with Nietzsche's ideas) and their secular ideologies fill this vacuum. Of course, Christians are not perfect either.

The difference, however, is that Judeo-Christian theism has the intellectual grounds for opposing disastrous value systems. Judeo-Christian theism provides a basis for moral dialogue. Secularism, *by definition*, stymies debate before it even gets started. Instead of being a rational debate, secular "dialogue" is reduced to a power grab (usually resulting in death camps, gulags, prisons full of the innocent, mass graves, and torture chambers). To the powerful go the spoils.

No demographic is more innocent and more vulnerable than the unborn. Because of this, the unborn are the most susceptible of any to the tyrannies of personally constructed value systems. Remember this the next time a liberal claims to be "standing up for the little guy."

Strength in Diversity? Not Likely.

The new addition to my Bumper Sticker Hall of Shame is the phrase "Strength in Diversity." Together with the phrase, "War Is Never the Answer," these two liberal battle cries are like nails on a chalkboard for me. The novel, arbitrary, noble-sounding ideas that modern liberalism considers virtuous are an interesting collection of misplaced half-thoughts; more often than not, they are self-referentially incoherent and extremely dangerous for humanity.

So often, modern liberalism takes a particular aspect of the legitimate worldview (Judeo-Christian theism) and elevates it as its own cause—a fundamental ideal that becomes an end in itself. This happens when basic foundational principles (objective truth) are rejected. In the grand scheme of things, diversity has its proper place; but on its own, disconnected from its function as part of a greater metaphysical objective truth, it ceases to be a virtue and becomes a false god whose arbitrary decisions have disastrous consequences for humanity.

Richard Weaver wrote in *Visions of Order*,

> What was a whole ceases to feel its reason for being a whole, and the different parts may suffer a random distortion—random just because there is no longer a unifying idea to prescribe fitness and size. Parts then get out of line and begin to usurp the places and roles belonging to other parts. This is the chaos that the true friend of culture beholds with deepest apprehension, not only because it deprives him of so much but because in the masses it can induce monstrous outbursts of irrationality.[6]

Without a unifying vision, the foundation of which is objective truth, diversity will become an irrational end in itself rather than a natural consequence of embracing the transcendent fact that humans have inherent value. Weaver writes that such observations (which include the fascist movements of Europe in the mid-twentieth century) "remind us that if no reasonable cultural unification is offered, an unreasonable one may be invented and carried to frightful lengths."[7]

C. S. Lewis takes a slightly different approach when he discusses this issue in his book, *Abolition of Man*. He labels universal, objective truth as the "Tao." Lewis claims that many ideologies adopt a particular aspect of the Tao and elevate it to ultimate superiority while rejecting the overall concept of the Tao. To Lewis, this is impossible. Once the Tao itself is rejected, the rug is pulled out from under all of its particulars, i.e. subsidiary claims.

For example, diversity is an ideal based upon the Judeo-Christian premise that human beings have inherent value (in virtue of the fact they are created in the image of God). Diversity is the logical outworking of respecting this inherent value in another human being. This presupposition demands that the individual's value be honored—regardless of race, religion or political persuasion. Thus, diversity is the presence of differing subsidiary beliefs in a society that agrees on the basic presupposition that individuals have inherent value. This does *not* mean that every subsidiary belief is correct or morally acceptable. It only means that the individual holding the belief has value. The possibility of legitimate diversity is removed, however, once the idea of *imago dei* is "cut out" of a worldview.

Within the context of the proper overarching, objective metaphysic (Judeo-Christian theism including the notion of *imago dei*), diversity is a virtuous *consequence*. Separated from its legitimate cause, however, diversity becomes "might makes right" tribalism where every belief is held as equally true and morally acceptable. Diversity (feel free to substitute

---

6. Weaver, *Visions of Order*, 13
7. Ibid., 13–14

in the word "tolerance") cannot survive as a virtue in itself. An effect will disappear if its cause is removed.

This is why, when we observe history, successful movements do not have diversity as their foundation. It is unity that breeds successful movements. The civil rights movement has been a success because diverse individuals rallied around a *common* ideal and acted on it to create a preferred future. The same thing happened during World War I and World War II (*any* successfully fought war for that matter). It wasn't the *differences* in our citizenry that led to the fortitude that defeated the Axis powers. It was the ideal of freedom *common* among diverse groups of people that united the forces of freedom.

Perhaps the most cogent examples are the founding fathers of the United States of America. The differences among the members of the Continental Congress were as deep and controversial as ours are today. Federalism, anti-federalism, loyalism, anti-loyalism, slavery, and a host of other issues deeply divided many early Americans. But it was the uniting ideals penned in the Declaration of Independence that brought together a diverse population to declare independence from the greatest world power at the time.

Our founding fathers concluded the Declaration with the words: "And for the support of this Declaration, with a firm reliance on the protection of divine Providence, we mutually pledge to each other our Lives, our Fortunes and our sacred Honor." The significance of such a declaration cannot be understated. These men and the individuals they represented were willing to sacrifice all of their earthly pleasures, property, lives, and honor for a common vision. Ladies and gentlemen, diversity does *not* create such a fervor. Common, uniting goals do. Diversity was put aside in the name of a vision common among those who believed in objective truth.

There is no such thing as "strength in diversity." Diversity is a side effect of *common* values, not diverse ones. The different branches of a tree grow from the same trunk. Remove the trunk, and the peaceful co-existence of its limbs disappears. Remove belief in the objective truth-claim that individuals have inherent value guaranteed by God, and the peaceful co-existence of diverse belief systems degenerates into postmodern "might makes right" tribalism.

Secularism's Need for Revisionist History

Have you ever wondered why revisionist history is so popular these days? The "de-religioning" of American history is an attempt to revitalize the secular enlightenment premise that the abolition of religious influence in society will lead to the decline of oppression and the inauguration of true freedom—a premise proved false by history itself.

Secular worldviews are rarely indifferent toward religion. More often than not, they view religion as either the cause of societal ills or an irrational response of those experiencing oppression. Either way, the alleviation of religion is good for society, either because it removes the major barrier to freedom or because it enlightens those who are experiencing oppression, which is the first step in reversing their fortunes.

Common to all secular worldviews is the assertion that religion is not healthy for society. A just, free society is attainable through purely secular means and the faculty of reason alone. Unfortunately for secularists, history is not on their side.

The fact is that religion played a vital role in the founding and establishment of the United States of America. The books, papers, and articles proving this fact are too voluminous to mention here. However, as this is an essay on the *motivation* behind revisionist history and not the case against its historicity, I need not beat a dead horse (or, at least, a horse that *should* be dead).

The underlying premise behind the motivation for revisionist history is the claim that the United States is a good thing (much to the chagrin of blame-America-first liberals). It is better for the United States to exist than not exist. Thus, if the United States is a good thing, it is a worthwhile endeavor to discover why and how it came to be. Perhaps there is something about the foundation and history of such a good nation that can be used as a standard for present and future culture and policy.

As a worldview, secularism predicts that secular philosophy rather than religion would be responsible for such a good society (because, according to secularism, religion prevents a good society from forming). The premises of secularism dictate this prediction. But, alas, upon historical inquiry, this is not found to be the case.

The secularist now has a problem. If the goal is to inculcate each succeeding generation with secular philosophy, it would be counterproductive to teach accurate American history, because it contradicts secularism's premises. If accurate American history is taught, many students may perceive the disconnect between how secularism claims the world works and how the world actually does work. Hence the need for a history that supports secularism's premises—a "de-Christianized" American history.

The transformation of religious American history to secular American history is a major coup for secularists who wish to proselytize the next generation of Americans. After all, a major step in realizing the liberal, socialist utopia is the removal of religion as a major influence in society. If people can be convinced that the foundation of good culture and policy is secularism, then the need for religion to be given a seat at the table of discussion (i.e., the free marketplace of ideas) is removed. Religion then becomes a private matter for those misguided few who have an inaccurate, nostalgic view of American history. Religion then becomes something that can be tolerated (because of that little, old, annoying Constitution), as long as it's not brought in to the public forum.

The case for secularism is severely damaged if, on the other hand, history teaches that the good society is based on transcendent moral truths—claims grounded in traditional religion. Throw in the 100 million murders in the twentieth century alone that were committed in the name of secular ideologies, and secularism *really* has an uphill battle to be convincing in the free marketplace of ideas.

Remember this the next time your child's history book emphasizes the sins of our founding fathers or diminishes the role of religion in the lives of those who formed our Republic. Obviously, not every founder was a saint nor even, perhaps, an orthodox Christian (although most of them were), but it is nonetheless historically accurate to state that the common public philosophy of the colonists and founding fathers claimed freedom and democracy were based on transcendent moral truths provided by the Judeo-Christian worldview.

Materialism Bad, Materialism Good: Which Is It?

Hardly a day goes by without some liberal politician screeching about the grave injustices perpetrated by "the rich." Phrases like "tax cuts for the rich," "non-livable wages," "corporate exploitation overseas," "the rich get richer and the poor get poorer," "there are two Americas," and numerous other class warfare slogans bounce off the walls of Congress like basketball players wearing flubber-laden shoes. The level of disdain with which liberals view those with money (*conservatives* with money, at least) is second only to their intense disdain for free-thinking black Supreme Court Justices.

Division and class warfare are the perfect divisive catalysts, because they play on the seemingly universal human traits of greed and envy. Liberals are masterful at directing the attention of a "have-not" toward something a "have" owns and convincing the "have-not" that what the "have" has is a fundamental right for everyone. (Modern liberals have come up with more "rights" in the last half-century years than I have excuses to not watch chick flicks.)

The "have-not" is told that he can be successful in life only if he possesses what the "have" has. Furthermore, the "have-not" is told that the "have" gained what he has through unfair exploitation of the "have-not." To top it all off, the "have-not" is told that he doesn't have the power within himself nor the resources to gain on his own what the "have" possesses. Whatever the particular object of desire is at the moment cannot be gained by the "have-not" himself. Rather, it must be given to him by the liberal politician. (Thus is the "vote in exchange for a program/program in exchange for a vote" phenomenon so necessary for the survival of the modern liberal politician.)

Apparently the relationship between having "stuff" and succeeding in life is a causal one. The liberal seems to think that if a person simply has enough "stuff" (money, free education, day care, condoms, on-demand abortion, a high wage, free health care, etc.) surrounding him, the road to spiritual, physical, emotional, and financial success is wide open. (Once again, human behavior is attributed to *systems*.)

This belief stems from the secular premise that human beings are simply products of their environment. If a person is placed in the ideal environment, success and prosperity are inevitable. If a person is placed in a less than ideal environment, however, poverty and failure are inevitable. Salvation lies in overthrowing systems rather than in changing individual hearts. This is why government-enforced redistribution of wealth and resources is so important for liberals. The salvation of humanity depends on it (as does the perpetuation of liberal power).

But wait a minute! In the minds of liberals, aren't "the rich" the bane of society? According to the modern liberal worldview, this shouldn't be the case. Those with enough "stuff" (i.e., "the rich") should be the perfect, well-adjusted human beings experiencing the salvation brought about by their environment.

Despite this, the modern liberal has declared war against CEOs, big businesses, corporations, suburbanites in gated communities, and "rich" people in general; yet these are the very same people they are trying to create via their wealth redistribution programs. Why do liberals want to create the very people they despise—the people who are the source of all the world's ills? Most likely two reasons exist: 1) Their power is contingent upon division. Without a victim and a scapegoat to blame, motivation for voting for a liberal disappears. 2) The worldview upon which they base their beliefs and agenda is wrong. Humans, as it turns out, are *not* simply products of their environment, but they are free-will beings not limited by naturalistic cause-and-effect paradigms.

Here's a perfect illustration of the definition of *oxymoron*. Fact One: Liberals despise the very people that, according to their own worldview, ought to be model citizens. Fact Two: Liberals are trying to increase the members of a demographic they despise.

So which is it? Is materialism good or bad? Those with the materials are despised, yet materialism is the way of salvation. How about picking one?

Child Rape and Weak Punishments: Who's to Blame?

If you've ever watched *The O'Reilly Factor* on Fox News, you're probably familiar with Bill O'Reilly's crusade against judges who deliver weak sentences to convicted child molesters. In the fall of 2006, there was a judge in Vermont who sentenced to four months in jail a man who admitted to continually raping a young girl for a period of years. In December of 2006, in Columbus, Ohio (in Franklin County), Judge John Connor sentenced Andrew S. Selva to probation after he confessed and pled guilty to two counts of sexual battery.

While it is true that Selva plea bargained down to two counts of sexual battery (technically considered a crime not as severe as rape), he still could have been sentenced to ten years in prison. The point of this discussion, however, centers upon the ideas that led to Judge Connor's decision.

In sentencing Selva to five years' probation, Judge Conner stated that Selva had a "disease" and would not receive any rehabilitation or treatment in prison. Conner also said that a prison term would serve no purpose except that of "revenge." In Judge Conner's mind, the criminal justice system isn't about punishment, but rehabilitation. Where does this idea originate?

Once again we must return to that pesky little thing called *worldview*. A worldview answers the most basic questions we have about the nature of reality. In this case, a worldview's answer regarding the nature of humans takes center stage. How someone views the human being will directly affect their beliefs, convictions, and daily decisions. This is especially true for those who, like Judge Conner, wield power.

A central premise of the secular worldview claims *all* that exists is physical stuff. Everything in the universe can be "naturally" explained through a series of causes and effects. There is no need for an appeal to the supernatural in explaining both natural phenomena (e.g., earthquakes, evolution, apples falling from trees, weather patterns, technological advancements, etc.) and questions regarding ethics, morality, meaning, or purpose. Everything can be explained using an "inside the box," cause-and-effect paradigm (i.e., a secularized version of the scientific method).

This includes humans. A person is a complex relationship of interacting chemicals and firing synapses. Just as the natural laws of the universe cause an apple to fall from a tree, the human is at the mercy of those same universal laws. A particular human's personality, thoughts, decisions, and behavior (the effects) are the dictates of internal (interacting chemicals, firing synapses, etc.) and external (the person's environment) causes.

Because every phenomenon within the universe can be reduced to a materialistic (physical "stuff") cause, there's no room for silly notions like the soul, the conscience, or free will. Thus, a person's crimes are not the result of a free-will choice, but the necessary result of a cause . . . which, in turn, is the necessary result of a prior cause . . . which, in turn, is the necessary result of a prior cause . . . and so on and so forth *ad infinitum*.

In short, a person is an automaton merely reacting to the stimuli that is input into a complex system of physical stuff, i.e., a human. Thus, to "fix" humans it becomes necessary to fix the causes of their behavior. It isn't the free will of a person that is responsible for crime, but the systems (or the genes) that shape him or her. (Although isn't it ironic that liberals claim homosexuals are born that way, while pedophiles can be rehabilitated? If one group's behavior is caused by genes and is unchangeable, shouldn't that be the case for other groups as well?)

This is why faulty or oppressive systems and/or societies are to blame for undesirable behavior such as murder, thievery, or child rape. Using this reasoning, the purpose of the criminal justice system isn't to hold the individual accountable for his behavior (because, ultimately, the individual isn't responsible for his own actions), but to rehabilitate or cure the individual from a problem (read: a "disease") that is out of his control—similar to curing a cold or the flu. The blame rests with the criminal's environment or surrounding system (including, but not limited to, bad parents, repressive religion, evil capitalism, poverty, lack of education, etc.).

By misunderstanding what a human being is, secularists form unworkable beliefs regarding systems of government, economic systems, the purpose of punishment, etc. This is Judge Connor's problem. He misunderstands the purpose of punishment, the criminal justice system, and civil government in general, because he is working from premises that don't accurately describe what a human is.

Until he alters his most fundamental beliefs regarding humanity, there is little hope of influencing his beliefs regarding subsidiary issues such as weak sentences for child rapists or the purpose of punishment in general. Of course, if the secularists are right, Judge Connor isn't to blame for the weak sentence . . . the blame falls on the same system of causes and effects that dictated the child rape in the first place.

Exploiting Katrina

The suffering wrought by hurricane Katrina in August 2005 took its toll on thousands of people. Even with all the technology and scientific advancements of modern society, we are still humbled by the power of nature. The best humanity can do is prepare and withstand. The amazing technological advancements of humanity can help shield us from many of the disastrous effects of nature's extremes, but technology's salvific power is extremely limited.

Natural disasters, however, are nothing new. In fact, they are often the harbingers of great opportunities for humans to show the loving, caring, and good side of their nature (the remnants of *imago dei* in this fallen world). The aftermath of hurricane Katrina was no different. Thousands of people were in the trenches helping complete strangers who were devastated by the hurricane. Millions more donated money to help people they had never met. The United States of America is the most generous nation the world has ever seen, and disasters like hurricane Katrina was an opportunity for America to shine.

Unfortunately, the human response to hurricane Katrina left much to be desired. However, this is not an essay criticizing the government's response to the hurricane. The government(s) could have responded much more efficiently than it did (especially the governor of Louisiana and the mayor of New Orleans). However, this will not be a litany of complaints about inherent government ineptitude or the general notion that it is the government's job to solve all our problems. This is an essay about the shameful response by some leaders and politicians.

Every time the glorious side of human nature is experienced, you can rest assured that the sinful side of human nature is not far behind in being exposed. If you've followed my essays up to this point, you probably know that I am of the opinion that modern liberalism perpetuates itself via exploitation. The response of many liberals to the aftermath of hurricane Katrina illustrates this claim perfectly.

Modern liberal leaders and politicians convince large groups of people that they are victims incapable of solving their own problems. Upon successful indoctrination of this notion, the politicians then hold themselves up as the only individuals capable of rescuing the victimized group. Thus, liberal leaders and the party and agenda they represent become the saviors of the "victimized" group.

Hurricane Katrina devastated the Gulf Coast, including Alabama, Mississippi, and New Orleans. For one reason or another, however, New Orleans took center stage . . . perhaps because the ineptitude of governmental bureaucracy and the decaying symptoms of the welfare state were most apparent there.

New Orleans was utterly unprepared for a category five hurricane such as Katrina. Local government officials such as the governor of Louisiana and the mayor of New Orleans were also woefully unprepared. Additionally, many of the private citizens in New Orleans were unprepared. The result was a great deal of suffering. People wanted someone to blame. And without fail, liberals never pass up opportunities to blame. This provided yet another tale of liberal victimization, division, exploitation, and scapegoating.

According to some, the suffering in New Orleans was caused by racist policy and racist government officials—not to mention a racist society in general (never mind the fact that the mayor of New Orleans at the time of the hurricane was a black liberal, that much of the policy and many of the government officials supposedly responsible for the suffering were liberal, that the massive welfare system in and around New Orleans was instituted by liberals, or that "white, fat, rich" individuals and corporations donated millions of dollars toward the relief effort). By providing a scapegoat (i.e., racist white people, racist government officials, racist government policy, racist capitalism, racist tax cuts, racist wars, and any other stereotypically conservative word that can be preceded by the word "racist"), liberals were dividing people based on race just as they have been doing regarding class for years.

By racially victimizing the victims of hurricane Katrina and appointing themselves as their saviors, liberals exploited that demographic for future votes. Liberals feed off of perceived victimization as well as class and racial division (although *any* type of division will suffice), because without such problems to solve, liberals and their saving medium (the government) lack the exploitative footing necessary to wield power. After all, how can you be the savior of someone who doesn't need to be saved?

This is why liberals played the "blame game." This is nothing new. Their entire ideology and source of power stems from the "blame game." Whether it's the war in Iraq, Social Security, poverty, terrorism, or any other challenge facing the American people, they are opportunities for liberals to victimize, divide, and exploit. And they never cease to take advantage of them. Liberals are excellent at criticizing the plans of others but notoriously inept at coming up with their own coherent plans for success. This is because their secular worldview limits possible solutions (to the world's ills) to shortsighted proposals that attempt to manipulate human behavior by using bureaucratic government programs.

Secularism: The Opiate of the Oppressor

Karl Marx believed religion was the "opiate of the masses." He believed religion encouraged the oppressed proletariat (the workers, i.e., the "poor") to passively accept its fate, thus allowing the bourgeoisie (those who control the means of production, i.e. the "rich") to continue its oppression of the proletariat. According to Marx (and many other secularists), belief in God and a final judgment dupes the oppressed (proletariat) because such beliefs convince them that their oppressors will eventually "get what's coming to them" in the *next* life. Therefore, the proletariat need not address *this*-worldly oppression because, in the end, God will judge the oppressors at the final judgment.

Realizing this, the bourgeoisie purposefully uses religion to perpetuate its power—which is maintained through the oppression of the proletariat. In this way, religion supposedly dulls the senses of its adherents and removes any motivation to overthrow the bourgeoisie oppressing them. Just as opium dulls the senses of its user and promotes passive acceptance of the user's situation (whatever or wherever that may be), religion encourages its adherents to passively accept their plight in life . . . thus perpetuating the exploitation needed for the bourgeoisie to continue oppressing the proletariat.

True to form, this is another example of secularism's claim that religion (indeed, *any* worldview claiming the existence of absolute truth) hinders freedom (along with the claim that secularism promotes freedom). Nothing new here. According to Marx, those who do *not* believe in God or the afterlife (i.e. secularists) are more likely to try to make *this* world a better place. Those who *do* believe in an afterlife are, theoretically, *less* motivated to attempt change in this world.

But what happens if we reverse Marx's "opiate of the masses" assessment? If religion encourages its proletariat adherents to passively accept the oppressive status quo, secularism surely encourages the same among the bourgeoisie. Secularism—bereft of any belief in God, judgment, or an afterlife—provides no motivation for the oppressors to change their behavior. After all, *this* world is all that matters. Oppressors have nothing to fear. They will never be punished for the oppression and misery they bring upon the proletariat. Moreover, those who comprise the proletariat have no inherent value and, thus, are not deserving of dignity and respect.

Only two things will motivate the bourgeoisie to voluntarily treat the proletariat with dignity and respect. 1) The belief that every person, regardless of class (and other factors), has inherent value and worth, and/or 2) The belief that something bad will happen to them in the *next* life if they mistreat the proletariat in *this* life. Neither of these beliefs are provided by secularism. In fact, both of these beliefs directly contradict secular presuppositions. Secularists who believe these two claims are (consciously or unconsciously) borrowing them from Judeo-Christian theism (no doubt to ease the tension created by the unexorcized portions of the *imago dei* within them). Secularism is truly the "opiate of the oppressor."

Even *if* secularism among the proletariat motivates the overthrow of the bourgeoisie (which is a questionable claim anyway), it provides no motivation, once the former proletariat becomes the new bourgeoisie, for the former proletariat to act differently than the former bourgeoisie. This is exactly why the French Revolution failed while the American Revolution succeeded. Religion (Judeo-Christian theism to be exact) motivated the American colonists to overthrow British rule. *After* the revolution was complete, the Judeo-Christian worldview of the colonists motivated them to construct a free society different from the one previously set up by their oppressors. French revolutionaries armed with secularism, however, were not able to set up a lasting free society as the Judeo-Christian American colonists did. Thus, Napoleon eventually came to power.[8]

Secular revolution is merely the switching of places. Freedom doesn't last when revolution is motivated by secularism. It merely results in a *new* oppressor and the *new* oppressed rather than the actual presence of liberty based on the value "all men are created equal." Revolution motivated by Judeo-Christian theism, however, goes beyond the mere motivation to overthrow oppressors. It provides the motivation to eliminate oppression

---

8. This point is also illustrated by the Russian and Cuban Revolutions—although the *initial* overthrow of Tsar Nicholas II in Russia wasn't communist in nature. The communists took control several months later.

8

Education
Institutionalized Indoctrination

Exorcizing God's Image

CHRISTIANS BELIEVE humans are created in God's image. What does this mean? Among other things, it means humans possess volition (free will), intelligence, moral acuity, as well as affective (emotional) and social (the need for relationships with God and other people) capacities. God's image in each of us is the ultimate foundation for the inherent value we possess. Without it, human life is not only valueless but also meaningless and purposeless. In a strictly materialistic world, there is no basis for the existence of objective or inherent value, meaning, or purpose. After all, these three things are non-physical and, therefore, outside the realm of human knowledge—*if* they exist at all. (On the other hand, if they are physical, they are reducible to physical "stuff" like chemicals and neurons and are, therefore, determined by physical laws. If this is the case, the terms lose their meaning anyway.)

As the dominant secular culture marginalizes religion in the public forum in its attempt to completely rid society of traditional religion and its influences, we should expect the ideas that go along with the banished worldview to disappear as well. Included in this banishment is the notion of the *imago dei* (being created in "God's image")—the foundation of value, meaning, and purpose. Since "the separation of church and state" has become hegemonic among legislative and judicial entities across the country (and embedded in the minds of much of the citizenry), the exorcism of the *imago dei* has been rampant. This is not an easy process, however, and secularists have had their hands full; but this doesn't mean they're not succeeding.

Why is this a difficult process? In short, because the *imago dei* has been imbedded into the fabric of the universe by the Creator. The *imago dei* is "real" in the same sense gravity is "real." Moreover, the *imago dei* is embedded into the essence of humanity—the very core of who and what each of us is. It is impossible, or at least very difficult, to avoid. Denying essential attributes of reality is an uphill battle and one requiring a multifaceted attack. Secularists, however, are up to the challenge.

The front lines of this battle are within the institution of education. Education, perhaps more than any other institution (at least nowadays), heavily influences the direction of American society and culture, because it plays a huge role in what each succeeding generation is taught. Thus, a takeover of the education system in this country was and is the main strategy for a secular cultural takeover. The beginnings of this educational coup, however, occurred in another institution: the judiciary. Once the judiciary was manipulated to subvert the will of the people, the secularists had the catalyst necessary to accomplish the primary goal in Operation Secular Culture: the expulsion of religious ideas and people from the public education system in this country.

The second goal was convincing the country that education is the salve for all our ills. This conclusion naturally stems from the secular denial of immorality (sin) as the cause of the world's problems. Instead of evil and suffering being *moral* problems, secularism claims evil and suffering are *ignorance* problems, i.e., results of a lack of knowledge (gnosis). And how do we solve the problem of lack of knowledge? That's right, through education. This is why no politician today could ever formally oppose "education" spending. It would be political suicide. In American society (and abroad), education has been granted the role of savior. Who in their right mind would stand against that which will save our society? (Even President Bush, a "conservative," buys into this thinking. He more than doubled the education budget from what it was during the Clinton Administration.) Along with the label of "savior" came the justification for gargantuan increases in education spending, a bureaucratic system run by elites who know what's best for us, and a massive public education system meant to "educate" every single person in this country. Goals 1 and 2 can be considered accomplished. So far, so good for secularists.

So now what do we have? We have a massive public education system charged with the role of savior that is void of God and his ideas. In short, we have a secular messiah attempting to save humanity through materialistic methods—a recipe for disaster if I've ever seen one (as illustrated in Chapter 6). Prescribing a medicine (secularism) based on a misdiagnosis (the claim that ignorance, rather than immorality, is the cause of evil and suffering) is, at best, ineffective and, at worst, disastrous. The modern institution of education is attempting to use an inaccurate view of reality to solve a problem for which it does not know the cause. For this reason, a secular education system is utterly incapable of solving *any* of society's problems.

Educating a child in a secular education system for twelve of his first eighteen years of life (or sixteen of his first twenty-two years if you include college) takes its toll on the mind. Slowly but surely, the *imago dei* written into the core of every person is exorcized. Secular ideas replace divine ideas "written on the heart." As a result, the values of society have changed drastically. The values that were once founded in the *imago dei* were banished from the public forum and replaced by a worldview that provides no such foundation. Values such as the belief in free will, moral acuity, and inherent human worth are lost forever, because the new reigning worldview (secularism) does not, indeed *cannot*, produce them. It's ironic that we cut out that which leads to virtue, then wonder why there is a lack of virtuous people in our world. C. S. Lewis wrote,

> And all the time—such is the tragi-comedy of our situation—we continue to clamour for those very qualities we are rendering impossible . . . In a sort of ghastly simplicity we remove the organ and demand the function. We make men without chests and expect of them virtue and enterprise. We laugh at honour and are shocked to find traitors in our midst. We castrate and bid the geldings be fruitful.[1]

The belief in free will is lost, because secularism's materialistic presuppositions preclude the existence of the non-physical—which is a prerequisite of free will. Secularism claims matter (physical stuff) is all that exists. Nothing supernatural or non–physical exists. Everything from thoughts to actions to social behavior can be reduced to something physical, i.e., internal factors such as chemical interaction, neurons firing, etc., and/or external factors such as oppressive systems or environments (e.g., capitalism, religion, abusive parents, etc.). If matter is controlled by physical laws and everything is matter (including humans), then everything is controlled by physical laws. In other words, if everything that exists is physical stuff, it follows that everything is subject to physical laws.

Therefore, that which was formerly attributed to free will (good *and* bad thoughts, actions, and social phenomena) must now be viewed as merely another effect within a closed cause-and-effect system ("closed" in the sense that nothing exists "outside" the physical universe). In order to break this necessary chain of cause and effect, something *not* at the mercy of physical law must exist. This "something" must be essentially

---

1. Lewis, *Abolition of Man*, 36–37.

non-physical—the existence of which is ruled out by secularism's most basic materialistic presupposition. Belief in free will is utterly unjustifiable within the secular paradigm. It is a luxury secularism simply can't afford.

The most obvious consequence of this conclusion is the belief that systems must first be changed in order to alter human behavior. This accounts for why secularists try to solve the world's problems by instituting massive systemic change (e.g., welfare, entitlement programs, socialist economic policy, massive educational institutions, diplomacy through reason at all costs, etc.) rather than by appealing to the heart of the volitional individual. Because individuals are the sum total of their physical environment, it is their physical environment which must be altered.

Moral acuity is the next value to be discarded, because, once again, matter is all that exists. Objective morality is not physical and, therefore, does not exist. This is often the most difficult attribute of the *imago dei* to exorcize. This difficulty is reflected by the fact that very few secularists actually live out the logical consequence of their materialistic presuppositions, which is a valueless (or moral-less) world. Deep down, no one (including secularists) wants to live in a world where there is no morality—where helping the poor is as morally neutral as murdering six million Jews. This deep desire is the *imago dei* gasping for air. But a valueless world is an accurate description of reality according to secularism. In fact, an entire ideology (secular humanism) has dedicated itself to justifying that which they can't seem to completely exorcise—God's morality "written on the heart." Of course, they reject traditional religion with its "strict moral codes," but they are quick to replace it with their own set of values—values arbitrarily borrowed from the Judeo-Christian religion that they unsuccessfully attempt to ground in secular presuppositions.

Many believe moralistic modernism (secular humanism) and postmodernism are different worldviews. This couldn't be further from the truth. Postmodernists simply complete what secular humanists could not, which is a full *imago*-ectomy. Both humanism and postmodernism are based on the same secularism. Postmodernism, however, is the only one that remains logically consistent with its materialistic presuppositions.

Without objective morality, moral relativism rules the day. To posit the existence of an objective right and wrong (a standard that can be used to judge the actions and lifestyles of individuals) becomes "intolerance." By the time someone finishes his twelfth or sixteenth year of public education, the belief in objective morality has been so thoroughly exorcized that it is *almost* perilous to retain the hope that it could be resurrected. The result? We will have generations of individuals with no moral anchor.

We will have whole societies that are unable to condemn and, thus, will be susceptible to believing disastrous ideas such as those of a Stalin, Pol Pot, or Hitler . . . ideas that, not surprisingly, thrive on secular college campuses across the country.

Lastly, the belief in the inherent value of a human being goes by the wayside. After all, if humans are merely physical stuff, and no objective values exist, then why cling to the intolerant idea that a person has inherent value regardless of his age, social standing, "usefulness" to society, strength, ability to defend himself, race, etc.? The only difference between a human being and a rock is the relative level of complexity. No fundamental difference exists between the two.

A secular educational institution that has successfully exorcized the *imago dei* from its ranks based on the faulty judicial interpretation of "the separation of church and state" will consistently produce individuals that reject free will (consciously or unconsciously), moral objectivity, and the inherent value of the human being. These beliefs directly influence the thoughts, beliefs, and actions of those who embrace them. Thus, the disastrous real-world consequences of these beliefs will inevitably be realized.

In the battle of worldviews, Judeo-Christian theism has an initial advantage by virtue of the fact that its basic values are "written on the heart" of every person. The *imago dei* stacks the deck in favor of Christianity. This advantage, however, can be snuffed out by years of secular indoctrination. This often results in a complete exorcism of the *imago dei* and its resultant values. At other times, it results in the manipulation (rather than a complete banishment) of the *imago dei*—as in the case of secular humanism and liberal Christianity. Christian values are warped because they are interpreted through a secular filter. This usually results in the attempt to realize Christian values through secular means, i.e., equality through socialist economic policy, peace through pacifist diplomacy, etc. Unfortunately, secular methods will never produce the manifestation of Christian values.

I realize my own worldview (Christianity) rejects the idea that human thoughts, beliefs, and actions are the sole consequences of physical laws and environment, so I cannot conclude that a direct cause-and-effect relationship exists between what the education establishment teaches and what its students believe. But I can say that someone's environment certainly *influences* what he believes and does. A person is influenced by a plethora of factors, such as personality, environment, etc. However, a person's free will is never compromised.

Our massive secular public education system, which is charged with saving society, is wrong-headed and incapable of fulfilling the task secularists have assigned it. It spends billions of dollars and years of time exorcizing the only thing that provides the values necessary to alleviate the ills of the world: the *imago dei*.

Open Mouth, Insert Joan Powell

In October of 2005, my community's local newspaper, *The Pulse-Journal*, had profiles on each of the candidates running for Lakota's (my local school district) school board. One of the candidates was the school board president, Joan Powell. Questions were asked of each candidate, such as "Who would you most like to meet?" Joan Powell responded by saying she would like to meet Abraham Lincoln.

Joan Powell responded that she would like to meet Abraham Lincoln because she would be interested to hear "his thoughts on how to bring a divided community together without going to war." I'll let that sink in for a moment. . . . Actually, I could probably end this essay right now. What could someone possibly say about a comment like that? Well . . . I'll give it a shot.

I think I'll ask Bill Clinton for his thoughts on telling the truth. Or maybe I'll go back in time and ask John F. Kennedy for his thoughts on marital fidelity. Maybe I'll ask Teddy Kennedy how to *not* drive drunk and drown a woman. Or perhaps I'll ask a union boss about encouraging hard work, ingenuity, and technological advancement. Catching my drift yet?

Not only couldn't Abraham Lincoln prevent war, but he also knew it was his only tool for forcing his Whig agenda on the populace (yes, I realize he was a Republican). Over 500,000 Americans and Confederates died in the civil war—America's bloodiest war to date. Lincoln did about as good a job of uniting a divided nation as Jimmy Carter did running the economy in the late 1970s.

What's interesting is that this wasn't the first time Ms. Powell put her foot in her mouth on public record. In November 2004, when the school levy failed, she told the local newspaper that the reason it failed was because so many people voted. (Don't you just hate when that happens?!) She then informed the public of the plan to put the levy back on the ballot the following March, when less people would be voting, thus increasing the levy's chances of passing.

How much time do you need for that one to set in? She was actually expressing to the public her desire to subvert the will of the majority by trying to sneak in a levy in a special election. I don't doubt for one second that that was the plan of the education folk who desperately want more money with which to play. But for the life of me, I can't figure out why she would inform the public of such plans.

Wait a minute—I know why. It's because the education elitists think the general public consists of a bunch of idiots who need to be enlightened as to what's best for their children. The masses aren't people with whom to work. They're people to enlighten and, as a last resort, dupe in a special election.

Ms. Powell's quote about Abraham Lincoln is one for the ages . . . and I, out of the goodness of my heart, couldn't resist sharing this little nugget with the world. Just be glad she never ran *your* school board.

"Less is More," "Addition by Subtraction," and Other Annoying Conservative Notions

Hanging on my mailbox one day in October of 2005 was a flyer distributed by "Yes Lakota"—a group that campaigned for the passage of a local school levy that had failed previously multiple times (the levy would increase local property tax in order to fund Lakota's public schools). The top of the flyer said, "Some people like the written word; others like the stats." Immediately underneath was the statement: "For everyone, we wanted to present Lakota by the numbers." Have you ever read something and then scratched your head in confusion regarding its underlying meaning?

Here were some of my questions: 1) What exactly did they consider the "written word"? 2) How was it different from the stats? 3) Did the "written word" not include statistics? 4) Did it take two failed levies for the education establishment to realize "the folks" might want to see some stats? 5) Are "the folks" incapable of researching the stats for themselves? As intriguing as these questions are, they are not the focus of this essay. The stats presented by the education establishment will be the focus.

The flyer was set up so a series of numbers were printed in bold, with smaller text explaining the significance of each number. For example, "520: Additional number of Lakota students enrolled just this year." Or "2109: The number of students enrolled in Lakota schools since the last levy passed five years ago." Or "1700: Approximate number of students attending class in converted custodial storage rooms and offices, locker rooms, hallways, stages and concession stands." I could go on, but you get the drift. Let's examine some of these statistics.

Education

- "65: Fewer dollars than the last levy request because Lakota refinanced and paid off bonds." (This number is in proportion to every $100,000.)

Question: Would the school district have refinanced if the previous two school levies didn't fail? Let's put it this way: When was the last time a *government program* held itself accountable, cut spending, reorganized, and paid off its debt out of the goodness of its heart? I venture to guess the answer is *never* (I will gladly eat my words if someone can show me a time when a government program voluntarily turned away funds, tax money, etc.). Even if such a miracle has occurred, however, it's probably possible to count the occurrences on one hand.

- "2,000,000: Dollars saved by a first-of-its-kind salary schedule negotiated between the Board of Education and the teacher's association."

Question: Would this renegotiation have occurred if the previous two school levies didn't fail? Let's phrase it this way: When was the last time a *union* voluntarily returned funds/benefits out of the goodness of its heart? Try *never*. I'm even more confident regarding this than the answer to the same question asked of government programs. In virtue of the district's description of the renegotiation as "first-of-its-kind," the establishment itself admits the answer is *never*.

- "-29: The number of teaching positions cut this year, even though we have enrolled enough students to fill a typical Ohio elementary school."

Question: When was the last time a district decreased the number of paid teachers in a school district out of the goodness of its heart? Similarly, when was the last time a teacher's union allowed the cutting of teachers' jobs out of the goodness of its heart? Once again, I venture to offer the answer, "Never." (On a side note: If the district subtracted -29 teaching positions this year, that means 29 new teachers were *added*. Perhaps this is why they don't usually venture into the realm of statistics.)

- "1700: Approximate number of students attending class in converted custodial storage rooms and offices, locker rooms, hallways, stages and concession stands."

The same question regarding government programs, voluntarily cutting programs, reorganizing, and turning away funds applies here. When was the last time a government program voluntarily used a closet when a new extension could be added to the building instead? Pardon me if I experience joy upon hearing that a government program is being forced to efficiently use all of its resources. (On another side note, it's time to cut concession stand funding if they're large enough to hold entire classes.)

The flyer begins to get interesting when the district brags about its performance. For example:

- *"533: The amount of money Lakota spends below what the average "Excellent" district spends in Ohio."* Similarly, on "Yes Lakota's" web site is the statement, "On average, Lakota spends over 6% less per student than other school districts in Ohio."

Does this mean that despite all these cuts, firings, closet/concession stand classrooms, and new students, Lakota is still performing exceedingly well? Surely that can't be the case. After all, isn't it true that as education spending decreases, so does the quality of education? Let me rephrase, as this might be an epiphany to those (liberals) who think throwing money at a problem will solve it. *The Lakota school district is spending less and performing extremely well.* Egad! If this gets out, what's next? Vouchers?

The goal of the flyer was to convince the voter that Lakota spent tax revenue efficiently. *Ipso facto*, voters should trust the district with *more* of their hard-earned money. Well, as outlined above, this incredible efficiency was brought about by *not* increasing funding. The district and the teacher's union were *forced* to become more efficient because many of the good people in their community don't subscribe to the, "If there's a problem, throw money at it!" mindset.

Can you imagine how efficient the district could have become if the levy continued to fail? In fact, I proposed that the community maintain the (then) current level of funding as long as possible, just to find out exactly how efficient the district could have become. What these statistics told me when I first read them was that despite the doomsday predictions (the supposedly disastrous consequences of the levy failing) spread by proponents of the levy the first two times around, Lakota was still turning out a great product. Those numbers told me that Lakota has what it takes to run an efficient school system. In fact, the flyer convinced me to have enough faith in the school district that I once again voted against the levy.

Levies are the government equivalent to the free market. In the real world of private business, corporations are motivated to be as efficient as possible. Why? Because if the company produces a sub-par product, it will go out of business. Government programs are not like this. Their existence is not dependent upon the forces of a free market. A government program could produce sub-par products for decades and still continue existing as long as some group of fat cat politicians continues to vote for the program.

The Whiny Liberal Gets the Grease

Has anyone ever had a child, a sibling, or a friend perpetually whine until he gets his way? Whining can take several forms. The most obvious forms are crying and complaining. Passive-aggressive forms of whining also occur, such as refusing to participate, giving the silent treatment, making life miserable for everyone around you until you get your way, and the ever-popular taking your ball and going home. Nobody likes a whiner (except fellow whiners).

In my community, the levy for the Lakota School District was put on the ballot three times, and it was rejected by the people three times. What did the education establishment learn from this? Judging from their behavior, absolutely nothing. Like a child who is told "no," the district just kept insisting. "Pretty please, with sugar on top?"

The school levy was put back on the ballot a fourth time, and it finally passed by about 1,500 votes. This was a war of attrition, not a battle of seeking the truth and the most efficient way to run a school system. The education establishment was going to pass this levy come hell or high water. It was just a matter of time. "Give me the levy, or give me death!"

Regarding the aforementioned forms of whining, the education elitists engaged in all of them. Every time the levy failed, they complained that the community simply didn't understand the information presented. Additionally, those who *did* understand the information (and voted against the levy anyway) "didn't want what was best for the kids or the community" out of selfishness, greed, or any other class warfare labels those of a liberal mindset repeatedly spew out.

As for being passive-aggressive, the district was dead set on making life as miserable as possible for the community until the levy passed. "Fine, if you won't let us play our way, we're going to make your life as miserable as possible." For example, they decided to cut busing. This levy wasn't about working with the community. It was about a group of education elitists (is there another kind?) who absolutely knew what was right for the community's children and were going to force their agenda on the people whether the people chose to be enlightened or not.

This became painfully obvious when Lakota's school board president Joan Powell told us that the reason the levy failed was because so many people turned out to vote. Because of this, the district planned to put the levy back on the ballot in a special election when less people would be voting, thus increasing the chances of its passage.

It's not often that someone actually steps out and tells a constituency he (or *she* in this case) is trying to subvert the will of the people to impose his own agenda. (Of course, this is the same woman who said she wanted to meet Abraham Lincoln because she wanted to know his thoughts on "uniting a divided community without going to war.")

At this point, I need not reiterate the arrogance of the education elitists, their inability or unwillingness to work with the community, or the idea that a government program will only be efficient when it's forced to be from external pressure. (For that, read the essays entitled "Less is More . . . ." and "Open Mouth, Insert Joan Powell.") I merely want to illustrate how the left works. The only thing better than beating a community over the head with multiple school levies would be getting a court to institute the levy via judicial *fiat*.

Now it's time to take a bit of a different look at the levy system.

Should John Kerry and Democrats be able to have another presidential election because they lost in 2004 . . . and continue having elections until they win? Should Republicans have been given the chance to win back congress when they lost it in 2006? Back in 1996, should Bob Dole and Republicans have been allowed to hold another presidential election because they lost . . . . and been allowed to keep holding elections until they won? Obviously, the answer is no. In such a system, elections would mean nothing.

If a school district puts a levy on the ballot, and the measure fails, should the district then be able to put that very same levy back on the ballot a month later? What if it fails again? Should the district be allowed to put that levy back on the ballot three months later? What if it fails again? Should the district be allowed to put the levy back on the ballot six months later? What if it fails again?

Should the losing party in an election be able to put their candidate back on a ballot (for the same political office, against the same opponent) just months after he or she has lost? What if he loses the election again? Should he be allowed to run again two months later? What if he loses again? Should he be able to run again six months later?

Here's my first proposal for my community: The citizens of West Chester and Liberty Townships (the townships comprising the Lakota School District) should issue referendums (I doubt getting the signatures to do so would be very difficult) to reverse the school levy that eventually passed. Let's hold a special election exclusively for this vote. If the vote fails to reverse the levy, we'll just have another referendum. If that referendum fails, we'll have another. If that referendum fails, we'll have another. Even if it fails 10 times in a row, we'll simply put it back on the ballot a few months later. We'll do this until it passes.

The education establishment would throw a fit if such referendums were repeatedly put on the ballot. I can hear the outcries now: "The people have already spoken on this issue." "We already had an election to decide this matter." "By voting on this again, we're wasting taxpayers' dollars."

Of course, all of these complaints would be hypocritical rhetoric on the part of education elitists who had no problem putting the levy on the ballot four different times. Why, then, weren't these complaints brought to the fore when they were descriptive of what the education establishment was attempting?

My second proposal is this: If a levy is put on the ballot and it fails, it should be a dead issue for however long the levy would have been active. If a levy would have been in effect continually, with no end in sight, and it failed to receive voter approval, then some amount of time should be allotted before the levy can be placed back on the ballot. Such elections would then carry weight. They would actually mean something.

For a narrow-minded education establishment, the current levy system is perfect. The district is never forced to change its mind, think differently, be held accountable, or work with the community. They can simply try and try again. When you have a group of people who all think alike, there isn't much innovation. This is the problem with the local, state, and national public education system. They educate their own, certify their own, and represent their own. It's a closed shop, a monopoly. Such environments don't breed innovation and certainly don't create quality products. They breed contempt for outsiders and an unwillingness to cooperate with those not privy to the educational gnosis bestowed on the elites.

Education, Elitism, and the Courts: The Rise of Statism

I often refer to the public education establishment in this country as "elitist." But what do I mean when I use the term "elitist"? An elitist is someone who believes he has unique access to special knowledge and treats with contempt those who don't possess such knowledge. This contempt in its milder cases usually takes the form of condescension. In its more extreme cases (which are becoming more and more numerous), it takes the form of force and the deprivation of rights. Elitists feel that they need to enlighten those not privy to their special knowledge and, if necessary, force them to be enlightened. It is not coincidental that such elitism is most often meted out through the courts.

Exhibit A: Judge Stephen Reinhardt of the Ninth Circuit Court of Appeals. Let me paint the picture for you.

In December of 2001, a letter of consent was sent home to parents at the Mesquite Elementary School in Palmdale, California. The letter was asking for permission from parents to administer a "confidential mental health survey" to their children. The survey was administered by Khristi Seymour, who had volunteered as a mental health counselor (she was in the process of getting a master's degree at the time).

The letter read:

> *Dear Parent or Caregiver,*
>
> *The Palmdale School District is asking your support in participating in a district-wide study of our first, third and fifth grade children. The study will be a part of a collaborative effort with The California School of Professional Psychology—CSPP/ Alliant International University, Children's Bureau of Southern California and the Palmdale School District.*
>
> *The goal of this assessment is to establish a community baseline measure of children's exposure to early trauma (for example, violence). We will identify internal behaviors such as anxiety and depression and external behaviors such as aggression and verbal abuse. As a result we will be designing a district wide intervention program to help children reduce these barriers to learning, which students can participate in. Please read this consent letter and if you agree, please sign and send it back to your school's principal no later than December 20, 2001.*
>
> *The assessment will consist of three, twenty-minute self-report measures, which will be given to your child on one day during the last week of January. This study is 100% confidential and at no time will the information gathered be used to identify your child. Your child will not be photographed or videotaped. You may refuse to have your child participate or withdraw from the study at any time without any penalty or loss of services to which your child is entitled.*
>
> *I* [the parent] *am aware that the research study coordinator, Khristi Seymour, one research assistant, the Palmdale School District, Director of Psychology, Michael Geisser, and a professor from CSPP, will be the only people who have access to the study's information. After the study is completed, all information will be locked in storage and then destroyed after a period of five years.*

I [the parent] *understand answering questions may make my child feel uncomfortable. If this occurs, then, Khristi Seymour, the research study coordinator, will assist us in locating a therapist for further psychological help if necessary. If I have further questions, I may contact Khristi Seymour at* [contact information]. *I understand that I will not be able to get my child's individual results due to anonymity of the children, but I may get a summary report of the study results.*

I have read this form and understand what it says. I hereby agree to allow my child to participate in this district-wide study.

Judging from the text of this letter, the study seemed innocuous enough. Some parents investigated further, however, when their children returned home asking them particular questions *after the survey was administered*. Included in this study was a section where the students were asked to rate the statements about their thoughts and feelings on a scale from "never" to "almost all the time." The following sex-related questions were included in this survey (keep in mind, these questions were asked of six-year-old children):

8. Touching my private parts too much
17. Thinking about having sex
22. Thinking about touching other people's private parts
23. Thinking about sex when I don't want to
26. Washing myself because I feel dirty on the inside
34. Not trusting people because they might want sex
40. Getting scared or upset when I think about sex
44. Having sex feelings in my body
47. Can't stop thinking about sex
54. Getting upset when talking about sex

The letter of consent specifically mentioned several areas of content included in the survey, such as violence, anxiety, depression, aggression, and verbal abuse. The letter made absolutely no mention that there would be sexual content in the survey. You're naive if you think such an omission was accidental. This public school didn't want to work with the parents in the community. School officials believed their agenda was right, and they didn't care what parents thought.

Interestingly enough, those conducting the survey (including the school district) felt that a child who would be uncomfortable answering those questions would probably be in need of further psychological help and therapy. Good heavens, people. *I'm* not comfortable answering those questions. Does that mean I'm in need of psychological help? (On second thought, don't answer that.)

The plaintiffs in the case sued, because they alleged that their basic constitutional right "to control the upbringing of their children by introducing them to matters of and relating to sex in accordance with their personal and religious values and beliefs" was violated. Judge Reinhardt ruled that, when it came to the public schools, parents have no such right. Judge Reinhardt wrote:

> *We agree* [with the lower court's decision], *and hold that there is no fundamental right of parents to be the exclusive provider of information regarding sexual matters to their children, either independent of their right to direct the upbringing and education of their children or encompassed by it. We also hold that parents have no due process or privacy right to override the determinations of public schools as to the information to which their children will be exposed while enrolled as students.*

Judge Reinhardt then cited a case decided by the First Circuit Court of Appeals, in which it was decided that parents have no rights when it comes to the design and implementation of public school curricula. The First Circuit Court decision reads as follows:

> *. . . the Meyer and Pierce cases, we think, evince the principal that the state cannot prevent parents from choosing a specific educational program—whether it be religious instruction at a private school or instruction in a foreign language. That is, the state does not have the power to "standardize its children" or "foster a homogenous people" by completely foreclosing the opportunity of individuals and groups to choose a different path of education. We do not think, however, that this freedom encompasses a fundamental constitutional right to dictate the curriculum at the public school to which they had chosen to send their children. We think it is fundamentally different for the state to say to a parent, "you can't teach your child German or send him to a parochial school," than for the parent to say the state, "You can't teach my child subjects that are morally offensive to me." The first instance involves the state proscribing parents from educating their children, while the second involves parents prescribing what the state shall teach their children. If all parents have a fundamental constitutional right to dictate individually what the schools teach their children, the schools will be forced to cater a curriculum for each student whose parents had genuine moral disagreements with the school's choice of subject matter. We cannot see that the Constitution imposes such a burden on state educational systems, and accordingly find that the rights of parents as*

described by Meyer and Pierce do not encompass a broad-based right to restrict the flow of information in the public schools.

Judge Reinhardt wrote:

In sum, we affirm that the Meyer-Pierce right does not extend beyond the threshold of the school door. The parents' asserted right "to control the upbringing of their children by introducing them to matters of and relating to sex in accordance with their personal and religious values and beliefs," by which they mean the right to limit what public schools or other state actors may tell their children regarding sexual matters, is not encompassed within the Meyer-Pierce right to control their children's upbringing and education. Accordingly, Meyer-Pierce provides no basis for finding a substantive due process right that could have been violated by the defendants' authorization and administration of the survey.

Reinhardt continues:

As the First Circuit made clear in Brown, once parents make the choice as to which school their children will attend, their fundamental right to control the education of their children is, at the least, substantially diminished. The Constitution does not vest parents with the authority to interfere with the public school's decision as to how it will provide information to its students or what information it will provide, in its classrooms or otherwise. . . . Perhaps the Sixth Circuit said it best when it explained, "While parents may have a fundamental right to decide whether to send their child to a public school, they do not have a fundamental right generally to direct how a public school teaches their child. Whether it is the school curriculum, the hours of the school day, school discipline, the timing and content of examinations, the individuals hired to teach at the school, the extracurricular activities offered at the school or, as here, a dress code, these issues of public education are generally 'committed to the control of state and local authorities.'"

In other words, once a child enters the door of the public school, parents have absolutely no rights whatsoever regarding what is taught. Not only do parents have no right to influence curricula, but they also have no right to know what their child is being taught. There is no legal responsibility requiring the school to inform parents of what their children are being taught. Parents also have no influence over or right to know how their children are being disciplined, what their children must/may wear, how and what their children are being tested on, who is teaching their children, or how long their children are at school.

Judge Reinhardt's (as well as the First Circuit Court's and Sixth Circuit Court's) decision is flawed in at least two ways: 1) Parents (and taxpayers in general) are the ones paying for the school system and have a vested interest *and right* in influencing what the schools teach. It is to the providers of funds that the public schools must be accountable. 2) The decision(s) is based on the presupposition that there is equal school choice.

It could be argued that the first flaw is addressed, in that parents (as well as communities in general) *do* influence curricula by voting on both local and state boards of education as well as state and federal legislatures. The problem, however, is that the courts have veto power. Even if local or state school boards of education or state or federal legislatures (elected by the people) adopt certain curricula, the courts can unilaterally reject such legislation. Once again, we see how non-elected judges overstep their democratic duty of interpretation by legislating from the bench, thus usurping the will of the people—in this case, school boards and legislatures.

The obvious hypocrisy of the education elitists, however, resides in the second flaw. According to Reinhardt and others, there is a fundamental right to choose where your child will go to school—whether it be a public institution, a private institution, or a home school. But once that decision is made, if you enroll your child in a public institution, parental rights disappear into the foggy quagmire of "Big Brother." Effectively, by sending your children to a public school, you are, in a legal sense, turning over temporary custody of your children to the public school system. The State retains the right to control what a society's children are taught and that to which they are exposed.

This seems practical enough. After all, a public school can't cater to every single idiosyncratic belief out there. As the First Circuit Court stated, *"If all parents have a fundamental constitutional right to dictate individually what the schools teach their children, the schools will be forced to cater a curriculum for each student whose parents had genuine moral disagreements with the school's choice of subject matter."*

Such a decision, however, presupposes a level playing field when it comes to education options. If parents really did have equal options regarding public school, private school, or homeschooling, the education elitists may have a point. But this is not the case. Nor do the education elitists want this to be the case.

As parents, you have the option of sending your children to a public school for "free." For us conservatives, however, we know there is no such thing as "free" education. My point, however, is that even those who pay little to no taxes have access to a public education system. The public education system is available to everyone regardless of how much they pay into the system. Thus, some parents can send their children to public schools for basically no charge. If parents who pay taxes into the school system choose to send their children to private schools (or to homeschool them), they simply lose that money, because it is not returned to them.

Homeschooling children or sending them to private schools, however, costs money (over and above the money paid in taxes to the public school system). Thus, it is much more difficult to send children to private schools (or to homeschool them). Additionally, there is a large segment of the population for which it is *impossible* to homeschool their children or send them to private schools (for financial reasons).

Thus, for them, public schools are the *only* option. For this population, parents are forced to enroll their students in a public school system in which their rights "beyond the threshold" are nonexistent. Even if these parents wanted to send their child to a private school that taught a curriculum more in line with their personal beliefs, they couldn't afford it.

What is important to realize is that the court decisions cited above *do* acknowledge the right of parents "to control the upbringing of their children by introducing them to matters of and relating to sex in accordance with their personal and religious values and beliefs" as well as to control other issues pertaining to the upbringing of their children. This right, however, is actualized when the parents *initially* choose where to have their children educated, *not after* the decision has been made. According to these court decisions, the parental right outlined above is not infringed upon as long as the *initial* choice is present.

But as we have already examined, a large segment of America's population has no such choice. For them, the right to control the upbringing of their children doesn't exist, because the choice is never *actualized*. Additionally, even for those who do have such a choice, the choice is not between equals. The choice is between a "free" option and options that are much more costly regarding time and money. In sports lingo, this is considered "fixing" the game. The rules are designed and enforced as to favor one team over another.

It would be like adding a $20 surcharge on every pack of Bubblicious gum, but not on Wrigley's spearmint gum. Wrigley's gum would cost $.75, while Bubblicious would cost $20.75. Which are you going to buy (especially if you're going to be paying $.75 anyway, regardless of which gum you actually chew)? Even if Bubblicious is the higher-quality gum, you're probably going to choose Wrigley's. Additionally, for many it would be *impossible* to purchase Bubblicious, because they simply could not afford it.

Here is where the hypocrisy enters the picture. The vast majority of the education elitists are against actualizing any kind of school choice. Two main reasons for this exist: 1) Public school teachers would decrease in number (due to lower enrollment in public schools)—something the teachers unions can't have; and 2) the stranglehold that liberal ideologues have on America's culture via the education system would be released.

Case in point: Vouchers. Instituting a voucher system is a way to actualize the right of all parents (especially the poor) to control matters regarding the educational upbringing of their children. Programs such as these would level the playing field because everyone would have their parental right actualized by being able to make the aforementioned initial choice (which is when the court says it is actualized). The current education system produces a monopoly free from accountability and competition. There is only one product to choose from . . . take it or leave it. Actually, it's more like "take it or take it."

If a right is never *actualized*, it doesn't exist. In this case, the parental right to "control the upbringing of their children . . ." is actualized (according to these court decisions) at the moment parents (or parent) choose which school to send their children. But because many Americans don't *actually* have such a choice, for them no such right exists. It would be like passing a law claiming black Americans have a fundamental right to a college education, while every college admissions committee rejects applications from black Americans. In *theory* the right exists, but *in actuality* it does not. Furthermore, even for those who can afford to homeschool their kids or to send them to private schools, it's not an equal choice, because it is much more costly regarding time and money.

If a system of equal educational choice existed, these judges and the liberals who support them *might* have a case. The problem is that such a system of equal educational choice does not exist . . . and the education elitists don't want such a system to exist.

Judge Reinhardt's decision was not merely about the wisdom of left-wing, socialist education agendas. It was about parental rights and the accountability of a public school system that is continually being wrenched from the hands of the communities who provide schools with both the children and the money. It's about the ever-encroaching State determining what a generation of children and later generations of adults will learn and believe. It's about not leaving parents with a viable option outside of a government-run school system. It's about using government coercion to manipulate culture.

At this point, I'm not railing against a public education system *in fact*. I'm arguing against the public education system as it currently *is*. Many claim the conservative movement is responsible for the deterioration of the public education system.

Guilty as charged.

The refusal to be held accountable results in deterioration.

Judge Reinhardt continues:

> *We conclude only that the parents are possessed of no constitutional right to prevent the public schools from providing information on that subject* [issues of sex] *to their students in any forum or manner they select.*

In his decision, Judge Reinhardt extended this right of public schools to issues other than sex. Thus, public schools have the legal authority to provide *any* information to students in *any* way they choose and with no legal responsibility to inform parents of either. Furthermore, parents have no legal right to object to *anything* the public schools teach, nor to any *manner* in which the public schools teach.

Unfortunately, Judge Reinhardt isn't alone in his opinion. This is an ideology that has infected a great number of those in the education establishment, and it can be seen all the way down to the local level.

Reinhardt wrote:

> *In fine, education is not merely about teaching the basics of reading, writing, and arithmetic. Education serves higher civic and social functions, including the rearing of children into healthy, productive, and responsible adults and the cultivation of talented and qualified leaders of diverse backgrounds.*

If this is true, is this the kind of job we want to leave to the State, its courts, and its bureaucrats?

In closing, it is interesting to note that Judge Reinhardt also rejected the plaintiff's second line of reasoning regarding why parental rights were denied. The plaintiffs claimed that parental rights concerning "the upbringing of their children . . ." are guaranteed by the "constitutional right to privacy." Reinhard ruled:

> *Thus, the right of the parents "to control the upbringing of their children by introducing them to matters of and relating to sex in accordance with their personal and religious values and beliefs" is not protected by the constitutional right to privacy, at least not as that purported right is understood by the parents in this case.*

Ironically, this same judge and many liberals who agree with his decision magically find a right to abortion under the guise of the same "constitutional right to privacy." Not only that, but a twelve-year-old has a constitutional right to have an abortion without her parents' knowledge. Apparently no constitutional right exists for that same minor to get her ears pierced, but she does have a constitutional right to undergo a dangerous medical procedure resulting in emotional and physical scarring, as well as the torturous death of her unborn child.

This is what happens when the wrong people are elected. This is what happens when non-elected judges legislate from the bench. Calling the Constitution a "living, breathing document" is simply a way to scrap the ideologies, values, and systems that allowed citizens to create the greatest country in the world.

In citing numerous rights that he claimed are protected under the "constitutional right to privacy," Judge Reinhardt wrote:

> We cannot overstate the significance of these rights. They symbolize the importance of our evolving understanding of the nature of our Constitution.

Without an objective, bedrock standard, the only standard is the "evolving" whim of those in power. Our Constitution provides an objective, non-evolving standard, and it is the greatest barrier to the liberal, statist agenda.

(Judge Reinhardt's decision is posted at http://www.ca9.uscourts.gov/ca9/newopinions.nsf/opinions+by+date?OpenView&Start=1&Count=100&Expand=1.1. The decision is entitled "Fields vs. Palmdale." It was filed on 11/2/05.)

Want to Compete? Lower the Standards.

I supported a decision of the Lakota School District (my local public school district)—most likely not for the same reasons that other people supported it, but I agreed with the decision nonetheless. In April of 2006, a letter to the editor in my local newspaper, *The Pulse Journal*, was written by a concerned resident (we'll call her Mrs. Smith to protect the name of the guilty) who addressed Lakota's grading scale. Apparently (I say *apparently*, because I wasn't aware of this issue until I read this letter to the editor), the district was entertaining the idea of changing from a seven-point grading scale to a 10-point grading scale. (For our purposes, we will ignore pluses and minuses)

The current seven-point grading scale is as follows:
- 100–93 = A
- 92–85 = B
- 85–77 = C
- 76–70 = D
- 69–0 = F

The 10-point grading scale is as follows:
- 100–90 = A
- 89–80 = B
- 79–70 = C
- 69–60 = D
- 59–0 = F

Mrs. Smith mentioned the fact that the Mason School District (a neighboring public school district) recently changed from the seven-point scale to the 10-point scale. Out of curiosity, Mrs. Smith inquired why Mason did this. Mason informed her that they had surveyed a number of schools in the districts in southwest Ohio and determined that the majority had converted to the 10-point scale.

Mrs. Smith wrote, "Mason wanted to give their students every advantage in competing in GPA with other schools and they felt that the 93–100 point scale hindered that." She went on to write, "Seems to me that Mason and other schools using the 10-point scale are more concerned with the success of their students and Lakota is more concerned with their image." Mrs. Smith concludes, "Maybe we as a school district should learn from other school districts on how to have Lakota students 'achieve to their fullest potential.'"

First, it is important to understand the difference between the two grading scales. Achieving higher grades is much easier on the 10-point scale than it is on the seven-point scale. A 90% on the seven-point scale is a B (3.0 grade point average [GPA]), while on the 10-point scale it's an A (4.0 GPA). Similarly, an 80% on the seven-point scale is a C (2.0 GPA), while on the 10-point scale it is a B (3.0 GPA). Additionally, there will be more passing grades on the 10-point scale than on the seven-point scale, because there is a wider range of possible passing percentages—40 and 30, respectively.

Taken as a whole, if a school district suddenly changes from a seven-point scale to a 10-point scale, each student's GPA will rise and more students will be considered "passing." Thus, the district-wide GPA will improve.

In this scenario, absolutely nothing objective will change. The students will not *actually* be performing any better. They will not have improved their academic performance. Yet, their grades will have improved literally overnight.

Why would a school district want to do this? One reason is that a school district may be lagging behind its neighbors in average student GPA. This reflects poorly on the schools (both locally and in the eyes of the universities where the district's students are applying). Thus, changing to a 10-point scale immediately raises the average GPA to a more "competitive" level.

Another motivation may be funding. If schools don't perform well in educating their students, they are often in danger of losing state and/or federal funding. Changing the grading scale is one way to more easily meet the state and/or national standards. Having a high average GPA is also helpful when those pesky school levies are put on the ballot.

Mrs. Smith claimed that by maintaining the seven-point scale, Lakota was only concerned about its image. It seems to me, however, that the Mason School District was the one concerned about image. School districts all over southwest Ohio are changing their grading scales. Maybe instead of increasing "competitiveness" by lowering standards, districts should consider doing what it takes to get their students to meet the current ones.

When corporations "cook the books" in order to increase the value of their shares or get around government regulations, the liberal outcry is almost deafening. Yet when public schools "cook the books" to falsely increase student "performance" for prestige or funding purposes, all is right with the world.

The fact that many schools are changing grading scales to falsely improve performance is, unfortunately, a microcosm of American culture in general. Objective standards that measure behavior and lifestyles are constantly being thrown out in the names of tolerance and relativism. After all, objective standards mean right and wrong, good and bad. In a relativistic culture, no one's behavior or "performance" is any better or worse than anyone else's.

Unfortunately for liberals, secularists, and relativists, there's never been an individual, school, state, or nation that has improved quality by lowering or doing away with standards.

This Just In! Having Children May Lead to "Lifestyle Changes" and "Adjustments"!

An April 2006 article in the *USA Today* newspaper entitled "High costs of child care can lead to lifestyle changes, adjustments" clued people in on a startling revelation: Having children leads to lifestyle changes and adjustments. Like any good Marxist treatment of the matter, however, the article focused on the economic aspect of the problem and hinted at a few economic solutions.

The article began by stating that Margaret Schwartz (a real-life example) would like to spend more time at home and maybe take a day or two off of work to be with her sons, "but she can't." You see, she spends $1,330 a month on child care. Does anyone remember the anti-drug commercial that revealed the cyclical life of a cocaine addict? The addict snorted cocaine so he could work long hours. He worked long hours so he could afford the cocaine. The lifestyle was a vicious cycle of never knowing which came first, the chicken or the egg. Ms. Schwartz was guilty of the same causal phenomenon.

The article cited that the average yearly child-care fees range from $3,803 to $13,480. The article reported that because of such costs, "working parents are basing major decisions about their jobs and families on how much care they can afford." In fact, to afford average-priced child care, a two-parent family would need to spend 10.6% of household income each year. A single parent, however, would need to pay almost $3 of every $10 earned. Hmmm, that's coming dangerously close to suggesting that a two-parent household is more efficient than a single-parent household (and that lowering the tax burden might actually help parents pay for child care).

The article discussed the methods that several families had utilized to pay the high costs of child care. One family, the Riveros, moved to a different town to find affordable child care. The Adams' were paying a nanny $2,400 a month to care for their son, Hunter (10 months of age) and $1,100 a month for Montessori school for Aiden, age 3. The nanny quit, however, which provided a "financial break." To help them with child care, they brought Mr. Adams' brother out from Nebraska to live with them.

The article then claimed that child-care workers earn low wages, the working poor bear the most burden, and very few companies help their employees by providing child-care subsidies or services. Nearly every cause *and* solution mentioned by this article was economic. Karl Marx would be so proud of this article.

The article discussed three potential solutions to the high cost of child care.

1) Taxpayers pick up the tab (also called socialism). In June of 2006, voters in California (no surprise there) voted on whether or not to support Proposition 82, which would tax "high" earners to provide pre-kindergarten child care to all four-year-olds in California. (Proposition 82 eventually failed.)

2) Force companies/employers to directly pick up the tab (again, socialism). The article quoted Rebecca Weingarten, co-founder of Daily Life Consulting, as saying, "It really affects careers and choices. . . . They feel helpless or are torn about how to afford the costs, but they feel alone. . . . Companies need to do more to help."

3) Have *other* family pick up the tab. The Adams' had a brother flown in from out of town to help. The article also suggested that, because of high child-care costs, parents are waiting until they are older to have children, "which means grandparents might not be physically capable—or live close enough—to help with child care." So by that statement, it would appear as if it's the grandparents' responsibility (if they are able) to help cover child care.

Perhaps *more* telling than the potential solutions mentioned in the article (although these potential solutions weren't necessarily endorsed by the article; they were more like forgone conclusions) were the potential solutions *not* mentioned in the article. *Nowhere* in the article was it mentioned that a parent might want to stay home with the child(ren) to address child-care needs. Apparently, the consideration that parents should raise their own children is completely lost on the author of this article.

The article began by mentioning the dilemma of Margaret Schwartz, a mother who wanted to spend more time with her children but couldn't because of child-care costs. She had to work to pay such costs. Like the situation of the cocaine addict caught in a vicious cycle, stopping either side of the cycle (working long hours *or* the cocaine addiction) would render the other side unnecessary.

Wait a minute! I think I've got it! I know a way Margaret Schwartz (or her husband) could spend as much time as she (or he) wanted with her (or his) children! She (or he) could put the career on hold (or simply choose raising children as a career) and personally take care of the child(ren). This would remove the high child-care costs, thereby making it unnecessary for her (or him) to keep her (or his) job.

Why is this concept so foreign to the author of this article and, no doubt, to so many others? Because of the denigration of the family. Modern liberalism teaches that the individual is the end-all, be-all of existence. Freedom is being able to create your own reality and live according to your own desires, whenever and wherever. An institution like the family, with its obligations and responsibilities, simply isn't conducive to such an ideology.

Feminism has contributed to this problem by denigrating the stay-at-home mother as second-rate (or no rate). For feminism, equality resides in shattering all differences between male and female, resulting in a uniformity of gender. Any job, i.e., motherhood and/or fatherhood, that smacks of "traditional gender roles" must be eradicated in the name of liberation.

If society creates a vacuum regarding who's responsible for raising children, who do you think will jump to fill that role? Various groups struggling for cultural dominance will make it a high priority on their agenda to fulfill such a function, because future cultural and ideological power comes with influencing children at such a young age.

Modern liberalism has already succeeded in doing so via their monopolistic public education system that "educates" children with liberal, secular ideals from the ages of five to 22. Why not go even younger? Of course, the only entity powerful enough to provide a medium for such an undertaking is the government (as we've seen with so many other liberal cultural takeovers—i.e., public education, socialized medicine and retirement programs, entitlement programs, wealth redistribution programs, the "separation of church and state," etc.).

A citizenry without virtue is totalitarianism's best friend. The powerful elite would like nothing more than a population of individuals shirking all obligation and responsibility. With every vacuum that is filled by government institutions or regulations, another step closer to totalitarianism we come. Thomas Jefferson was right. Eternal vigilance really is the price of freedom. When we cease being vigilant in our own obligations and responsibilities, we turn over such *freedoms* to someone else more than willing to fill the void and gain the power that comes with fulfilling the obligations and responsibilities formerly reserved for the citizenry.

9

The Judiciary
Circumventing the People

The Ideology of Choice?

IN HER column on August 17, 2005 ("Cindy Sheehan: Commander in Grief"), Ann Coulter quoted *New York Times* columnist Maureen Dowd as saying, "But his [Bush's] humanitarianism will remain inhumane as long as he fails to understand that the moral authority of parents who bury children killed in Iraq is absolute." I concurred with Ann Coulter when she responded to Dowd's comments by writing "Dowd's 'absolute' moral authority column demonstrates, once again, what can happen when liberals start tossing around terms they don't understand like 'absolute' and 'moral.'" You know that when liberals start using terms like "absolute" and "moral" in the same sentence, they've hijacked the language train and are heading off a cliff.

In his book, *Deliver Us From Evil*, Sean Hannity spends a chapter discussing how liberals are only pro-choice when it comes to abortion. When it comes to school choice, education curriculum, what to do with our own money, issues of church and state, guns, and a whole host of other issues, liberals believe they know what's best for everyone—and they usually get some federal judge to force their agenda on the American people. What makes Maureen Dowd's comment so comical is the fact that when it comes to parents' rights regarding most other issues, the "absolute moral authority of parents" magically disappears.

Which political ideology fights for the rights of twelve-year-olds to have abortions performed without parental notification? Which political ideology fights for the indoctrination of "safe sex" health "education" in public school without parental contribution? Which ideology fights against school vouchers that would allow poor parents to send their children to safer, more successful schools? Which ideology believes the government can better save for someone's retirement than the person who earns the money himself? Which ideology believes there should be a hefty tax on what parents can leave for their children's inheritance?

The answer to all of the above? Modern liberalism.

Modern liberalism doesn't believe in choice. It believes in the establishment of ideas thought up by elitists—ideas that are enforced through coercion via cultural institutions and government.

Star Parker's column, "Why We Need Conservative Judges," (July 25, 2005) is a great analysis of how liberalism views the law. The law's purpose isn't the protection of its citizens, but the social engineering of its citizens. For liberalism, the law and government are used to create the type of humans the liberal worldview says should exist. Unfortunately for liberals (and for the rest of us when liberals are in power), modern liberalism is trying to fit a square peg in a round hole.

If liberals truly wanted choice (especially parental choice), they would embrace the policies reflected in the series of questions listed above regarding parental notification, school choice, parental contribution to public education curricula, lower taxes, privatized Social Security, and the abolishment of the death tax—not to mention the acknowledgment of gun rights and the faulty interpretation of "separation of church and state."

The most recent example of modern liberalism limiting choice is the Supreme Court's recent decision (in Kehoe vs. New London) that allows the government to decide for people what should be done with their own property. According to the Supreme Court, as long as the new establishment would pay more in taxes, the current private property owner no longer has a right to his land or possessions. "Back in the day," the most prominent expressions and symbols of the existence of freedom were the ownership of a gun and a piece of land (private property) . . . two things modern liberalism claims are the bane of existence.

Judicial Activism and Abortion Rhetoric

While President Bush repeatedly insisted there would be no litmus tests for any of his judicial nominees, Senate liberals cannot say the same. When Senate confirmation hearings occur (when a president nominates a judge—Supreme Court or otherwise), this is what usually happens. Senate liberals repeatedly ask judicial nominees about their views on Roe v. Wade and gay marriage (for example). If judicial nominees do not answer these questions to the satisfaction of liberals, i.e., if they fail the litmus test, there is a liberal outcry.

Despite the fact that judicial nominees should not answer such questions in the first place, liberals will accuse the nominees of stonewalling their attempts to honestly learn about the nominee. Bush's nominees should be under no compulsion to answer ridiculous questions from liberals who will vote against their nomination anyway.

The President's right to appoint judges reflects the notion that elections actually mean something. Why liberals thought they had a right to determine who got appointed as judges when they had lost election after election (at the time) and represented a minority in the Senate (at the time) was beyond me. (Although the question of who controls the Senate is irrelevant in these cases because the Senate's "advise and consent" duty mentioned in the Constitution was not meant to be used as an ideologically-based stonewalling technique.) What was also beyond me was the fact that congressional Republicans yielded such an ability to the minority. When President Clinton appointed two far left judicial activists to the Supreme Court during his tenure, the Republicans didn't raise a stink. Why not? When Democrats control Congress, do you think they express a concern to "get along" with Republicans? While appeasing terrorists and criminals may be second nature to liberals, appeasing Republicans has never been a priority. Republicans should have returned the favor and forced a vote on President Bush's nominee(s). Let the Liberals cry foul. See if I care. I've grown accustomed to their whining and rhetoric over the years. Nothing new there.

Speaking of rhetoric. Liberals paint a picture of tyranny and disaster if Roe v. Wade is overturned. Abortion will become illegal, women will return to the back alleys, and the health of pregnant women will be prioritized lower than their unborn children. Is this really the case? Is this what liberals fear? I think not. Liberals are afraid of the will of the people. Overturning Roe v. Wade will not automatically make abortion illegal. All it will do is put the issue in the hands of the voters—and *that* is what liberals desperately fear.

The judiciary is so important to liberals, because it is only through the judiciary that they can "pass" their agenda. It's impossible for them to get their most cherished ideas (abortion on demand, socialist health care and economics, etc.) through the legislature (i.e., the people), so they must resort to forcing their agenda through judicial fiat—thus bypassing the people.

Some states will make most forms of abortion illegal, while some states will not. It's interesting that the liberal voices calling for "tolerance" and "diversity" mysteriously go silent when it comes to forcing the liberal agenda on the American people. If someone doesn't like the abortion laws in a particular state, he can, as Ronald Reagan said, "vote with his feet" by moving. States like California and New York will most assuredly legalize abortion (as will several others). If someone wants to live under such a law, they can move to a state that has such a law. But liberals fear a society where laws are determined by the legislature, i.e., the people. For that is a society largely absent of liberal policy.

Will Hypocrisy Never Cease?

Barely fifteen minutes after President Bush's announcement nominating John Roberts to the Supreme Court, the Democrats were at it again. Patrick Leahy and Charles Schumer each gave brief speeches chock full of liberal hypocrisy. Concerned with their "constitutional duty" not to rubber-stamp a judge with a lifetime appointment, they once again illustrated the depth of liberal politicking and double standards.

Any true conservative knows that a conservative who garners compliments from liberals is probably not truly a conservative. Case in point: Sandra Day O'Connor. After her resignation on July 1, 2005, liberals heaped praises on her as if she were a president who molested an intern and committed perjury.

She was classified a "mainstream conservative" by the left in hopes of encouraging Bush to nominate a similar type of "conservative." A "conservative" who believes the Constitution grants the right to brutally murder unborn children (even those whose bodies—except their head—are outside the womb) is a "conservative" liberals can compliment. Pardon me if I rue the day I'm ever complimented by a liberal.

Because liberals like Leahy and Schumer believed that John Roberts was a conservative that might have qualms about brutally murdering children who are half born, they immediately launched a political counterattack seconds after his nomination.

Senator Leahy praised O'Connor because "she didn't prejudge cases." Leahy then went on to say regarding the nomination process, "I really do not expect any issues that go to the qualifications, the honesty, integrity and of the fairness—the fairness—of a Supreme Court justice to be off-limits." You can rest assured knowing that Senate Democrats asked Roberts how he would vote in cases regarding abortion, gay marriage, and several other particular issues. When Roberts refused to answer such questions, he was berated by Senate Democrats for not answering their questions. Did Senator Leahy come to Roberts' defense because of his (Roberts') refusal to prejudge cases (like he did O'Connor's)? Of course not.

Senator Schumer stated, ". . . it is vital that Judge Roberts answer a wide range of questions openly, honestly and fully in the coming months. His views will affect a generation of Americans, and it is his obligation during the nomination process to let the American people know those views." I wonder if Senator Schumer will remember the Ginsburg standard. When Ruth Bader Ginsburg was asked specific questions regarding her would-be opinion regarding particular cases, she refused to answer. Apparently this was sufficient for Senate Democrats back then. Was such a standard sufficient when Roberts refused to answer those same questions? Of course not.

Why is it that the Supreme Court nominees of Democratic presidents fly through Congress (Ginsburg passed by a vote of 96-3, and Breyer passed by a vote of 88-9), while the nominees of Republican presidents are attacked mercilessly (e.g., Robert Bork and Clarence Thomas)? Democratic presidents push through flaming liberal activist judges like Ginsburg (General Counsel to the ACLU) and Breyer, while Republican presidents compromise and nominate pseudo-conservatives like O'Connor, Souter, Kennedy, and Stevens (now liberal activist judges themselves). Seven of the nine Supreme Court justices have been appointed by Republican presidents. That's hard to believe considering how liberal the Supreme Court is today.

Another Day Older and Deeper in Hypocrisy

Do people think before they speak? Or has the blinding influence of power and ideology so warped the politicians of this country that consistently telling the truth has become almost impossible?

On October 27, 2005, it was announced that Harriet Miers withdrew her nomination to the Supreme Court. She claimed her reason was because of documents the Bush administration wasn't willing to release for Senate scrutiny (a problem not for Miers but for senators). As White House counsel, all documents and conversations between Miers and Bush are protected under attorney-client privilege. Since she had no judicial record, it would have been difficult to learn anything about her judicial and legal philosophies, because the materials that would have revealed such information would not be released.

Let's get one thing straight: This withdrawal wasn't about documents. It was about the appointment of an unproven conservative and a person who reportedly didn't do well in interviews with Senate Republicans. The documents are a red herring. To be honest, I was never a big fan of Harriet

Miers' nomination. My reasons were the same as those of other conservatives. She was not a proven conservative with a record.

Senate minority leader (now majority leader), Harry Reid, cited Miers' withdrawal as a victory for the "radical right." He said that he hoped President Bush would not reward this kind of behavior by appointing a nominee in line with the radical right's agenda. God forbid there be a Supreme Court nominee who has similar views to a president who, in 2004, won a higher percentage of the popular vote than Bill Clinton ever received. (In his two presidential elections, Bill Clinton never received even 50% of the popular vote.)

Democratic senator, Dianne Feinstein, said that the attacks on Harriet Miers came from a group within a group, i.e., the radical right. Feinstein went on to say that people wouldn't have attacked a man like they attacked Miers. So now not only is the radical right responsible for Miers' withdrawal, but they also are sexists.

Let's see, according to Harry Reid and Dianne Feinstein, it is considered unacceptable behavior for a group to oppose a Supreme Court nominee because that nominee disagrees with them (which is what they accused the "radical right" of doing). Were these two Democrats born yesterday? Did they just blip into existence with absolutely no memory?

Does anyone remember the Robert Bork and Clarence Thomas nomination hearings? Bork was ridden out of town on a rail based on lies. Clarence Thomas was almost ridden out of town on a rail based on trumped-up sexual assault charges engineered by the Democrats as a last-ditch effort to reject his nomination. Bork and Thomas were treated horribly. They were the subjects of lies, and their names were dragged through the mud. Democrats tried to ruin their entire careers.

Question One: What sex were Bork and Thomas? Male. Question Two: Why did Democrats oppose Bork and Thomas? Because they disagreed with their legal and political philosophies.

Does anyone remember that Democrats filibustered appellate court nominations throughout the entirety of Bush's presidency? The Democrats opposed judicial nominees such as Priscilla Owens and Janice Rogers Brown because they were not "mainstream conservatives" (read: liberals). In fact, many of President Bush's judicial nominees were *never* brought to the floor for a vote. Why? Because the Democrats disagreed with the political and philosophical views of these conservative nominees.

That's right, the hypocrisy of modern liberal leaders. Liberal leaders readily point fingers at the "radical right," calling the group's behavior unacceptable, but they are strangely silent when the Democratic Party (currently controlled by the radical left) opposes judicial nominees for the exact same reasons.

How do Democrats constantly get away with such hypocritical behavior? Isn't there anybody out there who will call them out? Will Senate Republicans remember Harry Reid's comments the next time Democrats oppose a judicial nominee? Probably not.

The Democrats know what happens when a Republican president's nominee for the Supreme Court gets rejected. They usually get a more "moderate" or "mainstream" (read: liberal) nominee who, upon the nomination, trades in his principles for the power and influence available only through liberal judicial activism.

Gearing Up for a Fight
[written on 11/1/05]

Consider this my official endorsement of Supreme Court nominee Samuel Alito. In fact, I probably could have told you this yesterday before I knew anything about his judicial record. The simple fact that Democrats are coming out in droves in opposition to him tells me everything I need to know.

The first clue that Harriet Miers may not have been the best choice for the Supreme Court is the fact that Democrats were relatively silent after her nomination. Actually, that is one thing that worries me about newly appointed Chief Justice John Roberts as well. Only half of the Senate Democrats voted against him. In order for me to sleep well at night, I want every single Democrat in the Senate to vote against a Supreme Court nominee. In fact, I won't sleep easy until the Democrats filibuster a Supreme Court nominee. Only then can I rest assured knowing that a Supreme Court nominee is good for the country.

Do you remember that brawl that everyone was shaping up for—the knockdown, drag-out fight between Republicans and Democrats over a Supreme Court nominee that would divide the country? Well, folks, we might get just that this time around. . . . and I couldn't be happier.

Sure, it frustrates me to no end when Democrats spew out their rhetoric about "uniting the country;" selecting a "mainstream" conservative; Bush "giving in" to the radical right; and how conservative judges will roll back civil rights so as to reinstate slavery, rob women of their voting rights, and systematically kill off the poor, the disabled, and the secular.

For some reason, Democrats believe that they are entitled to keep the court at its current balance of six liberals and three conservatives (assuming Roberts turns out to be a conservative). For some reason, Democrats think that the president has to replace the outgoing justices with new justices who have the exact same political philosophy. Whence does this responsibility come?

Such a requirement is nowhere to be found in any founding documents, legislation, or precedence. In short, the president is required replace a liberal with a liberal, because Democrats want to maintain the *status quo* regarding the liberal stranglehold they have on the Supreme Court.

Make no mistake, the Democrats' definition of "mainstream" conservative is *liberal*. They continue to call for a nominee "in the mold of Sandra Day O'Connor," i.e., a liberal. A Democratic president, however, is free to appoint any radical left-wing judge he desires (read: Justices Ginsburg and Breyer), but a Republican president isn't permitted to appoint a conservative.

New York left-winger Charles Schumer said, "At first blush . . . Judge Alito does not seem to be a Sandra Day O'Connor." He said this in the context of expressing his disappointment that Bush nominated someone who would divide the country rather than unite it. Apparently it's only bad when conservatives divide the country. When liberals divide the country by undermining the war on terror, the war in Iraq, and a burgeoning economy . . . or exploiting the poor through class warfare . . . everything is fine and dandy.

Why wasn't the country divided when President Clinton nominated ACLU Council Ruth Bader-Ginsburg—a radical left-winger if there ever was one? Why wasn't the country divided when President Clinton nominated left-winger Stephen Breyer to the Supreme Court? Why does the country seem to be divided only when conservatives (i.e., Robert Bork and Clarence Thomas) are nominated for the Supreme Court?

Frankly, I get suspicious every time there's *not* division in Congress. Either the people I voted for aren't doing their jobs, or the people I voted for lost.

Supreme Court Epiphanies

In the first three days of the Alito confirmation hearings, I learned three things:

A Supreme Court Justice's Personal Opinion on Any Particular Issue Doesn't (or Shouldn't) Matter.

The only area where a judge's personal opinion matters is in the area of general legal philosophy. That is, what he thinks the role of the judiciary is, what the intentions of the founding fathers were when they crafted the Constitution, and what kind of document the Constitution is (i.e., is he an originalist, a strict constructionist, a judicial activist, etc.?). If a judge honestly answers these three questions, it is fairly easy to predict how he will decide on any particular case in the future.

Senate Democrats on the Judiciary Committee continually asked Samuel Alito what his personal opinions were regarding a number of particular issues (i.e., abortion, affirmative action, civil rights, etc.). What our liberal friends don't understand is that, for a conservative judge, personal opinion doesn't matter. It is the opinion of the *law* (the Constitution) that matters.

The proper question to ask Alito was not, "What is your opinion regarding abortion/affirmative action/civil rights?," but, "What do you think the *law* says about abortion/affirmative action/civil rights?" A good judge knows that questions of the former type are irrelevant in his capacity as judge. Nor should such questions be asked during the nomination process. Questions of the latter type are extremely relevant, because that is the duty of the judiciary: to interpret the laws *as created and passed by the legislative branch of government.*

Which brings me to my second epiphany:

Conservative Judges Base Their Decisions on The Law, while Liberal Judges Base Their Decisions on Some Vague Notion of "Justice."

This is why those who subscribe to a conservative judicial philosophy often use the words "restraint" and "modesty." A judge's decision regarding a particular case is restrained by the law. To invoke some standard beyond the law in issuing judicial decisions is to go beyond the role of the judiciary.

I read a column a while ago entitled, "The Only Good Constitution is a Dead Constitution," written by Jonah Goldberg. Goldberg discussed the danger in treating the Constitution as a "living, breathing document." What does categorizing the Constitution as a "living document" mean? Goldberg quoted Al Gore to summarize the position.

When asked what kind of Supreme Court justices he would appoint if he were elected president, Gore replied, "I would look for justices of the

Supreme Court who understand that our Constitution is a living and breathing document, that it was intended by our founders to be interpreted in the light of the constantly evolving experience of the American people."

Goldberg summed up the argument against viewing the Constitution as a "living document" by writing, "Once you accept the proposition that the words on the page can mean what you want them to mean, well, then the words of the page matter less than the views of those we select to interpret them. Once this happens, the Court in effect becomes an unelected and unaccountable legislature."

If the words of the Constitution have no meaning of their own and are not intended to be the standard throughout our country's history and future, then it is the will of a select few judges that will determine the laws and direction of the country. That is, whatever values adopted by the judiciary that are in vogue at the time will be the values that guide culture.

Goldberg quoted Robert Bork in citing the consequences of such a view. Bork wrote in his book, *The Tempting of America*, (as quoted by Goldberg) "The abandonment of original understanding in modern times means the transportation into the Constitution of the principles of a liberal culture that cannot achieve those results democratically."

Translated: What modern liberals can't pass through democratically (i.e., through Congress), they will force down our throats by way of judicial *fiat*.

When liberal judges invoke a standard outside the Constitution to interpret the Constitution, they have free reign to interpret the Constitution however they please. This is the great thing about appealing to some vague notion of "justice" in rendering judicial decisions. Doing so gives them *carte blanche* permission to infuse into the meaning of the Constitution whatever personal values they hold at the time. (This is also why liberal judges like to cite international law when interpreting the Constitution. Almost *any* personal opinion of a judge can be found in a codified law *somewhere* in the world.)

Simply Because a (Conservative) Judge Issues a Decision Doesn't Mean He Personally Agrees with that Decision. It Only Means that He Believes that This is The Law's Opinion of the Case.

This is another reason why a conservative judge's personal opinion regarding a particular matter is irrelevant. A conservative judge who properly views the role of the judiciary may issue a court decision that he does not personally agree with if the law in that case runs contrary to the judge's personal opinion.

If this is the case, what the law says trumps the personal opinion of the judge. *It is not a judge's role to determine the moral legitimacy of a particular law, only its legality. If a particular law is immoral, it is the job of the legislature, not that of the judiciary, to fix it.*

Herein lies a big difference between a liberal judge and a conservative judge. Very rarely, if ever, will a liberal judge issue a decision that is in disagreement with his personal opinion regarding the matter at hand. This is because modern liberalism acknowledges no authority outside the personal value construction of the individual. Conservatism, on the other hand, acknowledges an authority outside the values constructed by the individual: in this case, the law.

Random Thoughts on the Alito Confirmation Hearings

Why is it that liberals want a judicial nominee to have an open mind, yet, when it comes to liberal judicial mainstays such as Roe v. Wade, they expect a judge to assure them how he would rule in a future case? Once a judge declares his position on such a case, he would be beholden to that position regardless of the actual case brought before him in the future. Another important consideration is the fact that judges are appointed, not elected. In other words, they don't make campaign promises to those who would elect them. To do so would undermine the legitimacy (or what's left of it, at least) of the courts.

In January of 2006, Senator Patrick Leahy said that President Bush should have fulfilled his campaign promise to be a uniter and not a divider by appointing a judge from a list of hundreds that would receive unanimous support across the political spectrum. Of course, this is just political jargon meant to disguise his real wish for President Bush to appoint a liberal.

Leahy said that this list had numerous qualified candidates on it. He was either insinuating Alito wasn't qualified (which is ridiculous), or he was against him because of ideology. Ginsberg and Breyer were radical liberals, yet they were confirmed overwhelmingly by Republicans. The Senate's job is not to vote based upon the ideology of a judge, but upon his credentials. The particular ideology of a judge is decided by the person whom the American people elected as president . . . and a conservative was elected president in 2004.

The Judiciary

In order to convince us that Democrats are fair and balanced, Leahy went on to cite how Democrats stood up to Franklin D. Roosevelt when he tried to stack the Supreme Court with his own people by adding two seats to the court. Anyone who thinks the Democrats of today are like the Democrats of the 1930s is sorely mistaken. Leahy's comment that "we" (Democrats) stood up to FDR smacks of deceit and is probably a flat-out lie.

Ted Kennedy, the "morally pure, no-skeletons-in-the-closet" senator from Massachusetts, stated that the role of the Supreme Court is to be the guardian of civil rights. He said that the Supreme Court exists to check executive power. Of course, Kennedy failed to mention which branch of government, if any, serves to check the power of the Supreme Court itself.

Senator Joe Biden, merely falling in line with modern liberalism in general, goes on and on about how the racism and bigotry of today is just as rampant as it was in the 1960s . . . it just takes on different forms. Modern liberals must peddle this extreme overstatement to maintain the division and victim mentality so necessary in those who vote for liberals. Without divisive ideologies and victims to exploit, it's awfully hard for a liberal to get elected. After all, without a victim who cannot save himself, who can liberals exploit? If there are no victims out there, the liberals must simply convince us that there are.

Senator Dianne Feinstein believes that the Supreme Court shouldn't be moved to the right. She thinks it should represent "mainstream America" (or at least what *she* considers mainstream America . . . which isn't exactly represented by her home state of Soviet California). She stated that she believed that a majority of Americans agree with her political positions. (If this is the case, why don't liberals pass their leftist agenda through the legislature instead of the judiciary?)

In an interview after the hearings, Feinstein said that she believed Alito would limit congressional power by overruling legislation. Excuse me? I wonder if Feinstein knows the number of bills passed in Congress that went to legalize abortion. The answer is zero. Does she know how much state and federal legislation was overruled by Roe v. Wade? The answer: a whole heckuva lot. Liberals have never had a problem getting around the will of the people through the courts. If they did, they would never be able to actualize their leftist agenda—which has absolutely no chance of being approved by the people. Overruling the will of the people via the courts is their only hope.

Senator Charles Schumer claimed that the Alito confirmation hearings told us nothing substantial about Alito, because he refused to answer so many questions. The only assurance we have that he will respect precedence is a vague backing of *stare decisis*. Schumer claimed that a disrespect for precedence is reason enough to vote against a judge. He believes this because Supreme Court precedence has been liberal for the last 50 years. Following precedence—not the Constitution—is the only way to perpetuate the liberal agenda. A judge who is willing to overrule precedence in the name of constitutionality scares liberals, because he could undo years of liberal unconstitutional judicial *fiats* that have circumvented the will of the people. Had there been a conservative court issuing decisions over the last 50 years, Schumer would support a judicial nominee who did *not* respect *stare decisis*.

Schumer claimed that Alito would not disclose his opinion on abortion (assuming for a moment that Alito is pro-life), because it is unpopular. Such an admission would put him out of favor with the American people, which would make his nomination to the Supreme Court much more difficult. Alito did not answer questions regarding how he would decide a potential abortion case for two reasons: 1) He did not want to pre-commit himself to a particular position, because that would preclude him from judging a future case on its own merits; and 2) he knew that if he came out with his view of abortion in general, he would be "Borked."

On a side note, if liberals are so sure that the majority of Americans are pro-abortion, why don't they allow the American people to vote on the issue? Overturning Roe v. Wade would not immediately make abortion illegal. It would simply put the matter to local and state governments. For example, abortion would most likely remain legal in California, while it would probably become illegal (at least in most cases) in a state like Texas. The fact is that the majority of Americans do not support on-demand abortion, and liberals know this. This is why they must force their abortion agenda down our throats via the judiciary.

Senator Dick Durbin asked the question as to whether or not Alito would side with the poor and downtrodden or with the rich and powerful. Here's an idea: How about a judge that sides with the Constitution and the law? The legislative branch of government is the proper place to change the law, not the judiciary.

Senator Durbin also expressed concern that Alito would be replacing Sandra Day O'Connor, which would shift the court to the right. I've harped on this before, but I have no idea where liberals got the idea that a retiring judge must be replaced by a new judge with a similar ideology. Of course this isn't the case when a conservative judge retires . . . as illustrated when Ruth Bader Ginsburg replaced Justice Byron White. Liberals peddle

The Judiciary

this idea in order to maintain their stranglehold on the ideology of the Supreme Court.

This Just In: Supreme Court Crumbling

(The first article is a legitimate story reported by the Associated Press. The second, needless to say, is not.)

Supreme Court Marble Facade Crumbles
Monday, November 28, 2005
Associated Press

WASHINGTON—A basketball-sized piece of marble moulding fell from the facade over the entrance to the Supreme Court, landing on the steps near visitors waiting to enter the building. No one was injured when the stone fell. The marble was part of the dentil moulding that serves as a frame for the frieze of statues atop the court's main entrance.

A group of visitors had just entered the building and had passed under the frieze when the stone fell at 9:30 a.m. EST. Jonathan Fink, a government attorney waiting in line to attend arguments, said, "All of a sudden, these blocks started falling. It was like a thud, thud."

Ed Fisher, a government worker, said some of the marble pieces shattered, spraying the area with smaller chunks of stone. A group of students from Columbus, Ohio pocketed some of the fragments as souvenirs, Fisher said.

Mark Goodman, a Washington resident, said some of the people who picked up larger pieces of stones took them back. "We'll have to look on ebay tomorrow," Goodman said.

Earlier in the morning, dozens of people had lined up in hopes of getting a seat for arguments inside the court—a practice which is not unusual. Justices were back on the bench Monday following a two-week recess. The fallen marble lay directly in the center of the path up to the court entrance.

The 70-year-old Supreme Court building is undergoing a $122 million, five-year renovation project, although it does not appear that the accident was related to that work.

This Just In: Supreme Court Crumbling
Monday, November 29, 2005
James Abernathy

WASHINGTON – After over 200 years, the United States Supreme Court building gave way to gravity. On Monday morning, a large chunk of the Supreme Court building fell to the ground, almost killing a group of citizens walking beneath. It is thought that an ongoing disagreement between the building and gravity resulted in the falling of the marble chunk.

From his office a few blocks away, Senator Ted Kennedy (D – MA) responded, "This comes as a complete shock. We simply cannot let this stand. We must unite together as Americans and reverse this injustice perpetrated by gravity. By our sheer will, we will succeed."

In a statement issued earlier this afternoon, Representative Nancy Pelosi (D – CA) said, "Today we saw the disastrous fruits of gravity. Because of gravity, the Supreme Court nearly killed the citizens walking beneath it. We should heed this warning and come together to say 'No' to gravity. We must tell this contemptible foe that we will stand for it no longer."

The recent crumbling seems to be the result of an ongoing tension between the Supreme Court and gravity. Proponents of the Supreme Court building argue that it exists to preserve the rights and freedoms of buildings everywhere against un-American repression such as the invasive dictates of gravity.

Senator Charles Schumer (D – NY) said, "This is simply another example of gravity trying to force its own values on everything around it. If history has shown us anything, it's that monolithic cookie-cutter dictates forced on everyone never work. The Supreme Court must be allowed to continue its fight against gravity, and we must join this fight. Freedom itself depends on it."

Many, however, believe that a compromise can be reached and that a balance between the Supreme Court building and gravity is possible. In a joint press conference this afternoon, the so-called "Gang of 14," a bipartisan group of moderate Republicans and moderate Democrats, encouraged the Supreme Court building and gravity to sit down with one another to try to work out their differences.

Senator Mike DeWine (R–OH) said, "In the hope of uniting America and moving forward, we should encourage a compromise agreement which contains elements from both the Supreme Court building and gravity. I'm sure that once everyone settles down and becomes reasonable, cooler heads will prevail, and everyone will win—not just Washington-based interest groups."

Senator Arlen Specter (R–PA) commented, "In cases such as these, it's important to have balance."

Sara Johnson, a woman who was almost struck by the crumbling building, said that she didn't know the Supreme Court building was capable of such harm. Upon being released from the hospital where she underwent precautionary tests, she commented, "I had no idea. How long has this been happening? Why wasn't something done sooner?"

Frank Bowman, a social worker from New York who barely escaped the falling rubble, said, "If we solve the problem caused by trying to universalize gravity's values, we will address the root issue behind the crumbling building. Only then can we treat the abused building with the love and respect it deserves."

A member of the You've Got to Be Kidding Me Foundation, the Midwest-based think tank, asked Howard Dean, chairman of the Democratic Party, if the Supreme Court building should just be renovated. Dean responded by saying, "Renovating the Supreme Court building would be giving in to the radical demands of gravity. Such a cowardly act would set us back decades . . . back to the days when people were forced to believe restrictive dogmas like 'the sky is blue' and the laws of thermodynamics."

Film director and political activist, Michael Moore, chimed into the debate when he said that his next documentary is already in the works. "I've known about gravity and its exploits for a long time. In fact, I've already started production on my next documentary, *A Titanic Conspiracy Sunk: The Iceberg Lied, People Died!*, which exposes the oppressive conspiracy between gravity, icebergs, and the politicians and corporations that support them."

The newly elected president of the AFL-CIO, John Doolittle, who was three blocks away at the annual Reverse Collusion Conference, issued a statement that included a reference to gravity's harsh treatment of the marble that constitutes the Supreme Court building. "Gravity provides absolutely no benefits to those who get in its way. Gravity's ethical apathy and lack of tolerance toward those who think differently is staggering. Where are the labor laws that protect marble from the greedy ambitions of gravity to pull everyone down?"

The leftover rubble itself was quickly pocketed by those who were nearest the incident. Brian Smith, who witnessed the incident from a distance, commented, "After the piece of the Supreme Court building fell and shattered into little pieces, everyone frantically scrambled around, trying to grab a piece of the Supreme Court for themselves. Apparently, what's left of the Supreme Court is worth a pretty penny on ebay."

Jennifer N. Terpret, the chairwoman of People for the Separation of Church and State, issued a statement this afternoon. Miss N. Terpret stated, "This country was founded by people who wanted to respect gravitational diversity. Gravity may be fine for some people, but it's not for everyone . . . and the government shouldn't be kowtowing to the extreme wing of the gravitational party by constructing its buildings to favor gravity's agenda."

The outcome of this controversy is still very much up in the air, because debate in the Senate has virtually grounded to a halt. It doesn't look like a vote will be taken on the issue before Congress breaks for the winter. At the moment, the Republicans are either unable or unwilling to break the Democratic filibuster.

Senator Schumer told reporters, "Gravity definitely rises to the level of the 'extreme circumstances' that are required for a filibuster. Gravity's intolerance and lack of compassion for the individual rights of buildings to be built how they choose is not something Americans should tolerate. How a building is constructed is a private matter."

Calls to gravity's office were left unreturned . . . but reporters and officials expect to hear from it soon enough.

"Effecting" Change: Should Conservatives Be Pro-Abortion?

During the confirmation hearings on Judge John Roberts, liberal senators (especially Ted Kennedy) kept bringing up the phrase "effects test"—usually in the context of discussing the Voting Rights Act. The purpose of the Voting Rights Act is to prevent discriminatory legislation on both state and federal levels. Naturally, the question arose regarding the standard that should be used to determine whether or not a particular piece of legislation was discriminatory, i.e., unconstitutionally discriminatory against a particular group of people.

Two methods were discussed to determine whether or not a piece of legislation should be considered discriminatory and, thus, unconstitutional. The first was called the "intent test." A piece of legislation could be deemed discriminatory (and thus unconstitutional) only if it were shown that the legislation consciously *intended* to be discriminatory.

The second test was called the "effects test." This standard claimed that a piece of legislation was discriminatory (and thus unconstitutional) if the *effects* of the legislation were discriminatory, i.e., if they adversely affected any particular group of people. Thus, if the "effects test" is utilized, the intent of a piece of legislation is irrelevant.

Obviously, intent is much harder to prove in a court of law, because intent has to do with personal and/or mental motivation. Effects, on the other hand, are easier to prove because they are quantifiable (leaving out, for present purposes, the question of *whose* standard is used for determining what is and is not discrimination). Ted Kennedy is of the opinion that the "effects test" is vitally important when determining the constitutionality of legislation.

Let's see what happens when we apply the "effects test" to another issue of national interest and public policy: Abortion. (The following abortion statistics were gleaned from the Center for Disease Control [CDC] and a joint study done in 2005 by the Alan Guttmacher Institute [AGI] and Physicians for Reproductive Choice and Health [PRCH].)

It's been undisputed for a long time that the majority of abortions occur among minorities and the poor. This is not a controversial statement, although, depending upon the motivations of pro-abortion advocates, this fact may not be highlighted. In some contexts, however, liberals will cite this fact in an attempt to emphasize the role of racism and poverty in determining the decisions of individuals (rather than attributing moral responsibility to the individual himself). Here are some facts:

- 57% of those getting abortions are poor or low-income.
- Black and Hispanic women make up 51.8% of women having abortions.
- About 7% of women having abortions are Asian, Pacific Islander, or Native American.
- Thus, minorities account for nearly 60% of all abortions in the United States.
- Additionally, the poor and low-income account for nearly 60% of all abortions in the United States.
- About 75% of the United States population is white.
- The abortion ratio for black women (491 per 1,000 live births) is 3.0 times the ratio for white women (165 per 1,000).
- The abortion rate for black women (29 per 1,000 women) is 3.0 times the rate for white women (10 per 1,000), whereas the abortion rate for women of other races (21 per 1,000 women) is 2.1 times the rate for white women.

There are two possible premises regarding the value of legalized abortion. The first premise is that legalized abortion is good. The second premise is that legalized abortion is bad. Applying the "effects test" to the statistics above, legislation and court decisions that legalize abortion are unconstitutional regardless of which premise is held to be true.

If the first premise is true, the effects of current abortion policy are obviously discriminatory against the rich and white people, because a significantly lower proportion of the rich and white people benefit from the current abortion policy. In order for abortion policy not to discriminate, there must be a proportionally equal number of abortions in every possible racial and economic demographic. This is obviously not the case. Therefore, according to the "effects test," current abortion policy is unconstitutional.

If the second premise is true, the effects of current abortion policy are obviously discriminatory against minorities and the poor, because a significantly higher proportion of minorities and the poor are getting abortions. In order for abortion policy not to discriminate, there must be proportionally equal numbers of abortions in every possible racial and economic demographic. Seeing as a much higher proportion of minorities and the poor are being killed, it is obvious that, according to the "effects test," current abortion policy is unconstitutional.

If abortion is bad, current abortion policy discriminates against minorities and the poor. If abortion is good (or at least acceptable), current abortion policy discriminates against the rich and the white. It is obvious that current abortion policy has profoundly differing effects on different races and economic classes. As this is the very definition of discrimination, such policy is unconstitutional according to proponents of the "effects test."

In order for abortion policy to not be discriminatory, legislation must be drafted that *forces* the equal proportionality of abortions across the racial and economic board (as "nondiscriminatory legislation" does in the areas of business, education, military, etc.). If the "effects test" holds true, it is obvious that we must apply affirmative action principles to abortion policy, thus increasing the number and percentage of the rich and the white having abortions *or* restricting the number and percentage of the poor and minorities having abortions.

The "effects test" fails as a standard, because the potential causes of disproportional representation in any given context are numerous. I would also venture to say that disproportional representation in any given context, more often than not, has *nothing* to do with legislation but with the values, culture, and behavior of the under-represented or over-represented group. Additionally, some legislation is simply not categorically applicable to every group.

Here's what the "effects test" does: Once disproportional representation has been shown (which is not difficult to do), someone can insert any arbitrary, politically expedient "cause" as the alleged source of the disproportional representation. Not surprisingly, the solution that remedies the "cause" is found in the political agenda of the individual applying the "effects test."

"Effects tests" (including affirmative action, quotas, etc.) are outcome-based standards. Instead of judging a particular law or company policy on its own merits, the standard determining what is and isn't discrimination is removed from the actual law or policy. Institutionalizing a law or company policy such as affirmative action over and above a general antidiscrimination policy applied to particular cases is necessary only when the supposed oppressed group cannot find enough individual examples of discrimination that would prove the existence of widespread prejudice. A general antidiscrimination law enforced on an individual basis does not provide the environment where the supposed oppressed group can force moral acceptance of their lifestyle and/or receive special treatment resulting in unfair mobilization within a system.

Here are some facts concerning the reasons given for "terminating an unwanted pregnancy":

- Inadequate finances – 21%
- Not ready for responsibility – 21%
- Woman's life would be changed too much – 16%
- Problems with relationship; not married – 12%
- Too young; not mature enough – 11%
- Children are grown; woman has all she wants – 8%
- Fetus has possible health problem – 3%
- Woman has health problem – 3%
- Pregnancy caused by rape, incest – 1%
- Other – 4%
- Average number of reasons given: 3.7

Thus, the vast majority (96%) of abortions occur for reasons *other* than rape, incest, or the health of the mother, i.e., reasons that should be influential in preventing pregnancy and/or reasons of convenience. The United States of America is killing hundreds of thousands of minorities and poor each year—at a rate *much* higher than the rich and the white—out of convenience.

Knowing this, why do liberals support legalized abortion? Entire constituencies of individuals (i.e., minorities and the poor) that liberals make a business of exploiting never reach voting age. Can you imagine the landslide victories that liberals would have if they managed to exploit just 60% of those who are aborted (60% being a low-end estimate)? It seems as though the "party of the people" (although not unborn people) is shooting itself in the foot by robbing itself of its voting base.

Furthermore, if conservatives (Republicans in particular) are the minority-hating, poor-neglecting bigots whom liberals paint them to be, why do they oppose abortion? After all, the easiest and quickest way to establish a society of rich white people is to systematically eliminate minorities and the poor. What better way of doing that than killing them all before they are born? Sure, rich white people may lose a few of their own children in the process because of legalized abortion, but this is nothing more than friendly fire—an acceptable loss on the way to winning a war.

America used to be a place where "the tired, the poor, and the huddled masses" of the world could come to establish a hopeful life for themselves. Since 1973, however, we've been systematically killing them off—and we've been doing it out of convenience.

10

Terrorism and War
Secular Foreign Policy

Freedom and Death: Strange Bedfellows

I was watching the O'Reilly Factor on the Fox News Channel in the fall of 2006 and heard Bill O'Reilly say that the United States didn't lose the war in Vietnam. He made this comment in response to Ann Coulter's assertion that the United States lost the Vietnam War. Coulter responded by saying, "Bill, they are living under Communist rule!" I concur. The war was either won or lost, and seeing as the North Vietnamese communists now control the country, I'd mark that one up in the loss column. Although I suppose many Americans on the left would consider communist rule a victory . . . even within our own borders.

O'Reilly explained what he meant by his comment when he said that Vietnam wasn't a military defeat but a political defeat. Coulter responded by saying something along the lines of, "Exactly! But we still lost the war!" No sane person believes that the North Vietnamese were militarily superior to the United States. The United States lost the conflict in Vietnam because, 1) it was horribly run, and 2) the country lost its will. After years of media "reporting" about how the United States was losing the war and hours upon hours of liberal rhetoric lambasting the war effort, America lost its will to protect a country from a murderous communist regime (is there another kind?).

Now we see liberals at it again. Comparisons of Iraq and Vietnam are made almost off-the-cuff. Iraq is a "quagmire." Any student of non-revisionist history knows Iraq and Vietnam are nothing alike . . . right now. At the moment, the only thing the current situation in Iraq has in common with the Vietnam War is that liberals at home are attempting to undermine the success of the campaign. (In fact, Harry Reid, the Democratic Senate Majority Leader, said in April of 2007 that the war in Iraq has been "lost." Reid and Aymen al-Zawahiri seem to be on the same page. See the essay entitled "Phase One: Exit Stage Left" later in this chapter.)

The way the United States pulled out of Vietnam effectively sentenced thousands of South Vietnamese civilians to a brutal death. Leaving Vietnam in such a manner rendered 56,000 American deaths meaningless (if keeping South Vietnam free was the goal of the Vietnam War). (I realize this statement may seem out of character when considering my other opinions but I don't mean to say that these soldiers' *lives* were meaningless. They were fighting for a noble cause—a winnable cause had America had the right leadership and support from the citizenry. The fault lies entirely with how politicians ran the war and how the American people—a segment of the American people, at least—lacked the long term resolve to follow through . . . partially because of how the politicians ran the war. This is why it is vital to *complete the task*. It is the only way to honor those who have fought and died for a noble cause.) If Iraq becomes a "quagmire," it will be because liberals at home have made it such, once again rendering meaningless the deaths of our beloved soldiers. Iraq and Vietnam have the potential to have everything in common or nothing in common.

Both are/were worthy causes. Both objectives are/were achievable with resolve and efficiency. Vietnam took a turn for the worse for the aforementioned reasons. Let's hope Iraq doesn't follow. Terrorists know what happened in Somalia and Vietnam. They know their only chance of victory is to destroy the American will—a mission they hope to accomplish through the media, politicians, and American college campuses.

It's as if people think we're losing the war every time a coalition soldier dies. Unfortunately, this is exactly what war is like. As Ann Coulter mentioned on the O'Reilly Factor, no one stepped back after seeing the casualties list from D-Day and said, "Wow, what a great day!" War is hell. This is why it is so important to make sure the war is worth it. Iraq is worth it. Not only long-term, but also for the soldiers who have already died freeing twenty million people.

The reconstruction of Germany and Japan after World War II wasn't easy. It took years. Building free countries is a hard job. Freedom doesn't just pop out of nowhere to say, "Hey, here I am! Enjoy me!" The harsh reality is that freedom is the forced exception, not the rule. Historically speaking, very few people have lived in freedom. Consider the more or less "free" countries that exist today. How many of them, either at their creation or at some later point in their history, did not have to forcibly defend themselves with violence (or rely on another country to do that for them)? Good luck finding one.

I'm going to say something now that many people may find to be warmongering, shocking, and/or immoral. FOR FREEDOM TO EXIST, PEOPLE MUST DIE. The bumper sticker slogan, "War Is Never the Answer," is perhaps the most historically inaccurate, naive, ridiculous, and dangerous battle cry I've ever heard or seen in print. The shortsightedness and godlike faith in humanity that such a slogan reveals are staggering.

In my essay in Chapter 7, "No Ruts, No Glory," I discussed why an overinflated faith in reason and humanity is misplaced. Here, it will suffice to say that such a faith in reason and humanity is historical nonsense. Thomas Jefferson said, "Eternal vigilance is the price of freedom." Have you ever asked, "Vigilance against what?" The answer is vigilance against *people* who would rob us of freedom and prevent it from thriving. Why would Iraq be any different?

What did we expect terrorists to do when we launched a war against them after September 11, 2001? Lay down their weapons? Turn tail and run? Reason with us? Magically replace their hatred of us with gumdrop feelings of flowery bliss? C'mon, people . . . the terrorists are going to do the same thing every other freedom-threatening person in history has done when encountered with his own demise: *Fight back.*

As United States forces were approaching Japan near the end of World War II, the fighting became more and more fierce. Casualties were more and more frequent. Does this mean the United States was losing the war? Obviously the answer is no. As the Japanese began accepting reality, as their tyrannical way of life became threatened, as they came face-to-face with the forces of freedom, they fought more boldly than they ever had before. Casualties increased, and the enemy's vigor multiplied exponentially *precisely because* the United States was *winning*. It was during this time that American resolve was the *most* important.

Freedom doesn't come easily, and it's time liberals understood that. The foundation of freedom is blood, sweat, and tears. Modern liberalism is the spoiled child of hard-working parents who made a life for themselves with their own hands, burying their friends and family along the way. Too often, the offspring of freedom and affluence is tyranny, the result of freedom without vigilance.

Terrorism and Gravity: Apples and Oranges

Everyone claims they want to win the war on terror. Unfortunately, the mere statement, "We must win the war on terror!" without further elaboration tells us absolutely nothing about the beliefs of the one speaking.

Considering such elaboration is almost nonexistent in today's world of sound-bite politics, it is exceedingly difficult to learn much of anything about anybody.

Relativistic philosophies preclude the need for serious dialogue, thus dwindling the free marketplace of ideas. Besides, serious dialogue requires an intellectual rigor largely absent in today's culture. To once again quote Thomas Jefferson, "Eternal vigilance is the price of freedom." Such vigilance is required in every aspect of life—especially in the realm of ideas. Intellectual laziness among the citizenry is an overly ambitious government's best friend (as is an unarmed populace—but I digress).

When Ted Kennedy, Chuck Schumer, Nancy Pelosi, and Hillary Clinton say that we must fight the war on terror, they are saying something completely different from what George W. Bush, Dick Cheney, Condoleezza Rice, or Ann Coulter are saying when they claim the same. This is because these two groups of people think with completely different worldviews.

Let me illustrate by sharing a comment I've heard relatively frequently. The comment is, "In order to solve the problem of terrorism, we must first solve the problem of global poverty." What basic ideas about how the world works (presuppositions) underlie this claim?

One of the most important questions every worldview answers regards the status of humanity. That is, what is a human being? The comment above is based on the secular presupposition that no such thing as the supernatural exists, that nothing is "outside the box" so-to-speak. All that exists is physical "stuff." Thus, humans are subject to the same laws of cause and effect as every other object consisting of matter and/or energy. Just as gravity pulls an apple to the ground after it falls off a tree, scientific laws also dictate human ideas, decisions, and behaviors.

This presupposition logically leads to the conclusion that a human is a product of his environment, i.e., the systems around him. If the perfect system is present, it will create perfect human beings. Modern liberal ideology is based upon such secular presuppositions. This is why systems are so important to modern liberal philosophies and political ideologies. Systems are the sole catalyst for modern liberal soteriology.

For example, the previous statement is claiming that hatred and violence (terrorism) are caused by poverty and economic oppression. Once poverty and economic oppression are removed, hatred and violence will magically disappear. (Read my essay entitled, "Materialism Bad, Materialism Good. Which Is It?" regarding the contradiction this belief exposes in modern liberalism.) The claim here is that poverty *causes* terrorism. That is, those who are raised in a poverty-stricken, economically oppressive system are *externally caused* by their environment to become terrorists. Therefore, the way to rid the world of terrorism is to rid the world of what causes terrorism, i.e., poverty (and the tyrannical Western countries that cause Third World poverty via economic exploitation).

Conservatives, however, interpret the world using a different worldview—a worldview that sees humans as free-willed creatures who are capable of both great good and horrifying evil. This is not a worldview, however, that ignores the influence of environment. Systems play a role in the development of a human being, but they are by no means the "end-all/be-all." This is why liberals (whose worldview is secularism) are constantly trying to change the world by first changing systems and then human beings. Conservatives (those who embrace the Judeo-Christian worldview, consciously *or* unconsciously[1]), on the other hand, attempt to change the world by first changing human hearts, and then systems.

For liberals, fighting the war on terror means first changing the systems that (supposedly) create terrorists. This is largely the source of the "blame America first" tactic. After all, if America is exploiting the rest of the world, causing political and economic oppression, then America, in turn, is causing the systems that cause terrorists and, thus, terrorism itself.

For conservatives, fighting the war on terror means first killing the terrorists (the individuals responsible for terrorism) and then institutionalizing governments and laws that properly reflect the status of humanity. These two steps may be done simultaneously (as is being done in Iraq), but the former tactic must never be reduced to the latter.

This is why liberals can't be trusted with securing the United States. It's not necessarily because they don't want to make America safe (although there are some who don't). Every political leader claims to want to secure America. The problem is that liberals don't know how. Because they have a fundamental misunderstanding of what a human is, they have misdiagnosed the problem. When the root cause of a problem is unknown or misdiagnosed, it's cure will constantly be elusive. Solutions must address causes. (Cancer can't be cured by Rolaids, for example.)

On a side note, the next time someone suggests that poverty and economic oppression cause terrorism, ask him if he knows the financial status of a young, developing Osama bin Laden (who is a millionaire). Also, ask this person where all the first-, second-, and third-century Christian terrorists were. After all, if poverty and oppression cause terrorism, the quintessential examples of poverty-stricken and oppressed groups (not to

1. See Chapter 3.

mention persecuted) are the Christians of the first three centuries A.D. Is it crazy to think that terrorism just might have more to do with ideas than with environment? Perhaps we should rethink which religion deserves the label "Religion of Peace."

Phase One: Exit Stage Left

In the essay entitled, "Freedom and Death: Strange Bedfellows," I outlined the *potential* similarities between the Vietnam War and the current war in Iraq. I noted that America lost the Vietnam War because it lost its will, not because it lost militarily. No single country or fighting force in the world today could defeat the United States military. The defeat of the United States doesn't lie in defeating its military, but in destroying its resolve.

In July of 2005, American forces intercepted a letter written by Al-Qaeda's no. 2 leader, Aymen al-Zawahiri, to his top Al Qaeda deputy in Iraq, Abu Musab al-Zarqawi (who has since been killed). In the letter, Zawahiri outlined a plan to bring victory for Islamic terrorists. Let us take a look at some of the elements found within his plan.[2]

Stage One of the plan is simple: "Expel Americans from Iraq." Zawahiri knows that as long as American forces are in Iraq, the terrorists can't be victorious. He knows this because he knows terrorists can't defeat American military forces. The only way to victory is the withdrawal of American forces from Iraq. But why is Zawahiri, and terrorists in general, hopeful that the American forces will withdraw from Iraq? The answer is found within Zawahiri's own letter.

Zawahiri writes, "Things may develop faster than we imagine. The aftermath of the collapse of American power in Vietnam—and how they ran and left their agents—is noteworthy." America's past mistakes are providing hope for today's terrorists. The disgraceful withdrawal from South Vietnam, which sentenced hundreds of thousands to death, is a rallying point for today's terrorists who are, like the North Vietnamese, outmanned militarily. Just as patriotic Texans rallied around the cry, "Remember the Alamo!" today's terrorists cry out, "Remember Vietnam!"

We saw another example of this when President Clinton went into Somalia to apprehend a tyrannical warlord and pulled out unsuccessfully in the face of resistance. As the saying goes, "Everyone has a plan until you get hit." Well, America was hit in Vietnam and Somalia and lost its resolve to fulfill its plan. It is apparent that the terrorists have learned

---

2. The text of this letter can be found at http://www.msnbc.msn.com/id/9666242/.

from America's mistakes. The more disturbing observation is that many Americans haven't.

Zawahiri goes on to emphasize the importance of the media in undertaking jihad. He writes, "We are in a battle, and that more than half of this battle is taking place in the battlefield of the media. And that we are in a media battle in a race for the hearts and minds of our Umma [Muslim community]." Zawahiri understands the critical role the media plays in winning wars. He references the media regarding the broad public support that is needed from Iraqis to succeed within Iraq. After years of the media reporting only negative news from war zones, what effect will this have on public opinion?

Some Americans believe that withdrawing American troops from Iraq will decrease the violence and appease the anger of the terrorists. For those who don't see the idiocy of this statement outright, there are now words from the terrorists themselves, stating this is not the case. Zawahiri says that Al Qaeda must be ready to fill the void after the Americans leave. They must be prepared to continue the fight against those "un-Islamic" powers that will be vying for control after the Americans withdraw.

Zawahiri writes that the "mujahedeen must not have their mission end with the expulsion of Americans from Iraq, and then lay down their weapons, and silence the fighting zeal. We will return to having the secularists and traitors holding sway over us. Instead, their ongoing mission is to establish an Islamic state, and defend it . . . . If the matter is thus, we must contemplate our affairs carefully, so that we are not robbed of the spoils, and our brothers did not die, so that others may reap the fruits of their labor." Retreating from Iraq wouldn't decrease terrorists' hatred or violence. It would raise the hope of the terrorists (as the U.S. retreats from Vietnam and Somalia have done), steady their resolve, and usher in a new wave of violence.

Violence is a way of life for Islamic terrorists. We see this in the fact that after the first two stages of Zawahiri's plan (expelling the Americans and establishing an Islamic state in Iraq), stage three is bringing jihad to the surrounding Middle Eastern countries (violence). Additionally, stage four is conflict with Israel in an attempt to wipe it off the face of the Earth (violence).

The most important of these stages, of course, is expelling American forces from Iraq. How do they hope to do this? By weakening American resolve vis-à-vis Vietnam and through manipulation of the media. Does this sound familiar?

A war effort is undermined in two main ways: 1) By the media filtering only the negative aspects of the war to the public, and 2) A country's own politicians and leaders undermining the war effort. The terrorists are giddy with joy every time Ted Kennedy calls the war in Iraq a "quagmire." The terrorists come another step closer to victory every time *The New York Times* publishes a story on the failures of the war in Iraq. The terrorists have a crystal-clear vision of a future they want to realize. It will take a different vision, albeit just as clear, to ensure they are not successful. Where is such a vision from those undermining the war effort?

Zawahiri's letter should have been front-page news in every newspaper and TV news program in the country. It outlines exactly what the terrorists' plan is and how they're going to achieve it. It crystallizes the vision Islamic terrorists want to impose on the world. And it lays out exactly *how* they're going to achieve it. Unfortunately, the importance of this letter won't be emphasized. Do you think it might be because stage one of that vision is held by both terrorists *and* modern liberals?

War, Death, and Collateral Damage: Who is Responsible?

As I watched a documentary on the Manhattan Project on the History Channel, I was struck by an underlying theme running throughout. The narrator commented that Robert Oppenheimer, the man who led the project, set in motion something that couldn't be stopped. As August 1945 approached, it became more apparent that the hydrogen bomb was going to be used to end the war in the Pacific. So I asked myself, exactly what couldn't be stopped? The Allied war machine? The military brass? Humanity's warmongering nature? And what exactly did Oppenheimer start?

In his book *Resident Aliens*, Stanley Hauerwas (and coauthor William Willimon) suggests that the dropping of the atomic bomb on Hiroshima marked the beginning (or, at least, it was the symbolic downfall) of the degradation of American culture. It represented humanity's willingness to slaughter thousands of innocent people. It represented humanity's fallen nature and deviation from the Gospel. Just how far was the world from Christ's teaching? All one needs to do is observe the destruction wrought at Hiroshima and Nagasaki.

Let us take a step back for a moment and ask a few questions. First, why did the Manhattan Project exist? Why was the United States pursuing the ultimate killing weapon? Any answer to that question that doesn't include the fact that Nazi Germany was also pursuing such a weapon is historically ignorant and morally dubious. Had Hitler never started World War II, there would have been no Manhattan Project. Had Hitler not been pursuing the deadly potential of the atom, the United States would not have countered with a project of its own. (Even if America pursued the atom bomb and Germany didn't, however, America wouldn't have *used* it without provocation from oppressive regimes such as Nazi Germany and Imperial Japan—at least I hope not.)

Second, who was morally responsible for the innocent deaths at Hiroshima and Nagasaki? Obviously, the *direct* cause of the deaths was the hydrogen bombs dropped by the Americans in an attempt to end World War II. But who was *morally* responsible for the events? Those who blame America for dropping those bombs conveniently forget facts such as who started the war, who *else* was also pursuing nuclear technology, how many people (military *and* civilian) would have died during a land invasion of Japan, etc.

German and Japanese leaders brought the destruction of World War II on their own people. Obviously, this is not a rubber stamp for America to act in any way it wishes during wartime. But the Nazi and Japanese leaders who caused the war are morally responsible for *all* (military *and* civilian) those who died during World War II—unless America performed immoral acts of its own that cannot be attributed to Nazi Germany or Imperial Japan (for example, intentionally killing civilians for fun or due to hatred). In these cases, *nothing* absolves America from a moral responsibility not to engage in these acts. And yes, I realize such acts have occurred on a small scale (specific immoral acts in the context of a just war, for example) *and* a large scale (entire wars that are unjustified and immoral, for example).

Third, what *would have* happened had the United States not developed the hydrogen bomb? This is a more difficult question to answer, because it involves utilizing our imagination to picture a historical scenario that (thankfully) never arose. We already know that Germany and Japan had their own programs to develop nuclear weapons. Do you think they would have hesitated using them if such weapons were at their disposal? Judging from the war crimes perpetuated by both regimes, the answer is obvious. They would have rained hydrogen bombs from the sky, killing millions in the process.

Instead of condemning the creation of a hydrogen bomb by the United States, we should be thanking our lucky stars that Germany or Japan didn't develop the technology first. If America had not developed nuclear technology first, this world would be a very different place today—a much worse place.

So how is it that Robert Oppenheimer "set in motion" something that couldn't be stopped? The simple fact is that he didn't set anything in motion. The wheels of nuclear research and military technology were set in motion when Hitler invaded Poland. The road that led to nuclear proliferation began when Japan attacked Pearl Harbor. Oppenheimer didn't set anything in motion. He helped to bring closure to two totalitarian regimes that killed millions and would have certainly killed millions more if given the capability.

This is something many people today don't understand, and, unfortunately, this misunderstanding affects policy in the modern world. Whose fault is it when an American bomb inadvertently kills innocent civilians? Whose fault is it that we are fighting this war on terror? Whose fault is it that several thousand American soldiers have died in Iraq? Similarly, whose fault is it that 400,000 American soldiers died in World War II?

When evil rears its ugly head, the good people of the world have two options: 1) They can observe the situation with shortsightedness, or 2) they can establish a vision and maintain the resolve to realize that vision. While Hauerwas may condemn the United States for developing and using the hydrogen bomb, those who know better understand upon whom the condemnation *should* rest. Does Hauerwas actually believe that, had the United States not produced a hydrogen bomb, there would be no such thing as nuclear weapons today?

Can you imagine the liberal backlash if we were currently engaged in a war that was costing hundreds of thousands of lives? Modern liberals don't have the intestinal fortitude, nor the vision, to exact meaningful and lasting change in the world. They don't know what it takes to create free countries and maintain genuine liberty in the face of tyrants, murderers, and ACLU lawyers (see my essay entitled, "Freedom and Death: Strange Bedfellows").

In his farce of a "documentary" (*Fahrenheit 9/11*), Michael Moore attempted to bring home the reality of war by asking members of Congress if they would send their own children into war. Despite the irrelevance of his question, which ignores the fact that individuals may choose or not choose to join the military, the question does raise an interesting issue—namely, is it worth it? Are the allied casualties in Iraq worth establishing a democracy there? Are the deaths of young American soldiers worth the ousting of a dictator who tortured, raped, and murdered thousands upon thousands? The answer? It depends who you are.

For those whose plush surroundings are in their Hollywood Hills mansions, the war may not be worth it. For those who have had their wives and daughters tortured and raped, and their sons disappear—never to be seen or heard from again—it just might be worth it.

My Side of a Dialogue: The War in Iraq

The following is an e-mail I sent to an acquaintance who was debating with me (in 2005) about the war in Iraq. This isn't a direct dialogue, but a dialogue via e-mail.

So many issues, so little time. With that said, I'll try to address some of the issues you raised and the questions you asked me.

You claim you're a liberal "because I think what people do in their free time is their business." Interesting, that's the exact same reason I'm considered a conservative. Why is it that those leaders and politicians who claim that it's no one's business "what people do in their free time" are the ones trying to control our lives? Why don't they apply that standard when it comes to our money? Why don't they apply that standard when they force a monopolistic, hegemonic public education system down our throats? Why don't they apply that standard regarding a parent's right to know what their children are doing (read: minors getting abortions, parents sending their kids to the school of their choice)? Why don't they apply that standard regarding local and state government? Why don't they apply that standard when it comes to guns? Why don't they apply that standard when it comes to my private property? Why don't they apply that standard when it comes to health care? Why don't they apply that standard by allowing more freedom in the realm of health care, insurance, and what a community chooses to teach its children at the local school or do in "public" buildings? I could go on and on.

The fact is that those same people who claim they don't care what people do in their free time are the ones trying to control every element of society via coercion and government control. Liberals are only pro-choice when it comes to abortion. Yet, when it comes to every other issue, liberals think they know best and try to force their will on the people.

Regarding your first question: "Why are we in Iraq?" At the time of the invasion, the United States invaded Iraq because Saddam Hussein was thought to be a direct threat to our security. It's important to remember the fact that no one in the world disagreed with the claim that Saddam Hussein had weapons of mass destruction. The United Nations (UN) believed it. France believed it. Liberals believed it. Conservatives believed it. The issue wasn't whether he had them. The issue was what to do about it. The UN itself had seventeen resolutions telling Saddam Hussein that if he didn't disarm, there would be serious consequences. Additionally, the Bush administration made no attempt to connect 9/11 with Saddam Hussein.

So, at the time, the United States invaded Iraq because Hussein was thought to be a threat to our security (i.e., he could give weapons to terrorists, launch them against neighbors, etc.) and because the United States was enforcing the threat behind seventeen UN resolutions.

As we know today, the weapons of mass destruction were either moved out of Iraq or they weren't there. *If* the intelligence was wrong, did Bush lie to us? All I ask is that the world be held to the same standard as President Bush. Everyone in the world believed the same thing about the intelligence, so if Bush lied, then so did John Kerry, the UN, France, Europe, etc. Personally, I don't think any of them lied. I think the intelligence was either wrong, or the weapons were removed before allied forces were able to find them (or they are still buried in the desert somewhere).

Thus the question for us today is, Why are we *still* in Iraq? Like it or not, Iraq has become one of the main fronts in the war on terror. Whether or not America "created" such a front is irrelevant. The fact is, even terrorists themselves have identified Iraq as the center of the war on terror. Terrorists know they cannot defeat America militarily. They must win the battle of wills. This is exactly what happened in the Vietnam War. The Communists won the battle of wills, and America retreated. (Read my essay entitled "Freedom and Death: Strange Bedfellows" to understand that relationship and why pulling out of Iraq would be a huge mistake.)

You also claimed that we should use some kind of "2/3 standard" when it comes to deciding whether or not we should be in Iraq. It sounds as if you would prefer to base all your moral judgments on not only what's popular, but what's extremely popular (i.e., approved by 66% of any given group). Assuming, for a moment, that you are not saying this, I'll address the notion that "since Iraqis themselves don't want us there, we should leave."

How many Germans in the early 1940s thought that Americans should be in Germany? Not very many . . . and I would venture to guess hardly any. Besides the fact that no unbiased poll has been taken (at that time) concerning the opinion of Iraqis for or against the presence of Americans, such a "2/3 standard" (or any standard requiring popularity to precede action) is untenable to say the least.

You then appealed to the emotions by citing charred remains of children as a moral argument against military action (i.e. "collateral damage"). You ask me to pretend that the situation is reversed and envision my own little brother as that charred victim. Actually, it's a good thing you didn't ask us to envision our daughters and wives as charred victims, because under a regime such as Saddam Hussein's, they would have been murdered years ago—after, of course, they were repeatedly raped and tortured (as you can see, I can appeal to emotion too).

Besides the fact that the numbers of innocent people killed by allied forces have been grossly over-exaggerated for political purposes, attributing moral responsibility of such deaths to allied forces is morally dubious and ethically absurd. Who was oppressing these people? Who was responsible for raping, torturing, and murdering hundreds of thousands of innocent human beings? Who brought about the need for liberation in the first place? It is evil dictators and regimes like Saddam Hussein's who brought these things about, not America. Is America responsible for the deaths of World War II? No, Hitler and Tojo are responsible for all (including innocent people accidentally killed by allied forces) the deaths associated with a war brought about to end their horrific reigns (except for, as mentioned earlier, immoral acts perpetrated by coalition forces that were easily avoidable and/or immoral in nature).

When all is said and done, and if America sticks it out in Iraq, America and the allied forces will leave Iraq in the hands of Iraqis. Instead of citing your mysterious poll as evidence supporting pulling out of Iraq, why don't you wait until America leaves to ask them whether or not our "invasion" was desirable? Or better yet, why don't you cite the polls taken within days of the fall of Saddam Hussein as evidence? The answers to these questions are obvious. Instead of asking such a question to the very few whose innocent family members have been accidentally killed by allied forces, why don't you ask such a question to the men whose daughters and wives were raped, tortured, and murdered; or to the men whose sons or fathers were tortured and murdered because they disagreed with Saddam Hussein; or to the women whose husbands "disappeared," never to be seen again.

This war was against Saddam Hussein—not the Iraqi people. This war is now against terrorists, not the Iraqi people. You compared what America is doing in Iraq to a situation where someone would kill your neighbor because *you* murdered someone. The allied forces don't intentionally kill innocent people, which is what you're suggesting with that comparison. Common sense will tell anyone that that comparison is ludicrous.

On a side note, if you're consistent, you should apply your "2/3 standard" to domestic policy as well. If you did, you would be of the opinion that homosexual marriage should be illegal, because a vast majority of people support such policy.

Regarding your second question: "Who is paying for all this?" You complain that the debt is getting too large. Let me ask you this, What is debt? Debt is when you spend more than you have. I am wholeheartedly supportive of cutting the billions of dollars worth of government programs that contribute to this debt. The question that must be asked, however, is "What is the purpose of government?" I believe it is legitimate to spend money in areas where the government has a legitimate role, i.e., national defense, the courts, police, etc. (in other words, anything that helps *protect* our rights—not programs that *provide* our rights).

The first step in getting out of debt is to decrease spending . . . and I can think of a plethora of programs that we could cut right now in an attempt to balance the budget (e.g., welfare, social security, public education, etc.). Additionally, why is it that liberals only complain about the national debt in the context of discussing military expenditures? The debt problem magically disappears when they are discussing domestic entitlement programs.

You also made a comment about not needing your tax cut. Did you send it back? I doubt it. It is arrogant to think that because you don't need your tax cut, the millions of other Americans who received tax cuts don't need theirs. *Everyone* who paid taxes received a tax cut proportional to how much they paid into the system. Of America's population, 10% pay between 70% and 80% of all taxes. So don't lecture the rich on how they're greedy. Without the rich, there would be no government programs whatsoever. The welfare state exists because liberals, who claim "everyone can do what they want in their free time," steal from "the rich" and tell Americans what they can and cannot do with their money. It is also interesting to note that the majority of Americans would fall under the category of "rich" according to liberals' definition of "rich." But class warfare is an issue for another time.

Perhaps a quick lesson in economics is necessary. Here's a fact for you: Over the past year (2005) the federal government has brought in more tax revenue than in any year under the Clinton administration. The taxes under Clinton were as high as they had been since World War II, and they still didn't produce as much tax revenue as the economy under Bush's tax cuts. Why do you think that is? Lowering taxes increases production. Increased production means more people are making more money and spending/investing more. The more money people make, invest, and spend, the more is paid in taxes. The more that is collected in taxes, the more money government has to spend (i.e., for entitlement programs, military spending, etc.). Raising taxes decreases production, people are making less money and spending/investing less, less taxes are being paid, government tax revenues dwindle, and the government has less money to spend. Increasing taxes does not increase the tax revenue. This has been shown throughout history and makes common economic sense.

On a side note, the poverty rate halfway through Bush's eight-year tenure was a full percentage point lower than Clinton's was at the same time. The unemployment rate was lower than it ever was during the Clinton administration. Entitlement spending was more than double what it was under Bill Clinton. Education spending was also higher than it ever was under the Clinton administration. *And all this occurred with lower taxes!* Clinton's tax hikes never produced the prosperity and tax revenue Bush's tax cuts produced.

The Clinton tax hikes passed in his early years, before the Republicans gained control of Congress, started the recession before George W. Bush took office. The economic prosperity of the 90s wasn't caused by Bush Sr., but by Reagan's tax cuts and economic policy in the 80s.

So how do we pay for this? The answer is by decreasing taxes, thus increasing tax revenue, and cutting programs that are not in line with the basic purpose of government.

Regarding your third question: "Wouldn't it be better if our nation was viewed as the benevolent good guys?" Obviously the answer is yes. But in a world where values are messed up, "good" won't be recognized as such. No country in the history of the world has shed more blood for the freedom of others than the United States. No other country in the history of the world has freed more people than the United States. The United States spends more on international humanitarian aid than any other country in the world—even more than all of the Western European countries combined. To say that the United States isn't benevolent is a historically and morally ignorant remark. Whether or not the world recognizes the benevolence and generosity of the United States is out of our control.

You said, "I want a country where we are the good guys, we are the rescuers, we are the ones people can count on." My friend, you live in such a country. America has rescued more people than any other nation on earth. We spend more money to help the people of the world than any other nation on earth. America is by no means perfect. That is obvious. But to ignore the benevolence of the United States is to ignore reality.

You also asked, "If Christ were president, would we be in Iraq?" I've come to learn over the years that the only thing more useless than a hypothetical question is a hypothetical answer. That question cannot be answered . . . nor is it categorically applicable. However, I can tell you a few things about what the world will be like when Christ returns and assumes all power and authority under heaven. The unsaved will be eternally separated from God in torment and suffering. For those who are saved, there will be no more suffering, no evil, no murders, no rapes, no torturing, no machetes, no mass graves, etc.

If your standard for what is and is not legitimate government is based on the salvation Christ will bring (which, in my opinion, is not the function of civil government), you've got a lot of work to do . . . and a lot of people to damn.

11

Random Ideas
A Few Observations

Liberals, Kickball, and Playing Nice

I THINK I figured out why liberals are liberals. I think I finally figured out why they have a chip on their shoulder. I think I made a breakthrough in discovering the origin of the warped liberal view of "equality." Yes, ladies and gentlemen, I finally figured out why so many liberals are spoiled, bitter, and loud. My theory? As children, they were consistently picked last during recess. Follow me on this.

For the most part, especially on the recess playground, sports are a meritocracy. In the case of elementary school children, kickball is the culprit. The kids who can kick the ball the farthest and run the fastest are the first to be picked. The little fast guys and the power kickers (usually the kids with the most body hair) hear their names first, followed by the girls (unless you have a "picker" whose hormones have developed early) and the uncoordinated.

The recess playground time can be a catastrophic experience for the child, as it is often the first dose of reality the child experiences. Up until recess, the child is told how special and important he is. His self-esteem is coddled to the point of meaninglessness. And he is told his worth is not connected to what he does, but how he feels. All this goes out the window during recess. Only the best get to play. Recess kickball is a game of competition, identification, and exclusion—three things liberals despise.

First, the children are forced to compete. Their relative abilities and inabilities are exposed. Second, they are identified and judged based on their performance. Third, those not good enough to play are excluded (or put in right field, whereupon every member of the opposite team tries to kick it to right field). Sound familiar? That's right—this sounds suspiciously like the real world.

Now, there are a few options for the excluded. 1) They wait a few years, mature, and then join the game. 2) They go and do something else (i.e., collect bugs, talk to girls, hang out in the computer lab, etc.). An example of such a student is probably Bill Gates. He may have realized kickball wasn't his forte and nurtured a different, yet equally important, talent. 3) They run to the teacher, complaining about unfairness, and then return with that teacher, thus forcing the other kids to "play nice". . . whereupon the student gets to play but is then despised by his fellow playmates.

Which of these three groups do you think morphs into adult liberals? The answer is obvious.

The young liberal becomes envious of his classmates, wishing he had something his classmates had, and forces the authority figure to give it to him—thus making every classmate "equal." Of course, this results in our young liberal not having any friends, having been rejected by the very group he is jealous of—even while getting into the game.

This eventually produces a very large chip on our young liberal's shoulder. After all, his years of public education have told him that everyone is equal; no one is better than anyone else. Yet on the recess playground, this isn't the case. The young liberal's worldview has had a "close encounter" with a reality not beholden to his warped sense of egalitarianism.

This idea first entered my mind as an undergraduate at Miami University (Oxford, Ohio). I was on an ethics competition team that competed with colleges around the country. ("Ethics" was defined according to a secular philosophy department, of course.) We were practicing one evening, and a philosophy professor of mine told me that he didn't think athletics had any part in higher education.

It was obvious to me that this professor had never played competitive sports in his life. He didn't know about the positive influence that athletics can have on a young man or woman. I could actually sense bitterness in his comment. He was visibly upset. I thought to myself, *What could inspire such bitterness and anger?*

Liberals can't stand competition. They oppose discernment based upon gifts, differing abilities, and work ethic. Unfortunately for liberals, reality includes these things . . . and *should* include these things. Reality will pass you by if you don't acknowledge them.

So often in life, liberals seem to be on the outside looking in. Instead of getting involved on the recess playing field in a proactive way, they make the teacher force everybody to "play nice" . . . or they just sit there and complain about the situation, all the while pining for a world that will alleviate all discomfort.

This is why so many liberals have careers that are on the "sidelines." Think about it. What is the media? It's a group of people standing on the sidelines, observing and critiquing the players on the field—often warping or completely blocking the view of many sincerely interested onlookers, who may want to get involved themselves.

What is academia? It's a little enclave separated from the real world, where professors can theorize all they want about the ills and oppression of the world. What is public education? It's a place where children can be indoctrinated for years before they leave to enter the real world. What is a union boss? He's someone who produces nothing for society or the economy, yet lives off the work and production of others. What is an ACLU-like "freedom fighter"? He's someone who exploits the rights given him by true freedom fighters who came before.

This can be perfectly illustrated by the 2004 election. All Democrats did was critique the Bush administration. When it came to presenting a plan of their own, they were conspicuously silent. In one of the presidential race debates, Bush responded to such critiques by saying, "A plan is not a litany of complaints." What is the liberal plan to defeat terrorism? What is the liberal plan to triumph in Iraq? What is the liberal plan for Social Security? After months (even years) of debate, all we know is what their plans *aren't*—namely, whatever the Republicans come up with as a plan.

Find a playing field and join it. Obviously, every game needs to be held accountable. Every institution and association needs to be held accountable (as a conservative, I am constantly aware of this). But if you spend the vast majority of your time destroying rather than building, criticizing instead of critiquing, or complaining without an alternate plan, do everyone a favor and just keep it to yourself.

Teddy Roosevelt gave a speech entitled "Citizenship in a Republic" at the Sorbonne in Paris, France, on April 23, 1910, in which he said:

> It is not the critic who counts: not the man who points out how the strong man stumbles or where the doer of deeds could have done better. The credit belongs to the man who is actually in the arena, whose face is marred by dust and sweat and blood, who strives valiantly, who errs and comes up short again and again, because there is no effort without error or shortcoming, but who knows the great enthusiasms, the great devotions, who spends himself for a worthy cause; who, at the best, knows, in the end, the triumph of high achievement, and who, at the worst, if he fails, at least he fails while daring greatly, so that his place shall never be with those cold and timid souls who knew neither victory nor defeat.

As I'm sure you've noticed by now, this is about more than just kickball.

The Uniting Powers of God, Sports, and Kissing

Some people just don't get it. Some people don't understand why I'm in a bad mood the Sunday evenings (and often into the next week) after the Cincinnati Bengals lose. Some people don't understand how a game can so thoroughly affect the psyche of an individual. Some people just don't understand the passion of sports fans.

There are a few things in life I'm passionate about: my Christianity, politics, and sports. Those are probably the top three. What is interesting is when all three of these combine. For example, when I root more for an athlete because I know he is a Christian. Or when I decide which team to root against, based upon the respective number of liberals in each team's city or area. I find myself rooting more often for red state teams than blue state teams.

But something funny often happens when I'm engaged in a good sports discussion. I often start to forget about the other person's political opinions . . . which says a lot, considering the fact that I think modern liberalism and those who peddle it are doing an inordinate amount of damage to our communities, nation, and world.

Judging by the intensity or passion of my sports discussions, it can seem as though I'm just as passionate about the lack of pitching on the Cincinnati Reds as I am about overturning Roe v. Wade. Obviously, the latter issue is infinitely more important than the former, but I feel that the answer to the former issue is just as blatantly clear as is the answer to the latter issue . . . and I feel the need to voice my opinion regarding both.

For example, a recurring debate that used to occur at the poker table with one of my friends was whether or not Austin Kearns could become a great player for the Reds (although he was traded to the Washington Nationals in July of 2006). I was convinced that Kearns had the fundamentals and talent to become a perennial All-Star. All he needed was the opportunity to play an entire year (which meant that the Reds needed to trade somebody to open up an outfield spot). My friend (although he is a conservative) believed the jury was still out regarding Austin Kearns.

What is it about sports that can turn the best of friends into yelling arguers and sworn enemies into allies? Why am I addicted to fantasy sports? Why do I want at least one son with whom I can share my love of sports? Why do I read articles on the Bengals and Reds when I should be preparing lecture notes for my next class or writing a column that needed to be posted the day before? And most interestingly, why will I align myself with a flaming liberal who agrees with me that Austin Kearns has the potential to be a perennial All-Star?

For a few moments at least, it doesn't matter to me that his philosophical presuppositions and political ideology are contributing to the wholesale decline of Western civilization. What's important at this particular moment is that he agrees with me about Austin Kearns. Does Austin Kearns really have the power to unite warring cultures? Or is it something else?

People outside of the sports realm don't understand the impact athletics has on the life of a committed athlete. Sport teaches us about love, life, and God. Sport teaches us about relationships, about being part of a team, about commitment, about hard work, and about priorities.

When Carson Palmer throws a seventy-yard touchdown pass to Chad Johnson, I don't stop to consider the political ideology of the stranger sitting next to me before I hug him as if he had just given me twenty million dollars. When a group of Pittsburgh Steelers fans are obnoxiously mocking the Bengals' "Who-Dey" chant, the ill will that I wish on them isn't lessened by the fact that they may be diehard conservatives.

What is it then? Perhaps it's similar to whatever caused the excitement in me when I had my first kiss. It was during a game of truth or dare, and someone dared me to kiss a girl who was sitting across from me. At the time, I knew she was pro-abortion (I know, I know—why was a junior high kid already passionate about the issue of abortion? What a burden to bear.); but that didn't matter to me.

Aside from the fact that I was both attracted to and deathly afraid of females at the time (and still am), I put politics and philosophy on the back burner just so I could get some. What's wrong with me? (I still can't believe my first kiss was with a pro-abortion chick. Oh, the humanity!)

Maybe nothing is wrong with me. Maybe uniting themes are common to all humans—themes that have the potential to bridge the gap between hated enemies. Of course, these same themes also serve to divide as well. While mutual hate for the Pittsburgh Steelers could unite a liberal and myself, different team loyalty could also divide the best of friends. What's a politically active sports fan to do?

Of course, as a Christian, this should be nothing new. I should always be able to embrace a fellow Christian (or *anyone* for that matter) in love regardless of his philosophical or political beliefs. Of course, this doesn't mean that I must lend credence to his bad ideas. After all, shouldn't the loving action of the Creator of the universe—saving us from our sins on a cross—be able to unite me with my liberal opponent *at least* as well as Austin Kearns does?

If Godly love has the power to reconcile my sinful self with the sinless God of the universe, it certainly has the power to unite me with a liberal or a Steelers fan . . . maybe even a liberal Steelers fan.

Just as Jonah did when God called him to preach the saving message to Nineveh, I sometimes catch myself wishing destruction on my opponents rather than redemption. My goal shouldn't be to route my opponent, but to convert him. For in doing so, I have done both. Until then, however, I can only dream of a world full of Christian, conservative, Bengals fans.

Here's Some Bottled Water . . . and, Oh Yeah, Your Life is Meaningless . . . .

I was motivated to write this essay upon reading an article that had to do with President Bush's decision to add a faith-based initiative program (Office of Faith-Based and Community Initiatives) to the Department of Homeland Security. Bush did so in light of the destructive wake left by hurricane Katrina. Liberals, of course, are screaming bloody murder, claiming such an office blurs the separation of church and state.

Let's rewind things a bit.

Liberals agree on two things regarding hurricane Katrina: 1) Sport utility vehicle (SUV)-driving and environment-hating conservatives caused the hurricane; and 2) President Bush and the federal agencies (lackies hired by Bush) massively screwed up. Because they thrive on division, suffering, and victimization (even where none is present), liberal politicians focus on the negative of every situation and criticize every non-liberal leader in charge when something doesn't go perfectly. Thus, disasters (which the federal government is inherently incapable of fixing in the first place) are prime feeding grounds for these liberal sharks.

One of Bush's reasons for creating a faith-based initiative program within the Department of Homeland Security is to improve the response time and efficiency of services during and after a disaster. One would figure that to the degree the liberals have been griping about Bush's massive screw-up, they might want to look at faith-based groups as an option in fixing the problem. This would be true if liberal politicians were actually interested in solving problems. To do so, however, would be political suicide, because suffering and victimization (real or not) are necessary for them to maintain power.

There are two reasons people are against federal funding of religious organizations. One reason (a reason to which I am sympathetic) is that federal money always comes with strings attached. Government funding of religion is the perfect way for government to get its powerful claws into our churches and religious organizations.

Practical problems arising from this include churches and religious organizations being 1) limited in free speech because of politically correct speech codes; 2) being limited in freedom of association because of anti-discrimination policies (policies preventing churches from, for example, choosing not to hire a preacher because he is a homosexual); and 3) being limited in presentation of the gospel when providing services many communities need.

The other reason people are against federal funding of religious organizations is ostensibly based on the "separation of church and state" ideology (which we all know is code for "let's get religion out of the public forum altogether"). This ideology is embraced by secularists. Jeremy Leaming, spokesman for Americans United for Separation of Church and State, said, "No victim of a terrorist attack or a hurricane should have to hear a religious speech or profess a certain belief before receiving help that is backed up with tax dollars."

If Mr. Leaming had ever actually been to a religious outreach service, he would probably know that recipients of such services are never required to convert, nor are they subjected to "religious speeches" before they get the goods. In fact, most of the time, the only thing the recipient has to endure is seeing a sign or a T-shirt worn by the religious activist—or perhaps hearing "Jesus loves you."

Secularists (secular liberals usually) hate religion so much that they would rather a person or a family starve or go without shelter than be given food or a place to stay by a religious organization funded by tax dollars.

Mr. Leaming goes on to accuse faith-based groups of using disasters like hurricane Katrina to preach to its victims. Two observations:

1) Hardly a single day has gone by since hurricane Katrina that liberals haven't tried to exploit Bush's so-called screw-up to gain political points, or used hurricane Katrina to convince its victims that a) America is racist; b) "Bush hates the black man;" c) the federal government intentionally blew up New Orleans' levies (no, I'm not making this up); d) New Orleans is a "chocolate city;" e) SUVs and low fuel efficiency regulations are to blame for the hurricane itself; f) there wasn't a Federal Emergency Management Association (FEMA) employee at each victim's door with a five-course

dinner and $10,000 in cash the second after the hurricane was over, because those victims were black; or g) the Democrats could have prevented hurricane Katrina in the first place *and* could have immediately met all of the victims' needs after it was over.

2) Which message would you rather hear after a disaster? a) Here is some bottled water . . . and don't forget God loves you and there is hope after all; or b) Here is some bottled water . . . and all you are is a collection of chemicals and firing synapses with no ultimate meaning or purpose in this world . . . your suffering is also meaningless . . . and, oh yeah, Bush hates the black man.

Do you want to know the other threat that religious organizations are to government and secular service organizations? Consider this. There is only a fixed amount of suffering in this country and only a certain amount of help that needs to be administered. The more religious organizations help (especially religious organizations *not* funded by tax money), the less help is needed from government and secular organizations. That means less government jobs (and less union jobs). That means the government needs to raise less money through taxes (thus, lower taxes). That means a less powerful government. That means government has less say over the lives of Americans. All of these results are antithetical to the modern liberal agenda.

A volunteer for a religious organization once told me that the inner-city government programs designed to help the poor didn't like it when religious organizations tried to do the same. I didn't understand why at first, but now I do. Those who worked for the government agency or program would lose their jobs if the needs of the inner-city community were met through the private sector.

Once again we are brought back to the inevitable conclusion of the logical progression from naturalism to modernism to postmodernism: Look out for Number One. Well, that and the fact that modern liberalism needs a powerful government to do its bidding.

Environmentalism: An Ideology without Premises

This is an essay explaining why I'm not an environmentalist. I'm not an environmentalist, in the modern sense of the word, because both possible premises that explain humanity prevent environmentalism from being a coherent option.

The logical rule known as the "law of the excluded middle" states that an entity or phenomenon either is something or isn't something. For example, my television is either a duck or not a duck. It can't be in the middle. My computer is either the planet Mars or it isn't. One of these statements must be true. In these cases, my television is not a duck, and my computer is not the planet Mars. The law of the excluded middle can be applied to anything that exists. This includes humans.

For our purposes, we will examine two possible premises regarding the status of humans: 1) humans are special, and 2) humans aren't special. Most hardcore environmentalists reject the first premise (for a variety of reasons). Thus, we will discuss the second premise first.

This conclusion states that humans have not been granted special status among all the species on Earth. We are no more special than the monkeys in the jungle, fish in the sea, or the trees of the rain forest. We exist as equals with nature; indeed, we are no different from nature itself. Underlying this conclusion, most likely, is a belief in Darwinian evolution. Materialist Darwinian evolution requires the conclusion that humans are nothing special. This is why many environmentalists and animal rights activists equate the value of all living creatures with that of humans (i.e., trees, chickens, birds, insects, etc., have the same rights and value as humans).

The logical problem for environmentalists is the fact that if humans are nothing special, we have no obligation (moral or otherwise) to go out of our way to protect the environment or treat it with reverence. Furthermore, if humans are nothing special and, by definition, are a part of nature just like the lobster, snake, monkey, earthworm, and dandelions, it is impossible for humans to do anything "unnatural."

If what Carl Sagan said is true, that "The cosmos is all that is or ever was or ever will be," then it is categorically impossible for humans to do anything outside of or against nature. Only if humans were "outside of nature" or given special status within nature could we ever do anything "unnatural." But these are impossible conclusions if one starts with the premise that humans are nothing special (i.e., we are just physical "stuff" like everything else in the universe).

Therefore, if the second premise is true (that humans are nothing special), it is, by definition, "natural" when we bulldoze a rain forest to produce paper and building supplies, pollute a river with mercury, melt the polar icecaps, and "pave paradise to put up a parking lot." For something to be "unnatural," there must exist a standard by which one determines what *should be* (not just what *is*), and this standard must exist outside of, or separate from, what is being judged, i.e. nature—otherwise it is a meaningless, arbitrary judgment.

For the materialist who accepts the second premise, however, positing the plane of existence required for such a standard to exist (i.e., the existence of something or somewhere "non-natural") is an impossible conclusion. It is self-referentially incoherent for a materialist to accuse a human or group of humans of doing anything "unnatural."

In a materialistic universe, the Earth doesn't care what happens to it. It was here millions of years before humans showed up, and it will be here millions of years after we're gone. It doesn't care if we use up all its "resources" (I put the word "resources" in quotation marks, because it isn't the Earth that determines what is and isn't a resource—but rather human technology). The Earth doesn't care if we completely obliterate its ozone. It doesn't care if we melt its polar icecaps. And it certainly doesn't care if we kill every single spotted owl on the face of the globe. After all, it isn't just granting humans special status that's impossible within the materialist worldview. Granting *anything* special status is impossible. And that includes the Earth (or universe) itself.

Still, if an environmentalist insists that humans have a special, moral obligation to care for the environment, he *must* concede the truth of the first premise. It is here where the avid environmentalist becomes uncomfortable. If the first premise is true, and humans are special in some way, an explanation must be given to justify *how* humans have such a status . . . and I must admit, few things entertain me more than seeing a materialist squirm in his seat as he tries to justify, in first principles, why the world should adopt his high-minded ideals. If you haven't had such an experience, I highly recommend it.

Thus, environmentalism as a conclusion stemming from the first premise is impotent until the question of *how* humans acquired such a status is determined. This is because, presumably, whatever or whoever granted humans special status is also responsible for the standard by which humans should care for the environment.

I have no problem with a proper environmentalism that acknowledges a Creator and the special status given to humans by that Creator. That is a basic premise of Judeo-Christian theism. Such an environmentalism claims value is infused into nature not by nature itself or by humans, but by a Creator not reducible to his creation. Such is a theologically based, anthropologically centered environmentalism . . . which is complete nonsense to a materialistic environmentalist.

The second premise (that humans aren't special) renders the modern environmentalist agenda incoherent, while the first premise (that humans are special) so radically redefines environmentalism that it can be argued as being not environmentalism at all, but a spiritual orientation contingent upon the Judeo-Christian account of creation.

Preserving Civil Liberties

Benjamin Franklin said something to the effect of, "Those who are willing to sacrifice freedom in the name of temporary security deserve neither." I find it interesting that liberals employ thinking like this when it comes to military endeavors and fighting for freedom. But on matters of security that are not directly associated with killing bad guys, liberals are strangely silent. What are programs such as welfare, Social Security, Medicare, public education, economic regulations, farm subsidies, socialized medicine, etc., if not programs meant to *increase security?*

In a free-market system not dominated by government handouts, subsidies, and regulation—i.e., a *free* society—insecurity is part of the game. Individuals have to wake up every day, employ the right values, work hard, and be vigilant in creating and maintaining a secure life. Government doesn't exist to *provide* our rights; it exists to *protect* them. That is, the government exists to ensure that we can realize our rights *ourselves.*

Modern liberalism has been exploiting the fears of Americans for years under the guise of programs like "The New Deal" and "The Great Society." The left has been exploiting people's financial, career, and education insecurities for the better part of the century. They see such fears as the catalysts in bringing about a government that supposedly "takes care" of its people.

Liberals don't have a problem holding the government "accountable" (which is a liberal code word for undermining a war effort) when it is killing bad guys, fighting wars, and doing the other nitty-gritty things necessary to preserve freedom (i.e. fulfilling its proper role *protecting* our rights). Liberal "accountability" seems to disappear, however, when it comes to programs that increase the size and scope of government power within our own borders, i.e., programs that enforce the modern liberal agenda.

Liberals who decry patriotism (read: the Patriot Act) and the war on terror as attempts to take away our freedoms are being hypocritical. Why don't they classify their own Socialist domestic agenda the same way? Massive entitlement programs, public education, economic regulation, affirmative action, socialized medicine, and other bastions of illegitimate government power have ripped more rights away from Americans than any recent war on terror or act of patriotism.

The fact is that liberals are hiding behind a veil of vague politicking and scare tactics when they profess a concern for receding civil liberties in the light of war and patriotism. In their own little world, however, civil liberties are easily disposable when it comes to their own agenda.

On The Rebound

Have you ever been in a "rebound" relationship? If you don't know what that is, let me explain. A rebound relationship immediately follows a recently ended relationship. Sometimes the previous relationship ends badly, with not-so-nice feelings toward the ex-significant other. Sometimes the previous relationship leaves a person hurt. In the former case, a person often immediately finds someone new out of anger (perhaps with the intention of hurting the ex). In the latter case, a person often immediately finds someone new to fill the newly opened emotional void. Either way, there's nothing special about the new significant other. He/she merely fills a temporary need. The new significant other is called the "rebound" person.

This is exactly what happened with the 2006 midterm elections. There is nothing special about Democrats that caused them to suddenly become a viable alternative. The fact that their plan for America is simply to complain about Republican policy illustrates this point clearly. Have you ever asked a Democrat for a *specific* plan on *how* to win the war on terror? The only plan Democrats have today is the same one they have had for years: Raise taxes, pacify foreign policy and national defense, and marginalize religion into obscurity.

Of course, all this is peddled using language such as "affordable health care," "affordable education," "redeployment," "diplomacy," and "tolerance." All of this *sounds* good. It also *looks* good . . . which is usually the only real standard for a rebound relationship.

Things under the Republican Congress and White House weren't perfect. In fact, things are never perfect regardless of who is in power. But no matter how good things actually are, such imperfections often come to the fore when the same party is in power for a period of time. That party eventually gets blamed for everything that is going wrong, whether it is its fault or not. It takes imagination to envision what things would have been like had another party been in power—a quality sometimes lacking when a citizenry's resolve and vision are wavering.

Most people looking for a meaningful relationship don't want to be the rebound person, because they know the rebound person isn't there because of his or her own personality or qualities. Rather, the rebound person simply fills a need that *anyone other than the ex-significant other can fill.* Such is not a foundation for a long-lasting and meaningful relationship.

A Fox News Opinion Dynamic Poll that was done the day before the election illustrates this point. Of those who stated they were likely to vote Democratic in the election, 51% claimed they were doing so because they believed a change in leadership was needed. Only 21% claimed they were voting Democratic because they agreed with the Democrats' policies. If that isn't the very definition of a rebound situation, I don't know what is.

Like several guys I know, however, the Democrats don't care how they "get some," as long as they're getting some. A long-lasting, healthy relationship is not their top priority. *Power* is their top priority, because, once in power, they can implement their plan to raise taxes, pacify foreign policy and national defense, and marginalize religion. They'll gladly offer the proverbial shoulder to cry on, because they know what will happen next.

This is why Democrats constantly harp on what is wrong rather than what is going well. No matter how good things are (as they are right now in the United States), Democrats must convince the American people that there are constantly a myriad of things wrong that can only be solved by a liberalized government offering a helping hand. The citizenry is incapable of solving its own problems (*if* such problems even exist). This is why Democrats exploit things like the death toll in Iraq and, when necessary, invent hardships that don't exist—such as the myth that the current economy is in shambles (Nancy Pelosi said this administration's handling of the economy is the "worst since the Depression").

Ronald Reagan quipped once that someone asked him what the difference was between a small businessman and a big businessman. Reagan responded that a big businessman is what a small businessman would be if the government simply got out of his way. A liberal believes just the opposite. Success is only possible when the *system* in which a person exists causes it. The 2006 midterm election, while important, was most likely not very historically significant. *Hopefully* our Republican president can minimize the damage done by a Democratic Congress between 2006 and 2008. The 2008 election, however, will be much more historically significant than that of 2006. Not only will the White House be up for grabs, but the current tax cuts are due to expire in 2009 and 2010. Furthermore, it would be almost impossible to neutralize the damage Democrats would do to our country regarding the war on terror if they controlled both houses of Congress *and* the White House. Also, if Supreme Court Justice John Paul Stevens (age 87) doesn't step down between 2006 and 2008, he will most assuredly do so sometime between 2008 and 2012. The next Supreme Court Justice has the potential to end the stranglehold modern liberalism has had on the court for years. (If you think the liberals put up a fight against judges John Roberts and Samuel Alito, just wait.)

The silver lining for conservatives is that this backlash happened in 2006 (rather than in 2008, hopefully). This backlash would most assuredly happen in 2008 if Republicans had maintained control of both houses in the 2006 election. If conservatives have to choose which election to do well in, 2008 is the obvious choice.

The question is how the Republicans will respond. If we keep electing pseudo-Republicans like Mike DeWine and Lincoln Chafee, the conservative base won't see much difference between them and their Democratic alternatives. Moreover, neither will independents or moderates.

Hopefully after the citizenry has had its fill of the artificial feel-good "rebound guy," it will realize how good things were with the last guy (despite a few pseudo-conservatives and an annoying inability to unite against the Democrats).

A Beacon of Bigotry

I recently ran across a publication produced by an organization, Beacon Health, whose stated mission is as follows:

> *Beacon Health is dedicated to advancing the art and practice of home health care through ever higher standards of education, resources, and support for home health and hospice industry providers. We help homecare agencies and their people become more productive, prosperous, and professional by providing them with the knowledge and tools they need to achieve higher standards of business and professional practice.*[1]

The particular publication in question was distributed by a local home health-care agency to its employees (including home health aides and nurses). The title of the six-page packet is "Cultural Diversity."

The first section of the packet is entitled "The Facts about Cultural Diversity," wherein the term *culture* is defined. According to Beacon Health, *culture* "is a social pattern of behaviors, beliefs, and characteristics of a group of people that is passed on from generation to generation." Fair enough.

---

1. http://www.beaconhealth.org/.

The packet then rightly asserts, "Probably the biggest error in defining a culture is thinking in terms of race or gender. Far too often 'cultural diversity' is used to refer to the mix of male/female employees, or persons of a certain race. To assume that all members of a certain race share a common culture is never correct. The cultural diversity among members of any race is likely to be very large, since there are many factors making a culture." I wholeheartedly agree.

The packet then goes on to provide brief synopses of different cultures. Included are synopses of the following "cultures" (the packet rightly claims, however, that such descriptions rarely, if ever, fully describe any particular individual . . . the synopses are only to be taken as general overviews): Eastern Asian and Pacific Islander cultures; Haitian, Puerto Rican, Cuban cultures; Baptist culture (yes, the Christian denomination); Christian Science, the Church of Jesus Christ of Latter-day Saints, Islam, Jehovah's Witnesses, Jewish, Roman Catholic, and Russian Orthodox or Greek Orthodox cultures. Leaving out, for the moment, the standard used to decide which cultures the packet would assess, all this seems pretty harmless—maybe even helpful. But there is more.

The next section is entitled, "What This Means to You as a Home Health Aide," wherein some conclusions are drawn about the practical application of this newly garnered enlightenment regarding "culture." Included are notions that someone shouldn't draw conclusions about a patient based on his or her culture; instead the aide should learn about every patient as an individual and learn as much about other cultural groups as possible so as to better understand them. The aide should respect the rights of patients in their own homes and identify his or her own cultural beliefs, because those beliefs may affect the manner in which the aide approaches the patient. The aide must never try to change the patient's cultural beliefs and never try to "convert" anyone. Also included is the claim that if an aide believes that some cultural practices are harming the patient, he or she should notify the supervisor.

"So what's the big deal?" you may ask. Most of this sounds fairly inane. But there is more. Following the synopses and the calls for cultural sensitivity that are littered throughout the document, is a section entitled "Case Study: Cultural Diversity in Action."

In this case study (only hypothetical of course), a woman named Esther (a conveniently biblical name) is a new home health aide who has been asked to meet with her supervisor. The supervisor has received several telephone calls from Esther's patients and wishes to discuss the matter with her. The following were the complaints leveled against Esther:

1) Esther prays out loud.
2) Ester asks her patients to pray with her.
3) She had brought copies of the Bible to some of her patients.
4) Esther had criticized some of the foods her patients had eaten.
5) Esther has criticized some of the patients' way of life.

During her meeting with her supervisor, Esther made the following comments:

1) She began by saying how important her church is to her.

2) She said that some of her patients don't believe in Jesus and that she was only trying to help them.

3) She said, "Mrs. Goldstein is a Jew," then commented on the "crazy" ways they do things at Mrs. Goldstein's.

4) She commented that Mrs. Goldstein has two refrigerators and is particular about which foods go in which refrigerator "as if it really matters."

5) She noted that Mr. Johnson is a Catholic and has statues of Mary all over his house. Esther said, "He worships Mary instead of Jesus!"

6) "Mrs. González said that thing she wears around her neck protects her from spirits! I told her nobody but Jesus could protect her."

7) "And that Mr. Ahmed—I had to stop what I was doing because he said it was time to pray to Allah!"

8) About Mrs. Peters, Esther said, "She's one of those Mormons, and she wears the same underwear every day, and she wears it on top of her other underwear! I told her that was crazy and she shouldn't do that."

9) "And that Mr. Bevan Nyen—the smell of that food in that house. I don't know why they can't eat like the rest of us."

10) Regarding her patients in general, she said, "I know they are going to hell if they don't except the Lord Jesus Christ. I thought if I can help them, and give them a Bible, it would be a good thing. I can't understand why they would get upset."

11) About the other stuff, here is how I look at it—if you're going to live in America, then you better decide to act like an American. If not, then stay in your own country."

What can we gather about the identity or "culture" of Esther? Obviously, Esther is an evangelical Christian—and an "intolerant" one at that. She is completely ignorant of anyone's culture but her own. She doesn't respect any of her patients' privacy. She's ethnocentric. She's narrow-minded. She can't imagine how anyone could be different from herself. She inappropriately attempts to proselytize her patients and gives them Bibles. She prays so others can hear her, and she asks her patients to pray with her. She criticizes the foods her patients eat as well as their way of life.

Question: Is anyone really surprised that Beacon Health made the intolerant, bigoted, ignorant, uneducated, ethnocentric, arrogant home health aide an *evangelical Christian*?

Furthermore, the last comment (11) paints Esther as a patriotic American—in all probability a conservative Republican (as liberals stereotypically see them). Thus it is Esther—the intolerant, bigoted, ignorant, uneducated, ethnocentric, arrogant home health aide who is a patriotic (most likely a politically conservative Republican) and evangelical Christian, consistently attempting to "force" her beliefs on others. No doubt if this case study were acted out on a stage, Esther would have a Southern accent. Clearly, someone at Beacon Health has an ideological ax to grind. And seeing as Christians and Southerners (although she's not portrayed as a Southerner) are about the only two groups that can be ridiculed without repercussion, Beacon Health won't be admonished in the least for being intolerant.

Question: In the modern world, what group is most likely to force its beliefs on others? Evangelical Christians? C'mon. The answer is obvious. The answer is the "culture" previously listed under the synopsis "Islam" earlier in the packet.

Perhaps if Esther flew some planes into buildings, kidnapped some civilians, or cut someone's head off, she would receive the cultural immunity so often doled out by the liberal establishment to America-hating "cultures." But no, she prays aloud and hands out Bibles. She must be stopped!

Why Soccer Isn't America's Game

Sometimes people wonder why soccer isn't America's game, despite the fact that it is the world's most popular sport. After watching much of the World Cup in 2006, I came up with several reasons why soccer—while sometimes entertaining and definitely athletic—isn't America's game.

Reason 1: Taking dives
Why is it that *every* time a player is touched, he falls down and clutches some body part and screams in agony? Sometimes the player is carried to the sideline on a stretcher, whereupon he easily walks away from the stretcher uninjured. The reason, obviously, is to entice the referee to blow his whistle, thus giving the catastrophically injured player's team a free kick. We had a name for kids like this on the playground. We called them *pansies*—kids who were too small, unathletic, or weak to keep up with the better players (and they couldn't just deal with it). Because of this, they had to appeal to the teacher to forcefully level the playing field.

Thankfully, I observed that American players were not very often guilty of taking dives. The rest of the world's players, however (especially Europeans), fall to the ground faster than a Clinton administration intern. Americans, in general, aren't pansies (at least not yet), and we don't like games that reward pansy behavior.

Reason 2: The rules neutralize size and strength advantages.
In soccer, the rules are set up to equalize the size and strength factors. Being taller and stronger isn't much of an advantage in soccer, because the rules prevent physical play. Positioning is much more important than size or strength. In general, pushing and shoving is against the rules, because anything more forceful than a "lean in" brings a penalty. It's as if all the little guys on the playground got together and created a game designed to favor the kids who couldn't keep up with the bigger, stronger types. This is why a lot of the smaller athletes have such big mouths. They play a sport designed to protect them from those who would otherwise squash them like bugs as a result of their annoying small-man trash talk.

Americans like the biggest and the strongest in everything we do. Like communism, infomercials, and the rule in dodgeball that outlaws hitting someone in the face, games set up to forcefully favor the "little guy" deserve to be thrown into the "dustbin of history."

Reason 3: "Look, Mommy! No hands!"
It is against the rules to use arms and hands. Think about it. That which physically separates humans from every other species on earth—hands with opposable thumbs—is outlawed. That's right, the creators of soccer prevented the use of what God, in his eternal wisdom and glory, gave us to physically separate us from other species (or, if you prefer, what evolution spent millions of years crafting as the "fittest"). Thus, soccer represents either a step back in the evolutionary process or bad stewardship of what

the good Lord gave us. America has always been a place of progress. Soccer represents the opposite.

Additionally, one of the true tests of athleticism is dexterity of the hands. The three most popular sports in America (football, baseball, and basketball) all require skillful use of the hands. A sport that doesn't require dexterity of the hands is like sugar-free, fat-free cookies. No amount of artificial flavoring will ever make it better than the real thing.

Reason 4: Ties
Do you remember in 2002 when Major League Baseball's All-Star game ended in a tie? Bud Selig (baseball's commissioner who made the decision to end the game in a tie) received more criticism for that decision than for almost any other he's made as commissioner. Headlines everywhere read, "There's no *tying* in baseball!" This was a play on the famous line in the movie, *A League of Their Own*, that went "There's no crying in baseball"—a parody insinuating that tying in sports is as "girly" as crying in sports.

Ties were invented so no one would have to feel bad—so there would be no "losers." Unfortunately, there are no ties in real life. In every contest, there is a winner and there is a loser. I'm reminded of a scene in the television show *King of the Hill* where Bobby (about twelve years old) tells his father (Hank Hill, the main character) why he couldn't miss his soccer game (Hank was trying to convince his son to play football instead of soccer). Bobby said, "I can't miss the game, dad. I'm one of my team's eleven co-captains."

Now, it is important to note that I'm not referring to sports played by young children where the goal is as much to teach the children about life as it is to teach about sports. I'm talking about the highest level of professional competition. At this level, games are played to be won. At this level, competition brings the best to the top. Excellence is found in winning within the stated rules of the game—rules that ensure *fair play* rather than *forced egalitarian* play.

There is no "best" when there is a tie. No excellence. In line with the fact that America prefers the biggest and best in everything we do, the most popular sports in America don't allow ties (technically, football allows them; but they are extremely rare). Competitive sport at its highest level is about excellence, not self-esteem. Leave self-esteem for ten-year-olds and Title IX proponents.

Reason 5: That stupid "obstructing the goalie" rule.
America's second goal against Italy (shorthanded, I might add) was disallowed because one of our players was blocking the view of Italy's goalie. Is

it me, or is this rule just plain dumb? Can you imagine a rule in football preventing the defense from blocking the quarterback's line of sight? Or how about a rule preventing a hockey player from blocking the opposing goalie's view? If defenders don't want a player blocking their view, *move him*. Of course, as discussed above, this is not allowed in soccer. The goalie must have a "fair" chance to prevent a goal.

Having played soccer 11 years myself, I can attest that it is a lot of fun and physically demanding. But that doesn't mean soccer should be America's game. Nor was it *my* game. In short, soccer isn't America's game because it isn't "American" in any sense of the word.

Working for the Government

Every year near April 15, people scramble to put their taxes together to have them submitted by the federal deadline. Ironically, some taxpayers are still working for the government on April 15. In fact, many Americans work for the government well into May and sometimes June.

By "working for the government," I don't mean that such taxpayers have government jobs. I mean that the income they earn goes to the government ("for" meaning "on behalf of"). For example, if someone pays 25% of their income to the government in the form of taxes, that person "works for the government" through the month of March.

What a person pays to the government goes well beyond income tax. If one were to sit down and calculate how much of his own money goes to the government, he would have to calculate several different kinds of taxes, including (but not limited to) income tax, property tax, sales tax, etc. Additionally, if you include sales tax, you'll realize that the percentage of your income paid to government is much higher than you previously thought.

In light of the enormous amount of money that the government takes from its citizens at various levels, it's no wonder that the government takes the majority of it directly from someone's paycheck. Can you imagine the backlash if every citizen received his or her income *in toto* and had to personally write a check directly to the government? There would be massive tax reform by dinnertime. Perhaps the individual who came up with direct withdrawal of taxes is the *evil genius* spoken of centuries ago by Descartes. That said, let's examine the nature of two particular kinds of tax: sales tax and property tax.

Sales tax is the perfect example of double taxation. Every penny you pay on sales tax has already been taxed by the income tax automatically taken out of your paycheck by the government (federal, state, and local).

Depending on how much you spend, you could be adding significant percentage points to the portion of your income paid to the government.

Regarding property tax: Has anyone noticed the eerie similarities between paying property tax to the government and paying rent to a landlord? For example, what happens when a tenant doesn't pay rent? He gets kicked out of his apartment/home. What happens if someone doesn't pay his property tax to the government? (Although considering property tax is taken directly from a paycheck, that may not be possible.) He gets kicked out of his home (and potentially thrown in jail for tax evasion).

In the case of rent paid to a landlord, who owns the property? Obviously, the one to whom rent is paid and the one who has the authority to kick out a tenant. Using the same logic, who owns the property of the taxpayer? Presumably, the person (or entity) to whom the tax is paid and the one who has the authority to kick the taxpayer off the property.

From a functional standpoint, the tenant paying the rent and the taxpayer paying property tax do *not* own their respective properties. Thus, every property "owner" who pays property tax is merely a tenant paying rent to the real property owner, the government. Those who believe this relationship between government and citizen is no big deal misunderstands the vital importance of private property rights in a society.

For those on the left who deplore private property rights, this relationship isn't a problem. After all, in such a worldview the government is the *provider* of people's rights (rather than the protector). This includes property rights. In reality, the government owns everything (goods, services, people's incomes, health care, education, etc.) and distributes it according to a standard determined by those in power (or those who control the courts).

In the final analysis, there is no *good* way to tax—only the lesser of several evils. While sales tax combined with income tax is double taxation, sales tax *doesn't have to be* double taxation. Without income tax, sales tax ceases to be double taxation. A nationwide, graduated sales tax system would be much more fair and efficient than the current system. Another system that would be preferable to the current one is a flat tax or a fair tax system.

Either way, property tax is by far the *worse* of the evils (with income tax running a close second). Besides the fact that it is wrong in principle, it centralizes way too much power in the hands of government . . . which, I suppose, isn't a problem for those who believe government exists to provide salvation to a citizenry without bootstraps.

Moral Cannibalism: Tastes Like Liberal Chickens

I once read a quote that was attributed to Ayn Rand (I say *attributed*, because I haven't yet found where she wrote it . . . although it fits her philosophy). The quote is, "The moral cannibalism of all hedonist and altruist doctrines lies in the premise that the happiness of one man necessitates the injury of another." What does this mean?

The premise Rand decries as "moral cannibalism" claims that it is impossible to "move up" in society (i.e., acquire property, wealth, etc.) without *necessarily* injuring others. "Injury" is usually some kind of "exploitation" that most often takes the form of denying someone a supposed fundamental "right" (i.e., a "livable" wage, health care, abortion, child care, education, a job, overtime pay, clothing, food stamps, transportation, etc.).

Rand calls this notion "moral cannibalism," because it views economics as a zero-sum game where people are constantly feeding off of one another. A zero-sum game is one in which the end result is always zero. For example, if Sam and Joe are competing for a certain amount of money, say $10, the winner will be up $10 while the loser will be down $10. Thus, in the end, the result is still zero. This zero-sum game assumes there is only a fixed amount of capital to go around. (For the record, this is a thoroughly socialist notion—one that Rand properly labels "moral cannibalism.")

Creating wealth is *not* a zero-sum game. Liberals would like to believe that a fixed amount of wealth exists within a particular system and that that wealth must be equally distributed among the population. Liberals are ignorant of the fact that wealth must be *created*. If no one creates wealth, there is no wealth. If many people create wealth, then there's a lot of wealth. (Sounds a bit *too* simple, doesn't it?) Thus, there is no fixed amount of wealth in a system. It is dependent upon how much wealth is created by the people. Only *after* wealth is created (which is when the government gets involved) is it a zero-sum game. Wealth creation is not a zero-sum game, but forcefully distributing it certainly is.

If I invent a gadget that people want, and I go into business making the gadgets, whom have I exploited? If I hire employees at a rate they freely agree to, whom have I exploited? If I sell the gadget at a price the public voluntarily pays, whom have I exploited? If I spend my own money as I see fit, whom have I exploited?

The truth is this: The more "rights" the left thinks up, the easier it is to convince someone he is being exploited. If someone has a "right" to health care, and I, as an employer, don't offer it to my employees, I'm now exploiting them. If homosexuals have a "right" to marry, and I, as an employer, don't offer such coverage in my benefits, I'm now exploiting them. If someone has a "right" to child care, and I, as an employer, don't provide it for my employees, I'm now exploiting them. If someone has a "right" to a particular minimum wage, and I, as an employer, don't pay it, I'm now exploiting my employees.

This is also true on a larger scale. If someone has a fundamental "right" to health care, and government doesn't provide it, government is exploiting whoever doesn't get health care. If someone has a "right" to an education, and government doesn't provide it, government is exploiting whoever doesn't get an education. The constant creation of so-called "fundamental rights"—together with the notion that the role of government is to *provide* (rather than *protect*) such rights—is a prescription for big government and, eventually, totalitarianism.

Anyway, back to the point.

Wealth *cannot*, by *definition*, be created by government. Because government must use money garnered through taxes to do *anything*, there is *never a net gain in any system where the government is active*. The role of government isn't to actively pursue economic growth through heavy-handed legislation, but to create an unencumbered environment for the private sector to fulfill *its* rightful role of creating wealth. Even if there was an economic equivalent to the fabled perpetual motion machine in science, government could not, by definition, facilitate economic growth.

Here's why:

Let's say I earn $10 from mowing my neighbor's lawn. Let's also say that the government takes $3 of it to fund various programs existing (ostensibly) to spur economic growth, help the poor, etc. Even if all $3 is put back into the system (which we know is impossible due to government overhead, bureaucracy, ineptitude, and corruption) in the form of monetary aid for the poor, jobs during an economic crisis, etc., there is no net gain in the wealth of the system. This is because the government isn't *creating* wealth—it is only *distributing* it (and doing so inefficiently, I may add). (Only $1 gets to where it is meant to go, while $2 disappears into the government machine. Why not just let me walk across the street and give my neighbor $2? I save a dollar, and he gets a dollar more.)

By definition (once again), taxes only serve to siphon a portion of the wealth created by the private sector, thus slowing economic growth through the direct removal of wealth from the system and decreasing motivation for wealth creation within the private sector.

Government may be used for a few things, but economic growth is not one of them. This is why Franklin D. Roosevelt's policies lengthened the Great Depression, Lyndon B. Johnson's Great Society has never been successful, and why jobs created by the government do little to nothing in creating wealth.

But liberals don't understand any of this. They're too busy pitting us against one another and holding themselves up as the saviors that are worried about pesky economic realities. The very circumstances they decry as oppressive (i.e., poverty, etc.) are caused by the programs they claim will alleviate them.

Many dishonest liberals, however, know very well that the programs they support will do nothing to alleviate the problems they are said to address. The point of these programs is to increase government power by convincing the populace they are victims of forces they cannot overcome. Only with the help of government can the unfortunate overcome the impenetrable barriers brought to bear on them—by, no doubt, the "haves" of society who are exploiting them.

All the while, liberals demonize those who *create* wealth ("big" business such as Microsoft and wealthy CEOs), and they discourage new business creation (mostly small businesses) by instituting socialist economic policies. Politicians sit back and wait for the private citizen to engage in the work, risk, ingenuity, and thought necessary to create the wealth, and then they divvy up the plunder for their own political gain.

This is where we find contemporary economic rhetoric. Ask yourself this: When was the last time you heard something positive about the economy from the news media, academia, or public education (or any other bastion of liberal dominance)? It was probably a while ago—most likely not since the Clinton administration.

If the economy, or any realm of life, is doing well, liberals can't occupy the footing necessary to convince people they are victims in need of government help. This is why the Democrats are the party of "doom and gloom." After all, if everything were peachy-keen, the Democratic Party would not be necessary. So even when and where things are going well (such as the economy), they must convince the citizenry that things are really not going well.

Whoever has the loudest microphone has more ability to influence public thought. Modern liberalism has strategically taken control of the vital "microphones" in society—the media, education, the judiciary, etc. Thus, the "doom and gloom" message peddled by Democrats is the only message most Americans hear. This accounts for why Americans as a whole (in spite of the facts and their *personal* prosperity) believe the economy in general is not doing well. Once this lie is believed, liberals can offer their big government, socialist policies as the solution.

Here are some facts[2]:

1) Real gross domestic product expanded more than $1 trillion—or 11%—between the first quarter of 2003 and the end of 2005.

2) Five million new jobs were created—more than in Japan and Europe combined.

3) Real (after inflation) personal income has mushroomed up 5.7% on a compounded rate from the first quarter of 2003—almost $2,100 in more after-tax personal income per capita.

4) Industrial production is up $300 billion in the last three years (despite the cries of "You outsourced my job!").

5) Between the second quarter of 2003 and the end of 2005, 3.9 million new businesses were started.

6) Last year's total government tax revenue increased 15% from the year before. (Tax rates went down, yet the government collected more money.)

7) More domestic jobs were created by "insourcing" and from the capital gained by outsourcing than there were jobs lost from outsourcing.

8) The unemployment rate of 4.7% was lower than the rate *ever* was under the Clinton administration.

Instead of hearing about the myriad of indicators telling us that the economy is doing well, you'll hear how "the economy didn't create as many jobs as expected last month" or how "the jobs being created are not good jobs." (By the way, both of these statements are so vague that they render themselves meaningless.) You'll also hear about how many jobs have been outsourced, but nothing about jobs that have been "insourced" or the capital investment and jobs created by such outsourcing.

Sometimes Democrats get a bad rap for being negative. But their negativity shouldn't surprise anyone, because before they can hold themselves (government) up as saviors, they must tear down all that is doing well and all that creates prosperity. Only then can they offer their alterna-

---

2. http://www.foxnews.com/story/0,2933,195126,00.html.

tive—which is socialism—and the very policies that create and perpetuate the poverty that liberals depend on for their own survival.

Can anyone say "vicious cycle"?

12

A Bit of Theology
Civil Government and Narnia's Ancient Magic

A Narnian Revolution

I WENT to see the movie *The Chronicles of Narnia: The Lion, the Witch, and the Wardrobe*. The movie is based on the classic fiction book of the same name, written by C. S. Lewis. Overall, the movie does justice to the book's story (as much as any movie can, I suppose). The parallels between *The Lion's* story line and Christianity should be fairly plain to Christians, although people from any faith can enjoy the movie.

I would like to draw attention to the part of the movie when the White Witch (the villain) approaches Aslan (the lion, the "good guy") to demand the life of Edmund. (Edmund had earlier betrayed his brother and sisters by attempting to turn them over to the White Witch.) The White Witch cites the laws of the ancient magic that give her the right to demand Edmund's life.

According to the ancient law, the punishment for traitorous acts is death. By attempting to turn in his siblings, Edmund had broken the laws of the ancient magic. Thus, according to the ancient law, Edmund must lose his life. With the ancient magic as her leverage, the White Witch demands that Aslan release Edmund to her so she can carry out the sentence.

What's intriguing is that we soon discover that even Aslan is bound by the laws of the ancient magic. As you watch the scene unfold, you expect Aslan to sharply refute the White Which, sending her on her way with her wand tucked between her legs. This is not the case, however, as Aslan himself must yield to the dictates of the ancient magic. In one particular heated exchange, the White Which reminds Aslan of the relevant ancient laws. Clearly annoyed, and with a powerful voice, Aslan sharply responds, "Don't talk to me about the ancient laws. I was there when they were written!"

Upon hearing the demands of the White Witch, Aslan instructs her into his tent where they talk alone. When they emerge from the tent a few moments later, Aslan informs the onlookers that the White Witch has relinquished her claim on Edmund's life. Before the White Witch leaves with her entourage, she asks Aslan how she can be sure that he will follow through on his promise (regarding a deal Aslan and the White Witch brokered behind closed doors). Aslan's only response is an angry roar, which obviously frightens the White Witch and forces her into her seat.

A few scenes later, we learn that Aslan takes the place of Edmund under the knife. Aslan takes Edmund's death sentence upon himself, thus simultaneously satisfying the ancient magic and releasing Edmund from the penalty.

This is where the interpretation can get tricky. On the surface, it seems that Aslan must placate the demands of the White Witch. After all, it is the White Witch who is demanding Edmund's life and ultimately acts out the death sentence by killing Aslan. Aslan seems to submit to the White Witch. This, however, is not the case.

In this scenario, the White Witch has no authority. It is the ancient magic that has authority. Aslan is submitting himself to the laws of the ancient magic. The ancient laws demand Edmund's death, and Aslan must abide by such dictates. He has no choice.

The parallel lesson to be learned is that Edmund is every human being who has ever lived, Aslan is Christ, and the laws of the ancient magic are the very nature and attributes of God. The wages of sin (treason against God) is death, because God's holiness demands it. Christ's death didn't "pay off" Satan. It "paid off" God. God himself demanded that the penalty for sin be meted out. Christ's death doesn't set aside God's punishment for sin. Christ's death *is* God's punishment for sin.

The simple fact is that sin exists and we are all sinners. God's holiness demands that sin be punished. Therefore, every human has two choices: 1) Let Christ assume the punishment for your sin, or 2) Suffer the punishment for your sin yourself. Either way, the punishment for your sin is going to be doled out. It's inevitable. Even if God wanted to ignore sin by simply sweeping it under a rug, *He couldn't.*

It's up to each of us, however, to decide where our punishment will be directed: on Christ or on us. God's love provided the opportunity for the former; however, if we reject God's offer, it is the latter option that awaits us. As frightening as evil is, it pales in comparison to God's holy wrath. It is impossible to understand the loving grace of God without first understanding the holy wrath of God.

"What's the moral of the story?" you may ask; "What's your point?" My point is this: We live in a world where man is *not* the measure of all things. We don't construct our own meaning. We don't determine for ourselves what's real and not real, valuable or worthless, worthy or unworthy, true or false. Such "ancient" things have existed since time immemorial. The search for truth is about falling in line with reality, acknowledging that meaning can only be found in the truth that *comes to us* rather than the truth *created by us*.

My essay in Chapter 9 entitled, "This Just In: Supreme Court Crumbling" is a satirical treatment illustrating the absurdity of those who deny gravity in an attempt to construct their own ultimate reality. Just as it is absurd to deny the reality of gravity, it is equally absurd to deny the existence of objective right and wrong—a standard applicable to all people in all places at all times. While denying (or ignoring) the dictates of gravity brings disastrous consequences, they pale in comparison to the consequences of rejecting (or ignoring) the dictates of a morality woven into the fabric of the universe.

Just as Christ submitted to God, so should Christians submit to God. Propositional beliefs don't save us. Christ's blood saves us via our submission to the Creator of the universe.

Of course, this is nonsense to the secularist. But we've seen the consequences of man claiming to be the measure of all things. The argument, "Look at all the suffering brought about by religion!" has been ripped from the secularist's arsenal (especially following the twentieth century).

As Harry Blamires writes in *The Post-Christian Mind*, Christians ". . . can always reply without any qualms to the person who asks us, 'How can you believe in a good God in the face of the mess that the world is in?' We can turn the question back on the questioner: 'How can you expect the world to be other than in a mess when the good God and his laws are ignored?'"[1]

The War in Iraq, WMDs, and the Purpose of Government

The following are my responses to a few questions an acquaintance asked me via e-mail in 2005 (his comments are in italics).

Thanks for the e-mail. I hope you and your family are having a wonderful Christmas season. Let's see if we can take this issue by issue.

> *As far as your website, anything and all is of interest. My main concern is your values. Religion and pro-Iraq-war are two themes I see*

---

1. Blamires, *The Post-Christian Mind*, 12.

throughout the writings but I'm confused. I guess I'm confused on how someone so involved in religion is so in support of the war and violent solutions. I guess the first thing to help me understand where you're coming from is the principles of our religion that you see (and practice) as most important. Is it love, compassion, forgiveness, integrity, honesty, mutual respect, responsibility etc.?

At this point, the issue you want to address is the compatibility (or lack thereof) between war and Christianity. Because the question assumes the truth of Christianity, I can respond to your question by referencing the standard by which Christian truth is determined: Scripture.

In short, however, to answer your question, I don't value any one Christian principle over another. They are all of equal importance and validity. Therefore, I don't value honesty more than love, forgiveness more than compassion, mutual respect more than justice, forgiveness more than righteousness, etc.

The relevant question, however, doesn't concern which principle(s) I see as most important. Rather, the proper question has to do with *how* each Christian principle is to be lived out in our lives and in the world. To do this, we must understand the purpose of each principle, both in our personal lives and in the God-ordained institutions in his creation.

I find that most politically liberal Christians fall prey to what is often called the "Christological fallacy." Basically, the Christological fallacy is when a Christian attempts to construct his entire system of ethics based solely on the life and words of Jesus. Thus, someone's ethics regarding personal behavior, social behavior, family life, as well as issues surrounding the purpose of government, the legitimacy of war, and the criminal justice system are determined by referring only to the four Gospels that contain the ministry of Jesus Christ on the Earth.

This is a hermeneutical fallacy for the following reasons: 1) Jesus simply didn't address every single particular ethical issue. 2) The main purpose for the incarnation was not to "show us how to live." The purpose of the incarnation was to provide the opportunity for redemption by dying for our sins on the cross. (Of course, this is not to say that much of Christ's life is not applicable to our personal lives.) 3) And most importantly, the Gospels and the teachings therein are no more inspired than the book of Acts, Paul's epistles, Peter's letters, etc. For example, what Paul says in Romans 13 is just as binding for the Christian as what Jesus says in Matthew 24. The ethical ramifications of one should not be privileged over the other.

A Bit of Theology

Thus, in constructing an ethical system for life, the Christian must appeal to the entirety of Scripture rather than simply the Gospels. Therefore, the principles by which we as Christians live and by which we form our opinions regarding the issues before us today, must be garnered from a complete treatment of God's special revelation to humanity (the Bible).

When we do this, we notice that God has established certain institutions for particular purposes. For example, God ordained the family for a purpose, marriage for a purpose, and the church for a purpose (or purposes). We also see that God has ordained civil government for a particular purpose(s). More than that, however, God has also outlined civil government's role in the grand scheme of creation, as well as *how* civil government achieves that function.

The main passages in this discussion are Romans 12:17–21, Romans 13:1–5, and 1 Peter 2:13–14. If we apply only Christ's life and teachings to the role of civil government, then we must conclude that that role is to be fulfilled via love, compassion, mercy, forgiveness, etc. But, as we will see, according to the aforementioned passages, this is obviously not to be the case for civil government.

Let's begin by looking at Romans 12:17–21:

> Never pay back evil for evil to anyone. Respect what is right in the sight of all men. If possible, so far as it depends on you, be at peace with all men. Never take your own revenge, beloved, but leave room for the wrath of God, for it is written, 'VENGEANCE IS MINE, I WILL REPAY,' says the Lord.
>
> 'BUT IF YOUR ENEMY IS HUNGRY, FEED HIM, AND IF HE IS THIRSTY, GIVE HIM A DRINK; FOR IN SO DOING YOU WILL HEAP BURNING COALS ON HIS HEAD.' Do not be overcome by evil, but overcome evil with good. (NASB)

It is clear from this passage that Scripture instructs us to never take our own revenge. Instead, we are to treat our enemies with love (i.e., feed them, give them something to drink, etc.). This is how we as individual Christians are to treat those who wrong us.

Why should we do this? Because it is God who punishes. Paul instructs his readers to "leave room for the wrath of God" and quotes the Old Testament passage where the Lord says, "Vengeance is mine, I will repay." Paul is reassuring the Christians in Rome that wrongdoers will be treated justly. But it is not the individual Christian himself who ensures this justice. It is God who will distribute his wrath in accordance with the actions of wrongdoers.

Understanding Romans 12:17–21 is vital in understanding Romans 13. Without understanding the *context* of Romans 13, Paul's overall point concerning civil government in Romans 13 will not be understood. Thus, after instructing individual Christians to "leave room for the wrath of God," Paul immediately follows this exhortation with exactly *how* God will do this.

Paul writes in Romans 13:1–5:

> Every person is to be in subjection to the governing authorities. For there is no authority except from God, and those which exist are established by God. Therefore whoever resists authority has opposed the ordinance of God; and they who have opposed will receive condemnation upon themselves. For rulers are not a cause of fear for good behavior, but for evil. Do you want to have no fear of authority? Do what is good and you will have praise from the same; for it is a minister of God to you for good. But if you do what is evil, be afraid; for it does not bear the sword for nothing; for it is a minister of God, an avenger who brings wrath on the one who practices evil. Therefore it is necessary to be in subjection, not only because of wrath, but also for conscience sake. (NASB)

Pay attention to verse 4. Paul refers to civil government as "an avenger who brings wrath on the one who practices evil," i.e., the wrongdoer. But whose wrath is this? In short, it is God's wrath. Thus, Paul is stating that the purpose of civil government is to be an "avenger of God's wrath." Paul does not say that civil government is the avenger of God's compassion or the avenger of God's forgiveness. No, civil government is the avenger of God's wrath.

For some, it seems as though Paul takes up the subject of civil government at a random place in his letter to the Romans. When taken in context, however, Paul's placement of this discussion is not arbitrary. His discussion of civil government immediately follows his exhortation to Christians to leave the punishment of evildoers to the wrath of God. This exhortation logically leads to the question, "Okay, Paul, exactly *how* is God going to do this?" Anticipating such a question, Paul gives the answer a mere five verses later. Paul seems to say, "Good question. The answer is that God has established civil government to do this." (Obviously, the wrath of God meted out by civil government is not the eternal condemnation of nonbelievers to hell [eternal separation from God], but God's wrath in accordance with

A Bit of Theology

the evil deeds perpetrated by people in this world—based on the inherent value of every individual (regardless of race, religion, class, etc.).

Therefore, this interpretation is very different from the Islamo-fascist belief that Allah's followers (and the theocratic government) must mete out Allah's eternal wrath based on religious belief. According to Christianity, however, civil government does *not* perform this function (nor does the church). A so-called "Christian government" administers punishment based upon outward action rather than subjective factors such as religious belief, skin color, economic class, etc. (which is why "hate crime" legislation is "un-Christian"). The belief that having a "Christian government" means having a theocracy (such as the oppressive governments of many "Muslim nations") is completely and utterly false. It is a lie peddled by secularists who wish to use fear to marginalize Judeo-Christian theism.

But Paul doesn't stop here; he also discusses *how* the civil government is the avenger of God's wrath. In verse 3, Paul states that civil government should instill fear into those who would commit evil. How does the civil government do this? Paul states that civil government "does not bear the sword for nothing." This illustration pictures a soldier with a sword during battle. The soldier has a sword for a particular purpose—to use it! Thus, the civil government instills fear into those who would commit evil by punishing those who *do* commit evil.

Along the same lines, 1 Peter 2:13–14 reads, "Submit yourselves for the Lord's sake to every authority instituted among men: whether to the king, as the supreme authority, or to governors, who are sent by him to punish those who do wrong and to commend those who do right."(NASB) Once again, we see that it is the role of civil government to punish evildoers.

In 1 Timothy 2:1–2, we see that the goal of civil government is to provide a peaceful and quiet environment where people are free to live out "godliness and holiness," i.e., to do good. The passage reads, "I urge, then, first of all, that requests, prayers, intercession and thanksgiving be made for everyone— for kings and all those in authority, that we may live peaceful and quiet lives in all godliness and holiness." (NASB)

What we see in Scripture, then, is that government is an institution set up by God that ensures a peaceful and tranquil environment by punishing evildoers. Such punishment does not stem from the love, the compassion, or the forgiveness of God. It stems from the wrath of God (which is entirely separate from his love, compassion, mercy, etc.). It is justice—a justice that treats people as they deserve to be treated in accordance with their evil *deeds*. Such is the nature of the holiness of God. Such is the nature of civil government.

So how does this line up with Jesus instructing us to "turn the other cheek"? If our ethics concerning civil government are to be based on Christ's words alone, we must ignore what Scripture specifically says about civil government in the rest of the New Testament. Furthermore, if Christ's life and teachings regarding compassion, forgiveness, and turning the other cheek were meant to apply to civil government, the teachings of Christ are in direct contradiction with the New Testament teachings found in Romans, 1 Peter, 1 Timothy, etc.

So what is the Christian to do? Either Scripture blatantly contradicts itself, or Jesus Christ's teachings regarding love, mercy, compassion, and forgiveness were not meant to be normative ethical statements regarding the role and methods of civil government.

Therefore, to answer your question regarding which Christian principles I find "most important," I answer by saying that I hold to the equal importance of every Christian principle according to its rightful place within creation, its role, function, and purpose.

Thus, because of scriptural teaching, I value equally the principles of compassion and justice. But, also according to scriptural teaching, it is the role of civil government to ensure the latter rather than the former (it is the responsibility of individual Christians as well as the church to operate according to compassion, mercy, forgiveness, etc.). To do this, civil government must mete out God's wrath in the form of punishment . . . thus ensuring a peaceful and tranquil environment for those who do good.

Once the basic purpose for civil government is understood, it is easier to understand why extreme pacifism on the government level is not biblical *and* why principles such as mercy, compassion, and forgiveness are categorically misapplied to both the *why* and *how* of civil government. If governments cease to mete out God's wrath by punishing evildoers, they would no longer be fulfilling their God-ordained purpose. *By definition*, civil government is not pacifistic regarding criminal activity and other injustices.

On a side note, such governments described by Paul and Peter were not so-called "Christian" governments. Yet they were governments that nonetheless fulfilled their God-ordained purpose. Thus, for Christians today, instituting a biblical form of government does not require us to "Christianize" all of our leaders and/or offices. I would much rather have a conservative atheist in office than a Christian liberal (see Chapter 3).

For example, as Christians we are called to elect leaders not based on their personal faith but on their position regarding the purpose and methods of civil government (although being a Christian would certainly help). Case in point: Jimmy Carter was (and still is, I'm assuming) a born-again Christian, but his view regarding the purpose of government is so incredibly warped that a Christian would do better to elect a nonbeliever with a more biblical view regarding the purpose of government.

> *I think you also wrote about how the rest of the world thought Iraq had WMDs and that justifies us going to war over there. The problem is the rest of the world didn't attack Iraq preemptively without a majority of international support. And why did we stop searching for them so quickly? Why aren't we still searching for them now? The strongest military and economic power in the world (for now) and we had failed intelligence?!?!*

I'm not sure which column on my web site or article you are referring to here, but it was most likely in the context of defending President Bush against accusations that he was lying about pre-Iraq war intelligence. My point was aimed at those who were accusing the president of either manipulating the evidence or outright lying about it. My point was this: Use the same standard for every politician and nation who concluded Saddam Hussein had weapons of mass destruction.

If President Bush lied, then so did John Kerry, Ted Kennedy, Tony Blair, Jacques Chirac, the United Nations, as well as every other leader and country in the world. *Everyone* believed Saddam Hussein had WMDs. That wasn't the issue. The issue was *how* to deal with Hussein. Thus, to be consistent, if someone accuses George Bush of lying, he must also accuse the aforementioned politicians and countries of lying. If those other politicians and countries didn't lie, then neither did President Bush. At this point in the argument, I'm not concerned with whether or not President Bush actually lied. I am only concerned with using the same standard to judge the beliefs and statements of everyone else who said the exact same thing as President Bush.

Concerning your statement regarding international support: I don't use popularity as a standard when determining right and wrong . . . and I'm glad President Bush doesn't either.

Concerning your statement regarding the strongest military and economic power in the world having failed intelligence: Perfection is not a trait commonly found among the bureaucratic governments of the world. If the intelligence was wrong, the entire world was wrong—not just the United States. (Of course, this is assuming the intelligence *was* wrong and Hussein didn't simply take advantage of the six-month to one-year time frame he had to bury the WMDs or move them out of the country, i.e., to Syria.)

The pictures you have on your site are nice pictures from the war and should be taken into consideration. So should the number of soldiers that die outside of Iraq (in Germany) that the Pentagon doesn't count in the 2000 number we hear about all the time. So should the 20,000 plus dead Iraqi civilians (from us, not Saddam). Those pictures you have [of happy Iraqis celebrating the arrival of U.S. troops] *typically will not make it into the headlines because people don't watch and read the news for good news and philanthropy stories; people watch it because they want to know what's wrong.*

In these comments you don't really pose any argument. You simply describe a situation (although I would dispute your 20,000 civilian deaths reference). You state that the press doesn't promote pictures similar to the ones I have on my web site, but you attribute this to audience demand. The reason the press only reports on the negative aspects of the war is because the majority of the press is liberal and against the war in the first place.

The same thing happened in Vietnam. The North Vietnamese did not defeat the United States militarily. The North Vietnamese were triumphant because America lost its will for victory. And do you know what contributed heavily to this? Politicians at home undermining the war effort and a press determined to undermine the war by only reporting the negative, none of the positive.

Bibliography

Blamires, Harry. *The Post-Christian Mind*. Ann Arbor, MI: Servant Publications, 1999.

Cottrell, Jack. *What the Bible Says About God the Creator*. Eugene, OR: Wipf & Stock, 2000.

Eberly, Don. *Restoring the Good Society*. Grand Rapids, MI: Baker Books, 1994.

George, Robert P. *The Clash of Orthodoxies*. Wilmington, DE: ISI Books, 2001.

Hoeller, Stephan A. *Gnosticism: New Light on the Ancient Tradition of Inner Knowing*. Wheaton, IL: Quest Books, 2002.

Kurtz, Paul. *Humanist Manifestos I and II*. Amherst, NY: Prometheus Books, 1973.

Kurtz, Paul. *Humanist Manifesto 2000*. New York, NY: Prometheus Books, 2000.

Lewis, C.S. *Abolition of Man*. New York, NY: HarperSanFrancisco, 1974.

Marsden, George. *The Outrageous Idea of Christian Scholarship*. New York, NY: Oxford University Press, 1997.

McGrath, Alister. *The Twilight Of Atheism*. New York, NY: Doubleday, 2004.

Pearcey, Nancy. *Total Truth*. Wheaton, IL: Crossway Books, 2004.

Rudolph, Kurt. *Gnosis: The Nature & History of Gnosticism*. San Francisco, CA: HarperSanFrancisco, 1987.

Schaeffer, Francis. *A Christian Manifesto*. Wheaton, IL: Crossway Books, 1981.

Schaeffer, Francis. *How Should We Then Live?* Wheaton, IL: Crossway Books, 1976.

Sire, James. *The Universe Next Door*. Downers Grove, IL: InterVarsity Press, 1997.

Weaver, Richard. *Visions of Order: The Cultural Crisis of Our Time*. Bryn Mawr, PA: Intercollegiate Studies Institute, 1995.

Whitehead, John W. *The Second American Revolution*. Westchester, NY: Crossway Books, 1982.

Zacharias, Ravi. *Can Man Live Without God?* Nashville, TN: W Publishing Group, 1994.